Becoming an Addictions Counselor
A Comprehensive Text

Becoming an Addictions Counselor
A Comprehensive Text

Peter L. Myers, Ph.D.

Professor and Director of Addiction
Counselor Education Program
Essex County College

Norman R. Salt, M.A., CAC

Division of Addiction Services
New Jersey Department of Health

JONES AND BARTLETT PUBLISHERS
Sudbury, Massachusetts
BOSTON   TORONTO   LONDON   SINGAPORE

World Headquarters
Jones and Bartlett Publishers
40 Tall Pine Drive
Sudbury, MA 01776
978-443-5000
info@jbpub.com
www.jbpub.com

Jones and Bartlett Publishers
Canada
2100 Bloor Street West
Suite 6-272
Toronto, ON M6S 5A5
CANADA

Jones and Bartlett Publishers
International
Barb House, Barb Mews
London W6 7PA
UK

Copyright © 2000 by Jones and Bartlett Publishers, Inc.

Production Credits
Senior Acquisitions Editor: Paul Shepardson
Associate Editor: Amy Austin
Senior Production Editor: Lianne B. Ames
Manufacturing Buyer: Therese Bräuer
Design: Anne Spencer
Editorial Production Service: Joan Flaherty
Typesetting: AnnMarie Lemoine
Cover Design: Dick Hannus
Printing and Binding: Malloy Lithographing
Cover Printing: Malloy Lithographing

Library of Congress Cataloging-in-Publication Data
Myers, Peter L.
    Becoming an addictions counselor : a comprehensive text / Peter L. Myers,
Norman R. Salt.
        p. cm.
    Includes bibliographical references and index.
    ISBN 0-7637-0795-3
        1. Drug abuse counseling. I. Salt, Norman R. II. Title.

RC564 .M94 2000
362.29'186—dc21

                                                            99-053615

Printed in the United States of America
03 02 01 00 99   10 9 8 7 6 5 4 3 2 1

CONTENTS

Preface   xv
Acknowledgments   xviii

CHAPTER 1
Introduction to Addictions Treatment   1

Basic Characteristics   1
   The Focus   1
   The Client   2
   Practice Dimensions   2
   The Counseling Relationship   3
   Effectiveness of Treatment   5
Getting into Treatment   5
   Desperation   5
   Compulsory Treatment   6
   Natural Recovery   6
   Motives for Change   8
Uniqueness of the Field   11
Treatment Settings   12
   Recent Changes in Treatment Settings   13
   Case in Point: Funding and Treatment   15
   Types of Treatment Facilities   15
   Methadone-Maintenance Treatment   19
   Case in Point: Methadone and Other Drugs   20
   ▌ Activity 1.1 Tell me about your agency.   22
Models of Treatment and Recovery   23

v

▌ Activity 1.2 What's the system?   24

Self-Help Models   25

▌ Activity 1.3 What goes on in those meetings?   27

Inpatient Rehabilitation   27

Therapeutic Community   28

Models of Emotion   29

The Disease Model   31

A Progressive Disease   32

Relapse   32

Counseling Approaches   33

▌ Activity 1.4 Thinking about Counseling   33

Affect Management   34

Behavioral Change   35

Cognitive Change   35

Integration of Affect, Behavior, and Cognition   36

▌ Activity 1.5 The ABCs of Problems   38

Stages of Change   38

Motivational Interviewing   40

Addictions Treatment Comes of Age   42

References   43

CHAPTER 2
A Skills Approach to Counseling Addicts   53

Attitudes   53

▌ Activity 2.1 When I first heard the word . . .   54

▌ Activity 2.2 Words can hurt.   55

▌ Activity 2.3 Do I have attitudes?   55

Case in Point: It's a matter of attitude.   56

Categories of Attitudes   57

Sponsoring   57

Twelve-Stepping   58

Case in Point: The Start of Something Big   58

The Counseling Mystique   58

Limited Perspective   59

Individual Addictions Counseling Skills   59

Counseling Formats   60

Tailoring Counseling Skills for Addicted Clients   61

Engagement Skills   62

Active Listening Skills   63

    Paraphrasing or Restating   63

    Reflecting   63

    Simplifying   64

    Summarizing   64

    Reinforcing   65

❚ Activity 2.4 Am I a good listener?   66

    Reframing   66

Leading Skills   66

❚ Activity 2.5 That's a leading question!   69

    Counselor Self-Disclosure   69

❚ Activity 2.6 Do you know who I am?   70

Influencing Skills   71

    Interpretation   71

    Confrontation   71

❚ Activity 2.7 How do I influence people?   73

Timing   74

Process Recording   75

References   78

CHAPTER 3
Group Treatment of Addiction   81

Introduction   81

Group Culture   82

    ❚ Activity 3.1 Are you all together?   83

Developing Awareness of the Group Process   84

    ❚ Activity 3.2 Process or Content?   85

Intervening in the Group Process   86

    Involving Marginal Members   86

    Case in Point: Countering Isolation   87

    Encouraging Peer Leadership in the Group   87

    Case in Point: Peer Leadership   88

    Helping the Group Understand the Group Process   88

Developing Group Intimacy   89

    ❚ Activity 3.3 It made me who I am.   89

    ❚ Activity 3.4 Blowing My Image   90

Keeping the Group on Task   91

Staying on the Issue   91

Staying in Routine   91

Helping Group Members Explore Roles   93

Case in Point: Different Faces for Different Places   93

Personal Roles Enacted in Groups   94

Roles That Facilitate the Group's Work   6

▌ Activity 3.5 How do I see this group?   97

▌ Activity 3.6 In my family . . .   98

Helping the Group Deal with Defensive Behavior   98

Thinking through Defensive Behavior in Groups   98

Case in Point: Coming from a Different Place   99

Defense against Emotion   100

Formulating Treatment Plans for Group Members   102

Planning Formats   103

Impediments to Change   105

Roles   105

Process   105

Client Mix   106

Defenses   106

Case in Point: Throwing a Bone   107

Group Processing Recording   107

▌ Activity 3.7 How was group today?   107

References   108

CHAPTER 4

Ethics and Confidentiality   111

Introduction   111

▌ Activity 4.1 Easier Said Than Done   112

Gray Areas   113

Supervision and Consultation   114

Case in Point: An Unacceptable Excuse   115

Boundaries   115

Legal Issues   116

Confidentiality   116

Duty to Warn   117

Duty to Report   117

Case in Point: Eliza Fell through the Cracks   117

Informed Consent   118

Disclosure and Redisclosure   119

Case in Point: I can't give you that information.   120

Legally Incompetent Clients   120

Clinical Discussion   121

▌ Activity 4.2 What's the right thing to do?   121

Subpoenaed Information   122

Medical Emergency   122

Statistical Aggregates   124

Qualified Service Organizations   124

▌ Activity 4.3 Should I tell?   124

Training   124

Pending Legislation   125

▌ Activity 4.4 I'm wearing two hats.   125

Financial Ethics   126

The "Checkbook Diagnosis"   127

Representation of Services   127

Competence   129

Impairment   129

Lack of Preparedness   129

Lack of Responsibility   131

Professional Growth   132

Nondiscrimination   133

Objectivity   134

▌ Activity 4.5 Can't Handle That God Stuff   135

An Ethical Treatment System   135

References   137

CHAPTER 5
Case Management—from Screening to Discharge 141

The Marriage of Case Management and Counseling   143

Screening   144

Engaging   145

Screening Tools   145

▌ Activity 5.1 What do these people need?   149

Assessment   149

Intake   150

Biopsychosocial Assessment   151

    Components of Biopsychosocial Assessment   151

    ▌Activity 5.2 What's the best way to ask?   152

    Diagnosis   152

Treatment Planning   154

    Treatment Planning Process   155

    ▌Activity 5.3 What do we want to do here?   158

    ▌Activity 5.4 Okay, how are we going to do this?   158

    ▌Activity 5.5 Are these good objectives?   159

Progress Notes   159

Resources and Services   161

Impediments to Treatment   164

    Physical and Mental Abuse   164

    Ethnicity and Social Class   165

    Self-Assessment   165

    Criminal Offenses   165

References   168

CHAPTER 6
Considering Client Populations   173

Introduction   173

Age   174

    Childhood   174

    Adolescence   174

    Middle-Aged and Elderly   177

Sexuality   179

    Gender   179

    Homosexuality   179

Mentally Ill Chemical Abusers   180

    Myriads of Dual Diagnoses   182

    Issues of Medication   182

    Diagnostic Issues   185

    Schizophrenia   187

    Mood Disorders   189

    Case in Point: Ups and Downs   190

    Personality Disorders   191

      Antisocial Personality Disorder   191

      Borderline Personality Disorder   192

      Post-Traumatic Stress Disorder   194

      Attention-Deficit Hyperactivity Disorder   194

References   196

CHAPTER 7
Clinical Treatment Issues   201

Introduction   201

Denial: A Multifaceted Phenomenon   202

Denial by Chemically Dependent Individuals   204

    Motives for Treatment   204

    Labels and Stereotypes   206

    Social Standing   206

    Fear   208

      Fear of Exposure   208

      Fear of Rejection   208

      Fear of Change   209

    Impaired Memory   209

    Underdeveloped Social and Emotional Skills   210

    Neurological Impairment   210

    Case in Point: Do I know you?   211

Denial by Members of the Addict's Social Network   211

Recurring Denial   213

    Case in Point: It wasn't me!   213

Emotional Issues of the Counseling Relationship   214

    Transference   215

      Positive Transference   215

      Negative Transference   217

    Countertransference   218

      Positive Countertransference   218

      Negative Countertransference   219

    Case in Point: Everything's fine.   220

    Loss, Grief, and Regrets   222

    Case in Point: Sam's Story   222

    ▌ Activity 7.1 Is it OK if I feel this way?   223

    Setting Limits and Boundaries   224

Personal Space   225

Case in Point: What is that supposed to mean?   225

▌ Activity 7.2 How would you feel?   226

Physical Contact   227

Intangible Boundaries   227

Skills in Setting Limits   229

▌ Activity 7.3 Should I or shouldn't I?   230

References   231

CHAPTER 8
Family, Community, and Cultural Systems   233

Social Systems   233

The Family as a System   234

▌ Activity 8.1 In my family . . .   234

Status, Power, and Authority   235

Elements of the System   235

Definitions of Relationships   236

Conflict   237

Styles of Communication   237

Family Belief System   238

Harm to Nonaddicted Family Members   239

Expectations of Treatment   239

Privacy and Boundaries   240

Enabling, Codependency, and Roles in Families   240

Stress and Trauma   241

Family Roles   242

Scapegoating   242

Popular Views   243

Case in Point: Codependent or Mentally Ill?   243

Other Disorders   244

Cultural Patterns   244

Assessment of Addictive Family Roles   244

▌ Activity 8.2 How do I describe this family?   246

Addiction or Cultural Norm?   247

Charting the Family   248

The Genogram   250

Case in Point: Extended Families   251

The Family Map   251

Clinical Case: Hanna and Her Family   252
▌ Activity 8.3 How do you relate?   254
Family Intervention Skills   255
Family Education   256
Family Self-Understanding   257
Individuation and Personal Growth   258
Intervention Skills and Techniques   259
Sober Family Living Skills   260
Community Systems   263
Outreach Work   263
Case in Point: A Different Culture   264
Strengths and Weaknesses   265
A Professional Network   265
Community Profiles   266
Case in Point: A Drinking Community   266
Cultural Systems   268
Research   269
Cultural Competence   269
Ethnic Subgroups and Acculturation   274
Biculturalism and Code-Switching   275
Acculturative Stress   276
Suspended Ethnicity   276
▌ Activity 8.4 What's the neighborhood like?   277
References   278

APPENDIX A
Resources   287
Selected Journals   287
Web Resources   290

APPENDIX B
Self-Help Groups   295
Alcoholics Anonymous   295
Smart Recovery   297

INDEX   301

Preface

The authors of this text met in 1981when Peter Myers appeared before a counselor credentialing body for approval of a college-level addictions curriculum; Norman Salt represented the New Jersey Department of Health as director of addictions training. In that year, alcohol and drug treatment had separate governmental entities and different credentialing bodies for alcohol and drug counselors. Training was seldom organized within an academic or professional context, and treatment was too often based on tradition rather than on research.

Myers and Salt subsequently collaborated in a statewide higher education addiction consortium, and in directing a branch of the federal Project for Addiction Counselor Training (CSAT, SAMHSA, US DHHS) through the New Jersey Department of Health and Essex County College. It became clear that quality treatment and meaningful career ladders in addictions demand more college and university counselor training programs. The International Coalition for Addiction Studies Education (INCASE) took shape to advance college and university addiction studies programs, which are housed in departments of human services, psychology, counseling, sociology, education, criminal justice, and nursing, or as freestanding entities. In 1998 Myers was proud to represent INCASE on a National Steering Committee on Addiction Counseling Standards, which endorsed a consensus document on addiction counselor competencies (CSAT 1998). Addictions counseling had become a unified profession playing a critical role in reducing human suffering and social costs that totaled hundreds of billions of dollars yearly. Much research had shown that addictions treatment is effective in reducing alcohol and drug use, crime, and violence, and that every dollar spent on treatment is paid back many times over in social costs saved (CALDATA 1994; CSAT 1996; Tabbush 1986). The successes of treatments initiative for addicted offenders have been recognized by state legislatures (Egan 1999). Nevertheless, addictions treatment faces a fight for its life, since reimbursement for behavioral health treatment has dried up. The impact of mental-health services cuts are publicized more dramatically, with revelations that far more mentally ill people are in prisons than in psychiatric care (Kennedy 1999; Winerip 1999), whose medication and case management may not be addressed upon release (Bernstein 1999). Yet cuts have affected chemical abuse and dependency treatment even more severely.

At addictions conferences, many instructors have noted that although there are many excellent texts on the pharmacology, behavior, history, models, and theories of addictions, there are few on treatment. Especially needed is a basic, comprehensive, practical text that addresses knowledge, skills, and attitudes, and describes and reflects the field as it exists today.

With *Becoming an Addictions Counselor: A Comprehensive Text*, we aim to contribute to a training process that generates ethical, competent counselors who respond to clients' needs rather than impose "cookie-cutter" routines. Our training philosophy and goals are expressed throughout the chapters of this text in the following ways.

Counselors need to know why they do what they do. We encourage critical thinking about the assumptions that underlie the models counselors employ and their application to counseling practice, as well as the attitudes and feelings that counselors bring to the counseling situation. The nature of counseling models is introduced in chapter 1. An awareness of attitudes is introduced in chapter 2. The specific skills used in individual and group counseling are presented in chapters 2 and 3. Critical clinical issues regarding emotions, boundaries, and the phenomenon called denial are discussed in chapter 7.

We encourage experiential understanding through exercises and participation. To this end, structured activities offer opportunities to practice individual and group counseling skills (chapters 2 and 3), consider the ethical dilemmas that arise in treatment (chapter 4), and practice case management and treatment planning (chapter 5).

Training must generate ethical, competent counselors who respond to clients' needs rather than impose "cookie-cutter" routines. Ethics is the subject of chapter 4, individualized treatment planning is discussed in chapter 5, and culturally competent practice is outlined in chapter 8. Lack of familiarity with the diverse menu of treatment and self-help options is unethical, as is unfamiliarity with the treatment needs of different client populations. The most prominent treatment modalities and philosophies are introduced in chapter 1, and the challenges presented among different client populations are described in chapter 6, especially those of the mentally ill chemical abuser—difficult to treat yet underserved by a fragmented and overburdened service-delivery system.

Counselors must understand the broader context within which addictive behaviors and treatment occur. Many systems affect clients and counselors alike. Chapter 1 describes the historical and systems context of treatment and chapter 8 outlines the family, community, and cultural systems within which clients may be embedded, as well as techniques for working with these systems.

Training must reflect the rapidly changing realities of society, economics, and treatment technology. We encourage faculty and students to stay current by bringing the latest developments into the classroom from the daily media, which provide readable coverage of topics such as rapid detoxification methods (Priluck 1999), or through Web links. We also stress the importance of remaining current on developments in this dynamic field by reading professional journals and attending professional conferences. Following the example of a related Jones and Bartlett text *Drugs and Society, Fifth Edition* (Hanson and Venturelli 1998), we hope to promote learning and computer literacy by including an appendix of Web links and suggesting that instructors give Web-based assignments.

Becoming an Addictions Counselor: A Comprehensive Text is appropriate for use in college-level courses in addictions, alcoholism, drug or substance-abuse counseling, treatment, internship, and fieldwork, and case management. It can also be used in health and human service in-service programs and professional institutes, and as a self-help tool for those seeking entry to, credentialing in, or career enhancement in the addictions treatment field. The focus is on treatment of chemical abuse and dependency. Although we do not specifically address nicotine cessation or gambling problems, the basic counseling skills and techniques are certainly applicable beyond the strictly drug and alcohol venue. We also hope to communicate some of the complexity and the exciting nature of the addictions field, which combines grassroots movements, people who are recovering, professional and academic networks, and a wide variety of treatment settings.

Acknowledgments

The authors owe a great deal of thanks to Joan Flaherty, the developmental editor of this text. It was a pleasure to work with an individual of such talent, intelligence, knowledge, and humor. The authors also wish to thank the terrific staff at Jones and Bartlett, including Paul Shepardson, Lianne Ames, Amy Austin, and Jennifer Jacobson.

It is impossible to enumerate the many people from whom you learn during a professional career. Peter Myers wishes to thank the administration of Essex County College for its support of creative efforts by faculty to develop career and educational ladders that benefit students and communities; the addictions students who have tested, challenged, and provided illustrations for curriculum concepts; friends, colleagues, and former students in the network of treatment agencies in Essex County, New Jersey; friends and colleagues in the International Coalition for Addiction Studies Education; and Susan Briggs Myers, MA, MSW, CSW, for her loving support and clinical wisdom.

Norman Salt wishes to thank the late Ed Crawford, who taught him about the power and simple wisdom of self-help groups; Riley Regan, the retired director of the New Jersey Governor's Council on Alcohol and Drug Abuse, for giving him the opportunity to learn and teach about alcoholism and addiction; early mentors Vernon Johnson and Father Martin; his many students; and his wife Margie for her support and patience throughout the development of the book.

References

Bernstein, N. 1999. *"Back on the Streets Without a Safety Net."* The New York Times (13 September): B1, B6.

CALDATA. 1994. *"Evaluating Recovery Services: The California Drug and Alcohol Treatment Assessment (CALDATA) General Report."* Sacramento, CA: Department of Alcohol and Drug Programs.

CSAT (Center for Substance Abuse Treatment). 1996. *"National Treatment Improvement Evaluation Study."* Rockville, MD: Substance Abuse and Mental Health Administration, U.S. Dept. of HHS.

————. 1998. *"Addiction Counselor Competencies: The Knowledge, Skills, and Attitudes of Professional Practice."* Technical Assistance Publication 21. Rockville, MD: Substance Abuse and Mental Health Administration, U.S. Dept. of HHS.

Egan, T. 1999. *"In States' Anti-Drug Fight, A Renewal for Treatment."* The New York Times (10 June): A1, A26.

Hanson, G., and P. Venturelli. 1998. *Drugs and Society,* 5th ed. Sudbury, MA: Jones and Bartlett Publishers.

Kennedy, R 1999. *"Desperate for Treatment, and Battled Every Step: Addicts and Mentally Ill Seen as Vulnerable to HMO's."* The New York Times (26 May): B1, B5.

Priluck, J. 1999. *"I'm Too Old to Do This Again: Six days of Rapid Detox."* New York Times Magazine (25 July): 58.

Tabbush, V. 1986. *"The Effectiveness and Efficiency of Publicly Funded Drug Abuse Treatment and Prevention Programs in California: A Benefit-Cost Analysis."* Los Angeles: University of California.

Winerip, M. 1999. *"Bedlam on the Streets: Increasingly, The Mentally Ill Have Nowhere to Go. That's Their Problem—and Ours."* The New York Times Magazine (23 May): 42-48.

Introduction to Addictions Treatment

Basic Characteristics

Addictions treatment is an array of interventions, techniques, and organized services designed to initiate, facilitate, and support recovery from
chemical dependency. This section summarizes features of contemporary
addictions treatment and distinguishes it from other forms of counseling
and therapy.

The Focus

When an actively addicted individual enters counseling and treatment,
the addiction is treated first. Personal growth is unlikely when an individual is chronically intoxicated or when life revolves around the acquisition and use of drugs. It is difficult to facilitate a helping process with
an actively addicted individual. The saying in the treatment field is,

"You're just talking to a chemical." Addiction is not treated as a symptom of other problems, but as a primary condition in its own right. However, the treatment of addiction with coexisting psychiatric disorders dictates special considerations, which are discussed later (see chapter 6). Addictions treatment keeps chemical use and relevant issues as the prime focus.

The Client

People referred to addictions treatment programs vary tremendously on a spectrum of addictions severity, degree to which they have remained functional, and behavior patterns typical of people using depressants, stimulants, hallucinogens, or a combination of them (polyabuse). Addictions clients are usually barely emerging from chemical anesthesia and are typically more mentally confused and psychosocially and medically deteriorated than nonaddicted clients (excepting psychotics). Addicted clients may suffer from every sort of medical and social problem, and may resist or deny the need for help. Some are approaching a life-threatening situation. Typically, this client needs more guidance, care, and a wider scope of services than other clients, for example, an individual seeking help for a mild depression or adjustment problem.

Practice Dimensions

Addictions treatment includes, but must go far beyond, what many people call counseling. A sufficiently ecumenical definition of *counseling* and *psychotherapy* is a supportive and empathic professional relationship that provides a framework for the exploration of emotions, behaviors, and thinking patterns, and the facilitation of healthy changes. Addictions treatment certainly provides this service, and in fact, it provides individual, group, and family counseling. However, as indicated by the clinical assessment of a client, it may involve several levels of a multiphasic treatment system, which requires professional counselors who have detailed knowledge, skills, and attitudes in a wide variety of areas. The National Steering Committee on Addiction Counseling Standards, which represents the major accreditation, counselor, and educational organizations in the addictions field, chose as its consensus document, *Addiction Counseling Competencies: The Knowledge, Skills, and Attitudes of Professional Practice* (CSAT 1998). This document, authored by the Addiction Technology Transfer Center National Curriculum Committee, details eight practice dimensions of addiction counseling:

1. *Clinical evaluation*, which includes screening and assessment, knowledge of diagnostic criteria, assessment instruments, and treatment options
2. *Treatment planning*, in collaboration with the client, based on assessment

3. *Referral,* based on knowledge of resources
4. *Service coordination,* which includes implementing the treatment plan, consulting other professionals, and continuing assessment and treatment
5. *Counseling* individuals and groups, including families, couples, and significant others
6. *Education* of client, family, and community
7. *Documentation,* including management of records and preparation of reports, plans, and discharge summaries
8. *Professional and ethical* responsibilities

A competent addictions counselor must have a wide knowledge base, which the addictions consensus document (CSAT 1998) calls transdisciplinary foundations. These include familiarity with the range and effect of legal and illegal psychoactive chemicals, models and theories of addiction and treatment, cultural competency in working with a wide variety of client populations, standards of conduct in helping relationships, diagnostic criteria, insurance and health maintenance options, and the roles of family, social network, and community in recovery.

The necessity of mastering the multiplicity of administrative, or "housekeeping," tasks (in the broadest sense, case-management tasks) seems to shift the focus away from the counseling relationship and define the addictions counselor as little more than a caseworker. Yet this is far from the case.

The Counseling Relationship

The supportive, empathic counseling relationship is the glue that binds the client and counselor through assorted treatment stages, facilities, anxieties, and growing pains. The importance of the collaborative, therapeutic alliance cuts across and indeed supercedes the particular therapeutic approach or model employed. The counseling relationship in addictions treatment is fraught with emotional thunder and lightning. Emotional "baggage" that a client brings to counseling and the emotional response of the counselor are important in all counseling efforts. The client may approach the counselor with any of a number of newly tapped dependency needs, rage and resentment, grief and loss, evasive maneuvers, and attempts to manipulate or test the relationship. The counselor must develop skills to stay aware of his or her strong reactions to a client's behaviors and maintain a professional and helpful role.

Treatment of addicts in general is typically more directive, structured, and managed than counseling and mental-health services for nonaddicted and nonpsychotic individuals; early treatment is most directive. This also reflects the fact that in addition to the deteriorated and unclear state of addicts, much addictions treatment is interfaced with criminal-justice and social-service institutions that mandate treatment. *Directive counseling*, in this case, does not mean telling the client what to do. It means focusing on the client's short-term recovery and abstinence from addictive substances and trying to influence the client toward healthy behaviors and decisions. Such directive counseling uses simple, direct, and concrete methods and treatment concepts, which show some results in a relatively short span of time. Counseling modalities that are complementary to this approach tend to be chosen in addictions treatment.

Counseling methods for chemically dependent people are far from a standardized system. There is a strong influence of self-help groups from which formal addictions treatment emerged. As the field has become more professionalized, counselors and trainers have gravitated toward integrated, eclectic, and transtheoretical counseling models. Addictions counseling does not claim or attempt to be a comprehensive psychotherapy, yet the broad goals of psychotherapy complement those of addictions treatment. To achieve stable sobriety and avoid relapse, with professional help, the client must identify, communicate, accept, and manage emotions and learn nonchemical and assertive coping strategies, communications skills, self-efficacy, and responsibility. The client must unlearn catastrophizing and negative self-statements and other unhealthy thinking patterns.

Addiction specialists recognize that treatment is carried out in stages. In early treatment, deep-seated, painful, and threatening issues should not be forcibly introduced by the counselor, except as necessary to maintain the client's sobriety. Gradually, the client internalizes mechanisms to govern his or her recovery. Self-statements by clients progress from "I can't drink" to "I won't drink" and hopefully to "I don't have to drink" (Zimberg 1978, 17-9). Addictions treatment most approaches or converges with generic counseling and psychotherapy in the last stage. Counselors must pay close attention to the special treatment needs of each stage. For example, when treatment includes a phase of inpatient or intensive outpatient rehabilitation, there may be a tendency to consider later outpatient counseling sessions as less critical. This would be a dangerous mistake. "Factors that emerge during aftercare, such as changes in motivation, reactions to treatment, patient–therapist interaction variables, environmental cues, may be more important determinants of continued participation than factors present at the beginning of aftercare, with the possible exception of alcohol and drug use during intensive outpatient treatment" (McCay et al. 1998, 160).

Effectiveness of Treatment

The study of the effectiveness of counseling and psychotherapy is notoriously complex and controversial. There is a myriad of competing models of the human personality, its health and dysfunction, and methods of change. Each of these could be applied to hundreds of possible diagnoses and to variable populations according to gender, ethnicity, and so on. As Garfield and Bergin (1994, 6) point out, to assess the relative value of each approach in each situation would require millions of statistical comparisons. In the addictions field, some of the difficulties in evaluating the effectiveness of treatment outcome include

- variety in the patient mix that influences retention, completion, and success
- variation in definitions of success, for example, graduation, abstinence, stabilization of social functioning, moderation of use, and reduction in harmful effects
- programs that winnow out all but the most motivated, resulting in "graduates" who tend to stay abstinent
- outcome studies or analyses of outcome studies conducted by individuals strongly associated with one point of view, whose methods tend to confirm their biases

Most major addictions treatment modalities are associated with a significant drop in use of alcohol and other drugs (SAMHSA 1994) and in the associated health, social, and legal ramifications and costs. A widely cited study funded by the state of California (Swan 1995) found that every dollar spent on treatment saved seven dollars for taxpayers, largely due to the reduction in both crime and unreimbursed medical care.

Getting into Treatment

Initiation of addictions treatment involves some mix of desperation, compulsion, and natural recovery processes.

Desperation

Addiction creates a great deal of pain, yet hopeless and helpless individuals tolerate a great deal of pain on a daily basis. In early Alcoholics Anonymous (AA) groups, it was believed that the addict had to sink lower and lower until he or she "hit bottom"; until, that is, the alcoholic felt misery, illness, and pain that for the moment overshadowed the pleasures or perceived benefits of an addictive lifestyle. Early members of AA epitomized the desperate "low-bottom alcoholic," who was one step from "insanity or death." Later it became clear that earlier intervention was possible and preferable because it minimized medical and social damages and costs.

Addictions professionals increase an addict's desperation when they encourage relatives and peers to end their attempts to help the addict. By protecting and buffering the addict from the painful consequences of his or her behavior, these helpers enable the addiction to continue and progress. Examples of enabling include making excuses for the addict, paying debts and bills, posting bail, and dragging the addict into bed. Ending enabling is a key principle in helping to initiate recovery.

Compulsory Treatment

The need to use drugs and alcohol often leads to consequences that force clients into programs that they did not or would not choose on their own. In the vast majority of cases, initiation of treatment involves an element of involuntary or semivoluntary referral. Referral pathways may be

- through the courts, as alternatives to sentencing or incarceration, or as part of a child protective action
- from an employer, through an assessment and referral program called an Employee Assistance Program (EAP)
- from an alcohol and drug counselor at an educational institution with a Student Assistance Program
- from family and friends, through an organized intervention (outlined in chapter 8, "Family, Community, and Cultural Systems")

This compulsory element in initiating treatment is far more common in addictions counseling than in mental-health services, and has grown even more common in recent years, with the increased clientele from criminal-justice systems. This can be viewed as a disadvantage, because this client does not want to be in treatment and will resist and resent attempts to help. On the other hand, the client cannot disappear easily when pressure to change builds. Involuntary, or mandated, presence and other stipulations (e.g., progress reports to a child-welfare agency or to an employer) are elements of "therapeutic leverage." Some in AA call it "raising the bottom." That is, it creates initial incentive or pressure for the addict to accept treatment before he or she sinks to a more desperate level, from which there may be no recovery. Once in a drug-free environment, addicts are often engaged in treatment and may make profound changes in their lives.

Natural Recovery

A large proportion of addicts become abstinent or return to moderate use of psychoactive substances without treatment or after treatment has not effected recovery. As early as 1962 Winick described how heroin addicts often "mature out" of use. Note, however, that many switch to alcohol, which offers a less strenuous and illicit lifestyle. Since then, many authors have examined "natural recovery" (Granfield and Cloud 1996; Stall and Biernacki 1986; Waldorf and Biernacki 1977, 1981; Waldorf, Biernacki, and Murphy 1991; Winick 1962). Many studies of natural recovery or moderation of use were summarized in George Vaillant's landmark work, which includes his longitudinal study of "core city" (Boston) men (Vaillant 1983).

Various factors may contribute to someone's move away from active addiction with or without treatment. Addiction or abuse may be congruent with membership in a peer group or subculture. Once one is beyond it, there may be a tendency to mature out of a chemical-using lifestyle. For example, some fraternity members move beyond binge drinking after graduation (although many do not). The "pothead" clique becomes less attractive when one is 25, and therefore marijuana is not used as widely in the age brackets above 30. Some people may tire of the effects of a drug, a status often expressed as "I got sick and tired of being sick and tired." Young adults frequently weary of feeling "burnt" (apathetic, stupid, depressed, confused) from the effects of chronic marijuana use (Hanson and Venturelli 1998). For some, new affiliations provide a stake in breaking from addiction. The birth of a child or the possibility of a job may make someone a stakeholder in society (Waldorf et al. 1991).

Most addicts, whether they allow themselves to be aware of it or not, subscribe to aspirations for normality, positive relationships, and reintegration with a community. Having an intact social-support system to which one can return (Granfield and Cloud 1996, 50) and the motive to return to it can protect from severe decline into addiction and contribute to the ability to recover naturally from it. For some addicts, natural-recovery processes involve an affiliation through a dramatic conversion to a religious or other structured ideological perspective (Myers 1992). Innumerable individuals have ended alcohol or other drug abuse upon conversion to a religious or spiritual perspective, often when in dire straits or incarcerated.

Treatment advocates are sometimes uncomfortable with phenomena such as natural recovery, which they feel will prove harmful to their cause (Weisner and Room 1978) or will encourage addicts to "go it alone." In fact, those seeking to disprove the claims of treatment modalities seize on observations of natural recovery to illustrate the supposed uselessness of treatment or self-help roads to recovery. Nevertheless, a large proportion of addicts do not recover naturally, nor moderate their use. Attempts to control addiction disease without some facilitation of insight, contemplation of problems, identification of triggers for relapse, learning of coping mechanisms, and adequate social support are chancy. Natural recovery processes often lose out to the power of addiction, inertia, and despair, which is where formal treatment is necessary. Addictions treatment staff increasingly recognize the opportunities presented by natural-recovery processes in facilitating treatment. Rather than dismiss natural-recovery, current thinking stresses facilitation of a client's movement through stages of change (Prochaska and DiClimente 1992; Prochaska, Norcross, and DiClimente 1994), building on strengths rather than approaching the addict from the standpoint of his or her failure, pathology, and deficits.

The mixture of desperation, compulsion, and yearnings for recovery may outweigh the perceived benefits of continued use and the fear of change just long enough to create a window of opportunity to initiate treatment. This window may close if a client cannot be admitted quickly into a treatment program.

Motives for Change

No one personality type fits the addict. A wide variety of etiological and risk factors predispose, encourage, and drive chemical abuse and its progression into addiction (Doweiko 1999; Hanson and Venturelli 1998). Each client suffers from a unique mix of these factors.

Chemical abusers have bundles of conflicted motives for and against their patterns of use. The costs and benefits associated with change battle those associated with the status quo (Miller and Rollnick 1991, 23-24). This battle is like the classic approach–avoidance conflict, illustrated in Figure 1.1. This conflict as it works in an addict is illustrated in Figure 1.2.

Figure 1.1 The approach–avoidance conflict of an addict contemplating or beginning treatment. Far from the goal, gradient A, the motives to approach predominate; nearer to the goal, gradient B, the motives to avoid are stronger.

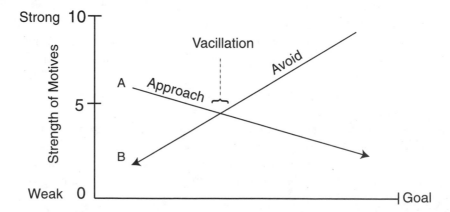

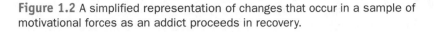

Figure 1.2 A simplified representation of changes that occur in a sample of motivational forces as an addict proceeds in recovery.

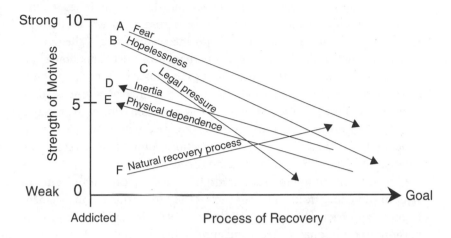

The approach–avoidance conflict was, first demonstrated by Neal Miller (1944, 1959), who alternatively fed and shocked mice on a runway and plotted how an animal's tendency to approach a goal (approach gradient) and retreat from it (avoidance gradient) both increased as it neared the goal. Avoidance motives increased more rapidly than did approach motives as it neared the goal. At a certain point they balanced out, and the mouse vacillated, darting back and forth. Analogies to the vacillating mouse are the nervous groom who feels increasingly anxious as the wedding day looms (or any individual who panics and flees intimacy which they also desire), and the person with a toothache who needs to go the dentist.

Addicts who are considering treatment have multiple elements in their approach–avoidance conflicts. Motives to attempt recovery include pressure from authority and loved ones, the painful consequences of substance abuse (muted by enabling), and natural-recovery processes. Motives to avoid treatment include short-term rewards in mood modification such as intoxication and chemical anesthesia, fear of physical withdrawal and change, association with drinking and drugging pals, hopelessness, and helplessness. The approach–avoidance analogy has limited application to the addict's struggle, because all of these motives fluctuate daily. More important, the emotional, cognitive, and sociocultural dimensions of human motivation cannot be reduced to a one-dimensional scale.

The mind of the active addict can be visualized as containing two opposing teams of motives in a tug of war, with the addiction counselor as coach and nutritionist for the recovery team. The initial job of the addictions treatment team is to manipulate the motives so that more of them aim in one direction than in the other. The job includes removing enabling buffers, mobilizing intervention and therapeutic leverage, and helping the addict identify and mobilize natural-recovery motives. A potential client's anxiety may cut in with increasing force as the day for intake approaches. A typical scenario is that the addict "cuts down" on drinking or drug use as part of an attempt to "get his act together," or enters detox and is sober for a couple of days. In either event, this alleviates some of the worst of the physical symptoms, which weakens one of the motives to approach treatment. This minor relief, coupled with anxiety, helps an addict decide to "do it myself." As one addictions counselor remarked, "The client seemed to hit bottom, but he bounced."

Various multiple-motives paradigms have become important in modern addictions treatments; one such is the Motivational Enhancement Therapy approach (Miller and Rollnick 1991). It leads toward major revisions of traditional concepts and approaches to denial and prevention of relapse. Just because the addict is enrolled in a treatment program, or has remained sober while under intensive supervision, or proclaimed allegiance to a self-help philosophy, does not magically eradicate all motives for drug use. As a saying in Narcotics Anonymous goes, "While you are in this meeting, your disease is doing push-ups outside the door."

Chemical abusers and addicts use very creative strategies to deny, minimize, rationalize, or avoid confronting their use. A wide variety of factors drive this array of avoidance behavior, which is much more often a problem in the treatment of addictions than of other disorders. The encounter with treatment personnel and institutions may, in fact, engender a defensive reaction. Moreover, the removal of chemical anesthesia itself in early treatment takes away the capstone of the system of defenses, which produces anxiety. Thus, the first step in ending addiction creates conditions for relapse. It is difficult to change and grow, and the process of dealing with addiction creates yet more discomfort. The counselor walks a fine line between the addict's denial and the premature unearthing of deep-seated, painful, and traumatic memories or problems (Wallace 1985, 37-8).

Regardless of the method of treatment, relapse is quite common. A majority of clients do not enter into permanent recovery at their first encounter with treatment; some never do. Many who now enjoy stable, long-term recovery from addiction had several "go-rounds" before it "stuck." Within the addictions treatment field, there is a range of opinion from those who feel that an addict is always an addict, so that vigilance against relapse and attendance at support groups must be lifelong, to those who believe that many can move beyond their identity as "recovering addict" in time. There is also a ferocious debate about whether the goal of treatment should be abstinence or whether moderate use can be learned and maintained by chemically dependent persons. Prochaska and DiClimente (1992) maintain that some degree of relapse behavior is a normal part of the spiral climb through stages of change.

Uniqueness of the Field

Most individuals treated for chemical dependency do not simply "go to a counselor." In the majority of cases, they participate in an organized treatment program. Programs and self-help fellowships provide a great deal of social support, an alternative to the culture of abuse, and the therapeutic effects of the milieu. Most treatment occurs in group settings, even aside from client participation in twelve-step programs such as Alcoholics Anonymous and Narcotics Anonymous.

There is a tremendous diversity in type, intensity, and length of stay in treatment. Some addicts qualify for admission to inpatient therapeutic communities funded to treat indigent clients, with a length of stay of eighteen months. Others participate in insurance plans that reimburse for only a five-day detoxification. Schuckit (1994, 3) remarked that "We function in a complex world where health-care providers must share scarce resources while reaching out to a pool of impaired individuals who, at least theoretically, have many more needs than we can possibly meet."

Treatment programs are part of or influenced by broader regulatory, economic, and political systems at state or national levels. Changes at these levels (e.g., legislative and funding initiatives, managed-care regulations) reverberate swiftly throughout the system of treatment providers, bringing rapid change in the status of facilities and employees alike. As a result of such regulatory changes, a large proportion of inpatient long-term rehabilitation facilities closed during the 1990s.

Who are addictions counselors? Thirty years ago most addictions counselors were nondegreed, recovering paraprofessionals. In the 1970s counselor credentialing systems emerged, and some states instituted separate certification for alcohol and drug counselors. Requirements were initially light, but have continuously added education, testing, and experiential requirements. National certification is available through state affiliates of the International Certification Reciprocity Consortium (ICRC) and the National Association of Alcohol and Drug Abuse Counselors (NAADAC). As of mid 1999, these two organizations were attempting to merge their accreditation systems. Today addictions counseling is a profession that requires rigorous preparation in a wide variety of areas. A tiered system has emerged in many states, ranging from paraprofessional credentials to master's-level licensure. Health-care delivery systems and reimbursement entities increasingly require professionally accountable treatment providers.

A large proportion of addictions counselors are still motivated by personal or family recovery issues, but most of them now have at least a bachelor's degree in a helping profession. The occupational niche for nondegreed paraprofessionals has been contracting, and is limited more and more to counselor aide positions in some large treatment programs. In response to these changing occupational needs, more than five hundred higher education programs in addictions studies have come into being. Training of addictions counselors has shifted gradually from a haphazard system of workshops and training programs into the academic mainstream. Many college addictions programs are affiliated with the International Coalition for Addiction Studies Education (INCASE 1997), which is preparing a comprehensive curriculum model and a mechanism for accrediting higher education programs.

Treatment Settings

There is a great range and variety of addiction-specific treatment settings, such as freestanding clinics, units in hospitals, mental health centers, and other social-service agencies. (Methadone-maintenance programs are discussed separately later in this chapter.) There are least three variables by which to classify an addictions treatment facility: model of treatment, level of care, and continuum of care.

Model of treatment is the treatment or recovery tradition upon which a program is based. These traditions and models, such as the therapeutic community and the Minnesota Model inpatient alcoholism program, are discussed later in this chapter.

Level of care is the intensity of treatment dictated by the severity of addiction and the degree to which the client's psychological and social functioning has deteriorated. The level of care is indicated by the number of hours per week of treatment, the degree of structure and supervision, and the scope of services. Facilities often specialize in providing a particular level of care. The evolution of a rational system of placement criteria to refer clients to an appropriate level of care is fairly new. Although use of such criteria may seem an elementary necessity, level of care has often been arbitrary, based on faith or tradition or the desire to curtail costs. The most widely accepted patient placement system is that of the American Society of Addiction Medicine (ASAM 1996). The types of facilities recognized by ASAM correspond to the following levels of care:

Level I: outpatient treatment

Level II: intensive outpatient treatment

Level III: medically monitored intensive inpatient treatment

Level IV: medically managed intensive inpatient treatment

To provide a simple example, a homeless, physically addicted, physically and mentally ill client would likely start out in a medically managed inpatient facility (level IV), whereas a full-time office worker with a family who has been identified as occasionally coming back from lunch in an intoxicated state would probably be referred to an outpatient treatment program (level I). Figure 1.3 (see p. 14) is an overview of ASAM's criteria for placement of adolescents in facilities with appropriate levels of care.

Continuum of care is the movement of addicts through a process of recovery. Although it may be woven out of treatment at disparate facilities, the ideal plan is to tailor a fairly seamless treatment "career." It may begin with intervention and referral from any of a variety of referring agents. Employee Assistance Programs in industry, Member Assistance Programs in organizations, and Student Assistance Programs in schools assess, intervene, and refer but do not treat addictions and substance abuse. The treatment career may include movement through several specialized facilities, such as a "detox," a "rehab," and a halfway house. Case management tries to ensure smooth continuity of treatment. As stated, initial referral and admission should be determined by assessment of the severity of the addiction and the client's needs, and should be to a facility that provides an appropriate level of care.

Recent Changes in Treatment Settings

The types and variety of facilities in which treatment takes place have changed in response to several factors. Three of them are cost-containment, tradition, and the correctional system.

Cost-containment efforts by managed-care entities have led to an overall move away from retrospective payment ("blind" reimbursement) and toward efforts to limit benefits for treatment services not considered medically crucial. Unfortunately, many mental-health and substance-abuse services are often seen as "not medically necessary." Some states have established parity for mental-health coverage with other medical care, but even among these some exclude substance-abuse services.

Since no research has demonstrated that inpatient rehabilitation is necessary for the vast majority of addicts, it has become easier for medical-reimbursement and managed-care entities to deny approval for inpatient care.

Figure 1.3 Adolescent Patient Placement Criteria for the Treatment of Psychoactive Substance Use Disorders

Criteria Dimensions	LEVEL I Outpatient Treatment	LEVEL II Intensive Outpatient Treatment	LEVEL III Medically Monitored Intensive Inpatient Treatment	LEVEL IV Medically Managed Intensive Inpatient Treatment
1 Acute intoxication and/or withdrawal potential	No withdrawal risk.	Manifests no overt symptoms of withdrawal risk.	Risk of withdrawal syndrome present, but manageable in Level III.	Severe withdrawal risk.
2 Biomedical conditions and complications	None or very stable.	None or non-distracting from addiction treatment and manageable in Level II.	Require medical monitoring but not intensive treatment.	Require 24-hour medical, nursing care.
3 Emotional/behavioral conditions and complications	None or very stable.	Mild severity with potential to distract from recovery.	Moderate severity needing a 24-hour structured setting.	Severe problems requiring 24-hour psychiatric care with concomitant addiction treatment.
4 Treatment acceptance/resistance	Willing to cooperate but needs motivating and monitoring strategies.	Resistance high enough to require structured program, but not so high as to render outpatient treatment ineffective.	Resistance high enough despite negative consequences and needs intensive motivating strategies in 24-hour structure.	Problems in this dimension do not qualify patient for Level IV treatment.
5 Relapse potential	Able to maintain abstinence and recovery goals with minimal support.	Intensification of addiction symptoms and high likelihood relapse without close monitoring and support.	Unable to control use despite active participation in less intensive care and needs 24-hour structure.	Problems in this dimension do not qualify patient for Level IV treatment.
6 Recovery environment	Supportive recovery environment and/or patient has skills to cope.	Environment unsupportive but with structure or support, the patient can cope.	Environment dangerous for recovery necessitating removal from the environment; logistical impediments to outpatient treatment.	Problems in this dimension do not qualify patient for Level IV treatment.

Levels of Care

Note: This overview of the Adolescent Admission Criteria is an approximate summary to illustrate the principal concepts and structure of the criteria.

This has quickly reverberated throughout the addiction service-provider industry. Since 1987 approximately one-half of inpatient residential treatment facilities have closed or converted to shorter-term treatment settings. In addition, there has been a decrease in the reimbursability for outpatient care as well, regardless of the need for more intensive care as assessed by addictions or medical staff.

As funding for addictions treatment has been cut at the national and state levels or has not kept pace with inflation, more funding has been available from correctional and other criminal-justice systems. Referrals for treatment of addicted offenders occur in the forms of pretrial intervention, alternatives to sentencing, serving sentence in treatment, and parole to treatment. In several states, drug courts and collaborative planning between criminal-justice personnel and addictions treatment providers has resulted in a new subfield for treatment of addicted offenders.

Trends in the treatment of addicted offenders vary by state. In Texas extensive initiatives were instituted, then reversed under a succeeding administration. Arizona reported extensive savings from a system to treat rather than imprison nonviolent drug offenders (Wren 1999). The Texas reversal was said to reflect a change from liberal to conservative government. Yet, as a New York Times editorial commented, "Arizona voters, tired of paying the exorbitant costs of imprisoning drug users and addicts who might be helped more cheaply, voted twice to provide a treatment alternative to jail. . . . Arizona is a politically conservative state. Its voters showed that they were tired of paying the costs of a bad idea. In requiring that drug offenders be treated before being freed of supervision, they may have made themselves safer" ("Arizona Shows . . .").

Case in Point
Funding and Treatment

Broad changes in funding are affecting the types of treatment that are available to addicts. For example, among the twelve major employers of students who graduated in 1988 from the Addiction Counselor Training Program at Essex County College in Newark, New Jersey, four have ceased operations, four have converted to serving primarily criminal-justice clients, and four remain relatively unchanged.

Types of Treatment Facilities

Most addictions treatment takes place in *outpatient treatment programs*. These are organized nonresidential treatment services in which the client visits the clinic at least once a week, and up to about ten hours per week.

There may be any number of activities such as individual, group, family, or didactic therapies. The multiple functions that may be served by outpatient facilities include:

- A setting in which the entire course of treatment takes place, as for the office worker in the example of level IV care, who may be stabilized and moved toward recovery without removal from the community or disruption of his or her occupational status.
- An initial point of contact for the many people who enter treatment at an outpatient treatment program, either as "walk-ins" or because that is the agency known to an employer or family member.
- Aftercare rehabilitation, usually of 28 days, which is only the very beginning of recovery. Upon discharge from an inpatient program, a referral is usually made to an outpatient treatment program that may last three to six months or even longer.

Intensive outpatient programs (*IOP*s), or intensive *outpatient treatment programs* (*IOTP*s), are more full and structured treatment settings in which the client is present from about ten to thirty hours per week. The broad category of intensive outpatient treatment may include programs that term themselves day treatment or, in a medical setting, partial hospitalization. Since the mid 1980s IOPs have sprouted geometrically (Washton 1997). This is a result of both cost containment by third-party payers and research that indicates that the 28-day inpatient stay, formerly the mainstay of addictions treatment, is a "faith" system not based on rational criteria. The IOP fills a large service gap in the treatment system between inpatient and outpatient care. Its cost is about half that of residential care, and it allows clients to continue in work and family life, promotes bonding among clients, and allows clients to practice relapse-prevention techniques in real-life situations. In addition, assessment of clients' readiness to complete treatment, and of their problems and progress, can be made in a realistic setting.

Clients of IOPs may be living at home, in a therapeutic or long-term residence of some sort, or in apartments as part of special programs. IOPs can even be operated in prisons. All of the components of rehabilitative treatment should be provided including counseling (individual, group, and family), treatment planning, crisis management, medication management, client education, self-help orientation, case management, discharge planning, and so forth (CSAT 1994; Gottheil 1992). IOTP is similar to "partial hospitalization." Both are ASAM PPC-2, Level 11-5.

Inpatient rehabilitation, or *intensive inpatient treatment*, involves a live-in setting. This category is quite diverse and includes therapeutic communities in which the length of stay varies from four to twenty-four months, and a variety of other rehabilitation units such as those based on the AA or Minnesota Model, which usually involve four-week stays. Inpatient treatment may be medically managed, medically supervised, or nonmedical. It also may involve a number of phases, such as orientation, treatment, discharge, and re-entry. Individual, group, and family treatment may occur, as well as considerable patient education and relapse-prevention training. Treatment plans are constructed collaboratively by client and counselor, who identify long-term and short-term goals that are continually reassessed and updated. Plans are made for re-entry into the community and ability to cope after discharge; they might include vocational, educational, and housing referrals, as well as continuing care as an outpatient of either the rehabilitation agency itself or another agency.

Detoxification, or *detox*, *units* may be freestanding facilities or inpatient medical units in which the client can be stabilized medically and can withdraw safely from drugs before entering a rehabilitation setting. Not all addicts or abusers require formal detoxification. Detoxification can also be an initial stage of inpatient rehabilitation, in the same unit. Detoxification is only the very first stage of recovery; it is not a complete or even a partial treatment process. Many addicts have detoxed repeatedly. The mistaken idea that detoxification is treatment contributes greatly to the idea that treatment is useless. Some addicts check themselves into detox units to reduce their level of tolerance, to "get their heads together" when they are homeless and cold, or to satisfy some impending legal proceeding. Others enter with the intention of recovery but retreat when the worst withdrawal symptoms have abated.

Detoxification from alcohol has traditionally taken place in inpatient settings. During the 1990s some outpatient detoxification units were set up, which appalled some addictions counselors. However, some studies (Hayashida et al. 1989) suggest that outpatient detoxification is not out of the question for a good chunk of the population in need (those with mild to moderate symptoms of alcohol withdrawal) and, in fact, it can free scarce resources to help more addicts. Nonmedical detoxification programs, sometimes called social-setting detoxification facilities or sobering-up stations, were common in the 1960s and 1970s but have fallen out of favor with regulatory and funding agencies since then, and thus have declined greatly in number.

Modern treatment of chemical dependency has an intermediate step between treatment and total re-entry into society. The *re-entry residence* is a built-in segment of the therapeutic-community treatment of drug addiction. In facilities that are derived historically from alcoholism there are halfway houses, which are therapeutically structured residential settings that follow rehabilitation; they usually require that residents work or pay a fee. The term *halfway house* is also used to refer to a variety of supportive and transitional residences for psychiatric patients and offenders just released from incarceration. Another type of transitional housing is the *cooperative living* arrangement for recovering alcoholics called Oxford Houses, which arose in the Capitol District in the late 1970s (CSAT 1992). These are democratically operated, financially self-supporting houses with no paid staff. They are essentially communes of alcoholics, living in buildings rented by the residents. This participatory democracy is believed to strengthen responsibility and end dependency, replacing it with self-sufficiency. The democratic operation of Oxford Houses extends to votes on admission of members and election of officers for six-month terms. The only house rule is sobriety, and use of any alcohol or other drug results in immediate expulsion. All the houses belong to the Oxford House, Inc., network. As a prerequisite to receiving federal block grants for alcohol and drug treatment, states must establish a revolving loan fund to help open new Oxford Houses. According to researchers at DePaul University (Jason et al. 1994), the Oxford House model builds autonomy, community, and self-esteem, and is underused and under-recognized.

Long-term residential care can be arranged for clients who are not yet capable of independent living; it is provided by the Salvation Army and many other nonprofit entities. Often these are little more than a structured shelter situation, although the "Sallie," as clients call it, also has a work requirement. Salvation Army residences may refer to themselves as rehabilitation programs, but this is a misnomer by most treatment-community standards.

Programs that serve special populations include those set up to treat the mentally ill chemical abuser, or MICA (see chapter 6), and those for pregnant addicts or addicted mothers and their children.

Continuity of care in the treatment career is essential. A large percentage of clients are "lost" when there is a gap between intervention and detox, detox and rehab, and so forth. Referring agents or case managers spend a great deal of time and effort struggling with the timing of available beds at the right time and place. For example, if a client referred by her Human Resources Department (HRD) needs to complete a 5-day detoxification program, followed by a 21-day rehabilitation stay at a facility with a 10-day waiting list, the client would have to wait 5 days before going into the detox so that she could slide neatly into the next phase, preferably transported directly between the facilities. Figure 1.4 shows the route this client's treatment would take.

Figure 1.4 The route of one client's treatment career, which is monitored by her case manager.

1. Meeting with EAP administrator
2. Evaluation at outpatient clinic
3. Inpatient detoxification (5 days)
4. Inpatient rehabilitation (21 days)
5. Aftercare at outpatient clinic
6. Ongoing reports to EAP

Methadone-Maintenance Treatment

Methadone maintenance (MM), perhaps miscategorized when called a treatment for opiate (narcotic-analgesic) addiction, is simply the systematic dispensation of a synthetic opioid that enables the addicted client to attain social stability, abdicate the criminal career, and enter the educational or occupational world. Last but not least, it reduces the risk of contracting or spreading HIV/AIDS by reducing the number of addicts who use and re-use hypodermic needles.

Methadone maintenance is effective because

- it is administered orally, in controlled doses.
- it can be administered only once a day.

- the rushes, highs, and lows that accompany much drug use are absent. The client can study, operate a vehicle, or file library books without nodding out or experiencing changes in mood or functioning.

There is tremendous variety among MM programs, for example, in counseling and other services offered, in the attempt to screen for alcohol and other drug use, and in attempts to taper the patient off to a truly drug-free status. Although MM programs wish it otherwise, many clients drink and use drugs, and many increase their use of alcohol and other drugs (AOD) if and when they taper off their methadone dosage. Higher dosages of methadone are associated with less illicit drug use (Hargreaves 1983).

Methadone maintenance occupies a peculiar position in addictions treatment. Although this modality serves more clients than drug-free treatment programs, MM is the shabby, outcast stepsister in the addictions field. Methadone-maintenance clients are stigmatized by the public at large, by the health-care system, and within the addictions field itself. To many, their participation in the dispensation of an opioid substitute denies them the honorific "recovering addict," but rather institutionalizes and ritualizes their addiction. This attitude dehumanizes clients and discourages the goal of abstinence.

Drug-free treatment models seem to make MM and treatment mutually exclusive categories. Yet methadone maintenance, whatever its shortcomings, need not be limited to a grim routine of early morning dispensation of the opioid. In fact, programs that are so limited often fail even in their mission to replace illegal opioids with a legal one.

Case in Point
Methadone and Other Drugs

A counselor at one program in the urban Northeast confessed that the vast majority of his clients drank fairly heavily, and at least half of them also consumed benzodiazepines and marijuana. He attempted to steer new clients away from the peer-group gatherings of the client subculture for fear that the new clients would progress in their overall polyaddicted status just as they were "stabilized" in their heroin addiction. Another program in the same region tested vigorously and randomly for fifteen substances and did not tolerate polyabuse.

Methadone programs vary along several axes, and so are difficult to compare. First, they may vary in the extent to which the program monitors and tolerates the use of other psychoactive substances. A philosophical paradox arises when drawing up standards for polyabuse behavior in methadone programs, which fall roughly under the rubric of the harm-reduction model. That is, as intolerance of other, non-opioid drugs increases, the number of clients decreases, as do the consequent benefits to society in terms of crime reduction and the reduced spread of HIV.

Another continuum along which MM programs fall is the degree to which there is individual, group, and family counseling. At one end of the spectrum are the programs that offer infrequent case-management sessions; in the middle are various levels of intensity to which programs attempt to involve clients in counseling processes; at the most treatment-intensive end of the spectrum are a few therapeutic-community (TC) day programs such as the Passages program (De Leon et al. 1993). MM violates the traditional, central community-treatment tenet of abstinence from the very start of treatment. The Passages program (De Leon et al. 1993) modifies the therapeutic-community format in terms of a more flexible phased schedule, a less confrontational style, and individualized case management. Integrating treatment with opioid substitution may seem to fly in the face of basic addictions treatment philosophy, which holds that one cannot treat an individual who is influenced by psychoactive drugs. How, for example, can an anesthetized person introspectively examine or communicate emotional states? However, while not the optimal situation, it is useful for a large segment of the MM treatment population to participate in a counseling milieu or process, the more comprehensive, the better. In this light, activities and techniques described in this book are not only applicable to MM settings, but are critical to enhance the ability of MM to achieve the goals of harm reduction or abstinence. Other MM program enhancements improve the retention rate and, indirectly, help reduce the spread of HIV. For example, substitution of this synthetic narcotic substance for intravenous drugs decreases associated needle sharing and participation in crime or sex industries to finance a habit (Anglin et al. 1993, 3-6).

Maddux (1993, 23-4) shows that a low or absent fee is associated with better retention, as is the clients' role in regulating their dosages. While some may suspect that an addict will maximize the dosage, it is unlikely because the methadone client is motivated to avoid withdrawal syndromes rather than seek a euphoric rush. The client may be re-entering the workforce and wish also to avoid excessive sedation. Maddux (1993, 24-5) reports that the client-regulated dose reduces conflict with staff as well as surreptitious return to illicit drug use, and that indeed, clients do not markedly increase their doses. Rapid admission is also a must in successful maintenance programs.

A standard methadone-maintenance program protocol may include

- intake
- annual medical examination
- attainment of increasing takc-home dose privileges, in stages
- monthly testing for drug use, with refusal to submit counted as a positive test (pregnant women tested more often, perhaps weekly)
- two one-hour counseling sessions each month, with crisis intervention sessions on request
- disciplinary detoxification resulting from any violation of program rules

Successful program enhancements cited by Anglin and colleagues (1993) should be designed to match an individual client's needs. These may include

- training for counselors and case managers
- intensive contact during the first month
- contingency contracts, that is, provision of rewards such as food or movie coupons for the client's compliance and progress
- enhanced program services such as bus passes, off-site psychiatric consultations, additional urinalysis (perhaps with swift on-site processing)
- high-risk counseling and support groups for HIV-infected clients, cocaine users, and women

Methadone-maintenance programs also vary in their attempts to wean the client completely from the addictive substances to this synthetic opioid. A combination of counseling and psychopharmaceutical support to methadone detoxification is most effective (Milby 1988). Although the rates of detoxification have improved gradually since the early days of MM, it is sad to report that some clinics do not encourage the ultimate goal of abstinence.

ACTIVITY 1.1 Tell me about your agency.

It is important for counselors to be familiar with the treatment providers in their communities and with the relationships among those providers. It is interesting and useful to visit an agency with which you are unfamiliar. Request an opportunity to interview a staff member or administrator. Your instructor may be able to provide a letter of introduction to help you get the interview.

To prepare for your visit, think about the information you want about the agency. Make a list of questions to elicit information about the following:

- agency philosophy
- agency policies and procedures
- administrative and clinical structure
- staffing patterns
- treatment philosophy
- treatment methods and modalities
- funding sources
- eligibility requirements
- length of stay
- cultural, class, and ethnic makeup of staff and clientele
- referral patterns
- success rate
- method of measuring success

Models of Treatment and Recovery

How do counselors know what to do to facilitate personal growth and recovery? The traditions and philosophies of addictions treatment are based on beliefs, concepts, and values concerning addiction, recovery, and the human condition, some of which are unwritten or inexplicit. It is important to be aware of these concepts, and the ways of organizing thinking about human problems.

The term *model* is used in science and philosophy to mean any representation or description of a phenomenon. Models identify

- parts or elements of what one is trying to describe, and their characteristics, whether atomic particles or family members.
- the interaction of these elements, and their places and roles in a system, structure, or process. How do members of a group communicate; why must they designate a scapegoat?
- boundaries of systems. How does an addicted family or an organization build enclosing barriers?
- changes that may occur in the system, whether evolution, adaptation, deterioration, or disintegration.

Although models are necessary, they have several pitfalls. A model is only a representation of a thing or process according to the builder's biases and thinking styles. It can easily oversimplify matters, leave out subtle connections, or include products of imagination. Robert Fancher (1995) states that while counseling and psychotherapy certainly help people, it is seldom for the reasons stated, and that their theoretical underpinnings are pseudoscientific accounts of how therapists *think* they help.

People approach work with a pre-existing model, and search for data to confirm it, tending to ignore contradictions. For example, if an addict resists a diagnosis, counselors will tend to attribute it to resistance and denial rather than fear of sanctions or stigmatization, cultural differences, or anger at a counselor's power over him or her (Taleff 1997).

Many models are part of elaborate systems of belief that have fierce adherents. These are called ideologies. An ideology can be interpreted in a dogmatic and rigid fashion, with hostility toward any different approach (Myers 1991). The addictions and psychotherapy fields have always been factionalized, polarized, and ideologized. In the addictions field, this is compounded by the fact that many people feel that their system of belief is necessary to save lives; anything else is a potential disaster. For example, many recovering alcoholics are horrified at approaches such as Moderation Management that countenance controlled drinking strategies. Yet the tendency to demonize differences goes far beyond personal experiences with alcohol and other drugs, and speaks to fears among the citizenry at large. Harm-reduction approaches, which include methadone maintenance, needle-exchange programs, and legalization of marijuana for medical purposes, are pilloried as pro-drug, and sympathizers are described as part of a conspiracy favoring drug use.

Models can also refer to a specific array of techniques or organization of services to achieve a certain goal, such as the MATRIX model for methamphetamine addiction. A term similar to model is *paradigm*, which carries the connotation of a pattern that governs behavior and thinking rather than a mere description.

Counselors must be skilled at thinking critically about models of addiction and recovery, counseling and treatment, rather than parrot what they have read or heard. It is unethical and dangerous to staff treatment programs with individuals who are not trained to evaluate critically the models they employ in counseling and treatment.

🄰🄲🅃🄸🅅🄸🅃🅈 What's the system?

Drawing on your experience in other coursework in the physical and social sciences, provide examples of

- elements of systems
- interactions of elements in systems
- boundaries of systems
- changes in systems
- theoretical models
- ideologies

Self-Help Models

Several movements for social and political change in the nineteenth and early twentieth centuries also had ideas about individual self-improvement. Most prominently, they attempted to influence people to be "temperate"; that is, cut down on the harmful use of alcohol. Temperance movements were linked in the second and third quarters of the nineteenth century to the Abolitionist (antislavery) movement. Temperance spokespersons included the famous abolitionist Fredrick Douglas. At the same time, societies of men known as Abstentionists sprang up and encouraged men to take an oath in church foreswearing alcohol. This was known as "taking the pledge." Societies of former drinkers, such as the Washingtonians and the United Order of Ex-Boozers, also anticipated the rise of AA in the next century. Because women did not have the freedom to buy and imbibe alcohol, most of these movements revolved around men. In fact, the idea of women as alcoholics was fairly unknown until the mid twentieth century.

In the early twentieth century, the votes-for-women movement, or Suffragettes, went tandem with the Temperance movement. Being newly political, these women joined the movement to ban alcohol outright, and were a key element in the Prohibitionist movement via a variety of organizations such as the Anti-Saloon League and the Women's Christian Temperance Union. Alcohol consumption declined for decades, and the United States went "dry" county by county, culminating in the passage of the Nineteenth Amendment to the United States Constitution in 1919, known as the Prohibition Amendment, which forbade the manufacture and distribution of alcoholic beverages. Paradoxically, in the 1920s a proto-feminist generation of women then helped organize the movement to gather a million signatures and abolish Prohibition. Congress acted upon this in 1933.

In the benchmark year of 1935 Alcoholics Anonymous (AA) was spun off by William Griffith Wilson and Dr. Robert Smith from the Oxford Movement, a religious organization. AA began to expand in 1941, when its success was widely publicized.

Alcoholics Anonymous is a peer self-help group, or fellowship, of alcoholics. In the 1930s, 1940s, and 1950s it remained the only help for alcoholics who otherwise would find themselves in psychiatric facilities, the drunk tanks in jails, or, if they were lucky, in shelters run by the Salvation Army or other religious organization. The defining characteristics of Alcoholics Anonymous, which are stated in the twelve steps to recovery (see Appendix B), include these principles:

- abstinence from alcohol as a requirement for recovery from addiction
- anonymity

- spirituality through a spiritual awakening and giving up control to a higher power
- self-identification as a sufferer from a lifelong, chronic disease
- staying sober one day at a time
- group support from a fellowship of alcoholics

The success of AA may be explained by its comprehensive network, which supports abstinence and recovery; frequent attendance at AA meetings where role modeling, confession, sharing, and support take place; and participation in the member network between meetings, including obtaining and relying on a senior member, or sponsor.[1]

Al-Anon, a fellowship for relatives and significant others of alcoholics, was founded in 1951, although it did not take off as a movement until 1962. Narcotics Anonymous (NA), the third of the three major twelve-step fellowships, was founded in 1953. It was relatively small throughout the 1950s and 1960s, with hardly any overlap with the therapeutic-community movement. It grew during the 1970s and even more during the 1980s. Although the basic text of NA, *Narcotics Anonymous* (NA 1988) was written in 1962, its section of personal stories dates from 1981. The language is more modern, more emotional, and more in tune with modern subcultures of drug use. The atmosphere of NA meetings is more emotional and "nitty-gritty" than that of AA. This is due in part to the fact that many members attended drug treatment programs that emphasize vigorous interpersonal interaction in group sessions.

A wide variety of twelve-step fellowships have spun off from AA and NA; the largest are Gamblers Anonymous and Overeaters Anonymous. Smaller fellowships include Debtors Anonymous, Sex and Love Addicts Anonymous, Sexaholics Anonymous, Obsessive-Compulsive Anonymous, and Attention-Deficit Disorder Anonymous. Addiction recovery fellowships that are not part of the twelve-step culture include Secular Organizations for Sobriety (Christopher 1989) and Smart Recovery (Trimpey 1992), which is based on the rational-emotive-behavioral therapy (REBT or RET) of Albert Ellis (Ellis et al. 1988), and which was originally called Rational Recovery (see appendix B). AA and NA are mistrustful of these non-12 step approaches and movements. As Pita (1996, 54-71) and others have noted, this is unfortunate because cognitive-behavioral methods can mesh nicely with the fellowship of AA (Horvath 1999).

---

[1] Many excellent histories and accounts of AA have been written, starting in 1939 with *Alcoholics Anonymous*, the "Big Book" (AA 1976). Others are historical volumes (AA 1957,1980) and books by writers and academics (Blumberg 1991; Kurtz 1988; Maxwell 1984; Robertson 1988; Thomsen 1975).

In Rational Recovery (RR) and Smart Recovery, members find it useful to conceive of the thoughts of drinking and irrational self-statements as an inner "addictive voice," which attempts to convince them to relapse. They simplify this concept as the BEAST, an easily remembered acronym as well as metaphor:

B = Boozing opportunity, when you think about drinking

E = Enemy recognition, when you hear the mental voice

A = Accuse the *thought* of drinking of being the real enemy

S = Self-control and self-worth are now yours for the taking

T = Treasure your sobriety; a lot is at stake (Bishop 1995, 149)

In the early 1990s, the founder of RR, Jack Trimpey, made the "addictive voice" concept the core of his approach to recovery, and has abandoned the entire REBT theory in favor of "Addictive Voice Recognition Training" (Bishop 1995, 143).

ACTIVITY **What goes on in those meetings?**

It is important for all addiction counselors to experience the atmosphere and process of a self-help fellowship. It is also a requirement of many certification and credentialing authorities.

Attend a self-help group with which you are not familiar, and write a two-page "reaction paper." Include a description of what took place, the format of the speeches, the customs you observed, the atmosphere before and after the formal meeting, and the feelings you had while attending.

Inpatient Rehabilitation

Alcoholics Anonymous steers clear of institutional affiliation. Early AA members, starting with Bill W., the founder, often filled their houses with those whom they were helping to "dry out." Eventually, inpatient rehabilitation programs based on AA principles grew out of this practice. These programs, which began in Minnesota in the 1950s, kept the AA philosophy but gradually added the professional framework of assessment-based treatment planning, as well as individual and group counseling. The length of stay for clients in Minnesota was 28 days. For decades afterwards, the dominant form of alcoholism treatment in the United States was based on this so-called Minnesota Model and a disease concept of treatment based on the philosophy of AA (Yalisove 1997). In the late 1970s and early 1980s a golden age of inpatient treatment was possible because of insurance reimbursement. Many expensive, private "rehabs" flourished.

Unfortunately, the excesses of that era were used to invalidate the inpatient approach, and many people in need of such a level of care have been denied that option.

Therapeutic Community

The term *therapeutic community (TC)* originally denoted an innovative approach in the inpatient treatment of post-traumatic stress disorder (PTSD) in the immediate post–World War II period. It instituted a therapeutic milieu among patients, as well as a structure that allowed patients' input into the management of the unit (Jones 1953, 1968; Rapoport 1960). However, the term is better known now for its application to the addiction field, as a demanding long-term, drug-free residential program run by recovering addicts. The therapeutic-community model began in 1958 in California when Charles Dederich, a recovering alcoholic, brought drug addicts into an AA group. He then split off to found his own organization, named Synanon after a mispronunciation of "seminar." It differed from AA in that it addressed primarily drug addiction, used confrontational methods, abandoned the spiritual component of AA, and was residential. The residential addict community was run totally by recovering addicts. This has been a feature in subsequent TCs, although there may be a supervising layer of professionals who may or may not be recovering addicts. Synanon developed a variety of harsh confrontational techniques that were designed to strip addicts of their "street" images and defenses. These included confrontational groups, then called "the Synanon guns." Other important features of this modality are work therapy and a hierarchy of rewards, privileges, and statuses up until graduation, which are designed to resocialize the addict into responsible and mature behavior (Yablonsky 1965). The stratification system goes beyond graduation; the TC graduate may return as a role model and often becomes part of the staff. Building on the principles of Synanon, the prototype of the modern therapeutic community was Daytop Village, developed by Daniel Casriel and David Deitch in 1964 and 1965 and founded on Staten Island, New York City. Other early therapeutic communities that developed in the late 1960s include Phoenix House in New York City, Integrity House in Newark, New Jersey, Marathon House in Exeter and Coventry, Rhode Island, Gateway House in Chicago, and Gaudenzia House in Philadelphia.

Reactions to TCs ranged from the predictable NIMBY (not in my backyard), to awe at the recently addicted clean-cut young men and women hammering, sawing, and scrubbing the sidewalk, to comparisons of TCs with religious revivalists. The Ford Foundation's Drug Abuse Survey Project (DASP 1972, 191-2) considered TCs "as much a quasi-evangelical movement as a drug-treatment modality. . . . The philosophy of the TC becomes the religion for the addict." It is true that at the time members used such phraseology as "living the concept" and "coming into the concept." The report also noted (DASP 1972, 192) that many TC practices paralleled the "encounter group" and "commune" movements of the time in the nonaddict society. Anthropologists studied Daytop Village as an interesting subculture (Sugarman 1974). Conflicts developed between emerging leadership of the rank-and-file recovering addicts and the professionals who often administered the TCs. In several instances the conflicts culminated in organizational schisms (Casriel and Amen 1971; Sugarman 1974, 119-27).

The TC model became dominant in drug treatment during the 1970s. There are hundreds of treatment programs that more or less follow the TC model. Therapeutic Communities of America, a national organization, has 58 affiliate programs. Many or most of the original, rather harsh practices have been modified considerably. The programs have seen the influence of social learning and cognitive psychology, and educational and occupational programs have been added to facilitate realistic re-entry into society. In addition, the model has been incorporated into many programs in prisons and programs designed as alternatives to sentencing, as intermediate sanctions, and as sentencing to treatment (Lockwood and Inciardi 1993). Unfortunately, the TC model is often stereotyped as an incredibly harsh environment, as if it had not changed since the 1970s (Deitch 1991).

Models of Emotion

A host of models of the human personality, its functions and dysfunctions, and of addiction underlie treatment methods. These models specify the components of and processes operating in human psyches and behaviors. These assumptions in addictions treatment may or may not be explicit or, by the time it filters down to counselors, the original rationale may be lost. For example, the use of intensive confrontation and emotional expression in group treatment is not grounded in research. Rather it is based on

- observations of tough street addicts in the 1960s, who were thought to be emotionally "encapsulated" behind a fortress of defenses, a character structure reinforced by chemical anesthesia.
- a self-help tradition of therapeutic communities.
- an old model of emotion as something tangible, stored in a system like water in clogged plumbing ("If you don't express all that anger you're carrying around, you're going to go out and shoot dope again!").

The "hydraulic" model of emotion has roots in the century-old psychoanalytic model, which was the only available description of the emotional system for many decades. If one subscribes to the view that stored-up feelings can psychically poison clients and lead to relapse, it follows that clients need to expel anger and pain forcefully by vigorous emotional expression such as shouting or crying. The culture of traditional therapeutic communities encourages, even demands, unfettered emotion to a greater extent than other programs do. While joining a twelve-step group like AA is often a transforming and cathartic experience, there is also concern that it is dangerous for a newly recovering alcoholic to dwell on anger and resentments. This is expressed in slogans such as "Turn it over to a higher power," "Let go and let God," "Take it easy," and "Live and let live." The format of twelve-step groups discourages group conflict; each member takes a turn, and there is a rule against interactions and reactions ("cross-talk") during presentations.

The point here is not to criticize group modalities, marathons, or crying in therapy, but to underscore that crucial assumptions often go unstated or unexamined. It is important to re-examine them (and all models of the psyche used in counseling and psychotherapy) in light of recent understandings about neurobiological function. Two well-known experiments highlight neurobiological influences in human responses and reactions. In one, the varying musical accompaniment to a grisly war film influenced the appraisal of and emotional reactions to the film as evidenced in measurements of physiological response (Lazarus 1966). In the second, subjects interpreted and defined the feeling they got from an adrenaline (epinephrine) injection according to situational cues (Schachter and Singer 1962). Such work led to the model that emotion involves

- the cognitive appraisal and labeling of external stimuli,
- a physiological response, and
- the appraisal and labeling of physiological states.

Studies such as those of Dutton and Aron (1974) support the hypothesis that people label their physiological states as emotions in accordance with cognitive explanations; yet, the cognitive appraisal hypothesis has limitations. Basic emotions or, more accurately, response systems evolved to deal with various social and environmental situations, such as anger, fear, joy, disgust, and surprise (Plutchik 1984). Neuroscientist Joseph LeDoux (1996, 16) explains that emotions are a way of talking about aspects of various systems that evolved separately and that involve separate neural systems that concern reactions to danger, procreative functions, sociability, and so forth. Cognition interpolates with this neural substrate in various ways, such as the interpretation of stimuli and physiologic arousal. However, cognition does not stand alone or have free reign; physiologic arousal that is of unknown origin tends to get a negative explanation (Marshall and Zimbardo 1979). Memory and associations also play a part in cognitive explanations of arousal (Maslach 1979).

Awareness of feelings and the ability to communicate these feelings reduce anxiety, loneliness, shame, and guilt. Awareness of thinking that contributes to a high level of negative feelings is also useful. In addition, it may be therapeutically valuable for someone to realize that he or she can demonstrate anger without falling apart, drinking, taking drugs, or experiencing terrible consequences. But emotions are not stored like old wine in an oaken keg to be tapped years later; nor does the volume always have to be turned up to an ear-shattering intensity for communication to be satisfactory.

In practice, none of this is particularly pertinent, helpful, or easily explained to the suffering client; nor does it diminish the client's very real and powerful emotions. It just argues against assuming that emotion is stored up as in a battery or flask, and questions the assumption that letting off steam or "getting out" anger in group therapy will solve problems, and whether understanding and modifying one's thinking can contribute to more manageable feelings and behaviors. Many counselors believe that a "menu" of techniques should be available for application to the particular needs of a client at his or her stage of recovery.

The Disease Model

The twelve-step philosophy of Alcoholics Anonymous and Narcotics Anonymous is not classified easily. It has elements of psychology, medicine, and spiritual teachings, and is also associated with the so-called disease model. In fact, there are many models that describe addictive disease. Many authors have examined various models of addictive disease (Conrad and Schneider 1980; Tournier 1979), and it is not within the scope of this text to review the history of moral, medical, psychological, and other models of addiction (see Thombs 1999).

As many AA members interpret it, the disease model states that addiction is a life-long disease, which is held in abeyance "one day at a time," and over which addicts are powerless. This dictates the need for complete abstinence and continuous membership in a recovery fellowship to ensure sobriety through reinforcement, support, and "keeping the memory green." The principle is that addiction is a disease that progresses inevitably.

A Progressive Disease

The concept of alcoholism as a progressive disease was formulated within the professional world by Jellinek, who described stages of alcoholic disease (1960). For members of AA and for those who have entered treatment in terrible shape after many failed attempts at sobriety, this certainly seems to be the case. But research with problem drinkers indicates that it is a mistake to generalize from that sample. Many addicts remain functional, many fluctuate in their levels of functioning, and others experience natural recovery or mature out of use (Granfield and Cloud 1996; Vaillant 1983; Waldorf and Biernacki 1997, 1981; Winick 1962). Some workers in the addictions field have avoided or dismissed information about spontaneous or natural recovery for fear it might damage the rationale for treatment or tempt patients to "go it alone." To the contrary, research by Prochaska and DiClimente (1982; Prochaska, Norcross, and DiClemente 1994) on recovery from tobacco addiction without formal treatment has provided tremendous help in improving addictions treatment.

Relapse

Some proponents of the disease-progression model point to the fact that some addicts who relapse after years of sobriety seem to move very quickly into a severe addicted state. They present this as evidence that the disease was progressing even *during* sobriety, which is hard to explain scientifically. Other people look to factors such as defeat, shame, guilt, and loss of social support to account for catastrophic relapse. Proponents of cognitive-behavioral treatment of addictions state that as part of the vicious cycle of relapse, the first use of alcohol (or other addictive substance) after a period of sobriety triggers thinking such as "Since I broke my abstinence, I might as well go on a binge" or "I can't face my AA sponsor and buddies after all this clean time" (Wright et al. 1993, 125). The cognitive-behavioral model of the relapse process (Marlatt and Gordon 1985, 38) can be summarized as follows: Individuals in a high-risk situation, who have not learned an adequate coping response, and who have low self-efficacy and positive expectations about using the substance, "pick up the first drink" (or drug). This triggers the Abstinence Violation Effect. The step of initial use is seen by the client as evidence of personal failure with attending guilt, shame, and embarrassment. That peers and professionals may indirectly convey agreement with this self-assessment only reinforces this sense of failure. Many clinicians feel that the ideology of "once a drunk, always a drunk" contributes to the expectation that relapse is inevitable or likely, and gives permission for a single drink to become a total, catastrophic relapse.

It would be a mistake to assume that members of AA or NA remain stuck in some "folk model." Many addictions counselors have blended twelve-step or therapeutic-community philosophies with professional research. For example, Marlatt and Gordon's relapse-prevention system (1985) promotes learning coping responses for high-risk situations, which increase self-efficacy about sobriety efforts, thus decreasing the probability of relapse. This is congruent with the twelve-step admonition to "Stay away from people, places, and things" associated with drinking or drugging, and "HALT: Don't get too Hungry, Angry, Lonely, or Tired." Prochaska, Norcross, and DiClimente (1994) see relapse as a normal part of the process of spiraling upward through stages of change.

Counseling Approaches

Counseling approaches, sometimes called theories of counseling or counseling models, are systems of ideas concerning the ways that change can take place. They can identify major goals and strategies of treatment. Some advertise in their name that they subscribe to a particular personality model. For example, the term *cognitive-behavioral therapy* indicates special attention to thinking (cognition), behavior, and the relationship between the two.

 ACTIVITY (**1.4**) **Thinking about Counseling**

Form small groups of no more than six people and elect a recorder and a spokesperson for each group. After a twenty-minute discussion, each group should have a consensus that

1. defines and describes counseling and
2. defines and describes addictions counseling.

Process: Group by group, define counseling first. Then describe what happens in counseling. How does this differ from other relationships and conversations? Note differences and similarities among groups. Which group members have gone to a professional for help of any kind (counselor, physician, nurse, lawyer, accountant, etc.)? Explore these relationships.

Many theoreticians champion their schools of thought, which postulate primary importance of affect (emotion), behavior, or cognition. Most therapists have come to acknowledge that each of these has a role in the human personality. Most therapists borrow from various clinical approaches, an approach that can be called eclectic, or integrative (Garfield and Bergin 1994, 8; Lambert and Bergin 1994, 143-4). A similar term is *holistic*, which simply means looking at and integrating all aspects of a system.

The counseling of chemically dependent people is far from a standardized system or method. Addictions counselors tend to gravitate toward counseling models that integrate or synthesize aspects of the personality and of change, not only because they are influenced by the trend toward integration of diverse techniques and concepts, but also because they see the practical necessity of covering all bases in combating a disease characterized by various vicious cycles and pervasive deteriorating effects. Some of these "bases" include affect management, behavioral change, and cognition.

Affect Management

When someone has lived for some time, perhaps during crucial developmental years, under the influence of an emotional anesthetic, he or she often suffers from "emotional illiteracy." This term refers to the fact that many people are simply naïve about feelings; they do not have the tools or habit of "reading" their emotional states, no words to describe them, and little practice in describing or communicating them. It is often better to describe this as a deficit of remediable skills rather than a pathology. Some tasks of counseling in the realm of emotion are to help the client

- identify and recognize emotions
- differentiate emotions from thoughts and actions
- accept emotions
- communicate emotions appropriately

Becoming emotionally literate offers relief from
- having to spend so much energy fighting emotions
- fearing buried or misunderstood emotions
- getting stuck in cycles of self-stimulating anxiety
- getting panicked by the experience of emotion
- fearing the outcomes of having emotion
- having "self-hate attacks" when "forbidden" emotions occur

Clients should learn that emotions are not catastrophes: "If you can think about it and talk about it, you don't have to drink about it." Cummings, Gordon, and Marlatt (1980) reported that three-quarters of alcoholic relapses involved either "unpleasant" emotions, interpersonal conflict (which arouses uncomfortable emotional states), and/or social pressure. Affect management addresses at least two of these high-risk situations. Much of this work takes place in group settings. Loss and grief are also major issues that emerge in recovery, from the loss of alcohol itself and all that entails (e.g., friends, places to go, some activities, emotional numbness) to the losses sustained while actively addicted (e.g., marriage, job, self-respect) (Goldberg 1985).

Behavioral Change

Addictive behavior is often defeated, self-defeating, and disorganized. Research shows that the outcome of treatment often depends on an increased sense of "self-efficacy" (Bandura 1997), a sense that what one does will make a difference. Meaningful recovery necessitates learning modes of behavior that help meet personal needs, or in popular terms, self-empowerment. In the self-efficacy theory of Bandura, clients change negative thinking by learning behaviors, performance, and coping responses via "homework" assignments (Bandura 1987). Other behavioral-change strategies include assertiveness training, which allows a direct, appropriate alternative to helpless, passive, aggressive, and passive-aggressive behavior. Many years of addiction leave a person without good grounding in stability and responsibility. The term *dry drunk* is used in AA to describe habitual, drunklike behaviors of a newly dried-out member, which might include impulsivity, moodiness, or irresponsibility. It also refers to a dangerous return to a state of mind or type of behavior that might lead to or forecast relapse. Behavioral approaches are also very valuable in relapse prevention. They involve identifying triggers of relapse and finding effective ways to deal with such situations. AA does this very simply by telling alcoholics to avoid "people, places, and things" associated with alcohol.

Cognitive Change

Beliefs, attitudes, thoughts, categories, and self-statements act as lenses through which to view and interpret the world. Cognition plays a large role in emotional responses by determining reactions to stimuli and providing labels for psychological states. According to rational-emotive-behavioral therapy, addictive thinking includes many irrational beliefs and negative self-statements, which can preclude positive action, force people to drive themselves unmercifully, and lead to chemical use. These beliefs and self-statements include demandingness, awfulizing, low frustration tolerance, and overgeneralizing.

Demandingness results from unfounded assumptions about requirements, usually expressed in terms of *should, must, ought to, have to,* and *need to.* Typical statements are "I can't tolerate anxiety" and "I must drink to get through the day."

Awfulizing is magnifying or exaggerating the badness of an event. Catastrophizing, panicky thinking styles, and cognition that follows what some professionals refer to as a "negative extrapolatory expectation pathway" found among a large subset of addicted persons. Catastrophizing or awfulizing can be a self-stimulating thinking cycle that creates paralyzing anxiety and easily contributes to relapse.

Low frustration tolerance, according to rational-emotive-behavioral therapy is not a neurologically based behavior such as in attention-deficit hyperactivity disorder, nor a personality dynamic. It is an irrational belief that a person cannot tolerate discomfort, frustration, or other unpleasant feelings, and thus must drink or take drugs to cope or become numb.

Overgeneralizing often applies to the future: "I will always be alone." "I will always fail." (Ellis and Dryden 1987; Ellis et al. 1988, 7-8). Overgeneralization can also apply to the past and present: "He always hated me." "Good things never happen to me." "She never once said a decent thing." "I screw up everything." "Everyone I ever knew believed in cheating on taxes."

According to Marlatt and Gordon (1985), decisions about when and how much people drink are shaped by expected outcomes of their behavior. One type of expectation is *alcohol-efficacy expectation,* which holds that people are more likely to drink if they feel a lack of power (self-efficacy). In such a situation they attribute the power to alcohol (alcohol efficacy) and believe it can help them get their desired outcomes (e.g., making friends, being relaxed at parties, calmly delivering a speech, enjoying a vacation).

Although there are apparent divergences between twelve-step and professional approaches, there are actually examples where twelve-step and cognitive psychology have *parallel* approaches to the kind of thinking that precedes initial relapse. Cognitive psychology (Beck et al. 1993) describes anticipatory beliefs that are triggered by internal states (boredom, sadness) or external stimuli (a bar, holidays). They include self-statements like "I can't have fun without pot" and "I won't be able to make it through the day without a drink." This in turn triggers drug craving, at which point a permission-giving belief is triggered, such as "One drink won't hurt," "I'll stop after one drink this time," and "I deserve it this one time." AA calls such beliefs "stinking thinking."

Integration of Affect, Behavior, and Cognition

Affect, behavior, and cognition are clearly interwoven. For example, a young man meets a young woman in his college class. They sit next to each other for much of the semester. He likes her very much, but avoids initiating any extracurricular recreation (i.e., dating). His thoughts (cognition) might include, "She will reject me," or "Even if she goes out with me, she won't like me," "I will feel worse when she rejects me than I would if I had never asked her out," and "I cannot tolerate the horrible feelings I will have," "It is hopeless to try," "I am not good enough for her," "I am too ugly to interest her." He feels (affect) ashamed, depressed, sad, lonely, and helpless. He acts (behavior) helpless and passive, or rather, he takes no action. The consequences of his failure to act are feeling worse, reinforced negative beliefs, lost opportunities, and so forth. This "learned helplessness" model of depression was introduced by Martin Seligman, who experimentally induced depression in animals (1962). Insights from the learned helplessness model have been some of the keys to understanding depression (Abramson, Seligman, and Teasdale 1978; Costello 1978; Depue and Monroe 1978; Seligman and Maier 1967). The major treatments for depression are psychotherapy, medication or a combination of both (Beck et al. 1993).

Several clinicians have formulated integrated strategies and applied them to the addictions. The best known integrative counseling model is rational-emotive therapy (RET), now known as rational-emotive-behavioral therapy (REBT). It was expounded in the 1950s by Albert Ellis (Ellis 1962) who applied it to the addictions during the 1970s (Ellis et al. 1988). It is the basis of Smart Recovery, a self-help network founded in 1996 as Rational Recovery. The other major school is cognitive-behavioral therapy (CBT), an approach associated with the names of Alan Marlatt (Marlatt and Gordon 1985), Peter Monti (Monti et al. 1989), and others. It is especially applied to relapse-prevention strategies. Rational-emotive and cognitive-behavioral approaches dissect the cascade of effects involved in triggers to drinking and drugging, ways of identifying and managing triggers to relapse, and ways of coping with cravings and maladaptive beliefs. It teaches behavioral and cognitive problem-solving strategies, and behavioral and cognitive skills such as assertiveness that counter helpless and hopeless behavior, thinking, and feelings.

One of the major themes of this text is the development of counseling skills that facilitate a helping, empathic, collaborative relationship between counselor and client. Cognitive-behavioral approaches do mention the use of empathy. Yet, in adaptations to short-term treatment, such an approach can lose the human dimension and be reduced to a set of "cookbook" routines, formulae, tricks, or gimmicks, against which the Project MATCH Research Group (NIAAA 1995, 8) specially cautions. Such routines soothe the counselor more than the client—another reason to focus on counseling skills. Techniques that address only cognition or that address emotion only in terms of the cognition involved are sketchy psychotherapies that skirt the pain and tragedies of clients. In warning against taking cognitive psychology's cool, common-sense approach to emotion too far, Fancher (1997, 195) quotes a line from Emily Dickinson, "There is a pain so utter, it swallows substance up."

ACTIVITY (1.5)   The ABCs of Problems

Break into three groups, then discuss the human dynamics in one of the following situations:

- A man fails to act on his wish to date someone
- A woman walks out of a family dinner when an argument arises
- A person cannot sleep the night before a promotional interview
- An assigned scenario
- A scenario you imagine

Identify affective, behavioral, and cognitive components, and the vicious cycles that connect these components. Take at least thirty seconds to visualize yourself in the situation before discussing in your small group the feelings, thoughts, and concerns with which you can identify. If time permits, the groups can report to the whole class.

Stages of Change

In the early 1980s James Prochaska and Carlo DiClimente (1982) posited an integrative model of change based on a study of cigarette smokers who quit without treatment, self-help groups, or other intervention. This is similar to the concept of natural recovery introduced earlier in this chapter. They identified six stages as common to all radical change in problem behaviors, including addictions, and applicable to any theoretical counseling approach. The stages are far more than periods of time; they represent a set of processes and tasks that must be done before moving to the next stage.

1. In the *precontemplation* stage, the individual resists change, denies the problem, and is demoralized. This individual may, however, be leveraged into treatment by environmental pressures, which may include significant others or authorities. At this point, information is helpful, particularly objective assessment data, not confrontation or advice.

2. In the *contemplation* stage, the individual is aware that he or she is "stuck," and acknowledges problems but is not ready to change, or even to prepare for change. The counselor's reflection of the client's ambivalence (see chapter 2 for a discussion of "reflection") helps the client move toward action.

3. The *preparation* stage involves some commitment to and anticipation of action, although the client may still be so ambivalent (have conflicting motives) that he or she falls back

from this position. (Prochaska and DiClimente originally called this the "determination" stage). At this point, probing and reviewing consequences of different decisions may be helpful.

4. The a*ction* stage involves real behavioral change. Support of healthy decisions and positive reinforcement of healthy behaviors are useful at this stage.

5. During *maintenance* the client consolidates the gains made during the action stage and institutes measures to avoid falling back, or relapse. The tasks here are learning how to "live in the world"; social skills such as assertiveness and communication skills are useful at this stage.

6. In the *termination* stage, the client moves past the problem-solving stage entirely. The focus here is still preventing relapse and dealing with many of the issues that surface in sobriety.

Prochaska and colleagues emphasize that growth is cyclical, best described in a spiral form. An individual may "fall back" from a stage he or she has attained into an earlier one, before moving up and further along. Thus, relapse or regression is seen as a normal part of the cycles of growth (Prochaska, Norcross, and DiClimente 1994, 47-50). With this approach it is important to assess carefully the stage that the client is in, and the pressures that may tend to keep him or her stuck in that stage or move him or her along to the next stage. Many, or most, in the addictions field do not think it is possible or desirable to move past a maintenance stage where one is perpetually vigilant and "keeping the memory green."

These stages of change have become popular in the world of counseling, and many eclectic counselors try to view their work as facilitating movement through stages of natural recovery. This is similar to Fancher's conception of the counselor as functioning as an "ancillary brain." "The clinician helps the distressed person perform the clearly legitimate task of puzzling out change intelligently. The clinician is necessary to this task because of the distress and debility under which the patient labors. . . .The therapist is simply a resource for ordinary activities undertaken in extraordinary circumstances" (Fancher 1997, 319).

Prochaska and DiClimente (1994) state that their "transtheoretical model" of stages of change is different from an eclectic model. They believe that rather than blended approaches, techniques of different theoretical approaches are most effective for specific symptoms, diagnoses, conditions, or problems.

Motivational Interviewing

Motivational interviewing (MI), or motivational enhancement therapy (MET), was developed by William Miller in the early 1980s. It asks what facilitates change, and recognizes that a counselor's style is a critical factor in providing conditions in which change is likely. It further asks why, if empathy is so important in psychotherapy and counseling of so many disorders, addictions treatment is usually based on some relatively aggressive form of confrontation, often including argumentation. MI/MIT sees the addict as (naturally) ambivalent about change and fluctuating considerably in the state of readiness to change. It uses a set of cognitive-behavioral methods to tip the scales in the direction of change and facilitate movement through stages of change. Many addicts are in the precontemplative stage and can be educated about their problem in order to enter the contemplative stage, in which they often "seesaw between reasons to change and reasons to stay the same" (Miller and Rollnick 1991, 16, 38). Motivational interviewing is a complex and sophisticated system. Before attempting to implement this approach, counselors should read the works of Miller and Rollnick in their entirety. According to Miller and Rollnick (1991, 55-63), the general principles of MI/MET are the following:

1. Express empathy through skillful reflective listening, with acceptance and respect, which builds a working relationship and supports the client's self-esteem.

2. Develop discrepancy between present behavior and the broader goals identified by the client, and explore the consequences of present behavior. That is, help the client perceive the rewards of change, as opposed to the costs of maintaining the status quo. The client, not the counselor, should present the arguments for change.

3. Avoid argumentation. Accusing clients of being in denial, resistant, or addicted is, in this view, countertherapeutic. Accepting the label "alcoholic" or "addict" will not guarantee change. In fact, the attempt to cajole a client into accepting such a label often creates resistance to change rather than helps change along.

4. Roll with resistance. That is, do not battle with the client over each disagreement, but continue to work around these areas, maintaining a working relationship.

5. Support self-efficacy. "You can do it. You can succeed." There is hope in the range of alternatives.

Some of the best contributions of MI are the identifications of therapeutic "traps" (Miller and Rollnick 1991, 64-71) that clients often get caught in, such as the following three traps:

1. In the *confrontation-denial trap*, the therapist takes responsibility for the problem and for changing it. This elicits resistance from the client who denies the problem and the need for change. This becomes a vicious cycle in which the therapist turns up the heat and the client defends with more vigor, eventually feeling trapped.

2. In the *expert trap*, the therapist's knowing attitude edges the client into a passive role, rather than encouraging exploration of his or her ambivalence and choices for change, not allowing the client to set the pace.

3. In the *labeling trap*, a power struggle also elicits resistance. The behavior or attitudes that counselors call resistance may be generated by their insistent, even combative, stance that the client accept particular labels. Taleff (1997) goes into much greater detail about resistance.

Motivational interviewing can be adapted to short-term counseling through a system summarized in the acronym FRAMES:

F = Feedback on their current status, providing a message of

R = self-Responsibility and giving

A = Advice to make a change, offering a

M = Menu of alternative strategies to meet his or her special situation with

E = Empathetic listening, reinforcing a client's

S = Self-efficacy, or belief in the ability of the client to change.

Motivational interviewing and the Stages of Change Model illuminate the cyclical, fluctuating nature of motivation and the simultaneous approach and avoidance of recovery goals. Many clinicians recognize that a new model can be oversimplified into a faddish gimmick. Barber (1994, 44) and Nealy (1997) have warned against ignoring the broader context of change, which includes emotions, self-esteem, dependence on large and impersonal social institutions, "the strengths and weaknesses of our interpersonal relationships, the extent of our social support networks, the stability of basic survival needs" (Nealy 1997, 12). Later in this text we show the role of the group milieu as a dynamic influence (chapter 3), the case-management framework that propels the client through a treatment process (chapter 5), and the framework of family, community, and culture (chapter 8).

Addictions Treatment Comes of Age

As Emile Durkheim stated a century ago, "All preconceptions must be eradicated" (Durkheim 1964, 31). Counselors should not take psychological
or addictions models on faith, without critically evaluating the assumptions that underlie them. Rigid adherence to any ideological model can
lead to overlooking diagnoses that do not fit its narrow interpretation of
behavior. For example, the manic-depressive, or bipolar, mood disorder
of one individual was ascribed to unresolved codependency issues. Another
was chalked up to a dry drunk. Severe attention-deficit hyperactivity
disorder of adolescent TC residents resulted in such things as failing to
turn off a light; the adolescents were thrown into the category "irresponsible behavior" and subjected to a severe verbal reprimand or "haircut"
(Myers 1991, 131). Counselors need to examine and continually re-
examine the philosophical bases of treatment interventions, to determine
what helps rather than rely on hallowed tradition or sacred ritual. Indeed,
the popular concept of codependency has been tremendously useful to
people whose lives revolved around the addiction of another, harming both
in the process. Nevertheless, everything from communism to manic-
depression has, at one time or another, been attributed to codependency.
Counselors must remain mindful of the limits of explanatory models, and
the dangers of dogmatically cutting everything to a single form. Keep in
mind the myth of the Procrustean Bed. King Procrustes cut down his guests
or stretched them on the rack to fit a single sized bed.

Gradually, much of the dogmatism and factionalism surrounding
addictions treatment has abated. Today there are programs combining therapeutic-community approaches with cognitive-behavioral relapse-prevention models (Lewis et al. 1993), and even therapeutic communities with
methadone clients (De Leon et al. 1993). The field is maturing and
professionalizing and, as in clinical psychology, addictions treatment is
increasingly putting together what is best from all models. This includes
the structure and love in the therapeutic community, the recovery charisma
and emphasis on vigilance against relapse of AA and NA, and the strategies to avoid relapse and to bolster self-efficacy of cognitive-behavioral
approaches. Regardless of the philosophical mix adopted, all treatment
conducts assessment-based, collaborative planning and assigning clients
to an intensity of treatment that matches the severity of addiction. Even
methadone program administrators have found that the success of their
efforts is related directly to enhancement with counseling and other
services (Anglin et al. 1993; McLellan et al. 1988).

References

AA (Alcoholics Anonymous). 1957. *Alcoholics Anonymous Comes of Age.* New York City: Alcoholics Anonymous World Services.

AA (Alcoholics Anonymous). 1976 (orig. 1939). *Alcoholics Anonymous.* New York: Alcoholics Anonymous World Services.

AA (Alcoholics Anonymous). 1980. *Dr. Bob and the Good Oldtimers.* New York: Alcoholics Anonymous World Services.

Abramson, L. Y., M. E. Seligman, and J. D. Teasdale. 1978. "Learned Helplessness in Humans: Critique and Reformulation." *Journal of Abnormal Psychology* 78, 1 (February): 49-74.

Alibrandi, L. A. 1987. "The Folk Psychotherapy of Alcoholics Anonymous," chap. 13 in *Practical Approaches to Alcoholism Psychotherapy*, 2nd ed. S. Zinberg, J. Wallace, and S. B. Blume, ed. New York: Plenum Press.

Anglin, M., et al. 1993. "Enhanced Methadone Maintenance Treatment: Limiting the Spread of HIV among High-Risk Los Angeles Narcotics Addicts," in *Innovative Approaches in the Treatment of Drug Abuse.* J. Inciardi et al., ed. Westport, CT: Greenwood Press.

APA (American Psychological Association). 1997. "Tailoring Treatments for Alcoholics Is Not the Answer." *APA Monitor* 6.

"Arizona Shows the Way." Editorial. *New York Times*, 24 April 1999, A18.

ASAM (American Society of Addiction Medicine). 1996. *Patient Placement Criteria for the Treatment of Substance-Related Disorders*, 2nd ed. Chevy Chase, MD: Author.

Bach, G. R. 1966. "The Marathon Group: Intensive Practice of Intimate Interaction." *Psychological Reports* 18: 995-1002.

Bandura, A. 1987. "Self-Efficacy: Towards a Unifying Theory of Behavior Change." *Psychological Review* 84: 191-215.

———. 1997. *Self-Efficacy: The Exercise of Control.* New York: W. H. Freeman.

Barber, J. G. 1994. *Social Work with Addictions.* New York: New York University Press.

Bart, P. B. 1964. "Ideologies and Utopias of Psychotherapy," chap. 1 in *The Sociology of Psychotherapy.* P. Roman and H. Trice, ed. New York: Jason Aronson.

Beck, A., et al. 1993. *Cognitive Therapy of Substance Abuse.* New York: Guilford Press.

Bishop, F. Mischler. 1995. "Rational-Emotive Behavior Therapy and Two Self-Help Alternatives to the 12-Step Model," in *Psychotherapy and Substance Abuse*. A. M. Washton, ed. New York: Guilford Press.

Blumberg, L. U. 1991. B*eware the First Drink: The Washington Temperance Movement andAlcoholics Anonymous*. Seattle: Glen Abbey Books.

Carkhuff, R. R. 1969. *Helping and Human Relations 2:, Practice and Research*. New York:Holt, Rinehart, and Winston.

Casriel, D. 1966a. S*o Fair a House: The Story of Synanon*. New York: Prentice-Hall.

————. 1966b. "New Success in Cure of Narcotics Addicts." *Physicians Panorama* (October): 1–4.

Casriel, D., and G. Amen. 1971. *Daytop: Three Addicts and Their Cure*. New York: Hill and Wang.

Chiauzzi, E. J., and S. Liljegren. 1993. "Taboo Topics in Addiction Treatment: An Empirical Review of Clinical Folklore." J*ournal of Substance Abuse Treatment* 10: 303-16.

Christopher, J. 1989. *Unhooked: Staying Sober and Drug-Free*. Buffalo: Prometheus Press.

Conners, G. J., K. M. Carroll, C. C. DiClimente, et al. 1997. "The Therapeutic Alliance and ItsRelationship to Alcoholism Treatment Participation and Outcome." *Journal of Personality and Social Psychology* 30: 510-7.

Conrad, P., and J. W. Schneider. 1980. "Alcoholism: Drunkenness, Inebriety, and the Disease Concept," chap. 4 in *Deviance and Medicalization*. St. Louis: Mosby.

Cormier, W. H., and L. S. Cormier. 1991. I*nterviewing Strategies for Helpers*. Pacific Grove, CA: Brooks/Cole.

Costello, C. G. 1978. "A Critical Review of Seligman's Laboratory Experiments on Learned Helplessness and Depression in Humans." *Journal of Abnormal Psychology* 87, 1 (February): 21-30.

Cournoyer, B. 1996. *The Social Work Skills Workbook*. Pacific Grove, CA: Brooks/Cole.

CSAT (Center for Substance Abuse Treatment). 1992. *Self-Run, Self-Supported Houses for More Effective Recovery from Alcohol and Drug Addiction*. Technical Assistance Publication Series 5, Rockville, MD: Department of Health and Human Services, Substance Abuse and Mental Health Services Administration.

CSAT (Center for Substance Abuse Treatment). 1998. *Addiction Counselor Competencies: The Knowledge, Skills, and Attitudes of Professional Practice.* CSAT Technical Assistance Publication Series 21, Rockville, MD: Substance Abuse and Mental Health Administration.

Cummings, C., J. Gordon, and G. A. Marlatt. 1980. "Relapse: Prevention and Prediction," in *The Addiction Behaviors.* W. Miller, ed. Oxford: Pergamon Press.

DASP (Drug Abuse Service Project). 1972. *Dealing with Drug Abuse: A Report to the Ford Foundation.* Washington, DC: Author.

Deitch, D. 1991. "Training Drug Abuse Treatment Personnel in Therapeutic Community Methodologies." *Psychotherapy* 30, 2: 305-15.

DeLeon, G., S. Sacks, and R. Hilton. 1993. "Passages: A Modified Therapeutic Community Day Treatment Model for Methadone Clients," in *Innovative Approaches in the Treatment of Drug Abuse.* J. Inciardi et al., ed. Westport, CT: Greenwood Press.

Depue, R. A., and S. M. Monroe. 1978. "Learned Helplessness in the Perspective of the Depressive Disorders," *Journal of Behavioral Psychology* 87, 1: 3-20.

Doweiko, H. 1999. *Concepts of Chemical Dependency,* 4th ed. Pacific Grove, CA: Brooks/Cole.

Durkheim, E. 1964 (orig. 1895). "The Rules of Sociological Method," chap. 1 in *What Is a Social Fact?* S. Lukes, ed. New York: Free Press.

Dutton, D., and A. Aron. 1974. "Some Evidence for Heightened Sexual Attraction under Conditions of High Anxiety." *Journal of Personality and Social Psychology* 30: 510-7.

Egan, G. 1998 (orig. 1975). *The Skilled Helper,* 6th ed. Pacific Grove, CA: Brooks/Cole.

Ellis, A. 1962. *Reason and Emotion in Psychotherapy,* Secaucus, NJ: Citadel Press.

Ellis, A., and W. Dryden. 1987. *The Practice of Rational-Emotive Psychotherapy.* New York: Springer-Verlag.

Ellis, A. et al. 1988. *Rational-Emotive Therapy with Alcoholics and Substance Abusers.* Boston: Allyn and Bacon.

Fancher, R. 1997. *Cultures of Healing: Correcting the Image of American Mental Health Care.* New York: Freeman.

Fiedler, F. 1950. "A Comparison of Therapeutic Relationships in Psychoanalytic, Non-Directive, and Adlerian Therapy," *Journal of Consulting Psychology*, 14: 436-45.

———. 1951. "Factor Analyses of Psychoanalytic, Non-Directive, and Adlerian Therapy." *Journal of Consulting Psychology*, 15: 32-8.

Garfield, S. L., and A. E. Bergin. 1994. "Introduction and Historical Overview," chap. 1 in *Handbook of Psychotherapy and Behavior Change*, 4th ed. A. E. Bergin and S. L. Garfield. ed. New York: Wiley.

Gerstein, D. R. 1994. "Outcome Research: Drug Abuse," in *The American Psychiatric Press Handbook of Substance Abuse Treatment*. M. Galanter and H. D. Kleber, ed. Washington, DC: American Psychiatric Press.

Goldberg, M. 1985. "Loss and Grief: Major Dynamics in the Treatment of Alcoholism," in *Psychosocial Issues in the Treatment of Alcoholism*. D. Cook, ed. New York: Haworth Press.

Gottheil, E., ed. 1997. *Intensive Outpatient Treatment for the Addictions*. New York: Haworth Press.

Granfield, R., and W. Cloud. 1996. "The Elephant That No One Sees: Natural Recovery among Middle Class Addicts." *Journal of Drug Issues* 26, 1: 45-61.

Hanson, G., and P. Venturelli. *Drugs and Society*, 5th ed. Sudbury, MA: Jones and Bartlett.

Hargreaves, W. A. 1983. "Methadone Dose and Duration for Methadone Treatment," in *Research on the Treatment of Narcotic Addiction: State of the Art*. NIDA Treatment Research Monograph Series, DHHS pub. no. ADM-83-1281, J. R. Cooper et al., ed. Rockville, MD: National Institute on Drug Abuse.

Hayashida, M., et al. 1989. "Comparative Effectiveness and Costs of Inpatient and Outpatient Detoxification of Patients with Mild-to-Moderate Alcohol Withdrawal Syndromes." *New England Journal of Medicine* 320 (9 February): 358-65.

Hester, R. K. 1994. "Outcome Research: Alcoholism," in *The American Psychiatric Press Handbook of Substance Abuse Treatment*. M. Galanter and H. D. Kleber, ed. Washington DC: American Psychiatric Press.

Horvath, T. 1999. *Sex, Drugs, and Gambling, and Chocolate: A Workbook for Overcoming Addictions*. San Luis Obispo, CA: Impact Publishers.

INCASE (International Coalition of Addiction Studies Educators). 1997. Draft of "Areas of Study in Addictionology." January 1997 Curriculum Conference, Las Vegas, Nevada.

Ivey, A. 1971. *Microcounseling: Innovations in Interview Training.* Springfield, IL: Chas. C. Thomas.

————. 1988. *International Interviewing and Counseling,* 2nd ed. Pacific Grove, CA: Brooks/Cole.

Jason, L. A., M. E. Pechota, and B. S. Bowden. 1994. "Oxford House: Community Living to Community Healing, " in *Addictions: Concepts and Strategies for Treatment.* J. A. Lewis, ed. Gaithersburg, MD: Aspen.

Jellinek, E. M. 1960. *The Disease Concept of Alcoholism.* New Brunswick, NJ: Hillhouse Press.

Jones, M. 1953. *The Therapeutic Community.* New York: Basic Books.

————. 1968. *Social Psychiatry in Practice: The Idea of the Therapeutic Community.* Baltimore, MD: Penguin Books.

Kazdin, A. E. 1994. "Methodology, Design, and Evaluation in Psychotherapy Research," chap. 2 in *Handbook of Psychotherapy and Other Behavior Change.* A. E. Bergin and S. I. Garfield, ed. New York: Wiley.

Kurtz, E. 1988. *A. A.: The Story.* San Francisco: Harper and Row (rev. ed. of *Not-God,* Harper and Row, 1978).

Lambert, M. J., and A. E. Bergin. 1994. "The Effectiveness of Psychotherapy," chap. 5 in *Handbook of Psychotherapy and Other Behavior Change.* A. E. Bergin and S. I. Garfield, ed. New York: Wiley.

Lawson, G. W., D. C. Ellis, and P. C. Rivers. 1984. *Essentials of Chemical Dependency Counseling.* Gaithersburg, MD: Aspen.

Lazarus, R. S. 1966. *Psychological Stress and the Coping Process.* New York: McGraw-Hill.

"Learned Helplessness as a Model of Depression." 1978. *Journal of Abnormal Psychology* 87, 1.

LeDoux, J. 1996. *The Emotional Brain.* New York: Simon and Schuster.

Lewis, B., et al. 1993. "Four Residential Drug Treatment Programs: Project IMPACT," in *Innovative Approaches in the Treatment of Drug Abuse,* J. Inciardi et al., ed. Westport, CT: Greenwood Press.

Lockwood, D., and J. A. Inciardi. 1993. "Crest Outreach Center: A Work-Release Iteration of the Therapeutic Community Model," in *Innovative Approaches in the Treatment of Drug Addiction.* J. A. Inciardi et al., ed. Westport, CT: Greenwood Press.

Maddux, J. F. 1993. "Improving Retention on Methadone Maintenance," in *Innovative Approaches in the Treatment of Drug Abuse.* J. A. Inciardi et al., ed. Westport, CT: Greenwood Press.

Maliver, B. 1973. *The Encounter Game.* New York: Stein and Day.

Marlatt, G. A., and J. R. Gordon. 1985. *Relapse Prevention.* New York: Guilford Press.

Marshall, G. D., and P. G. Zimbardo. 1979. "Affective Consequences of Inadequately Explained Physiological Arousal." *Journal of Personality and Social Psychology* 37, 6: 970-88.

Maslach, C. 1979. "Negative Emotional Raising of Unexplained Arousal." *Journal of Personality and Social Psychology* 37, 6: 953-69.

Maxwell, M. A. 1984. *The AA Experience.* New York: McGraw-Hill.

McAndrew, C. 1969. "On the Notion That Certain People Who Are Given to Frequent Drunkenness Suffer from a Disease Called Alcoholism," in *Changing Perspectives in Mental Illness.* S. C. Plog and R. B. Edgerton, ed. New York: Holt.

McCay, J. R., et al. 1998. "Predictors of Participation in Aftercare Sessions and Self-Help Groups Following Completion of Intensive Outpatient Treatment for Substance Abuse." *Journal of Studies on Alcohol* 59, 2 (March): 152-62.

Meier, S. T., and S. R. Davis. 1993. *The Elements of Counseling,* 2nd ed. Pacific Grove, CA: Brooks/Cole.

Milby, J. B. 1988. "Methadone Maintenance to Abstinence: How Many Make It?" *Journal of Nervous and Mental Disease* 176: 409-21.

Miller, N. E. 1944. "Experimental Studies of Conflict," in *Personality and the Behavior Disorders,* vol. 1. J. M. Hunt, ed. New York: Ronald.

———. 1959. "Liberalization of Basic S-R Concepts," in *Psychology: A Study of a Science,* vol. 2. S. Koch, ed. New York: McGraw-Hill.

Miller, W. R., and S. Rollnick, ed. 1991. *Motivational Interviewing: Preparing People to Change Addictive Behavior.* New York: Guilford Press.

McLellan, A. T., et al. 1988. "Counselor Differences in Methadone Treatment," in *Proceedings of Committee on Problems of Drug Dependence.* L. S. Harris, ed. NIDA Research Monograph no. 81, DHHS pub. no. ADM 88-1564. Rockville, MD: National Institute on Drug Abuse.

Monti, P. D., et al. 1989. *Treating Alcohol Dependence: A Coping Skills Training Guide.* New York: Guilford Press.

Myers, P. 1992. "Cult and Cult-Like Pathways out of Adolescent Addiction," in *Special Problems in Counseling the Chemically Dependent Adolescent.* E. Smith Sweet, ed. New York: Haworth Press (orig. appeared in *Journal of Adolescent Chemical Dependency* vol. 1, no. 4, 1991).

NA. 1988. *Narcotics Anonymous.* Van Nuys, CA: Narcotics Anonymous World Service Office.

Nealy, E. C. 1997. "Early Intervention with Active Drug and Alcohol Users in Community-Based Settings." *Journal of Chemical Dependency Treatment* 7, 1/2: 5-20.

NIAAA (National Institute on Alcohol Abuse and Alcoholism). 1995a. *Project MATCH Monograph Series, 3: Cognitive-Behavioral Coping Skills Therapy Manual.* NIH pub. no. 94-3724. Rockville, MD: NIAAA & U.S. Dept. of Health and Human Services.

Pita, D. 1996. *Addictions Counseling.* New York: Crossroads.

Plutchik, R. 1984. "Emotions: A General Psychoevolutionary Theory," in *Approaches to Evolution.* K. H. Scherer and P. Ekman, ed. Hillsdale, NJ: Erlbaum.

Prochaska, J. O., and C. C. DiClimente. 1982. "Stages and Process of Self-Change in Smoking: Towards an Integrative Model of Change." *Psychotherapy* 20: 161-73.

Prochaska, J. O., J. C. Norcross, and C. C. DiClimente. 1994. *Changing for Good.* New York: William Morrow.

Rapoport R. 1960. *Community as Doctor.* Springfield, Il: Chas. C. Thomas.

Robertson, N. 1988. *Getting Better: Inside Alcoholics Anonymous.* New York: William Morrow.

Rogers, C. 1951. *Client-Centered Therapy.* Boston: Houghton Mifflin.

————. 1970. *Carl Rogers on Encounter Groups.* New York: Harper and Row.

————. 1986. "Client-Centered Therapy," in *Psychotherapists' Casebook: Therapy and Technique in Practice.* I. Kutash and A. Wolk, ed. San Francisco: Jossey-Bass.

Rosenthal, M. 1980. "Therapeutic Community Models 3: Phoenix House," in *The Therapeutic Community.* E. Jansen, ed. London: Croom Helm.

SAMHSA (Substance Abuse and Mental Health Services Administration). 1994. *Cost of Addictive and Mental Disorders and Effectiveness of Treatment.* DHHS pub. no. 2095-94. Rockville, MD: Substance Abuse and Mental Health Administration.

Schachter, S., and J. E. Singer. 1962. "Cognitive, Social, and Physiological Determinants of Emotional State." *Psychological Review* 69: 379-99.

Schuckit, M. 1994. "Goals of Treatment," in *The American Psychiatric Press Handbook of Substance Abuse Treatment.* M. Galanter and H. D. Kleber, ed. Washington, DC: American Psychiatric Press.

Seligman, M. E. P. 1972. "Learned Helplessness." *Annual Review of Medicine* 23: 407-12.

Seligman, M. E. P., and S. F. Maier. 1967. "Failure to Escape Traumatic Shock." *Journal of Experimental Psychology* 74: 1-9.

Solomon, L. N., and B. Berzon, ed. 1972. *New Perspectives on Encounter Groups.* San Francisco: Jossey-Bass.

Stall, R., and P. Biernacki. 1986. "Spontaneous Remission from the Problematic Use of Substances." *International Journal of the Addictions* 21: 1-23.

Stoller, F. H. 1968. "Marathon Group Therapy," in *Innovations to Group Psychotherapy.* G. M. Gazda, ed. Springfield, IL: Chas. C. Thomas.

Sugarman, B. 1974. *Daytop Village: A Therapeutic Community,* New York: Holt Rinehart, and Winston.

Swan, N. 1995. "California Study Finds $1 Spent on Treatment Saves Taxpayers $7." *NIDA Notes* 10, 2 (March/April): 34.

Taleff, M. J. 1997. *A Handbook to Assess and Treat Resistance in Chemical Dependency.* Dubuque, IA: Kendall-Hunt.

Thombs, D. 1999. *Introduction to Addictive Behaviors,* 2nd ed. New York: Guilford.

Thomsen, R. 1975. *Bill W.* New York: Perennial Library, Harper and Row.

Tournier, R. 1979. "Alcoholics Anonymous as Treatment and as Ideology." *Journal of Studies on Alcohol* 40: 130-239.

Trimpey, J. 1992. *The Small Book: A Revolutionary Alternative for Overcoming Alcohol and Drug Dependence* (rev. ed.). New York: Delacorte Press.

Vaillant, G. E. 1983. *The Natural History of Alcoholism: Causes, Patterns, and Paths to Recovery.* Cambridge: Harvard University Press.

Waldorf, D., and P. Biernacki. 1977. "Natural Recovery from Opiate Addiction: A Review of the Incidence Literature." *Journal of Drug Issues* 9: 281-90.

———. 1981. "Natural Recovery from Opiate Addiction: Some Preliminary Findings." *Journal of Drug Issues* 11: 61-74.

Waldorf, D., C. Reinarman, and S. Murphy. 1991. *Cocaine Changes: The Experience of Using and Quitting.* Philadelphia: Temple University Press.

Wallace, J. 1987. "Critical Issues in Alcoholism Therapy," in *Practical Approaches to Alcoholism Psychotherapy,* 2nd ed. S. Zimberg, J. Wallace, and S. B. Blume, ed. New York: Plenum Press.

Washton, A. M. 1997. "Evolution of Intensive Outpatient Treatment (IOP) as a Legitimate Treatment Modality." *Journal of Addictive Diseases* 16, 2: xxi-xxvii.

Weisner, C., and R. Room. 1978. "Financing and Ideology in Alcohol Treatment." *Social Problems* 32: 157-84.

Winick, J. C. 1962. "Maturing Out of Narcotic Addiction." *Bulletin on Narcotics* 6:1.

Wolan, B., ed. 1989. *Dictionary of Behavioral Science,* 2nd ed. New York: Academic Press.

Wren, C. 1999. "Arizona Finds Cost Savings in Treating Drug Offenders." *New York Times,* 21 April, p. A12.

Wright, F. D., et al. 1993. "Theoretical Rationale," in *Behavioral Treatments for Drug Abuse and Dependence.* NIDA Research Monograph 137, NIH pub. no. 93-3684. Rockville, MD: National Institute on Drug Abuse.

Yablonsky, L. 1965. *Synanon: The Tunnel Back.* New York: Macmillan Prometheus Books.

Yalisove, D. 1997. "The Origins and Evolution of the Disease Concept of Treatment." *Journal of Studies on Alcohol* 59: 469-76.

Zimberg, S. 1987. "Principles of Alcoholism Psychotherapy," in *Practical Approaches to Alcoholism Psychotherapy*, 2nd ed. S. Zimberg, J. Wallace, and S. B. Blume, ed. New York: Plenum Press.

A Skills Approach to Counseling Addicts

Attitudes

An *attitude* is a state of preparedness or a mind set to make a particular response. It has cognitive, emotional, and behavioral components. Many attitudes involve evaluations of persons, groups, or institutions. For example, you may believe that your uncle is smart or well informed, you may feel affection for him, and you may be predisposed to act respectfully and interested in what he says. His co-workers might disagree, dislike him, and act indifferent to him. As a result of prejudicial attitudes some people are judged superior and enjoy the benefits, and others are judged inferior and suffer the effects of discrimination.

People are rarely aware of the complex of attitudes that help govern their behavior. Attitudes are acquired from early experiences, parental and peer influence, media, education, and belief systems. They are often self-fulfilling prophecies because a counselor's approach to clients often leads them to act in ways that counselors expect. Moreover, people may ignore information that does not fit their preconceptions (Taleff 1997). Attitudes toward addicts and addiction are especially endowed with meanings, emotional attributes, and ideology—all of which combine to act as a lens coloring the way people think about them. The CSAT's consensus document itemizes attitudinal components that pertain to each dimension of counseling addicts.[1]

The alcoholic is often seen as the "town drunk" or as a "bum," rarely as the banker or minister. This cognitive appraisal encourages an emotional response such as disgust, pity, anger, or fear. These attitudes and feelings are then carried into the professional realm (usually outside of the awareness of the professional) and bear on how clients are treated.

ACTIVITY 2.1   "When I first heard the word..."

Memories can give us clues to our unrecognized attitudes, and to their sources.

LEADER: Relax, close your eyes, and take a few deep breaths. Let go of present concerns as you let out a deep breath. Remember as far back as you can to the first time you heard the word *alcoholic*, or *a drunk*, or *an addict*. Remember the situation as clearly as possible. Take a few minutes to do this.

LEADER: How old were you? Who was present? What was going on at the time? What was being said? Who was saying it? Most important, what were you feeling?

Process: Return to the here and now and regather either in small groups or in one large group. Volunteers share their experiences. Note the variety of experiences. It might be useful to have someone write on newsprint or chalkboard the opinions and feelings.

Discuss: How do our early experiences color our views of alcoholics and drug addicts? In what ways do we stereotype? In what ways might our beliefs keep us from seeing a problem that does not fit our stereotype? Why might drug addicts and alcoholics feel stigmatized?

---

[1] The 1998 addiction competency consensus document (CSAT 1998) is subtitled "Knowledges, Skills, and Attitudes of Professional Practice." This underscores the importance of attitudinal training to complement the knowledge and skills that are the traditional domains of addictions (and other) counselors.

Follow-up: Think about your first encounter with an alcoholic or a drug-addicted client. What were your fears, concerns, expectations, and other feelings and thoughts? What happened and in what ways did your experiences and biases affect the encounter?

Aside from the beliefs and attitudes that counselors have, it is important to be aware of general, societal attitudes about drugs and alcohol. Attitudes differ by culture, but in general, American society provides very conflicting and inconsistent messages about the use of, abuse of, and addiction to drugs.

 ACTIVITY (**2.2**) **Words can hurt.**

As a group, brainstorm (for 5 minutes) a list of synonyms for to get drunk. *Have someone record responses on one half of the board or newsprint. Next, brainstorm (for 5 minutes) to think of synonyms for* a drunk. *Have the recorder write all these responses on the remaining half of the board or newsprint.*

Process: What did you notice about the list of words? Usually the words about getting drunk—*smashed, bombed, stoned,* and so on—seem violent but exciting. The words associated with a drunk—*a bum, a no-good, a lush,* and so on—are usually derogatory.

Discuss: What messages do the media give about alcohol, tobacco, and over-the-counter drugs? What messages do the media give about alcoholics and drug addicts?

Another aspect of attitudes is the judgment of the social and behavioral characteristics of subgroups of alcoholics, drug abusers, and addicts. This is often related to personal value systems being applied to the behavior of stereotyped clients. When engaging clients in treatment, counselors need to identify their own reactions and biases to situations. The variety of these includes sexual and physical abuse, exploitation of others, criminal behavior, and sexual orientation.

 ACTIVITY (**2.3**) **Do I have attitudes?**

Read the following description of the fictitious people and rank them from 1 to 10 on the basis of how strongly you feel about their negative characteristics. Number 1 would represent the character you feel has the most negative characteristics and number 10 would have the fewest negative

*characteristics. For example, one might rank a person who deliberately
gives a child an apple in which she has hidden razor blades as number 1
and a person who cheats on his diet by having a candy bar as number 10.*

1. Rita is a mother who uses diet pills, tranquilizers, and booze, but
   gets upset when her kids use drugs.
2. Mrs. Elling, a school counselor, tells the parents of a student who
   has confided in her about his involvement with drugs.
3. Stan is a good provider, but gets drunk occasionally and beats his
   wife.
4. Jackson sells a mixture of Nestlé's Quik and saccharine as mescaline
   for $3 a hit.
5. Mariah obtains a large supply of "reds" (barbiturates) and passes
   them around at school.
6. Mohammed, a 22-year-old man, has been drinking heavily at a
   party and decides to drive his buddies home in his parents' car.
7. Police Officer Gaudette knows of a 9th-grade drinking party and
   decides not to investigate because "kids will be kids."
8. A 17-year-old Lee turns his 12-year-old brother on to drugs.
9. Eldon constantly argues with his wife and causes family problems
   because he drinks and cannot hold a job.
10. Janice is addicted to heroin and steals in order to support her
    habit.

Process: After each of you has ranked all the people in the list, break into
groups of four to six members. In your group, see if you can come up with
a consensus ranking. Think about criteria you used to decide ranking. Discuss
the values and attitudes that went into the ranking.

Case in Point

It's a matter of attitude.

A methadone-maintenance client was known to regale the staff with hilarious interpretations of the political sexual scandals of 1997 and 1998. One
day this client showed a different side; he gave a somber account of a close
friend at this MM program who had cancer. He and his friend had visited
a prestigious research and treatment center, which had initially offered the
friend medical attention. When they saw from the voluminous charts that
the patient was also an addict being treated on MM, the admitting staff
abruptly asked them to leave. The MM client then took in his friend the
cancer patient, and cared for him until his death.

Categories of Attitudes

The addiction competency consensus document (CSAT 1998) lists attitudes in every subarea of each practice dimension. For example, there are nine subareas of the practice dimension of screening, each of which enumerates from one to four attitudes. The entire document names close to 300 attitudinal elements of counselor competency. We have categorized these elements for an overview of broad goals of attitudinal training in addiction counseling. Almost all of the attitudes in the CSAT document fall into the following categories:

- Respect for or sensitivity to clients' needs, perceptions, interests, rights, and input
- Collaborative work and rapport with clients
- Understanding of and respect for the importance or value of each practice dimension and subdimension
- Flexibility, which is demonstrated by being open to a variety of approaches
- Professionalism, including collaboration with colleagues, patience and perseverance, and recognition of personal biases and limitations

The last category leads to a consideration of how the motives that prompt individuals into addictions counseling can shape attitudes toward the counseling role and toward clients. Many individuals are influenced, perhaps unwittingly, by the social stigma imposed by "deviant" identities such as addict, mentally ill, or offender. In a counselor, these attitudes may predispose dislike or distrust of clients, which would preclude establishing the necessary supportive or empathetic relationship, and might well create the expectation of failure.

The addictions counselor who is also in recovery brings attitudes that affect the ability to play an objective and professional counseling role. There are many avenues by which recovering individuals enter the counseling occupation. For example, a graduate of a therapeutic community may have been hired immediately as a counselor aide, or an individual recovering from personal or family addiction may have pursued a degree in addictions counseling. The emotional experience of recovery or codependency can exert a powerful influence on counseling attitudes, as the following examples show.

Sponsoring

The counselor who has been a member of a recovery fellowship and has sponsored new members finds it gratifying to "give back" some of what was offered to him or her, and extrapolates this into the counseling role.

Among addictions students in Newark, New Jersey, enrolled in the Project for Addiction Counselor Training (sponsored in the early 1990s by the Federal Center for Substance Abuse Treatment), the majority had sponsored recovering addicts in the fellowships of AA and NA, and the number of individuals each student had sponsored ranged from two to five.

Twelve-Stepping

Reaching out and helping other addicts, twelve-stepping, is a cornerstone of maintaining one's sobriety. If counseling is seen as an extension of twelve-stepping, then the counseling role is seen (although the counselor may not be aware of this) as a means for the counselor to maintain abstinence. When a client fails, does not make progress, or relapses, the counselor may perceive that as a threat to his or her own sobriety, which might result in fear, anxiety, or anger.

Sponsorship and twelve-stepping involve a level of intimacy that is helpful and healing, but it is inappropriate in a professional counseling relationship. A confusion of these roles can lead to unprofessional attitudes toward the counseling relationship. (Attitudes toward counseling by recovering individuals are also surveyed in chapter 6.)

Case in Point

The Start of Something Big

In 1935 William Griffith Wilson, a sporadically employed stockbroker, was traveling alone through Akron, Ohio. An alcoholic whose drinking had almost destroyed his life, he had finally stopped drinking, but feared for his sobriety. He contacted Robert Smith, a physician whose practice was suffering as a result of his deteriorating alcoholic state. They talked for hours, and not only did Bill Wilson stay sober, Dr. Bob put down the bottle as well. Alcoholics talking to alcoholics began Alcoholics Anonymous, and it remains a core feature of "the program." Step Twelve encourages carrying the message to other alcoholics and, as it did for Bill, reinforces sobriety. In times of stress and doubt, members are encouraged to go out and speak with suffering, active alcoholics. Service, sponsorship, twelve-stepping, and meetings are all therapeutic components of the fellowship of Alcoholics Anonymous and other self-help programs.

The Counseling Mystique

The experience of recovery can create a counseling mystique on the part of recovering individuals, leading to unrealistic expectations about the job (Lawson, Ellis, and Rivers 1984, 4). Frequently counselor trainees, aides, and new counselors "crash" from the charismatic experience of seeing someone come off the street and announce, "My name is Tom. I'm an addict and I haven't used in a week," to disillusionment when they encounter repetitive paperwork, bureaucracy, and other routines of social-service agencies. Such an individual, especially if his or her training has not been through an accredited institution of higher education, may not have "recognition of the value of accurate documentation" (CSAT 1998, 37).

Limited Perspective

The counselor whose training was focused on only one model might not have an attitude of "willingness to consider multiple approaches to recovery and change" or "open-mindedness towards a variety of approaches" (CSAT 1998, 37, 41). Such training limits the acquisition of a wide variety of counseling skills and strategies. This observation applies equally to any single-focus or dogmatic training model, whether derived from a recovery tradition or a school of clinical psychology such as psycho-analysis or behaviorism.

Individual Addictions Counseling Skills

Despite great effort over the years, no research has been able to demonstrate the superior efficacy of a particular school of thought or format in counseling and treatment. The specific school of thought to which a counselor subscribes and the counseling format are less important than rooting his or her practice in basic counseling skills. These can establish and maintain a good working relationship and involve the client in his or her recovery—moving from a problem-ridden and helpless state through an exploration of alternatives, gaining insights and motivation, and taking action for personal growth.

Counselors need to examine their understanding of how and why professionals support and motivate an individual to change. Psychotherapy research indicated as far back as 1950 that the therapist's theoretical orientation and educational background were not crucial factors in treatment effectiveness (Fiedler 1950, 1951). However, many practitioners have been too invested in their theoretical identities to pay much attention to such studies. Hundreds of studies, summarized by the technique of meta-analysis, show that many different therapies help clients, and that a number of supportive, learning, and action factors common to many therapies are associated with a positive outcome. Many of these factors pertain to the quality of the therapeutic relationship, including the therapeutic alliance and interpersonal skills (Kazdin 1994; Lambert and Bergin 1994).

The "client-centered-counseling" of Carl Rogers (1951, 1986) was one of the first approaches to emphasize empathy and the client's potential growth, shifting away from an attitude of therapist as high-and-mighty expert and putting a "human face" on the therapeutic process. In the 1960s vocational and educational counselors began to develop a subfield known as *counseling psychology*. They were interested in short-term, concrete changes in clients rather than long-term psychotherapy, and were among the first to emphasize counseling qualities such as respect, warmth, concreteness, empathy, and genuineness.

Twenty-five years ago, Carkhuff (1969 a, b), Ivey (1971), and Egan (1998) were principal pioneers in investigating counseling qualities from a behavioral perspective. They studied exactly what counselors did or said that demonstrated helping qualities. This research led to a skills approach to counseling. The behaviors and skills necessary for effective counseling can, in fact, be taught to a large proportion of intelligent, motivated individuals. The skills are those of communicating, not of providing perfect advice, answers, or brilliant commentary. (Another term is *process skills*). Today, training of most mental-health workers, social workers, and counselors is grounded in one of the several generic counseling approaches. This approach includes learnable skills to facilitate a counseling process that helps clients to achieve insight, feel better about themselves, and change behavior patterns in directions that get them what they need (Cournoyer 1996; Egan 1998; Corey and Corey 1998). Recent meta-analytic studies of treatment effectiveness, appear to validate such an approach. Nonetheless, many addictions counselors, not to mention many other mental-health professionals, have no formal training or preparation in specific counseling skills.

Counseling Formats

Individual counseling sessions may to some extent follow a certain predictable routine, which may be based on a particular counseling or self-help model. Counseling formats translate treatment plans into digestible and understandable steps for client and counselor alike, in the individual counseling setting. The format may also represent an adaptation of a favorite model to accommodate limitations of reimbursement. *Format* refers to both the sequence of sessions and the structure of the counseling session.

The sequence of sessions in cognitive-behavioral therapy, for example, may entail a long-term relationship or it may be limited to seven sessions. Such a seven-session sequence might be the following:

1. introducing coping skills
2. coping with cravings and urges to drink
3. managing thoughts about alcohol and drinking

4. learning to solve problems
5. learning drink-refusal skills
6. planning for and coping with emergencies
7. consequences of seemingly irrelevant decisions
   (NIAAA 1995, 19)

The structure of the counseling session may or may not follow a predictable routine. Beck and colleagues (1993, 97) recommend the following elements as the structure of a cognitive therapy session:

1. setting the agenda
2. checking the mood
3. bridging from last session
4. discussing today's agenda
5. using Socratic questioning
6. offering capsule summaries
7. assigning homework
8. giving feedback in the therapy session

This example shares with many psychotherapies a concern for budgeting time, linking the present session to previous and future sessions, and application of insights gained in the session to the life of the client. Yet a breakdown into eight segments is an unusually complex format. Moreover, routines may exist but not be immediately apparent. Students should observe counseling with the aim of determining whether there is an unspoken routine, such as a typical lead question or cooling-off segment toward the end to provide an appropriate emotional return to the world.

Tailoring Counseling Skills for Addicted Clients

There are many ways of itemizing, categorizing, and defining counseling skills and subskills. Definitions of skills overlap considerably, and it is dangerous to try to isolate or memorize definitions. Such a robotlike approach neglects the actual interpersonal process that these skills should facilitate. In fact, it is possible to defeat the purpose of a skills approach by memorizing definitions and using stock phrases.

The skills discussed here roughly follow tasks and stages of addictions counseling. They also fall across a continuum from less pressure to more pressure, from passive to active. Cutting across the various models, an addictions counselor must first engage the client and build a therapeutic alliance. This provides a safety zone within which the client can reveal feelings and find support for recovery. Then the counselor can facilitate the client's gradual self-awareness and finally self-direction.

Addictions counseling is directive counseling. It is concerned with influencing clients toward healthy behavior; therefore, it is concerned with the process of change. As discussed in chapter 1, Prochaska and colleagues (Prochaska and DiClemente 1982; Prochaska, Norcross, and DiClemente 1994) identified stages of positive change—precontemplation, contemplation, determination, action, and maintenance—that many people undergo with or without professional help. Performance of counseling skills can be judged best by their efficacy in helping people move gradually through stages of personal growth.

Engagement Skills

Engagement skills are crucial to establish a positive counseling relationship. To reach treatment goals, a counselor must be able to make personal contact and develop a working alliance with a client (Meier and Davis 1993, 2-3). Because the typical addict is isolated emotionally, the counseling bond can be healing; investment in this relationship is a major factor in carrying a client through the rough shoals of early recovery. Engagement can be facilitated through qualities of genuineness, immediacy, warmth, and a nonjudging attitude. These qualities are demonstrated when the counselor has developed the skill of attending. Cited in some form in almost all training protocols, *attending* refers to providing cues that demonstrate concern, warmth, respect, interest in, involvement in, and awareness of the client's communications. These cues can be nonverbal such as eye contact, an involved and relaxed body posture, and interactive gestures. Or the cues can be verbal such as an animated rather than a flat tone of voice or reassuring and encouraging vocalizations such as "hmm," "aha," and "go on."

Development of a working alliance also requires the counseling tasks involved in orientation and training of clients. Orientation is one of the core functions of the International Certification Reciprocity Consortium. Although orientation is not related to particular skills, it is necessary. Part of the engagement process is explaining counseling, which Meier and Davis (1993, 4-6) consider part of "role induction," or socialization into the client role. The idea of talking openly about problems and feelings with a person who is not a family member or close friend is often a new one. The client may expect to be interrogated and given answers, rather than be aided in the process of self-exploration. The interactive nature of the counseling process needs to be explored, and the client needs explanations of confidentiality, treatment goals, and therapeutic culture. The alliance is developed further and cemented by explaining the process by which the counselor and client will develop a treatment plan based on long-term and short-term goals. Even the involuntary client can see the helpful intent and possibilities inherent in this scheme. Thus, successful engagement prepares the client to benefit from treatment.

Active Listening Skills

Using active listening skills (Egan 1998), the counselor connects to and can reflect emotions, thoughts, and attitudes of his or her clients. This cluster of skills is known as attending skills (Ivey 1988) and reflective listening (Miller and Rollnick 1991). By providing a clear mirror to the addict, the counselor interjects an "observing ego" that may be lacking.

Paraphrasing or Restating

The therapeutic qualities of empathy (the ability to perceive another person's experience and communicate that perception back to the person) and warmth can be developed by acquiring the skill of paraphrasing. *Paraphrasing* refers to a counselor's verbal response that rephrases the essence of the client's message. It allows the client to hear what he or she has just said, either in parroted form or with added clarity. This interactive process increases trust and reduces resistance. The following interchange is an example of a counselor's clarifying a client's message and restating it:

CLIENT: I started to do the bills, but I couldn't stand it and made a phone call instead. I started again, but I decided to have a snack.
COUSELOR: You kept finding ways to avoid doing the bills.

Reflecting

When the content being restated is emotional, it is a *reflection of feeling*. The counselor captures and expresses to the client the essence of what the client is feeling. This facilitates the exploration and identification of emotional needs and states. The emotional message may have been stated directly; however, the client may not be aware of his or her own emotional output, or of how his or her emotional message was understood. Reflection of feeling shows the client that the counselor has understood the message. An alert, nonjudgmental, and friendly ear also acknowledges and validates a client's feelings, allowing him or her to own and accept the feelings and claim the right to have them. The counselor should be careful not to interpret the client's feelings. When reflecting an expressed feeling, the counselor remains neutral, not offering opinions, judgments, or advice. Neither does a counselor tell a client what he or she is feeling. The following interchange shows a counselor's reflection of a client's expressed emotion:

CLIENT: When he told me that, I just lost it. I pushed my plate away and stormed out.
COUNSELOR: You sound very angry with him.
CLIENT: You bet! I could have thrown it in his face!

Not only does the client become more aware of his or her emotions and the emotional content of his or her utterances, but there is also the implicit message that "it is okay to be angry" (or sad, happy, lonely, etc.). Reflection of feelings helps the client establish, maintain, and affirm the habit of communicating feelings directly and appropriately rather than resorting to unproductive responses such as violence, drinking, or drugging. Some counselors use the expression, "If you learn to talk about it, you won't have to drink about it." If the client is ready, the counselor may move to *leading* skills (discussed later in this chapter).

Reflection of feeling has a particular twist in addictions treatment. Addictions counselors must be aware of temporary physical states in withdrawal and early sobriety that should be identified to the client, rather than interpreted as personal or interpersonal issues. For example, a person may drink too much coffee or take too much decongestant medication and have a reaction that is misperceived or misinterpreted as anxiety pertaining to some real issue. During withdrawal from depressant drugs including alcohol, the central nervous system undergoes rebound activity, which may also be experienced as anxiety and apprehension.

Simplifying

Reflection and restatement also have the important benefit and function of *simplifying*. Simplification removes confusion, avoids intellectualizations and convoluted explanations, and helps the client stay focused on concrete feelings and problems in the here and now. The famous AA slogan "Keep it simple" expresses this key element in self-help and counseling systems. Steve de Shazer, founder of the short-term, solution-focused school of therapy, quipped that one should edit the motto "Simplify, simplify, simplify" down to the single word "Simplify" (Berg and Miller 1992, 9).

A further function for reflection of feeling and restatement of content is to show the client that the counselor understands and is following the client's stream of consciousness. Egan (1998) calls this "pacing" the client, an image borrowed from sports training that connotes a more active form of "attending." It gives a sense of teamwork and collaboration and, in general, builds a positive feeling about the counseling experience. Clients who have clarified their feelings and thoughts from their counselors' restatements and reflections, which they have listened to and absorbed, leave the sessions feeling clearer and more at peace.

Summarizing

A higher level of abstraction in restatement and reflection is *summarizing*, or tying together the main points, themes, and issues presented by clients during part or all of a session. Miller and Rollnick (1991) see an added benefit of skilled summarizing: illustrating clients' ambivalence to them, allowing them to see the "positives and negatives *simultaneously*, acknowledging that both are present" (79).

An elaborate summary of the positives and negatives of using alcohol and drugs is a technique suggested in motivational enhancement therapy and Beck's cognitive therapy. To arrive at this summary, the counselor enlists the client in enumerating contradictory motives in the "decisional balance" (Beck et al. 1993, 137-9; Miller and Rollnick 1991, 23-4, 78-80, 95). Beck suggests a four-cell "advantages-disadvantages analysis" of quitting and not quitting. This summary can serve as an assessment tool for the counselor, who can then choose the best way to "tip" the decision toward sobriety. A major shortcoming of this approach, acknowledged by Miller and Rollnick (1991, 24), is that many of the forces driving addictive behavior are not enumerated easily by rational reflection or introspection. These include enabling behaviors and cultural factors, as well as short-term forces such as psychological discomforts of hangover or withdrawal, which "fall off the chart." Another shortcoming of this technique, not mentioned by the motivational or cognitive theorists, is that there is no means provided for measuring the relative strength of these motives. Also, one cannot simply measure pain, grief, love, and other emotional associations against motives, habits, consequences, or memories. Still, a written list of costs and benefits of change compared to costs and benefits of the status quo is a nonthreatening activity that can serve to focus the thinking of addicts in the precontemplative stage.

Reinforcing

Many counselors simply affirm, support, and even praise the client for whatever steps he or she has taken. While this is not exactly a listening skill, it is a nonthreatening form of engagement and involvement. Miller and Rollnick (1991, 78-9) list it as an important technique. Examples of reinforcing include statements such as:

"I appreciate how hard it must have been for you to decide to come here. You took a big step."

"That must have been very difficult for you."

"You're certainly a resourceful person to have been able to live with the problem this long and not fall apart."

"It must be difficult for you to accept a day-to-day life so full of stress."

Such praise must be genuine or it will sound patronizing, disengage the client, and reduce support.

ACTIVITY (2.4) Am I a good listener?

After reading through this activity, form groups of three. In each group, one person will play the role of the client, one the counselor, and one the monitor. The "client" will talk about a personal problem or issue, or something he or she would like to change. Where possible, keep the focus on issues related to use of drugs or alcohol. The "counselor" will counsel the client, practicing active listening skills (approximately 8 minutes). The "monitor" will give feedback, noting what skills were observed and where they were or were not used appropriately (approximately 1 minute). Note that the purpose of this activity is to practice active listening skills. It is not designed for solving problems or probing deep emotions or secrets.

Discuss: After all groups have concluded their role-plays, return to the large group and discuss your feelings about the performances of the roles. Identify specific listening skills.

- What other counseling skills did you observe?
- Were they used appropriately? If not, why not?
- Would the inappropriate use you observed be harmful or just ineffective? Explain.
- How would you have done it differently?

Reframing

Reframing is different from reflection or restatement because this skill interprets a client's experience in a new light or in a reorganized form. For example, reframing can facilitate the perception of an event in a more positive light, or a "bad" situation can be seen as a challenge and a potential learning experience.

Reframing is emphasized in psychotherapies that are based in cognitive techniques, such as rational-emotive therapy, or RET (Ellis 1985; Ellis and Dryden 1987; Ellis et al. 1988). The counselor should take care, however, not to apply this technique in a manner that seems to trivialize or glibly explain away a client's loss and grief in the face of tragedy or adversity. An example of reframing, via patient education, is the client who begins to see alcohol- and drug-related behavior not as bad or shameful, but as symptomatic of a disease. Reframing gives the client a different perspective, and this reduces the heavy shame-based feelings with which the client is often burdened.

Leading Skills

Categorizations of helping or counseling skills vary among human services. The category of "leading" skills discussed here is much broader than the definition found in many counseling textbooks.

Leading skills are ways of encouraging and suggesting connections that help the client move along in self-exploration and keep the client thinking about his or her acts, thoughts, and feelings. These skills also help the client develop the habit of self-reflection.

By using leading skills, addictions counselors help the client gain personal insights. To do so, counselors merely facilitate steps taken by the client in exploring emotions, behavior, and cognition. Leading is effective only if the client has some self-awareness; no one can progress from point A to point B until he or she has gotten to point A. For example, it is premature to discuss the implications of angry feelings if the angry person has not identified and acknowledged those feelings! In addition, leading questions should be open-ended and begin with *what, when, where,* or *how.* Various schools of thought, including MET (Miller and Rollnick 1991, 71-2) and cognitive therapy of addictions (Beck et al. 1993, 104-5), stress the importance of open-ended questions such as "What else?" "Anything else you can think of?" "Such as...?" They encourage thinking, talking, contemplation, and exploration. These types of questions can

- lead to other examples of a behavior or feeling, which may suggest a pattern. "Do you think that you may do this in other areas of your life?" "Do you feel this way in other situations?" "Do you often feel like this?"
- lead to elaboration of the original statement. "Tell me more about that feeling." "What was that like?"
- lead clients to reflect on what they think and feel in particular situations. "How did you feel about that? Him? Her? Yourself?"
- lead toward links among thoughts, feelings, and behaviors. "How do you act when you feel this way? "Does that thought make you anxious?" "How do you feel after you do that?"
- lead toward an understanding of consequences, and implications of behavioral choices and patterns. "What would happen then?" "What would that mean?" "Is it OK to have those feelings?" "Why aren't you entitled to your feelings?"
- lead back to the crucial topic, the here and now, the topic at hand, and addiction-specific concerns. "How does that relate to . . . ?"
- lead to discussions of plans and behaviors. "What are you going to do about it?"

The "downward arrow" technique used in the cognitive therapy approach to addictions counseling is based on questions that lead the client through an identification of self-statements or unarticulated assumptions about "domino effects" of their choices. This model states that there are layers of "automatic thoughts" triggered by specific situations which can lead to, among other things, catastrophizing or all-or-nothing thinking. Using this technique, the counselor asks repeatedly about the meaning, consequences, or implications of an idea or situation to "deconstruct" the chains or layers of belief. In one example (Beck et al. 1993, 140-2), a man is afraid of not drinking at an upcoming office party. By asking him a series of questions, each a variation on the question, "What does that mean to you?" (e.g., "What would the implications be?" and "What would the consequences be?"), the counselor finds that the man doesn't think he'd be fun sober, that no one would stick with him, that his sales career would suffer, and he'd lose his house and family!

Focusing is important due to the time-limited nature of addictions treatment, especially in the managed-care era. It may be a gentle or more active nudge, as in the probing/questioning skill discussed later. A crucial topic to attend to and focus upon is the counseling process itself. The counselor facilitates awareness of and open discussion of the client's experiences in the session, and what happens between the parties. This is perhaps the most curing growth experience that is possible in counseling, far outweighing advice, answers, and therapeutic sleight-of-hand. A popularized expression is "staying in the here and now." As Meier and Davis (1993) advise, "When in doubt, focus on feelings" at a level appropriate to the stage of treatment and with full awareness of anxiety or even pain that this may necessitate. "How does that make you feel?" is a here-and-now question.

The other crucial topic to lead the client to is the relevancy to recovery and relapse of the content under discussion or the process just revealed. "Do you think this discussion can help you stay sober?" The skilled counselor lets the client make the connections.

Leading the client to discuss plans and behaviors helps him or her see the link between his or her actions and getting results. It leads to self-efficacy, the confidence that one has some power over one's life. By encouraging the client to make plans assertively, counselors facilitate movement toward the point of taking action to effect his or her recovery.

In developing skills to help clients develop self-awareness, a counselor must pay attention to the timing of questions, as well as how assertively he or she pursues the point. The term *probing* carries the connotation of going underneath a surface feeling or idea into deeper, perhaps buried material. In choosing to move faster or more aggressively in leading, counselors tread the fine line between leading and confrontation. It is seldom appropriate for counselors to force clients to "spill their guts," that is, to suddenly access and ventilate intense rage and pain, especially in early treatment. Counselors may feel that the client is ready to go further, ask various questions that lead into new territory, and then sense anxiety that signals them to back off for now. Several concerns affect the decision of whether to pose potentially threatening questions:

- the stage of treatment
- the degree to which the client has become engaged and invested in treatment
- the degree of coercion involved in the client's participation in treatment
- awareness of nonverbal cues provided by clients that indicate that the counseling process is generating anxiety

ACTIVITY 2.5 That's a leading question!

After reading through this activity, form groups of three. In each group, one person will play the client, one the counselor, and one the monitor. The "client" and the "counselor" will discuss a personal problem or issue the client would like to change (5–10 minutes). Keep the focus on issues related to drugs and alcohol. The "monitor" will then give feedback about which skills he or she observed (1–2 minutes).

Remember that the purpose of this activity is to practice leading skills, not to solve problems. Also remember that all information shared here is confidential.

Discuss: After all groups have concluded their role-plays, return to the large group and discuss your feelings and observations about the performance of the roles.

- Identify specific leading skills.
- Were they used appropriately? If not, why not?
- Would the inappropriate use you observed be harmful or just ineffective? Explain.
- How would you have done it differently?

Counselor Self-Disclosure

In the addictions field, *counselor self-disclosure* often means the counselor shares his or her recovery from addiction. In generic counseling, the term refers to a counselor's sharing his or her relevant feelings, attitudes, opinions, or experiences for the benefit of the client. Counselor self-disclosure can benefit the client because it

- reduces shame, guilt, and sense of isolation by showing the client he or she is not uniquely horrible

- aids in maintaining a here-and-now focus
- provides an example of intimacy to a client who has never experienced intimacy or who has lost a sense of how to be intimate

Counselors never use self-disclosure to impress the client, nor in response to the counselor's need to confess or ventilate. Skillful self-disclosure is relevant in content, occurs in an accurate context, and is timed effectively.

Self-disclosure of a counselor's recovery from addiction has been the subject of an ongoing debate in addictions counseling. Some see this disclosure as a crucial contribution of the recovering counselor in providing hope, inspiration, and role models. Paradoxically, some nonrecovering counselors feel that an agency milieu in which counselors disclose their recovery status puts them at a disadvantage. However a client who is bent on devaluing the counselor will come up with a reason for each type of counselor (i.e., "You're just a drunk like me, how can you help?" or "You never went through it, how can you help?"). In either case, the counselor should respond by encouraging the client to identify and communicate his or her needs and goals, and explore how the treatment plan and counseling process will facilitate movement in this direction.

The term *self-disclosure* can refer not only to revelation of recovery status but also to the sharing of any information or feelings by the counselor. Some of the goals of counselor self-disclosure are facilitation of intimacy, identification, and reduction of shame or guilt about feelings. If done appropriately, it can open up people's "hidden spots." Counselors may wish to tell clients how behavior affects them in order to bring out some emotion, tension, or discrepancy. For example, a "chatterbox" client communicated tension and forced cheerfulness to the counselor, who remarked, "While you're telling me all these great things, I'm starting to feel anxious, and I wonder why that is." Chapter 7 discusses the emotional reactions of counselors to their clients.

ACTIVITY **2.6** **Do you know who I am?**

Consider the surface and visual issues that make people seem different (hair color, skin tone, accent, manner of dress, size, etc.). Pair up with someone who seems very different from to you. In pairs, share a significant experience that made you what you are. These experiences might include a terrible loss, an act of kindness from another person, getting or leaving a job or home, getting married, or divorced.

> **Process:** After 5 to 10 minutes regather to one larger group and discuss: Were there similarities in your experiences? Did the physical differences begin to be less significant or more? Did one person feel more comfortable than the other in divulging personal information? Did the person who went second feel easier about self-divulging after hearing the first person's story? How did you feel as you listened to your partner's story?

Influencing Skills

Simply being in a counseling relationship exerts an influence on clients. But sometimes counselors actively intervene to influence their clients. This is dangerous territory. Great skill and thoughtfulness are required to exert a positive influence that furthers the client's treatment.

Interpretation

Interpretation is a technique used by counselors to provide a new "frame of reference" or alternative ways of looking at situations. Interpreting involves seeing connections between situations, beliefs, feelings, and behavior. It involves understanding the influence of experience and the dynamics of different personalities. Of course, it is preferable for the client to develop insights and self-understanding than to be told things about himself or herself. As Meier and Davis (1993) emphasize, avoid advice and avoid premature problem solving. Counselors can cheat clients out of the wonderful therapeutic experiences of struggling with old ways of thinking, uncovering feelings, seeing new connections, and having exciting realizations if they supply pat answers—even when clients demand them and are angry when refused. Growth is liberating.

Confrontation

Confrontation is a deliberate use of a question or statement by the counselor to induce the client to face what the counselor thinks the client is trying to avoid. The "therapeutic lens" now attempts to correct shortsighted distortions. The technique is designed to provide an opportunity for change. Confrontation usually points out discrepancies

- within the client's statement or beliefs.
- between statements and behaviors.
- between strengths and weaknesses.
- between what a client states and what the counselor heard or observes.

The process skill of confrontation involves five elements: timing, staying concrete, estimating, forcefulness, and keeping tabs on the counselor.

Effective *timing* of the confrontation occurs when the client can see the possibility of change or when resistance is causing stagnation. Confrontation can break resistance, which might cause boredom, and can weaken or eliminate a desire to leave treatment. Poor timing for confrontation would be during the throes of major depression, suicidal ideation, and after a major defeat. There is no formula for timing of confrontations. Rather, it is related to the counseling skills of attending to the clients' verbal and nonverbal cues that provide information on their emotional states, and to correct gauging of the development of a therapeutic alliance.

Staying concrete and *providing hope* are very important in confrontation. Counselors should remember that the goal of confrontation is to facilitate change. Vagueness, lectures, and pontification can create confusion or even despair. Rather, it is important to make simple and concrete remarks, and to imply or incorporate the possibility of specific change. This can move the client forward, past the discomfort of the confrontive moment and toward taking the next step. An example is, "Is your behavior getting you what you need? Can you think of other ways of feeling good?"

Estimating how much to confront and how forcefully is also critical. Meier and Davis (1993, 12) offer a rule of thumb, "You may confront as much as you've supported." In addictions treatment, the client is often a mandated involuntary participant, denial is practically universal, and the amount of time available for the treatment is limited. Although involuntary treatment certainly does not make it permissible to use harsh and unpleasant methods, it does make counselors a little less fearful of being frank with their comments. The supportive addictions counselor provides an opportunity for change without boxing the client in a corner to the point of being abusive or destroying the possibility of a therapeutic alliance.

Although it is easy to confuse with rage and raised voices, confrontation can be done with the utmost gentleness. Drug treatment in particular has been associated with extremes in confrontation. Counselors who are habituated to strong confrontational methods may find them ill-suited to other milieux. Their methods may have to undergo modification as those counselors seek employment in agencies with different philosophies of treatment.

Monitoring the counselor's emotional state and motives is very important. Confrontation should always be motivated by a desire to help the client change. That is, counselors must confront clients out of concern rather than rage, annoyance, demonstration of power, or self-glorification. Counselors must honestly assess their motives and feelings when initiating a confrontation (this is discussed in chapter 7 in the section on counter tranferrence).

Ellis and colleagues (1988, 56-7, 72-4) encourage counselors to confront irrational, unhelpful cognitions. They refer to this as *disputing*, which may include:

- challenges to evidence produced by clients
- identifications of distortions in thinking
- development of more accurate explanations of events (reattribution)
- argument in favor of irrational beliefs to bring out the lack of validity for this position
- disputation of catastrophizing or awfulizing modes of thought, which may generate so much anxiety as to pose a threat of relapse

Figure 2.1 is an example of the disputing technique as applied to awfulizing.

Figure 2.1 An Example of Disputing

IB (Irrational Belief): *It's awful when I don't drink and therefore I have to feel anxious.*
DC (Disputing Counselor): *Why is it awful?*
IB: *Because it is so* uncomfortable.
DC: *And you run the universe, right?*
IB: *No, but I* should *be able to control my own discomfort.*
DC: *That would be great. But, really,* must *you?*
Client: *No, I guess I do not* have to have more comfort.

Source: Ellis et al. 1998. *Rational-Emotive Therapy with Alcoholics and Substance Abusers.* Boston: Allyn and Bacon.

ACTIVITY **2.7** **How do I influence people?**

After reading through this activity, form groups of three. In each group, one person will play the role of the client, one the counselor, and one the observer. Role play one of the situations listed below. The "counselor" will counsel the client, practicing active influencing skills (approximately 8 minutes). The "observer" will give feedback, noting what skills were observed and where they were or were not used appropriately (approximately 1 minute). Remember to keep the focus on issues related to use of drugs or alcohol. The following list suggests some situations to role play.

- A court-mandated client in an intake session is denying or resisting the need for treatment.

- A client who has been sober and drug-free for two months has skipped counseling sessions and stopped attending support group meetings. The client is somewhat withdrawn and shows some of the signs of impending relapse
- A client is getting into trouble on the job, flying into rages at home, and acting sullen and brooding in the session.
- A client who has been sober and drug-free for four months has not made progress on a goal in the treatment plan (e.g., finding a job, making friends, taking a vacation, repaying a debt, etc.).
- Enact situations that your instructor suggests.

Discuss: After all groups have concluded their role plays, return to the large group and discuss the effectiveness and impact of influencing skills.

- Identify specific influencing skills. Were they effective? Why or why not?
- Would you recommend handling the situation another way? How? Why?
- What feelings were invoked in the "counselors" and "clients"?
- What other counseling skills did you observe?
- Did the influencing skills of the counselors facilitate change in the clients? How?

Timing

The discussion of probing skills stresses being aware of the client's level of anxiety and knowing when to "advance" and "retreat." Throughout the application of all counseling skills, it is necessary to know how far to go, how to time comments well, and how to match the intensity of feelings and anxiety a counselor might arouse with the stage of treatment and the client's mood.

The "art of counseling," unlike the "science" or "technique" of counseling, depends very much on timing, which depends on the comfort level and skill of the counselor. Nevertheless, there are some ground rules. When clients come into treatment, their anxiety is usually high and they need anxiety-reducing responses (reassurance, explanation, attending, listening, and support). Later, when clients become complacent and comfortable, techniques that *increase* some level of anxiety (probing, confrontation) are useful to motivate a client. As Wallace points out in his classic piece "Critical Issues in Alcoholism Psychotherapy" (1987, 37-49), addictions counselors continually walk a fine line between allowing clients' denial to continue too long and pushing them prematurely toward self-disclosure.

Process Recording

Process recording is a way that counselors keep track of, look back at, reflect upon, think about, and analyze what is going on in the counseling process. It is more than a simple recording of events; it is recording and processing what is going on, leading to an evaluation of the use of techniques and the client-counselor relationship. It allows counselors to "attend to" and "pace" themselves. It is a standard training method in social-work and mental-health settings, but unfortunately often absent in the chemical-dependency practicum. It is an invaluable tool in the fieldwork or practicum component of counselor preparation. Process recording is quite useful in supervisory sessions. Figure 2.2 is an excerpt from a process recording.

Figure 2.2 Excerpt from a Process Recording

Sandra Baskin (SB), a counselor at an outpatient addictions facility, wrote the following as part of her process recording of an individual counseling session with Michael Gerrity (MG). Her process comments are in parentheses. She uses the following abbreviations: Dx=diagnosis, Tx=treatment, ASP=antisocial personality, DA=district attorney.

MG entered the room.

> *(I was feeling burned out and irritable since this was the fourth client in a row, the last one being very hostile. I hoped that my mood didn't show.*

MG: Hey, what's up? Mind if I duck outside on the terrace for a quick smoke?

SB: Hey, you know we can't do that!

MG: Nobody will know, come on Ms. Baskin.

(Now I'm starting to really get annoyed at MG.)

MG (smiles broadly): Well, it could be worse! I'm alive! And with my favorite counselor!

> *(I felt disarmed by Michael's impish smile and smiled back. Now I remembered that Michael had a Dx of ASP and could be very charming and manipulative. I was mad at myself for being conned even for a moment. Got to check charts before client comes in. Maybe make red flags for important info. MG is also coming up for a court hearing . . .)*

(continued)

SB: Are you feeling ready for your hearing with Judge Madsen?

MG: Only if you are. (a teasing reference to my role in preparing the agency report on MG's cooperation, participation and progress in Tx).

SB: Do you feel that I'm on your side here? (MG still tends to view me as another cop, my attempts at empathic engagement must be a con job like MG would pull.)

MG: Ummm (suddenly loses his glib repartee).

SB: I was in your position once. (Oh, crap. Why did I blurt that out? I'm so anxious to make a connection with Mike that I jumped over a boundary. Did NOT need to share that. There's that over-identification/codependency issue kicking in . . . my little brother MG is not . . . Now I'm feeling anxious and out of control.)

MG: Yeah? (smiles again, more authentically) Maybe we can be buddies after all. (An alliance or a con? What is the difference for him? My comment helped, but at what price later on?) Well, I'm pretty stressed about it. You know, Madsen gets into his Hanging Judge bag, get-the-dope-fiends-off-the-street thing.

SB: Maybe we should concentrate on concrete steps in your treatment plan that will help you stay clean, AND out of the clutches of the DA. And an agency plan for an alternative to sentencing.

MG: I guess I can't go wrong with that. Thanks, doc. (MG calls me 'doc' when he is feeling positive about our relationship. I think I rescued the situation.)

(Looking back at this section, I realize I'm spending a lot of energy on second-guessing everything I say and do, and on the client's response, micromanaging myself. So much for the here and now!)

Process recording, progress notes, and case presentations are different things. *Process recording* is a transcript or summary of everything that went on between the participants, and the emotions evoked by their interactions. *Progress notes*, or *chart notes*, document that appropriate tasks or interventions were completed, and provide background for the next worker. The *case presentation* demonstrates the ability to muster an overview of an addict's entire treatment career, and mastery of the entire scope of treatment.

The process recording should begin with a brief description of the client and where he or she is in the "client career," a brief summary of treatment goals that are being implemented, and any other information that can provide context for the listener or reader. After this, the process recording breaks down into two tracks, the content track and the process track. The content track is a transcript of the verbal and nonverbal behavior of the client (e.g., client came in ten minutes late, tapped his fingers rapidly while speaking, said "I hate you!" in a loud, high-pitched voice). The process track includes such items as the following, in the order that they occurred or were observed:

- observations about a client's emotional state
- broader inferences about how the client's expectations, transference issues, and transcultural issues affected the client's actions in the session
- the counselor's emotional reactions (e.g., "I felt . . . and this is probably related to a similar experience or relationship I had.")
- itemization of the counseling skills applied at each point during the session
- observations of how the counselor's use of particular approaches influenced the process

Process recordings can alternate paragraphs or make columns (content and process) to record the tracks. Typically, the column system results in some blank spaces in the content column, because the commentaries usually run longer. Cournoyer (1996, 210) uses a multicolumn analysis to prepare a transcription of an audio- or videotaped session: content, skill used, counselor's gut reaction, and counselor's analysis.

The final section of the process recording contains suggestions for treatment (improvement) based on the counselor's observations. Examples of suggestions are more client education on the treatment process, further discussions of his or her expectations of treatment, focus on the here and now, avoid data and war stories, stay with more modest session goals, remember to budget time for "patching up" the client after heavy self-disclosures, learn more about the client's ethnic background, do something about that burnout, use attending skills more and influencing skills less.

Process recording is governed by legal and ethical guidelines. Preparation and use of the document must be done in collaboration with the agency's administrators. The agency should determine whether the sensitive document should be kept in the files, since it could be subpoenaed for use in legal proceedings against the agency, its employees, or the client.

R E F E R E N C E S

Bandura, A. 1987. "Self-Efficacy: Towards a Unifying Theory of Behavior Change." *Psychological Review* 84: 191-215.

Beck, A., et al. 1993. *Cognitive Therapy of Substance Abuse.* New York: Guilford Press.

Berg, I. K., and S. D. Miller. 1992. *Working with the Problem Drinker: A Solution-Focused Approach.* New York: Norton.

Bishop, F. M. 1995. "Rational-Emotive Behavior Therapy and Two Self-Help Alternatives to the 12-Step Model," in *Psychotherapy and Substance Abuse.* A. M. Washton, ed. New York: Guilford Press.

Carkhuff, R. R. 1969a. *Helping and Human Relations 1: Selection and Training.* New York: Holt, Reinhart, and Winston.

———. 1969b. *Helping and Human Relations 2: Practice and Research.* New York: Holt, Reinhart, and Winston.

Corey M. S., and G. Corey. 1998. *Becoming a Helper,* 3rd ed. Pacific Grove, CA: Brooks/Cole.

Cormier, W. H., and L. S. Cormier. 1991. *Interviewing Strategies for Helpers.* Pacific Grove, CA: Brooks/Cole.

Cournoyer, B. 1996. *The Social Work Skills Workbook.* Pacific Grove, CA: Brooks/Cole.

CSAT (Center for Substance Abuse Treatment). 1998. *Addiction Counselor Competencies: The Knowledge, Skills, and Attitudes of Professional Practice.* CSAT Technical Assistance Publication Series 21, Rockville, MD: Substance Abuse and Mental Health Administration.

Cummings, C., J. Gordon, and G. A. Marlatt. 1980. "Relapse: Prevention and Prediction," in *The Addictive Behaviors.* W. Miller, ed. Oxford: Pergamon Press.

Egan, G. 1998. *The Skilled Helper,* 6th ed. Pacific Grove, CA: Brooks/Cole.

Ellis, A. 1962. *Reason and Emotion in Psychotherapy.* Secaucus, NJ: Citadel Press.

———. 1985. "Expanding the ABC's of Rational-Emotive Therapy," in *Cognition and Psychotherapy.* M. Mahoney and A. Freeman, ed. New York: Plenum.

Ellis, A., and W. Dryden. 1987. *The Practice of Rational-Emotive Psychotherapy.* New York: Springer-Verlag.

Ellis, A., et al. 1988. *Rational-Emotive Therapy with Alcoholics and Substance Abusers.* Boston: Allyn and Bacon.

Fiedler, F. 1950. "A Comparison of Therapeutic Relationships in Psychoanalytic, Non-Directive, and Adlerian Therapy." *Journal of Consulting Psychology* 14: 436-45.

———. 1951. "Factor Analyses of Psychoanalytic, Non-Directive, and Adlerian Therapy." *Journal of Consulting Psychology* 15: 32-8.

Garfield, S. L., and A. Bergin. 1994. "Introduction and Historical Overview," chap 1. in *Handbook of Psychotherapy and Behavior Change*, 4th ed. A. E. Bergin and S. L. Garfield, ed. New York: Wiley.

Ivey, A. 1971. *Microcounseling: Innovation in Interview Training*. Springfield, IL: Charles Thomas.

———. 1988. *International Interviewing and Counseling*, 2nd ed. Pacific Grove, CA: Brooks/Cole.

Kazdin, A. E. 1994. "Methodology, Design, and Evaluation in Psychotherapy Research," in *Handbook of Psychotherapy and Behavior Change*, 4th ed. A. E. Bergin and S. L. Garfield, ed. New York: Wiley.

Lambert, M. J., and A. E. Bergin. 1994. "The Effectiveness of Psychotherapy," in *Handbook of Psychotherapy and Behavior Change*, 4th ed. A. E. Bergin and S. L. Garfield, ed. New York: Wiley.

Meier, S. T., and S. R. Davis. 1993. *The Elements of Counseling*, 2nd ed. Pacific Grove, CA: Brooks/Cole.

Miller, W. R., and S. Rollnick, ed. 1991. *Motivational Interviewing: Preparing People to Change Addictive Behavior*. New York: Guilford Press.

NIAAA (National Institute on Alcohol Abuse and Alcoholism). 1995. Project MATCH Monograph Series, 3: *Cognitive-Behavioral Coping Skills Therapy Manual*, NIH Pub. no. 94-3724. Rockville, MD: U.S. Department of Health and Human Services.

Prochaska, J. O., and C. C. DiClemente. 1982. "Stages and Processes of Self-Change in Smoking: Towards an Integrative Model of Change." *Psychotherapy* 20: 161-73.

Prochaska, J. O., J. C. Norcross, and C. C. DiClemente. 1994. *Changing for Good*. New York: William Morrow.

Rogers, C. 1951. *Client-Centered Therapy*. Boston: Houghton Mifflin.

————. 1986. "Client-Centered Therapy," in *Psychotherapist's Casebook: Therapy and Technique in Practice*. I. Kutash and A. Wolk, ed. San Francisco: Jossey-Bass.

Taleff, M. J. 1997. *A Handbook to Assess and Treat Resistance in Chemical Dependency*. Dubuque, IA: Kendall-Hunt.

Wallace, J. 1987. "Critical Issues in Alcoholism Therapy," in *Practical Approaches to Alcoholism Psychotherapy*, 2nd ed. S. Zimberg, J. Wallace, and S. B. Blume, ed. New York: Plenum Press.

Group Treatment of Addiction

Introduction

Just about any gathering of clients is liable to be called a group or group therapy. In this chapter the term *group treatment* applies to interactive groups that have an observable group process and in which the clients' talking to each other is the major activity, directly or indirectly facilitating personal growth and recovery from addiction. A variety of didactic and educational groups can also have important roles in addictions treatment, but in such settings interaction among members is not a central or defining characteristic.

Most alcohol and drug treatment occurs in group settings, which are well suited to the needs of recovering addicts. Groups break down isolation and encourage relatedness, social re-emergence, and the identity of the "recovering addict." They provide hope, motivation, peer pressure, and support on recovery issues. Tension, shame, and guilt are reduced greatly when members bring out concealed feelings, thoughts, and behaviors, which are often shared by others in the group. Clients can form attachments and loyalties to something larger than the one-to-one, sometimes overdependent counseling relationship, thus forming a counterbalance to the user/abuser milieu. Groups allow observation of real behavior patterns and replaying of roles, and reflection on them. They are tremendously cost-effective, and "are also great fun" (Blume 1985, 75).

Although addictions groups are specialized among the group therapies in their focus on recovery issues such as denial and relapse prevention, they also touch on many of the emotional, behavioral, and cognitive issues found in all group modalities (Frank 1985). Group counseling methods are as diverse as those of individual counseling. Groups vary tremendously in focus, content, intensity, client characteristics, stage of treatment, format, and philosophy. Emotions may be screamed or politely discussed; behavioral changes may be harshly mandated or merely suggested; clients may interact freely or be discouraged from "cross-talk." The way in which a group is conducted is often based on a hallowed tradition within the agency milieu. Some addictions professionals feel that rigidly following tradition may clash with the individual needs of clients and research-based treatment design.

Group Culture

Societies and groups have systems of behavior, values, and ideas that professionals refer to as their culture. The culture of a counseling group includes theme, content, group process, lore, format, and often a philosophy of human nature. A group's culture may derive from a particular tradition such as twelve-step, psychoanalytic, confrontational encounter group, and Gestalt psychology, or it may be a synthesis of styles. Agency and group culture is often summarized and transmitted in the form of slang, mottoes, and aphorisms (e.g., When you think you're looking bad, you're looking good! You're as sick as your secrets. It gets better. Keep it simple. Bad feelings get in the way of good feelings.). As happens in any culture, therapeutic culture engenders many concise descriptions of, among other things, the group dynamics and process. For example, protection from confrontation is described at Daytop Village (New York) as "red-crossing," and at Integrity House (Newark, NJ) as "band-aiding."

Group cultures vary in the ways they map out personality dynamics. As discussed in chapter 1, models of the personality, although not always directly stated, are crucial influences on clinical approaches and should be recognized and critically evaluated. For example, anger is handled differently in different group cultures. The twelve-step model in a group setting may influence the identification of anger as a relapse trigger; members might then be encouraged to "turn it over to a higher power" or put it aside. In contrast, the therapeutic-community model, which also sees anger as a sign of potential relapse, recommends that such emotions be forcefully purged from the system in the group. Some clinicians (Brown and Yalom 1977, 452; Wallace 1985a, b) caution against pressuring clients to engage in extreme emotional outbursts in addictions groups because they are far too threatening and overwhelming, and call for premature self-disclosure by clients.

Addictions agencies often have formal orientation to group rules and group culture. Group orientation facilitates the group process. For example, the almost universal rules of "No violence or threats of violence" and "Everyone stays in his or her seat except for a group exercise" reassure the members that this is a safe place where, unlike some family and community environments, expressions of opinion or anger will not meet with physical retaliation or abuse. Orientation and ground rules also provide structure and reassurance for the recently active alcoholic or addict who may retain some fear of losing self-control and physically acting out when angered. Other group norms that are commonly introduced in an orientation include the importance of regular attendance and punctuality, the rule against sexual contacts among group members, and strict confidentiality. While it is tempting to gossip, "Everything stays in this room."

ⒶⒸⓉⒾⓋⒾⓉⓎ **Are you all together?**

Sometimes it is difficult to assess "groupness." For instance, is a band a group? Is a baseball team? A family? Audience at a concert? Usually a group has some shared goals, some development of trust, norms of how to behave toward each other, some sense of leadership, and methods for making decisions. Probably most important of all is that members think of themselves as part of a group.

Form groups of six to eight and draw a picture of "a group" and of "a collection of people." How do your pictures differ? Small groups can post their pictures and describe them, differentiating the qualities of "group" and "collection of people."

Process: Did all of the small groups come up with similar definitions? What processes took place in the small groups during the assigned task? Did some people push for completion, take over leadership, bring up other topics?

Developing Awareness of the Group Process

Group process refers to all patterns and styles of interaction in the group. *Content* is what a group is discussing. It may be the problems or concerns of members or perhaps the tasks they are trying to accomplish. Although content should always be relevant to group objectives, even more important is the healing that goes on.

In order to help the group facilitate healthy behaviors, healing, and recovery from addiction, the counselor must be skilled in observing and evaluating the dynamics at work in the group.

First of all, counselors should think about how people present themselves. From these behaviors alone, none of which would be discernible in a transcription of the group, counselors can deduce the tone or atmosphere of the group (e.g., accepting, supportive, rejecting, tense or edgy, repressed, avoidant, or overly polite) and the level of participation by each member. Behaviors to observe include:

- *Voice:* How do people sound? Listen to the voice qualities that members use.
- *Expression:* What are the facial expressions: smiles, frowns, raised eyebrows, sneers? If a person smiles, is it spontaneous, tight-lipped, fixed?
- *Posture:* What postures are adopted: bunched up, tipped back in chair, close or distant from the speaker or the next person in the circle?
- *Contribution:* Who talks a lot? Who seldom talks? Who talks only when probed?
- *Visual focus:* Where do people look when they talk? At others? At one person? At the leader? At the floor or ceiling? Out the window? Eyes closed?

Second, counselors should observe regular patterns of social interaction: how decisions are made and tasks are accomplished, agreements made and kept, roles developed and enacted. Patterns to observe include:

- *Influence:* Who influences whom in the group? How? What's their style of influence?
- *Rivalry and conflict:* Is there animosity or conflict between members? Is it open? Covert? Passive-aggressive? Aggressive? Constant or intermittent?
- *Level of participation:* Who takes part? Always the same people? How much? How often? Is participation encouraged or discouraged? How do members respond to nonparticipation by other members?

- *Decision making:* How are decisions made? Does one person dominate or take the lead? Does everyone have something to say or a chance to say it? Do decisions in the group come easily or with conflict?
- *Teamwork and productivity:* How are tasks accomplished, or not? Is the group following up on crises that have been mentioned? Are commitments being kept? Does everyone show up? Is everyone on time?
- *Roles:* What roles are developed? Why and how do people play parts such as "scapegoat" and "hero"? Who is "in trouble"? Examples of members who are in trouble include those who cannot get a turn to speak, are cut off before finished, are going to leave the group very upset, or are the target of derision or disrespect and cannot respond adequately.
- *Covert agreements:* Are there unspoken understandings such as taboo topics, nonconfrontation, and resistance to progress? Does this occur in subgroups or cliques, or on the part of the entire group?

Group process is a powerful tool; it can be healing and facilitate growth or it can be devastating. Knowledge of group processes and continuous attention to process enable counselors to fulfill the ethical responsibility of promoting and safeguarding clients' welfare, emotional safety, and progress in recovery. The major role of an addictions group leader is not to give information, advice, or counseling but to facilitate the group process.

Group development is complex and slow, and should not be rushed or mandated. Tension, conflict, resistance, and regression are expected; they provide important learning opportunities for the members. When members do not feel that they are being helped or feel stalemated in their attempts to progress, they may make the leader their scapegoat. Anger at the leader is a normal stage in group development, and the ability to express such feelings can be a growth experience for members (Ormont and Strean 1978; Stokes and Miller 1980, 124-5; Yalom 1975, 306-11).

 ACTIVITY (3.2) **Process or Content?**

Decide if each statement in the following group conversation is focused on process or content. Take about 10 minutes to read over the items and make notes where appropriate. Then discuss responses to the items.

MARY: Let me tell you about my last slip.

TOM: How does everyone feel about talking about this?

JOHN: I don't like the word "slip." I prefer "relapse."

MARY: It happened when I ran into my old girlfriend.

SUSAN: I had a similar experience with my boyfriend.

BILL: How does Terry feel about our discussion?

TOM: I noticed Mary back off when you asked Terry to talk about it.

MARY: He's always criticizing my decisions.

TERRY: Tell us more about your reactions to Bill.

SUSAN: I'd get a lot out of more discussion of resentment.

Intervening in the Group Process

It is important to realize that group process is always going on. The counselor or anyone designated as the leader or facilitator must decide when, if at all, to intervene in the group process. This decision depends on what the group leader sees as necessary to make the group interaction healthier and more productive, to encourage more interaction, to remind the group of its goals and rules, and to focus the group on process or recovery issues. Group leaders can choose to intervene in many ways and at various levels. They can choose between content (e.g., adding information to the discussion) or process (e. g., commenting on the silence, anger, or lack of involvement). They can also choose to address one, several, or all the group members or encourage members to respond to one another.

Involving Marginal Members

Group membership is an important issue for each member. Members, particularly new members, are always struggling with whether they belong. To what extent they should or could share about themselves is a critical concern. Sharing of self is risky and requires trust of other group members and a belief that the benefits from the group outweigh the risks. Although new members of a group should not be forced to plunge directly into interaction, counselors must try to phase in their involvement. Waiting more than two group meetings sets a precedent that can dilute the group process below therapeutic levels. Moreover, marginalized members receive less help than they could, feel no investment in the group, and are in danger of leaving treatment or of relapse. Although they may not have articulated it, even to themselves, they feel extremely lonely and left out. In many cases, it is a relatively simple task for the counselor to help them initiate some contact with the group. One can, if no major pathology or other serious problem is suspected, gently force the issue. Subtle nudges include noting shared problems among members and asking the isolates to comment on their reactions to particular disclosures. At the very least, a counselor can note a group member's silence so that he or she does not feel invisible. Although many new members are overwhelmed by the self-disclosures and open exchange of emotions in group, it is important to identify other reasons for marginality and isolation. Possible reasons include fear of self-disclosure in a sensitive area such as sexual orientation, violence committed while intoxicated, or concomitant psychiatric diagnosis. These issues may be determined best in individual counseling. If an individual stays isolated and sees no way out of isolation and feeling unwanted, he or she will eventually leave unless compelled to stay.

Case in Point
Countering Isolation

At an agency that employed one of the authors, clients filled out confidential questionnaires asking with whom they preferred to associate. These connections were charted, and those who were not "on the chart" (called sociometric isolates by social psychologists) were rightly gauged as at risk of being "splittees" (individuals who leave treatment). Remedial interventions such as those discussed in this book were conducted to bring them into contact with other members.

Encouraging Peer Leadership in the Group

Counselors need to encourage a greater proportion of member-to-member interactions at the expense of leader-to-member interactions. This applies both to content (e.g., advice, confrontation, feedback) and to facilitation of group process.

If clients are still embedded in the drug culture, it may predominate over identification with a recovery program. Simply putting them into a room and expecting group therapy to occur is unrealistic, and may in fact be asking for trouble. If clients have developed some measure of therapeutic alliance with counselors, the group is much less likely to go out of control. However, a large proportion of senior, committed clients is less often found in the current world of short-term and mandated treatment. The situation faced by the counselor whose client bragged of "skin-popping" (see "Case in Point: Peer Leadership") may be more typical. Luckily, the counselor in that situation was rescued by a senior staff member who developed a positive, healing group process by focusing on issues of common concern, such as teen parenting and parental abuse.

Case in Point

Peer Leadership

The importance of peer leadership and positive peer culture was made clear early in the career of one addictions counselor, who was trained at a branch of an adolescent intensive outpatient program where senior group members trained, confronted, and helped new members. The leader, in fact, had little to do. Interventions by peers were much more effective than interventions by authority figures. The following month the counselor was placed at a new branch where he and another staff member had to conduct a large group of teenagers who were not socialized to group culture and process, nor to drug-free norms and goals. They watched in horror as a member bragged to a receptive audience of having "graduated" from sniffing heroin to subcutaneous injection ("skin-popping").

It is important for counselors to examine whether they behave in ways that centralize the group around themselves, and if so, why. For example, a counselor may fear that silences signal that the group is not functioning and will fail, or that time will be wasted, or that a point will be missed unless he or she makes it in the (theoretically) correct or most articulate way. A counselor may be afraid of losing control of the group or feel gratified by playing the role of revered leader, wise oracle, or healer. Of course, clinical or legal emergencies that require quick decisions by the staff override preferences for letting the group process develop at a natural rate.

Helping the Group Understand the Group Process

Group members are primed during orientation to focus on what is going on in the room. During orientation, as well as during the first few group sessions, clients learn slogans and terms that describe group processes. In order to encourage the group's reflection on its process the counselor must be aware of his or her own feelings in the group and how they reflect the prevailing atmosphere. The leader can and should comment on his or her observations of group processes, but it is more powerful for members to have and communicate these insights. The best facilitative interventions are those that encourage the group to observe itself and discuss the group process, often called a here-and-now focus. Such observations offer growth experiences for addicts; they provide insight as to how one actually behaves and how others react, and they reveal or highlight the consequences for one's identity, addiction, or recovery. Such a focus creates involvement, relevancy, and excitement. It is the basis for many group benefits listed in the introduction to this chapter.

Developing Group Intimacy

An atmosphere of intimacy is necessary for individuals to feel trusting, which is a precondition for taking the risks involved in curative self-disclosure of information and emotion. Under ideal conditions, it happens this way—orientation, developing trust, calling members on violations of rules, nudges by the counselor, reminders, and so on. Unfortunately, most groups, especially addictions groups, operate under restraints. Groups are most often limited by financial issues, such as a member's number of group sessions or the reimbursable fee being limited by his or her insurance company. Therefore, structured ice-breaking activities can accelerate the process in the early stages of a group.

Activity 3.3 and others have been developed (Napier and Gershenfeld 1973; Stokes, Tait, and Miller 1980) and used successfully for decades to help a group move quickly to intimacy. Activity 3.4 was developed in the late 1960s at Daytop Village, Inc., to help addicts shed their street or "dope fiend" images, which were thought to impede recovery. It allows people to shed stereotyped perceptions of themselves, known as their "jackets" (a term based on the manila file folder of information that follows the person in the criminal-justice system). This of type sharing allows people to explore intimacy in a nonthreatening manner, lessens group defensiveness, and establishes an atmosphere of trust.

ACTIVITY **3.3** **It made me who I am.**

Form pairs based on differences that you perceive in the other. First, discuss the criteria you chose to define "difference," and then discuss a pivotal or critical event in the formation of your personalities or lifestyles, regardless of whether it was positive or negative.

Process

- Was it hard to share the critical event with your partner?
- Did you quickly censure your choice of events and settle on an easy one?
- Do you feel closer to your partner now? If you do feel closer, how does that closeness or intimacy affect you?
- Does it make you feel vulnerable, embarrassed, or anxious to have disclosed personal information to your partner?

3.4 Blowing My Image

"The Philosophy" is ascribed to Richard Beauvais (1965) and was read at the morning meeting of Daytop Village. Read "The Philosophy," or ask someone to read it aloud.

The Philosophy

We are here because there is no refuge, finally, from ourselves.
Until a person confronts himself in the eyes and hearts of others,
He is running.
Until he suffers them to share in his secrets,
He has no safety from them.
Here, together, a person can appear clearly to himself,
Not as the giant of his dreams, nor the dwarf of his fears,
But as a person, part of a whole with a share in its purposes.
Here, together, we can at last take root and grow,
Not alone anymore as in death, but alive in ourselves and others.

Discuss: What does "the dwarf of our fears" represent? Some answers might be that we are afraid that what we have to offer is insufficient or not good enough, that we can't measure up in the eyes of others. Some counselors humorously refer to an unrealistically poor self-image as "delusions of inferiority."

Can low self-esteem, poor self-efficacy, or fear of being attacked make a person feel as if he or she needs to put up a mask, present a false image, or maintain a grandiose or tough exterior? Can this in turn make a person feel unknown, dishonest, or not liked for who he or she truly is? Do you think people can see through images to know what people really need?

What does "the giant of our dreams" represent? Here the giant symbolizes what we would like to be; it is a wish-fulfillment image.[1]

Process

1. Each member receives feedback from the group on the image he or she presents to the world.
2. Each member then honestly recounts his or her self-image and secret, wish-fulfillment image.
3. Each member performs a simple task that changes his or her image in the eyes of others. For example, a person perceived as super serious tells a joke or does something silly, a "good guy" admits a nasty impulse, or a "tough guy" admits to vulnerability or fear.

---

[1] Wallace (1985) describes a "reactive grandiosity" that compensates for an addict's sense of inferiority, although this process is certainly not unique to addicts. The point is that all of these images are inconsistent. Cognitive dissonance creates anxiety and the need to deny one or another of the dissonant images.

4. Each member briefly explores how the self-disclosure and having his or her image blown made him or her feel. Others may offer brief reactions.

Keeping the Group on Task

Staying on the Issue

A goal in the development of a well-functioning group is that the group members themselves realize when the discussion has gone astray, and point it out. Until the group can do this, however the counselor needs to refocus the group on recovery issues. This is particularly a task in groups composed primarily of beginners, such as those in detox units.

Many groups emphasize feelings in the here and now. This helps the clients become aware of their emotions, identify them, differentiate them from thoughts and attitudes, learn to communicate them assertively and appropriately, feel comfortable with them, and learn to ventilate and share them rather than chemically anesthetize them. Feelings are hard work; they are also threatening. It is natural to drift into an easy-going discussion about sports, clothes, or even drugs. Counselors monitor this so that every moment of the group is used in a productive way, maximizing the gains each client can achieve. Effective group counselors do not stamp out all utterances referring to past events; however, they help to distinguish between war stories of addiction, which are not productive for interactive groups, and accounts that evoke emotion in the speaker and other members of the group.

Staying in Routine

The counselor has the task of gently assuring that the group format, to the extent that there is one, is followed. Format refers to the way the group's time is structured. There are an almost unlimited variety of formats, including the following examples:

- *Open discussion:* Members take random turns as they wish, without cross-talk; a format found in twelve-step fellowships.
- *Rigidly timed segments:* Each member has the same amount of uninterrupted time to speak.
- *Loosely timed segments:* The length of time each member speaks shifts from client to client according to the issues and emotions that arise.
- *Unstructured interaction.*

Within the overall group format, the individual client's turn in groups may also follow a predictable routine, as does the personal "story" or "drunkalogue" in AA. There are various approaches to how a client should use the time in a group. Aside from attempts to help a client focus on relevant issues, there may be some attempt to structure the turn taken by a client. For example, it may be considered important to ensure that the client gains insight into his or her behavior, thinking, and emotions, or that the client sees the connections among these areas. Years before formal schools of psychotherapy and counseling attempted such a broad synthesis, some addictions programs staffed by recovering addicts structured groups so as to "cover all the bases." In one such format, clients took their turns to be helped by focusing first on a specific problem, then feelings related to the problem, then positive behavioral changes they could attempt, and finally identification and feedback from group members. This cycle could be repeated for each client who took a turn "on the hot seat."

In the format just described, the *problem* segment could address an issue raised by a client or an observation by another group member of behavior seen as problematical, in a concerned inquiry or confrontation. The *feeling* segment could involve helping the client identify, evoke, communicate, and accept her or his emotions concerning the issue. It may entail

- simple questions such as, "How did you feel about that?"
- focusing and clarifying questions.
- going around the room and telling everyone present the feeling, speaking to someone not present,[2] or speaking to a person playing the role of the absent subject.[3]
- venting an emotion by shouting or crying.

The third segment of this format is commitment to a plan for behavioral change or experimentation broken down into specific behavioral steps, as well as contingency planning. These are written down to so that the group can follow up on them in the next meeting. The commitment may be as simple as getting phone numbers of two group members and calling them during the week.

Identification and feedback come through supportive comments from others. Group behaviors in one segment may provide material for the next member's turn. There are two functions to such a segment:

1. In one study (Feeney 1976) alcoholics rated identification with others as the most helpful element of group therapy. It is a tremendous relief for a client to realize that his or her problems and feelings are shared by many others, that others have "been there, done that," and they can empathize with what the client is going through.

---

[2] This is the "empty chair" technique (Perls 1969).
[3] This activity has roots in psychodrama; some grounding in essentials of pschodrama would improve its effectiveness.

2. A "cooling-down" phase involves closure and summation of the segment. If the client is upset, an attempt is made to sooth ("patch up") him or her prior to the end of his or her segment. Cooling-off and closure segments are found in many group counseling approaches; they provide a transitional period from the vulnerability of deep emotion to the outside world.

In formatting the entire group meeting, time should be budgeted for possible crises, for a cooling-down phase, and at least a moment for each member to be noticed and acknowledged.

Helping Group Members Explore Roles

Roles are patterns of behavior, sets of expectations, and parts played in a social system. As in physical systems (such as the solar system), the parts interact and resonate with each other. Members of addictions groups can benefit tremendously by reflecting on how their behavior in group replays, repeats, or transfers from another situation, past or present. The counselor needs the skill of facilitating this self-reflection. When counselors attempt to analyze a system of roles, they look for motives that the individual members of the group may have for each person to play an assigned part. The benefits accrued to one or more members may be obvious, indirect, or even based on false perceptions. However, the group leader should take care not to fall into glib formulae that interpret behavior in terms of simple transference from other roles. A group member's behavior may be a situational adaptation not typical of other settings.

Case in Point

Different Faces for Different Places

People play various roles. Someone can loom larger than life in one setting, then fade into meekness in another. One example is an assistant principal who is the terror of the classroom, but is timid in the presence of peers at the faculty lunch table. Another example is the camp director whom all acclaim as "easy to work with and wonderful with the kids," but who has no time, energy, patience, or understanding for her husband and children.

Groups offer the possibility of learning to be accepted based on authentic feelings and reactions, not some image someone thinks he or she needs to erect. This has a humanizing effect, lowers anxiety, and reduces the need to self-medicate with psychoactive substances.

Personal Roles Enacted in Groups

The role a member takes in a group has roots in his or her emotional history. The following roles are often cited as parts played in families, which can be transferred into other group settings. Again, it may be glib and deceptive to interpret all such behaviors as transferential of family issues or patterns. In the following sampling of roles typically found in addictions groups, it is important to note the variety of motivations that generate or maintain such behaviors.

The term *scapegoat* is perhaps the most common example of a group role. The name comes from the Biblical book of Leviticus and refers to the goat driven out into wilderness bearing the sins of the tribe. As originally described by Jackson and Bateson of the "Palo Alto group" in family therapy (Satir 1967, 33-5), an individual brought into therapy as the identified patient may be the scapegoat in a dysfunctional family.[4] Both professional and folk psychotherapy systems have long recognized the advantages of scapegoating for group members, such as

- deflecting attention from their own behaviors,
- forestalling possible attacks on themselves, and
- and creating a convenient, cathartic whipping-boy.

People commonly chosen as scapegoats include different, weaker people or those who are new to the system. Although one would not expect an individual to seek out such a role, some might find it convenient to justify leaving the program in order to relapse. Orientation sessions and written rules for groups in addict-run therapeutic communities have long included injunctions against scapegoating. Groups use many terms to identify destructive scapegoating behavior. In its most egregious forms, when a group "jumps on" a person and bombards him or her with criticism, it may be called "rat-packing," "rat-raging," or "piling on." There is also a more subtle holier-than-thou form of criticism, which serves to scapegoat other members. The latter is identified and thwarted by the slogan, "If you can spot it, you've got it."

The *leader*, *protector*, or *pseudotherapist* role involves taking responsibility for the problems of others. It also sets the individual apart from and above the ranks of the group members. There are many motivations behind adopting such a role. It might stem from

- a recapitulation of the super-responsible or family hero role in the addictive or other type of dysfunctional family.
- a fear of intimacy (i.e., a way of holding people at arm's length).
- a wish to avoid confrontation and direct the focus away from self.

---

[4] The group of researchers that has become well known as the Palo Alto group is officially the Western Behavioral Science Institute.

- a feeling of not being entitled to acceptance and attention as an ordinary group member, but only in this special, exalted position.
- faulty thinking such as, "If I'm not on top, I'm a flop."

Approaches by the facilitator to the member who consistently adopts this type of role should start with encouraging the member to take time for him- or herself, to ask for help with problems, and to make statements that include "I feel. . ." or "I need. . . ." Once the member has gained that skill, the group can explore which motivation might apply in this case. Another type of approach is for the facilitator to encourage members to turn the tables on the "leaders," confront them, and strip them of their carefully constructed images.

The *provocative, hostile,* or *resentful* role may represent, to some extent, recapitulation of a scapegoat role in the family of origin. Other motives that bear exploration include

- a "counterdependent" defense, fear of intimacy, or vulnerability.
- testing of limits and quest for imposition of structure.
- wishing others to really prove their concern despite the unpleasantness.
- wishing to be ejected—an excuse for avoidance or relapse.
- lack of skill in better ways of getting attention.

The group should not rise to the bait of the provocative member, but defuse the situation by asking what the provocateur really needs from the group or from specific members of the group. The group can help a hostile member understand that he or she is actually painting him- or herself into a corner of isolation.

The *class clown* or *joker* role may be generated by

- anxiety
- fear of intimacy
- boredom
- fear of confrontation
- a need for attention, lack of skill in better methods of getting it
- hostility, a wish to provoke
- unrecognized attention-deficit hyperactivity disorder (ADHD)
- a need to compete with the leader

The class clown often attempts to involve others in his or her act, and searches for an audience, sidekick, or straightman. Again, the group can defuse this role by asking the joker what he or she really needs or wants from the group or from specific members of the group, and encouraging statements that begin "I feel" or "I need." Finally, every attempt to provide a bit of humor need not be denounced as a pathological role!

The "weakest" group member, or the "sickest" one, may be pathologically dependent, and have come to this role through

- the feeling that he or she is entitled to attention only if very sick or in crisis.
- the need to regress, be babied, or get permission to not be responsible.
- the fear of termination; if one gets healthy or grows up, one has to leave the group, and be independent.
- hoping to find an enabler in the group to feed, promote, encourage, and justify weakness.
- identification with addicted parents in the family of origin, who modeled the sick behavior.
- hope that less will be expected of him or her in the group, which may come from fear that he or she can't do what is expected and can't measure up.

Roles That Facilitate the Group's Work

Another approach to analyzing and categorizing roles in groups has to do with how members focus on facilitating the accomplishment of group tasks or on satisfying their own needs. Such an approach is less personal and clinical, but focuses on the needs of the group as a living "organism." This approach to categorizing roles was developed by early group dynamics theorists (Benne and Sheats 1948; Deutch 1953). It became the basis for human relations training (Nylen, Mitchell, and Stout 1967) and was later borrowed for group counselor training adapted for alcoholism counselors (Stokes, Miller, and Tait 1980, 78-80).

Group facilitators or group maintainers typically engage in

- *harmonizing* to reconcile differences and reduce tensions (usually associated with the placater or peacemaker role in an addictive family).
- *gatekeeping* to keep communication channels open, and facilitate communication by others.
- *compromising* to reconcile conflicts and help people admit errors.

In contrast, self-oriented roles tend to interfere with the group's mutual efforts. These behaviors include

- *dominating* by monopolizing the group, not listening to others, and trying to make all the decisions.
- *withdrawing* and making no contributions, appearing apathetic or afraid or having no affect.

- *blocking*, usually by being aggressively critical, attacking others' opinions, and being hostile.
- *Seeking recognition* and trying to be the center of attention, the entertainer, and by frequently straying off task and topic (perhaps related to the class clown).

It is more difficult to get members to appreciate the importance of focusing on tasks in groups than on emotions, behavior, and lives of the individual members. Obviously, tasks do not have the personal impact of, for example, realizing that one is being scapegoated or recapitulating a family role. Approaches to educating members on healthy approaches to the work of the group need to be reduced to basic questions such as, "What are we trying to do right now?" and "Is this helping?" Such questions encourage direct and assertive communication of needs and feelings and helps to short-circuit manipulative or self-serving behaviors.

According to Carroll and Wiggins (1997, 68-9), the dominator or monopolist is the most troublesome role for novice facilitators to change. The usual alternatives are letting the monopolist get his or her way, or allowing resentment to build and boil over into angry confrontation. Asking the monopolist what he or she wants or needs from the group, or how he or she perceives the group's responses to him or her is a better strategy.

 ACTIVITY (3.5) **How do I see this group?**

Form a group of six to eight volunteers and play roles that facilitate the group's work (approximately 15 to 20 minutes). As observers, other members of the class identify the roles. Observe the levels of trust and self-disclosure, the levels of participation, the decision-making process, the levels of loyalty, and the sense of belonging. Then, six new volunteers form a group and play roles from the list of self-oriented or so-called negative roles. Again, the rest of the class can offer observations. Discuss what was different. Questions for discussions can include

- What roles are being played or enacted here?
- What levels of trust or self-disclosure were displayed?
- What was the level of participation?
- What was the level of loyalty, sense of belonging?
- What was the decision-making process?
- How did other members react to blocking of the group process by a member? Did they adopt a unified reaction, did they overcome it, or did it lead to chaos?

- What feelings were evoked during the enactments by actors and observers?
- How might the group facilitate the adoption of productive roles for themselves and group members?

 ACTIVITY (**3.6**) **In my family . . .**

Use the same format as in activity 3.7; however, use family-style roles. By drawing slips of paper, you can be assigned one of the broad roles such as scapegoat or class clown. Other members or observers identify the role or defense being enacted.

Helping the Group Deal with Defensive Behavior

Thinking through Defensive Behavior in Groups

A wide variety of strategies and tactics are used to protect the self from unwanted or feared intrusion, exposure, and demands, or unpleasant emotions or realizations. Aspects of the group process may be perceived as threatening, attacking, or potentially painful. Moreover, counselors emerging from self-help movements, as well as traditionally trained clinicians who specialize in group treatment of addictions, will concur with Marsha Vannicelli that addicts "have well-developed skills for evading limits and for shifting or diffusing the focus" (1982, 19).

Since addictions groups in particular have a "gangbusters" tradition, it is important to answer four questions when dealing with behaviors that members consider defensive: Why are we calling this behavior a defense? Why are we attacking this defense? Why are we adopting this strategy, and might another approach be better? Will the member feel overwhelmed and leave the group? (This issue is explored in greater detail in the "Denial" section of chapter 7.)[5]

Why are we calling this behavior a defense? Basic sociology holds that there is a predictable social routine in which behaviors that do not meet the ideal norms of a group or that generate anxiety are labeled deviant or abnormal. In many groups someone whose behavior stands out from others can become isolated, even by not fitting in with the flow of interactions due to hesitancy at expressing feelings in terms the group finds satisfying. This person can even become the focus of group frustrations and a convenient target for venting negative feelings. In this scapegoating process, "difference" becomes "deviance" and "defensiveness." The group

---

[5] Michael Taleff (1997) provides a lengthy treatment of these issues in *A Handbook on Treatment of Defensiveness and Resistance in Chemical Dependency Treatment*, Dubuque, IA: Kendall/Hunt.

then proceeds to stigmatize, scapegoat, punish, and segregate the "deviant" individual. The group needs to ask the following three questions:

1. Could the disliked behaviors be harmless idiosyncrasies that do not need to be eradicated in order for recovery to proceed?
2. Could the "defensive" behaviors result from cultural differences?
3. Is the defense or resistance a refusal to accept a label preferred by the group (e.g., a problem drinker does not accept the label of alcoholic)? Not sharing the mental map of group members is not, ipso facto, a true defense or resistance.

Unfortunately, group facilitators can be sucked into this process as a result of their own frustrations in trying to help the nonconforming member. A few guidelines to keep in mind are that the counselor needs to keep tabs on his or her own feelings, help members to do the same, and act out of concern for all members.

Case in Point
Coming from a Different Place

In a high-energy encounter group for volunteers at an addictions program on Staten Island, New York, in which some recovering addicts participated, a young Scandinavian woman had difficulties convincing the other members that she was upset. Time and again they challenged her statements by observing that she "acted like she had no feelings," "acted like a zombie,'" and "seemed stoned." Finally, the psychotherapist who was facilitating the group stated that one would not expect the nonverbal cues of "upset" Scandinavians to be as dramatic, on average, as those of the Mediterranean, Latino, and Jewish people who formed a majority of the group members.

Why are we attacking this defense? Allowing that the behavior of a member could bear "tuning up," the group needs to check out the group process before constructing a strategy to deal with the "defensiveness." Is there a need to create sinners or saints in the group? Is the group bored and craving diversion and excitement? Is the behavior provoking anxiety the group doesn't want to face or handle? The group might ask, why are we finding the faults and why are we excoriating the faulty? Is it to help someone overcome a behavior that impedes growth or to meet other personal or group needs? To provide a simple example, almost everyone can recall being yelled at when a parent or the boss was angry about something else.

Why are we adopting this particular strategy, and might another approach be better? Construction of strategies to handle resistant or defensive behavior in groups is not value free; it is based on a model of human behavior and behavioral change. Traditionally, many addict groups have used the mechanism of confrontation to deal with resistance and defensiveness. This is based on the paradigm that addicts are character disordered and encapsulated in a fortress or prison. Others feel that confrontation amplifies the adversarial quality of the group and thus, defensiveness itself. They prefer instead to defuse defensiveness with identification and making the member feel more secure.

Helping a group member gradually drop his or her defensive posture can also be facilitated by encouraging reflection on exactly what he or she is getting from this self-defeating stance. Some helpful questions are, "Do you feel good about doing what you're doing?" "Are you getting what you need?" The group's questions should be designed to develop the client's understanding of his or her goals and behavior patterns, and the discrepancy between them. Finally, the client should be encouraged to explore other behavioral routes toward meeting needs and goals.

Will the member be overwhelmed and leave the group? A group may force a member into a confession or into crying and consider it a great victory. Nevertheless, it is important to consider whether the attacked member will feel so overwhelmed, crushed, threatened, or humiliated that he or she will never return. The degree to which confrontation or a hard-nosed approach can be employed must consider the investment that members have in staying, therapeutic leverage such as mandated attendance, and the supports available (e.g., a long-term, inpatient setting has different support systems than a weekly group has).

Defense against Emotion

It is often difficult to be vulnerable, trusting, and emotionally open to a group of relative strangers. It is also hard work. Labeling a new member defensive may not be helpful. Participation in the group process and natural reverberations to the expressed emotions of others should gradually help the new member share his or her emotions. In responding to "defensiveness," there are two extremes to avoid. One is egregious time-wasting and unspoken agreements not to discuss threatening or challenging topics. The other is pounding away at clients until they are exhausted, hate the group, or are traumatically and prematurely stripped of carefully constructed defenses. Spots of humor can provide a respite from the hard work of revealing emotions. The group format may include a built-in mechanism that moves toward and away from anxiety-provoking content (see the section "Staying in Routine" earlier in this chapter).

Groups help to build emotional literacy, which is the ability to identify, acknowledge, experience, and communicate emotions (Goleman 1995). A large proportion of group norms, mottoes, and exercises concern emotion; treatment groups tend to be charged with emotion. Yet individuals invest a lot of energy in defending against emotion, for a wide variety of reasons. In groups, defenses to avoid emotion can be grouped into three categories: blunting or negation of feeling, staying in a cognitive or informational channel, and playing a role that enables avoidance of emotion.

Blunting or negating feeling. A variety of mechanisms can be employed to blunt or negate threatening or painful feelings. It is important to distinguish such defenses from unfamiliarity with the vocabulary of emotion and from the blunting of affect that may be symptomatic of depressant abuse or schizophrenia. Emotions can be negated by

- denying emotion
- withdrawing and isolating
- staying vague or confused
- using program jargon and clichés

Staying in a cognitive or informational channel. By providing only cognitive and informational content, a group member can avoid his or her emotions. Varieties of this defense include

- intellectualizing
- barraging the group with data
- telling "war stories"
- not venturing beyond the ritualized AA drunkalogue or "story"

Playing a role. People can avoid their emotions by playing particular roles. This includes

- being a joker or class clown
- remaining belligerent
- acting as pseudotherapist
- being fragile, weak, or a victim
- insisting on uniqueness
- staying the outsider, perhaps underscored by behavior such as repeated lateness

Defensiveness is not an emergency, although an anxious counselor may perceive the situation in such terms. The counselor and the group can simply wait for a defensive individual to identify with others and respond to her or his need to integrate with the group. To this end, the group should reward nondefensive communication. Members can help the individual explore reasons for avoidance of emotions, such as fear of acting out rage (may have occurred during active addiction), fear of retribution, guilt, and so forth. They can also patiently point out the defense in session after session so that all members are familiar with it. The counselor should not demand change, but simply aid the member to observe and acknowledge his or her behavior. It can even become part of group humor. Eventually, the subject will wish to discard that identity.

Addictions group treatment varies greatly in the degree to which pressure is applied to clients exhibiting "defensive behavior." Some favor a proactive, pressure-cooker strategy. Some components of such an approach are explored in the section "Personal Roles Enacted in Groups." They include eliciting simple here-and-now feelings, asking focusing questions, prompting clients with such statements as "that would make *me* mad," and exploring how the individual may be recapitulating a family role in the group.

Formulating Treatment Plans for Group Members

Groups are shaped by the agency's preferences and traditions. Ideally, these can be reconciled with, to borrow corporate phraseology, a management-by-objectives approach; that is, start with basic recovery goals and formulate strategies based on individual treatment plans and contracts, stages of treatment, and client mix.

One of the major tasks in planning group treatment is to make sure that issues and individual clients' concerns are addressed in the group, including issues emerging in individual counseling that warrant group attention (making sure to observe confidentiality). Likewise, information, issues, and problems that emerge in the group need to be forwarded to individual counseling, when necessary. Clearly, staff need to function as a treatment team. There are three canons of long-range treatment planning in groups:

1. Phase goals appropriate to each stage of treatment.
2. Anticipate feelings that are likely to be evoked at each stage.
3. Make sure the approach is congruent with or appropriate to the setting or modality (e.g., an intensive outpatient treatment program, a residential program, a half-way house).

One example of rather predictable feelings is "the terrible twos." This phrase refers to the second year of recovery. In recovery milieux, it is a humorous analogy to the difficulties parents often have when their "little angels" exhibit stubborn behavior or tantrums when they are two years old. In early recovery, the addict is often on a "pink cloud," having ascribed all problems to the former addiction. When problems (inevitably) reassert themselves and result in cognitive dissonance or some attempt to set the blame on some lingering aspect of addiction, the client must begin to face his or her disappointment that recovery is not nirvana. These issues can be brought out and shared in the group setting. Another example of predictable feelings is the approach of termination. When a member is preparing to leave the group, he or she may have anxieties that are manifested in regression, threat of relapse, or behavior that covers up needy feelings (such as a show of independence or denigration of the group or leader). In addition to monitoring the departing member, the counselor should observe the group's reactions to the impending departure of the member, to determine whether the group is motivated to undermine growth, emphasize weakness or danger, or "break the wings" of the client.

Planning Formats

The formats for planning treatment for groups that appear in figures 3.1, 3.2, and 3.3 are based on some of the most important sets of goals for addictions groups. It is not realistic to expect counselors to chart all of their group goals, strategies, and impediments, especially in a short-term treatment setting, nor to follow any chart very closely in an interactive, unpredictable group. However, counselors should be prepared with appropriate interventions at each stage of treatment and anticipate the potholes and bumps that inevitably crop up when traveling these paths.

Figure 3.1 Plan 1 for Group Treatment

Goals *(apply to early treatment)*
- *Manage uncomfortable physical and psychological states of early sobriety.*
- *Manage the desire to drink.*
- *Manage the anxiety and stress of being in an institutional setting, in a hospital unit, or in the group.*

Strategies
- *Establish group norms of sharing.*
- *Use role models by pointing to more senior clients who have moved beyond acute withdrawal.*
- *Provide information about withdrawal and abstinence.*

Trouble-Shooting Areas

Problems: *denial of desire to drink, flight into health*
Resolution: *identification given by others more experienced, sticking with first-stage issues, reiteration that feelings are normal and natural*

Figure 3.2 Plan 2 for Group Treatment

Goals *(appropriate to later treatment)*
- *Develop the ability to engage in conflict and resolving conflict without withdrawing, drinking or drugging, or becoming violent.*
- *Related Objective: Learn to be angry in a socially appropriate way, without anxiety, guilt, or acting out.*

Strategies
- *Orient to the group norm: No violence or threats of violence. Stay in your seat. One person talks at a time.*
- *Orient to group culture, including the mottoes: Bad feelings get in the way of good feelings. You are entitled to all of your feelings. If you talk about it, you won't drink about it. It's not that you're not good enough, only you is good enough!*
- *Discuss old ways of dealing with resentments and triggers for violence.*
- *Orient to a simplified version of assertiveness concepts: it is not hostile or aggressive behavior, passive behavior, or indirectly hostile (passive-aggressive) behavior.*
- *Encourage "I" statements: "I need . . .," "I feel . . . "*
- *Reward direct expressions of anger. Show the positive aftermath.*

Trouble-Shooting Areas

- *Fear of rejection*
- *Conflict defined as part of "old, bad" ways*
- *Passivity, depression, and learned helplessness*
- *The low-conflict style of Alcoholics Anonymous*
- *Fear of own feelings, panic at premature self-disclosure*
- *Denial of feelings*

Figure 3.3 Plan 3 for Group Treatment

Goal *(appropriate throughout treatment)*
- *Stability and responsibility, which are the broad behavioral objectives*

Strategies
- *Use punctuality and attendance as group material.*
- *Explore reasons for difficulty in establishing responsible behavior patterns. Link to chemical intoxication, addictive lifestyle, and hopelessness.*
- *Discuss difference between being "dry" and real recovery. Use the AA concept of the dry drunk.*

- *Discuss behavioral problems and specific commitments made to group for follow-up.*
- *Prioritize goals and objectives, breaking down behavioral changes into simple, nonthreatening, concrete steps to be taken one at a time.*

Trouble-Shooting Areas
- *Explore the impediments to changing behavior-habitual roles, process variables, and client mix.*

Impediments to Change

Regardless of the planning format, counselors must observe, assess, and monitor the enormous variety of impediments to changing behavior. These include habitual roles, process variables, and the mix of clients in the group.

Roles

Almost any of the roles adopted by group members can create impediments to behavioral change. For example, some may be afraid to relinquish a "sick" role that offers some comfort. Others may engage in "rescuing." Rescuing enables the avoidance of confrontation or other uncomfortable situations. Such "red-crossing" or "band-aiding" in drug rehabilitation programs is often a problem with new members who identify with people "on the hot seat" and become anxious when others are pressured. It can also be a form of "flag-waving" (i.e., signaling that the rescuer needs help), presentation of a nice-guy image in order to be liked, or the habitual reprise of codependent and enabling behavior of the addictive family. Crying in particular is certain to bring out rescuing behavior. It is good material for group discussion when it occurs. A useful tool is the therapeutic-community concept of responsible concern (similar to the tough-love concept), which is that rescuing is not helpful to the individual or to the group. In behavioral confrontation, counselors are always steering a course between scapegoating and rescuing.

Process

Aspects of group process that can impede behavioral change include mutually protective, tacit agreements among members not to "make waves" or reveal certain information, "pulling covers." Some programs call these negative contracts. They often reflect a relationship outside of the group. Entire groups can also develop a tacit understanding to avoid uncomfortable or pressuring areas and topics. So-called higher-level groups of experienced members are prone to this. While it may appear that the group process is well developed and group affiliation and solidarity is optimal, it is important to examine whether, on a deeper level, the group is resting on its laurels and resisting the difficult, anxiety-provoking work necessary to progress further. Scapegoating and steamrolling of a weaker, newer, annoying, or different member is another example of a group contract.

At Daytop Village members link the two concepts: It is sometimes thought "red-crossers" were "hustling for a contract." In more familiar language, people may do favors such as rescuing and protecting others in the vague or explicit hope that this will be reciprocated. Assertiveness skills training (Lange and Jakubowski 1976, 23-4) refers to this as the "hidden bargain."[6]

Client Mix

A group may include those who are severely deteriorated in their personal and social skills. Others do not have a stable early behavioral base or model and require habilitation as much as rehabilitation. Others suffer from long-term hopelessness and/or disabling major depression and have difficulty acknowledging improvement. Individuals with attention-deficit hyperactivity disorder often fare poorly in therapeutic environments that punish small "irresponsible" infractions.

Defenses

Any of the defenses may come into play, such as deluging the group with data; offering a ferocious, hostile image (one who will retaliate); and presenting a weak, fragile, and guilt-evoking image (which Al-Alon groups have aptly labeled "the poor me," or "throwing a pity party"). A seductive or flattering member may also succeed in soft-pedaling confrontation. Experienced group members may present a super-honest, super-confessing image. The counselor should consider whether this is a subtle form of resistance, especially when real and difficult behavioral changes should be on the agenda. Another defense is the raising of distracting information or side issues, sometimes called "throwing a bone." This phrase can also refer to presenting real information in a skewed way in order to have something to say. See the "Case in Point: Throwing a Bone." In such as case, the group's response could help the client overcome his timidity and reticence in interpersonal, dating, and sexual matters or it could make him feel more inadequate and alone. Group process in a confrontational-style group can set up a self-fulfilling prophecy: When the group relishes pouncing upon defenses, participants may feel anxious and evasive and become more defensive. Much of the behavior that is called denial is simply a reaction to anxiety.

---

[6] Assertiveness skills training is a long-established system of learning appropriate, nonthreatening, and effective approaches to dealing with conflict, potential conflict, and communication of negative emotion. See Lange and Jakubowski (1976) for training options for this area.

Case in Point

Throwing a Bone

At an addictions group in a young adult intensive outpatient clinic based on the therapeutic-community model, a young man who had problems initiating romantic relationships had not spoken in weeks and was prodded for an update. He sadly recounted a steamy encounter that culminated in frustrating rejection. Then a friend remembered that this incident had taken place two years earlier. It was revealed that he had not, in fact, been dating for some time and in anticipation of "flak" on this score was "throwing a bone" to the group. The group met the discovery with derision, ridicule, and gales of laughter.

Group Process Recording

Recording group process is more difficult than recording individual process. There are several participants and a multiplicity of relationships. Moreover, note-taking during group sessions is rarely allowed. Notations on the content of sessions and on the process taking place in the group are often a summary of what the counselor recalls with detailed descriptions of events that were particularly dramatic or as especially illustrative of the process. Like individual process recording, a group process recording can be laid out in two columns (content and process) or it can be written in alternative paragraphs for the same purpose.

ACTIVITY **3.7** How was group today?

To practice recording the content and process of a group you can use the processes at work in a real treatment group or in a "fishbowl" group set up in the classroom. In the latter situation, a circle of students observes a smaller group that is conducting a scripted role play, or a group that is simply discussing their feelings in the here and now. Do not take notes during the role play. Later in the day, write your process recording of the group. When the class meets next, compare the perceptions and descriptions you wrote with those of your classmates. How do your descriptions of each component agree and disagree? What accounts for the differences in perception of group processes?

References

Benne, K. D., and P. Sheats. 1948. "Functional Roles and Group Members." *Journal of Social Issues* 4, 2: 41-9.

Blume, S. 1985. "Group Psychotherapy in the Treatment of Alcoholism," in *Practical Approaches to Alcoholism Psychotherapy.* S. Zimberg, J. Wallace, S. Blume, ed. New York: Plenum Press.

Brown, S., and I. D. Yalom. 1977. "Interactional Therapy with Alcoholics." *Journal of Studies on Alcohol* 38, 3: 426-56.

Carroll, M. R., and J. D. Wiggins. 1997. *Group Counseling: Back to the Basics.* Denver: Love Publishing.

Deutch, M. 1953. "The Effects of Cooperation and Competition upon Group Process," in *Group Dynamics,* 3rd ed. D. Cartwright and A. Zander, ed. New York: Harper and Row.

Feeney, D. J., and P. Dranger. 1976. "Alcoholics View Group Therapy." *Journal of Studies on Alcohol* 37, 5: 611-9.

Frank, D. J. 1985. "Therapeutic Components Shared by All Psychotherapies," in *Cognition and Psychotherapy.* M. Mahoney and A. Freeman, ed. New York: Plenum Press.

Goleman, D. 1995. *Emotional Intelligence.* New York: Bantam.

Lange, A. J., and P. Jakubowski. 1976. *Responsible Assertive Behavior: Cognitive/Behavioral Procedures for Trainers.* Champaign, IL: Research Press.

Levinson, V. 1979. "The Decision Group: Beginning Treatment in an Alcoholism Clinic." *Health and Social Work* 4, 4: 199-221.

Napier, R. W., and M. K. Gershenfeld. 1973. *Groups: Theory and Experience.* Boston: Houghton Mifflin.

Nylen, D., J. R. Mitchell, and A. Stout. 1967. *Handbook of Staff Development and Human Relations Training.* San Diego, CA: University Associates.

Perls, F. 1969. *Gestalt Therapy Verbatim.* Moab, UT: Real People Press.

Satir, V. 1967. *Conjoint Family Therapy.* Palo Alto, CA: Science and Behavior Books.

Stokes, J. P., R. C. Tait, and L. P. Miller. 1980. *Group Skills for Alcoholism Counselors: GFTP Trainer Manual.* Rockville, MD: Dept. of Health and Human Services, National Institute of Alcohol Abuse and Alcoholism.

Taleff, M. J. 1997. *A Handbook to Assess and Treat Resistance in Chemical Dependency.* Dubuque, IA: Kendall/Hunt.

Vannicelli, M. 1982. "Group Psychotherapy with Alcoholics: Special Techniques." *Journal of Studies on Alcohol* 43, 1: 17-37.

Vinogradov, S., and I. D. Yalom. 1989. *A Concise Guide to Group Psychotherapy.* Washington, DC: American Psychiatric Press.

Wallace, J. 1985a. "Working with the Preferred Defense Structure of the Recovering Alcoholic," chap. 2 in *Practical Approaches to Alcoholism Psychotherapy.* S. Zimberg, J. Wallace, and S. Blume, ed. New York: Plenum Press.

————. 1985b. "Critical Issues in Alcoholism Therapy," chap. 3 in *Practical Approaches to Alcoholism Psychotherapy.* S. Zimberg, J. Wallace, and S. Blume, ed. New York: Plenum Press.

Yalom, I. D. 1975. *The Theory and Practice of Group Psychotherapy.* New York: Basic Books.

4

Ethics and Confidentiality

Introduction

Ethical principles define and govern the right, good, and moral behaviors that are expected in proper professional relationships. Ethical standards are developed and maintained by associations and credentialing bodies of real estate brokers, lawyers, helping professionals, and others. They are motivated by a desire to protect clients, to avoid governmental interference and malpractice suits, and to develop public confidence in general and client confidence in particular.[1]

---

[1] We are deeply indebted to William White, whose landmark book Critical Incidents (1993) has brilliantly outlined the areas of ethics training for addictions counselors. His "critical incident" method sets a standard for ethics training and has significantly influenced the format of this chapter.

There is a compelling necessity for ethical standards in the counseling relationship. Counselors hold a great deal of power over clients; mechanisms are necessary to ensure that this power is not abused. The overall objectives of counseling ethics are to maintain client welfare as foremost, to do no harm (physical, emotional, or financial), and to maintain standards of responsibility, integrity, and accountability.

Although confidentiality is the area most regulated by legal statutes, not all critical areas of ethics are formulated into legal statutes. Professional conduct can be legal but not ethical!

Many addictions counselors, like their clients, participate in addiction recovery milieux. This and other relatively informal aspects of the addictions field blur boundaries and roles, creating possibilities for ethically compromising situations.

Ethical standards supersede all other considerations. All counseling actions and decisions must be considered from the standpoint of and be governed by these standards.

In the preparation of addictions counselors, specialized ethics training is the area most often cited as inadequate. Furthermore, internal agency discussion of ethical issues is sometimes muted out of shame, fear, confusion, or expediency; this can be summed up by the term "institutional denial" (Myers 1992; White 1993, i, 1). Counselors must bear in mind that institutional systems of the agency and broader society generate a climate and a range of options that bear on individual ethical choice.

ACTIVITY (4.1) Easier Said Than Done

In a large or a small group, each person states one principle or guideline by which he or she lives (in the broadest sense, an ethics statement). Typical responses are "I never lie," "I never kill or hurt someone," and "Honesty is the most important to me."

Discuss: Consider the following questions and discuss your answers with each other.

- Do you subscribe to the statement "Thou shall not kill?" Have you killed an animal or put a pet to sleep?
- Do you believe it is wrong to steal? Have you copied an audio- or videotape or a CD instead of buying your own?
- Have you ever covered up for a friend's mistakes or lateness at work by lying to a supervisor?

- Have you ever been aware of mistreatment or neglect of a child but did not communicate this information to authorities, nor confronted the perpetrator?
- Have you taken an office item home from work or photocopied a personal item at the office?
- What other small or big actions reflect your ethics?

Process: Can you identify connections among the ethics statements you made, your values and morality (preferences and judgments), group customs (traditional ways of doing things), and laws (standards set by legislative authority)? Are ethical choices absolute? For example, are there circumstances in which it would be permissible to plan to kill someone?

The mandatory orientation of a client that takes place during the intake process includes information about the agency's confidentiality guidelines and practices. The client receives a summary of regulations concerning confidentiality and signs the summary to attest that he or she has understood. The client and the agency each keep a copy of the signed form. At the same time, for the purposes of case management, the counselor may request that the client sign a Consent for Release of Information form that stipulates exactly what client information can be released and to whom. When information is divulged legally to a third party, that third party cannot release it to anyone. The two most common uses of the consent form are

- to allow continuity of care when different facilities are involved in the client's treatment (e.g., detoxification and rehabilitation units) and
- to report a client's compliance to a referring agency (e.g., EAP administrator or parole officer).

Gray Areas

Activity 4.1 shows the impossibility of composing precise rules for human behavior. In ethical counseling, *knowledge* of guidelines must be supplemented by the *skills* of interpreting complex situations and of *applying* ethical standards to them. Also pertinent to ethical counseling are the skills discussed in chapter 7, which involve developing and maintaining awareness of the counselor's personal needs and feelings, evaluating how they color the counseling relationship, and ensuring that clients' interests are held foremost. Often, counseling situations occur in which there are competing ethical and/or other obligations. Moral dilemmas arise out of conflicts between two or more beliefs, values, laws, or standards. In resolving such dilemmas, it is useful to establish a hierarchy of ethical standards, that is, a list of ethical concerns rated according to which predominate or take precedence over others. Lowenberg and Dolgoff (1988) present such a hierarchy of ethical standards:

1. protecting human life
2. fostering independence and freedom
3. fostering equality
4. promoting a better quality of life
5. protecting the right to privacy
6. truthfulness
7. abiding by rules and requirements

Standards vary in their attempts to be specific. Some are brief and sketchy; others go into great detail to cover every eventuality. For example, the American Counseling Association thought it important to stipulate that professionals engaging in intensive short-term training and counseling experiences (e.g., marathons and encounter groups) ensure "that there is professional assistance available during and following the group experience" (ACA, 1981, B17).

Supervision and Consultation

Consultation with supervisors or other professionals is necessary to ensure a continuing ethical relationship between counselors and their clients, especially in situations where there appears to be a conflict among ethical standards or between ethical and other considerations. Seeking appropriate consultation is considered an ethical necessity in most helping professions (NASW 1980, II8). Not to seek advice from others can be unrealistic, stubborn, unwise, and even unethical. One may need to speak to experienced peers or clinical supervisors, or call on the expertise of those trained in other helping professions such as psychiatry or neurology. Consultation should come sooner rather than later. Unfortunately, counselors are often compromised ethically and legally by pride and embarrassment.

Consultation with supervisors about ethical considerations, when carefully documented in clients' records, helps protect both the counselor and the agency in litigation and governmental audit. "Failure to consult" is a subcategory of negligence in malpractice law (Hogan 1978).

Guidelines for supervision of counselors in private practice vary considerably among the helping professions. Failure to provide adequate supervision is unethical and a basis for action under malpractice law (Hogan 1978). "Supervision" has both administrative and clinical dimensions. Although it would be ideal to separate these roles so that there is a space where counselors can feel safe airing their self-doubts, problems, and errors, in the real world the immediate supervisor serves both administrative and clinical functions. This reality challenges the supervisor's own ethics when he or she must weigh the factors of a situation that puts clinical and administrative concerns in conflict. Probably the most typical example of this conflict is that a client needs more personal attention and a longer stay in treatment, but the supervisor is charged with encouraging counselors to see as many clients as possible during a workday, and discharging them from treatment as quickly as possible.

Ethical supervision must be adequate and nonvindictive, and facilitate growth. The supervisory process should be based at least in part on routine procedures and objective criteria for evaluation, a structure that helps to avoid but cannot prevent all personalistic or subjective processes. Some addictions treatment agencies hire graduates of the program as counselors. Objective evaluation may be compromised if supervision is assigned to a former primary counselor of this individual. The supervisor should share evaluative data with supervisees on a regular basis, and the supervisees need an opportunity to respond.

Case in Point

An Unacceptable Excuse

A clinician treating a very hyperactive preadolescent failed to diagnose attention-deficit hyperactivity disorder. She felt increasingly angry and frustrated, which compromised her ability to counsel the child. Instead of withdrawing from the case, she ended up in a physical struggle with the child, in which she administered a spank. When confronted by the parents, the clinician brought in a post-hoc "consultation" with an eminent psychologist that justified the events that had transpired.

Documented consultation should not be used to excuse egregious violations of ethical standards, nor as part of an ongoing plan for expedient but unethical practice. Unfortunately, such misuses of consultation do occur with alarming frequency and are a violation of ethical standards.

Boundaries

Addictions treatment is unique because a large proportion of staff are also in recovery from that which they are treating. Boundaries are a theme in all realms of counseling but come to the forefront more often and more easily in the addictions field, because recovering counselors and clients share similar histories, issues, and even membership in self-help fellowships. Such an issue cuts to the core of the professional counselor-client relationship. With the best will in the world, failure to delineate and differentiate these identities destroys the professional identity and role, and leads to any of a number of ethical compromises, violations, and manipulations. Regardless of the setting, but especially in addictions counseling, counselors are counselors—not bowling buddies, lovers, or business associates. Counselors cannot paint clients' houses, sleep with them, treat them to lunch, let clients stay in their homes, lend them money, or borrow money from them (not even $1 for a cup of coffee). The recovering counselor faces a continual strain in maintaining boundaries, but that eases in time.

Although there are some very strict standards about personal boundaries, there are also gray areas. For example, how much self-disclosure by counselors is appropriate or ethical? How about hugging, which is permitted and encouraged by many support and self-help groups? Touching a client with the appearance, implication, or suggestion of sexuality is clearly an ethical violation, but is it always wrong to hug or put an arm around a client? Obviously, this is an area where ethical standards vary (Pope and Vetter 1992, 401; Rhodes 1992, 43-4). (The area of boundaries is explored in detail in chapter 7.)

Legal Issues

Confidentiality

A major legal and ethical obligation of addictions counselors is to maintain a zone of privacy around information revealed by clients, whether it be in written records (charts, memos, notes, messages, e-mail, and electronic files) or verbal communications. The counseling relationship, like that of lawyer and client, cleric and penitent, is "privileged," legally covered with a code of silence. Federal laws protect clients' identities and records.[2] Quite extensive federal guidelines were published in July 1975 and came into effect August 1, 1975. They were amended in August 1986 and published in the Federal Register, vol. 52, no. 110, on June 9, 1987. Violations may bring fines ranging from $500 (first offense) to $5,000. State regulations vary and the law of privilege has, in recent years, been strengthened in some states but threatened or eroded in others. Where there is a conflict between these statutes, federal guidelines prevail. Every counselor must be informed as to how specific state regulations interpret federal statutes. (See the section "Professional Growth" later in this chapter.)

The governing principle is that all information communicated by clients in programs or individual treatment is privileged and confidential. This principle is based not only on the right to privacy, but also on the likelihood that clients will accept and succeed in treatment if they can be

---

[2] Federal guidelines are set forth in Title 42, Part 2 of the Code of Federal Regulations, often referred to by their abbreviation, 42CFR-Part 2, and also in Title 42 Section 290dd: 3, US code.

confident that information is protected. There are a few, clear exceptional circumstances in which information revealed by clients can be communicated to others.

Duty to Warn

When information reveals a clear danger to the client or others, such as suicidal or homicidal intent, a professional obligation called the Duty to Warn medical personnel or police supersedes confidentiality. In addition, in most states it is a legal obligation to inform the police if any crime is threatened or committed against an agency's staff. Penalties for failure to warn vary from state to state. Individuals harmed by such failure often seek compensation by instituting lawsuits.

Duty to Report

Initial reports of child abuse and neglect are stipulated by the federal Child Abuse Prevention and Treatment Act of 1974, which denies federal grants to states that do not comply with reporting standards. The Duty to Report to child-protective agencies in a region overrides or supersedes confidentiality rights.

The duties to warn and to report child abuse do not throw open agency files; they merely mandate the provision of specific information to the appropriate authorities. State regulations define what constitutes child abuse. Anyone who works with children is a "mandated reporter" of abuse, even abuse that the professional observes on the street or in the home of a friend or relative. However, there is considerable variation in how mistreatment of children is initially perceived, often influenced by the cultural background of the staff involved. In several instances paraprofessional child-welfare workers in New York City overlooked what later was identified as serious physical abuse of children. In some agencies, a nondegreed counselor identifies abuse that is then "called in" by another staff member.

....

Case in Point

Eliza Fell through the Cracks

The mother of six-year-old Eliza Izquierdo was a mentally ill crack cocaine addict who believed her child was possessed by evil spirits. Eliza was kept home from school, neglected, and abused. She died from beatings in November 1995. Warning signs had been missed or ignored by her school and her caseworker. Her death became a rallying point for social-service reform.

The Child Abuse and Protection Act also mandates confidentiality regarding specifics of child-abuse cases, which has been frustrating to those seeking to root out negligence and neglect. Therefore, Congress amended it in 1992 to facilitate effective investigation and prevention of abuse. Specific implementing regulations were released in 1996 by the U.S. Department of Health and Human Services.

In New York, the Social Services Law has interpreted in even more stringent terms the stipulation of total secrecy. When child-welfare authorities refused to testify in hearings on cases of severe child abuse that "fell through the cracks," legislators concluded that the state regulations functioned to protect bureaucratic bungling or inaction. After checking with federal regulators to verify they were in line with the 1996 regulations, New York enacted modifying legislation (Eliza's Law, see "Case in Point: Eliza Fell through the Cracks") to permit more disclosure for investigative purposes.

Informed Consent

Informed consent means that the client has been educated as to the nature and form of disclosure. A client can give specific and written consent to the release of information. Every agency has a printed consent form that is explained carefully to every client (see Figure 4.1). It is signed by the client and by the individual performing the intake procedure, and dated. The intake procedure, or the paperwork involved, may be implemented by an addictions counselor or a specialized intake worker. Blanket consent to release any or all information, or from or to any party, is acceptable in the CFR. Written consent specifies the type of information that may be released, who is to release it and to whom, and for what purpose. It should include a statement that consent can be withdrawn. A client can usually withdraw consent verbally as well as in writing, although the time frame within which this occurs varies by state. The release must be signed and dated.

Confidentiality is not limited to the time of treatment. It starts when the client applies or calls to apply, even if he or she does not make an appointment. Confidentiality responsibilities do not end when the client exits treatment, whether from completion, relapse, administrative discharge, or other circumstance, or if the client dies. The counselor and other staff must ensure that records are kept in such a manner that confidentiality will be preserved. The disposal of records presents the same expectation. "Dead" files cannot, for example, be taken in cartons to the street or left in unlocked cabinets in a storage room (ACA 1981, B2). They must be shredded or incinerated.

Figure 4.1 Informed Consent

Macedonia Memorial Medical Center
Release of Confidential Information
Consent Form

I, _____, a patient in the Addiction Services Unit at
Macedonia Memorial Medical Center, hereby authorize the following
disclosure of information from my treatment records/files:

I authorize Macedonia Memorial Medical Center to release information listed
below to (name, title, organization to which disclosure is to be made):

_____

Purpose or need for disclosure (as specific as possible): _____

_____

Nature or extent of information to be disclosed (as limited as possible): _____

_____

This consent will terminate upon (date, event, or condition): _____

_____

I understand that my records are protected under federal regulations
governing confidentiality of alcohol and drug abuse records, 42 CFR Part 2
and cannot be disclosed without my written authorization unless otherwise
provided for in the regulations. I also understand that information disclosed in the
party listed above may not be disclosed to a third party without a separate signed
consent, and that I may revoke this consent at any time except as legally proscribed.

Signature of Patient: _____
Signature: ___ Parent ___ Guardian ___ Authorized Representative

_____
Signature of staff person: _____
Date: _____

Disclosure and Redisclosure

Release of information with a client's informed consent binds the party
to whom it is released not to release it to a third party (see Figure 4.2).
The information is bound by the confidentiality guidelines. Information
disclosed by consent should be limited to that needed for case management, diagnosis, referral, and rehabilitation, and to process insurance
claims or aid in the disposition of criminal proceedings.

Figure 4.2 Prohibition of Redisclosure

> This information has been disclosed to you from records whose confidentiality is protected by Federal Law. Federal Regulation (42 CFR, Part 2) prohibits you from making any further disclosure of it without the specific written consent of the person to whom it pertains, or as otherwise permitted by such regulations. A general authorization for the release of medical or other information is NOT sufficient for this purpose. The Federal rules restrict any use of the information to criminally investigate or prosecute the patient.

The fact that clients are in treatment at a particular agency cannot be revealed, without written consent of the client or a court order, regardless of who is inquiring. Relatives cannot simply call to speak with Joe, or ask if Joe has arrived. Nor can staff always trust that a caller is who he or she claims to be.

Case in Point

I can't give you that information.

One of the authors called a large treatment facility to inform a staff member of a scholarship. The man who answered the phone gave a detailed and helpful account of the counselor's comings and goings, and how best to contact her. When he was asked, "Whom am I speaking with?" he responded "I'm sorry, I can't give you that information, I'm a client."

Even when a counselor or other professional refers a client to treatment, once the client has completed intake at the treatment agency, staff are following correct practice if they no longer communicate information about that client to the referring party, unless the client has given consent for release of information.

Legally Incompetent Clients

If the client is incapable of understanding his or her rights and responsibilities, that client might be judged legally incompetent. Special consent provisions are made for legally incompetent persons and for minors; a legal guardian signs (or refuses to sign) consent form(s) (see Figure 4.1). In the case of releasing information about a deceased client, consent forms are signed by the person who has the power of attorney. A medical diagnosis does not constitute legal incompetency: It is only a piece of the evidence presented in courtroom procedures to determine a person's "competency." It is the responsibility of the agency's administration to ensure that privileged information is not released unless appropriate forms have been presented to document such legal determination, according to federal and state statutes.

Clinical Discussion

Confidential information can be discussed for clinical and supervisory purposes. If such agency functions took place only in a strict chain of command, this would be quite clear. However, peer supervision, case conferences, and shift reports multiply the number of people who have access to confidential information. These factors, as well as the informal organization of the profession, make it difficult to define appropriate boundaries of secrecy. A baseline principle should be established that disclosure is on a need-to-know basis, as opposed to freely exchanging information with any and all personnel. Sharing of information cannot occur outside of a treatment unit in a larger institutional setting. For example, a nurse in detox cannot tell her friends on the maternity floor about her hallucinating patient. In addition to people involved in the client's care, the people who deal with billing and other record keeping may legally receive limited confidential information.

Any counselor or agency must establish clear guidelines for access to confidential records by secretarial workers and volunteers. If they must have access, they must fully understand and implement confidentiality guidelines. The CFRs apply to all support personnel, administrators, volunteers, interns, and so on.

ACTIVITY 4.2 What's the right thing to do?

Phil is a counselor in an intensive outpatient program where you work. He has been employed in the field for three years and has been in recovery for six years. You have been close to him for most of that time. A month ago, Phil's son was killed in an automobile accident. In his grief, Phil went out and got drunk. He immersed himself without delay in his recovery fellowship as well as in short-term bereavement counseling, and he has confided only to you about the situation. State regulations mandate that counselors have at least two years uninterrupted "clean time." Phil is very afraid that if the agency finds out about his relapse, he will lose his job.

Discuss

- How do you feel about this situation?
- What would you say to Phil?
- Can you consult someone about this to get advice on your position?
- What should or can you say to the agency administrators?
- When is withholding information a breach of honesty?
- If you fail to disclose Phil's relapse, do you think you'd lose your job?
- How can you reconcile, on one hand, the trust and confidence of a friend and, on the other, loyalty to the agency and safety of clients?
- What do you think would be the best thing to do for your friend?
- What would be the right thing to do? Does this conflict with what you think would be best for Phil?

Subpoenaed Information

The pendulum has been swinging back and forth in recent years in regards to legal use of client information. In some legal decisions, the need to uncover evidence regarding criminal activity has superseded confidentiality of the client-counselor relationship, while in other cases the opposite interpretation has been made. In the early 1990s the subpoena came to overrule the client-counselor privilege and the anonymity of twelve-step fellowships.

An example of the latter is the 1994 Cox case in New York. Seven members of Alcoholics Anonymous testified under subpoena that another member had told them of his emerging memories of killing a Larchmont couple as they slept in their home (Hoffman 1994).

In 1996 the U.S. Supreme Court ruled that federal courts must allow psychotherapists and other mental-health professionals to refuse to disclose patients' records in judicial proceedings. This ruling created a new type of "evidentiary privilege" (Scarf 1996). *Privileged information* is information that remains within the confines of a professional relationship, such as between an individual and his or her minister, priest, lawyer, or psychotherapist. The term *evidentiary privilege* simply refers to the fact that by its "privileged" status, information cannot be used as evidence in court. The person holding that information cannot be forced to reveal it.

Medical Emergency

Medical information usually shielded by confidentiality regulations may be released when necessary for evaluation and treatment of a medical emergency. For example, a diabetic woman may lose consciousness if her blood sugar is too high or too low. The fact of her diabetic status must be communicated without hesitation if the client has such an emergency.

Another example is that of a man having great difficulty breathing or appearing to have some sort of heart attack. A counselor is obligated to inform paramedics or other medical personnel about the medications the man takes (see Figure 4.3).

Figure 4.3 Client's Rights to Confidentiality

ESSEX COUNTY COLLEGE STUDENT AFFAIRS AREA
Health Services Department
Office of the Substance Abuse Coordinator
877-3129

THIS PROGRAM IS REQUIRED TO COMMUNICATE TO EACH CLIENT THAT FEDERAL LAW AND REGULATIONS PROTECT THE CONFIDENTIALITY OF ALCOHOL AND DRUG ABUSE PATIENT RECORDS. A SUMMARY OF THE LAW AND REGULATIONS MUST BE GIVEN TO EACH CLIENT.

<u>YOUR SUMMARY OF THE LAW IS PROVIDED BELOW.</u>

The confidentiality of alcohol and drug abuse patient records maintained by this program is protected by federal law and regulations. Generally, the program may not say to a person outside the program that a person attends the program, or disclosed any information identifying a cleint as an alcohol or drug abuser *unless*

1. The client consents in writing
2. The disclosure is allowed by a court order, or
3. The disclosure is made to medical personnel in a medical emergency or to qualified personnel for research, audit, or program evaluation.

Violation of the federal law and regulations by a program is a crime. Suspected violations may be reported to appropriate authorities in accordance with federal regulations.

Federal law and regulations do not protect any information about a crime committed by a client, either at the program or against any person who works for the program, or about any threat to commit such a crime.

Federal laws and regulations do not protect any information about suspected child abuse or neglect from being reported under state law to appropriate state or local authorities. (See 42 U.S.C. 290 dd-3 and 42 U.S.C. 290 ee-3 for federal laws and 42 CFR - Part 2 for federal regulations)

I HAVE RECEIVED A COPY OF THE ABOVE SUMMARY.

_____
(Client's signature)

Date: _____

Source: Victor B. Stolberg, M.A., Ed.M.

Statistical Aggregates

Information may be provided for statistical aggregates for research or audits, such as the percentage of clients who are entering treatment for the first, second, or third time (see Figure 4.3). In releasing confidential information for these purposes, clients' names and other information that could identify clients cannot be released.

Qualified Service Organizations

The services of outside agencies such as laboratories and accounting firms are often required. Such agencies, known as qualified service organizations, receive information that is necessary to perform their contracted functions. They are governed by a signed Qualified Service Organization Agreement, or QSOA, under which they agree to abide by federal and local regulations concerning confidentiality.

ACTIVITY 4.3   Should I tell?

Your 28-year-old client discontinued treatment. Then you read in the newspaper that he committed suicide. His grief-stricken father called you, requesting any information you have that would help the family under-stand why his son killed himself. They speculate over what they did or did not do that was responsible for his death. Your memories and notes clearly show that his suicide was related to factors over which they had no control. What do you do? Since the client is no longer alive, can it hurt to share information with the family?

Discuss

- How should you respond to this family's wishes?
- Do you have an ethical responsibility to your client's family?
- Do you have to maintain this client's confidentiality even though he's dead? After all, you have information that would definitely lighten their grief.
- If the police investigate this unnatural death, what would you contribute to their fact finding?

Training

Where case information or material is used for training counselors, the identity of the client must be disguised. Individuals who participate in such training must be informed as to the need to maintain confidentiality. Unfortunately, participants in training who work at a local agency occasionally recognize a client, and accidentally blurt out either the name or information that provides a substantial hint to the client's identity.

Pending Legislation

Counselors should be aware that specific state regulations that apply to minors, school-based programs, and other institutional settings might differ from those in effect for treatment agencies. These vary considerably from state to state, and litigation is pending concerning the role of parental consent and information that is provided to parents.

Finally, there is also considerable debate, as well as pending litigation regarding the access of managed-care entities to client information. Many people believe there has already been considerable rapid erosion of confidentiality by managed-care audits (Lewin 1996; Scarf 1996), which has resulted in harm to clients and decline of trust as to the privacy of the client-counselor relationship.

ACTIVITY **4.4** **Wearing Two Hats**

Two hats is a term for an individual who has dual roles. Employees of addictions agencies often talk about two-hat problems to denote the staffer who is in a recovery fellowship with clients.

> Don is a recovering cocaine addict who works at Reality Lodge, a large long-term treatment program staffed largely by graduates of this therapeutic community. Don attends Narcotics Anonymous to maintain and strengthen his own recovery from addiction. At one meeting, a young woman named Cheryl makes a comment after the main speaker, in which she shares the difficulty she is having in staying drug-free. Cheryl happens to be a court-mandated client at the outpatient department of Reality Lodge, and Don knows that she has not shared these minor relapses with the staff.
>
> As an NA member, Don would never carry that information outside of the meeting, but as a counselor he would notify his agency and then the court. Which hat decides what he does?

Discuss

- What if Don calls the client on this and urges her to come clean herself? What if Cheryl tells him to mind his own business and warns Don not to break the confidentiality of NA?
- Should Don tell the agency staff what he heard at the NA meeting regarding this client's lack of sobriety? In weighing the anonymity of NA and the confidentiality of Don's agency, which carries more weight? What information can he share legally?

- What federal or state (use your state) regulations are relevant to Don's decision?
- Can you write a guideline for this type of situation to state clearly the agency's obligations?
- What, if anything, should Don say to Cheryl?

Financial Ethics

In a national survey of "ethically troubling incidents" among psychologists, confidentiality-related problems were the largest category, followed by blurred, dual, or conflicting relationships. The category we are about to consider, the financial realm, ranked third (Pope and Vetter 1992).

Commissions or rebates (kickbacks) for referrals and fee-splitting are unethical and illegal (NAADAC 1992, Principle llc). It is out of line for a counselor to seek or accept private fee arrangements with a client who is working with his or her agency. A counselor may not treat a client in an agency-run group and then see him or her "on the side" for a fee; nor can a counselor who has a position with an agency list that position on a brochure or print it in other literature (business card, stationery) to recruit clients to a private practice.

A counselor may not use client contacts to promote a personal commercial enterprise or that of a relative or friend. For example, a counselor who learns that his client needs a good lawyer cannot refer that client to his sister the attorney, even with all the goodwill and honesty possible. Or a counselor cannot help out her senior citizen client who has plumbing problems by getting him a good deal with her uncle in the septic tank business.

Borrowing money from a past or present client is a form of financial exploitation by the counselor who is using his or her position of power. It is unethical to accept gifts or tips from clients or their families (NAADAC 1992, Principle 11d). For example, a counselor, even in a gesture of generosity, cannot lend money to a pregnant client for a taxi ride so she doesn't have to struggle with public transportation to get home. Or a counselor, while knowing the therapeutic value of a client's giving, cannot accept tickets to the ball game.

A counselor or other staff member should not regularly obtain meals from an agency's commissary designed for clients' meals, unless this is considered a convenience of employment, stipulated by contract or by-law, or at least approved by the governing board or other legal authority.

Regrettably, each of these practices occurs in the treatment community, usually involving some combination of (1) lack of clarity on the part of the treatment agency regarding ethical guidelines, (2) personal or recovery relationships between worker and administrators, leading to enabling of these behaviors, and (3) premature counseling role for an individual in early recovery. Such individuals may have unsolved problems such as compulsive gambling, overidentification with clients that leads to blurring of boundaries, overextension and burnout, or a need to compensate for low self-esteem by grandiose or narcissistic posturing.

The "Checkbook" Diagnosis

Counselors may recognize that a client needs treatment, yet policy guidelines or gatekeepers of their medical coverage exclude all but the most severely afflicted. Agencies may be tempted to provide a billable or "checkbook" diagnosis. This phenomenon, also called diagnostic creep, can be motivated by a desire to obtain help for suffering individuals or by the wish to fill available beds and keep reimbursement flowing to the agency coffers. The alternative is to deny care, refer elsewhere, or prematurely discharge clients whose problems are so severe that they might drain agency resources while bringing little reimbursement. Agencies that receive governmental support are often required by state regulations to set aside a certain proportion of treatment slots for "uncompensated care" or "charity care," that is, treatment of clients who have no medical coverage. Providing something other than an objective and proper diagnosis is unethical and if egregiously inaccurate could open an agency to fraud.

A related practice to diagnostic creep is to use an adolescent addictions unit as a catchall for adolescents with problems, such as giving chemical dependency diagnoses to one-time LSD users or without sufficient data. This is an unethical business practice. In addition, labels take on a life of their own: It is unfair, stigmatizing, and self-fulfilling to call teen drug experimentation an addiction. (White 1993, 53, 112)

Representation of Services

Claims made for the helping process in general and for the process in addictions counseling in particular must be realistic. Addicts range from the vulnerable to the desperate, who have completely "hit bottom," or at the very least live in chaos, disarray, and unhappiness. Counseling must not be presented as a miracle-working process or cash in on New Age or other trends. It should not claim other than the modest and realistic, addiction-specific, facilitation of recovery. A counselor or an agency should pay careful attention to how it represents itself, the services it offers, and professional qualifications of employees.

Clients and prospective clients must understand the scope of treatment—what is and is not treated—methods of treatment, length and cost of treatment, and limitations of treatment. The client must be informed fully at the onset of counseling, if not before, about the purposes, goals, techniques, and procedures involved (ACA 1981, B8). The addictions counselor's core function of orientation is, then, prompted by an ethical standard. One corollary of this principle is that the client cannot be unknowingly or involuntarily be the subject of any type of experiment (ACA 1981, B15, D5, D6).

Neither addictions counselors nor agencies should claim or imply treatment for nonaddictive psychiatric disorders, related areas such as reduction of stress and anxiety, or solutions to problems of living. However, relapse prevention may draw upon techniques used in psychotherapies such as relaxation methods or assertiveness training for the specific purpose of reducing the risk of relapse (ACA 1981, A7).

Unethical marketing of services is quite common. This includes advertising every kind of specialized care where little is actually present. Examples include a general care unit that is promulgated as having a special women's program or a cocaine addiction program; patients being admitted to a "detoxification program," which is actually a general medical floor of a hospital with one part-time alcoholism counselor; and toll-free numbers that offer "free assessments," then tell all callers that they are addicts and refer them to their own programs or to those that have paid to be a designated agency. William White (1993, 32, 40-1, 45) chronicles many such examples.

Any representation of service must not engage in grandiose impression management that suggests, implicitly or explicitly, charismatic or other special qualities of the counselor (Vermont 1980, Principle 9). The guru pose should be avoided.

Testimonials from satisfied customers are, in general, ethically inappropriate (Vermont 1980, Principle 9).

Claims made for counselors' credentials should be specific and not misleading or inflated (ACA 1981: A4). The basis for use of terms such as *clinician, therapist, certified,* and *licensed* must be clear. Some states have a tiered system that recognizes a minimal level of preparedness for the entry-level employee or addictions screening worker in a general social-services setting as well as a professional counselor certification. It is unethical to represent the minimal credential as a board certification.

In-house job titles that are abbreviated after names (e.g., "John Smith, S.A.C." for an in-house title of Substance Abuse Counselor) must not be printed on agency stationery or business cards to imply certification or licensure. Some unethical misrepresentations include individuals employed in other than counseling roles at an agency who state or imply that they are counselors; volunteers who imply they are staff; aide positions that are represented as full counseling positions; and counseling roles that are represented as administrative (NAADAC Principle 4a).

An "official seal" of twelve-step fellowship should not be claimed to attract clients. An agency should never give the impression that it is an "AA" agency, or that many staff members are AA members. Alcoholics Anonymous would be the very first to object to this! Twelve-step fellowships neither recommend nor endorse agencies or organizations. (See the Twelve Traditions in the appendix.). Neither should personal membership in fellowships be used to enhance recruitment. Not only is this practice unethical, it leads to confusion about the roles of fellowship peers, sponsors, and counselors.

With the managed-care system, treatment options have come under severe limitations. Some managed-care entities have discouraged or even forbidden health-care providers from talking freely with patients about their treatment options. Providers feel that such "gag rules" put blinders on patients, preventing them from intelligently participating in decisions that affect their lives, and contradicting the principle of informed consent. For physician providers, it may even violate the Hippocratic Oath which states, "First, do no harm." Gag rules on providers are being challenged in litigation in several states.

Competence

One of the key functions of ethical standards is to ensure that those entrusted to help are indeed reasonably ready and able to do so. Competency issues include counselor impairment, issues that cloud objectivity or distract from focus on the client's interest, and preparedness in a variety of knowledge and skills areas.

Impairment

Counselors are impaired if they suffer from conditions that cause measurable decrements in clinical performance or that compromise their counseling status. These include various psychiatric and neurological syndromes that render the counselor less than competent to perform counseling functions, as well as possible relapse into substance abuse. NAADAC Principle 3(d) (1997) states that professional impairment needs appropriate treatment, and the addictions counselor certification boards in many states stipulate that recovering counselors must abstain from addictive substances (AODACCBNJ 1990, 7a, b). In New Jersey, relapses must be reported to the certification board and a two-year suspension imposed.

Lack of Preparedness

Lack of or inadequate training is a form of incompetence that jeopardizes clients' recovery. To put it even more strongly, because addictions are chronic, progressive, often fatal diseases, the incompetence of treatment staff can threaten the lives of clients. Various incompetent actions, such as "improper treatment, inadequate treatment, negligence in use of technique, inadequate diagnosis" (Hogan 1978), are the basis of many malpractice suits. However, competencies of addictions counselors have been a gray area. The definition of adequate preparedness has varied from state to state and from agency to agency. At the end of the 1990s unified models of addiction counselor competency are becoming standard, as seen in the federally sponsored and published document "Addiction Counselor Competencies: The Knowledge, Skills, and Attitudes of Professional Practice" (CSAT 1998), which has been endorsed by the major addictions counseling constituencies (NCRC/AODA 1991).

It is natural for grateful, recovering persons to wish to assume a counseling role and give back to the community what they have gained. In fact, the addictions field was founded and developed by recovering addicts in a self-help milieu, whose commitment, energy, and skills at engaging and motivating addicts are often the envy of "straight" staff. The certification process was not linked initially to professional training such as that required in nursing, social work, or psychology. The competence of nonprofessional or paraprofessional recovering counselors has been a great debate in the addictions field for at least thirty years (Krystal and Moore 1963; Lemere et al. 1964). However, few would claim now that personal recovery alone is sufficient preparation for the counseling role. Bissell (1987, 4) quotes a half-way house director as saying, "Just because you had your appendix out doesn't qualify you to take out mine!"

The nondegreed addictions counselor faces disadvantages in completing paperwork, writing case presentations, and dealing with the certification process—topics that are taught in educational programs that lead to degrees. There are also questions regarding service to clients. For example, does lack of knowledge about psychiatric diagnoses or the DSM-IV on the part of a counselor who interacts with possibly mentally ill chemical abusers constitute incompetence? Addictions counselors who have had no training in screening concurrent psychiatric diagnoses are increasingly rare. In the past, bipolar (manic-depressive) clients were occasionally mislabeled as "dry drunks" (a term used in recovery milieux to denote the disorganization, impulsivity, and mood swings that may be the aftereffects or consequences of long-term addiction). In 1990 a college intern, who had acquired basic knowledge of psychiatric symptoms from his coursework, observed a sober client seemingly in the throes of a manic state. His suggestion that a psychiatric consultation be obtained was rebuffed initially by naïve staff. He prevailed by petitioning the agency director; the consultation did confirm his suspicion of a mood disorder (Myers 1991). Failure to refer clients appropriately keeps them from proper treatment and jeopardizes their safety and lives.

On the other hand, addictions counselors bitterly note that other health-care providers, including supervisory medical personnel, often sorely lack first-hand knowledge of addictive disease, miss the diagnosis, and cannot see through denial and deception. In 1988 at a public hospital in Brooklyn, New York, new graduates of foreign medical schools routinely overdiagnosed paranoid schizophrenia among crack addicts in an inpatient psychiatric unit.

The responsibility for ensuring staff competency lies primarily with the agency. Some agency administrators are happy to use untrained, newly recovering individuals, sometimes graduates of their own programs. Their motives usually combine elements of naïveté and the opportunistic use of a cheap labor pool (Bissell 1987, 5-6). To get a foot on the career ladder, many people might be glad to be so "exploited." Some argue that such hiring practices are not necessarily unethical, if the employer offers or requires a systematic and mandatory program of continuing education, professional growth, and certification. Unfortunately, such programs have often been absent. Hiring untrained individuals generates unsophisticated, clinically limited "hothouse plants" who cannot function occupationally outside of a certain type of recovery program, can hardly differentiate themselves from clients, are prone to ethical compromises or burnout, and have limited writing skills and unsophisticated clinical skills.

Lack of Responsibility

Irresponsible or careless behavior is incompetent and unethical. For example, a counselor's chronic lateness results in inadequate services, impairs the counseling relationship, and demonstrates a bad example to people who are emerging from the personal chaos of addiction. Poor record keeping, frequent interruptions of sessions to take phone calls, and failure to follow up in case management are ineffective and disrespectful practices that constitute unethical treatment.

It is no shame to recognize the limits of competence. A counselor may be very good at what he or she does, but should not feel impelled to tackle every skills area. Ability to identify one's limits of competency, as well as goals for further growth and training, is a clinical and ethical imperative, usually requiring some guidance and input from clinical supervisors. Not everyone can repair computers or perform brain surgery; why should any counselor who has not been trained as a family therapist feel compelled to assume the role of marriage counselor? Getting drawn into acting in areas outside of the scope of one's competency compromises ethical standards (ACA 1981, A7). Again, this can also harm clients and make the agency liable to lawsuits.

Many guidelines (NAADAC 1992, Principle 3b; AODACCBNJ 1990, Standard 8c) consider it a duty to report incompetence to certification authorities. Private practices, agencies, and hospitals should have guidelines for dealing with incompetence.

Professional Growth

Continued growth and ongoing education are tenets of ethics in most helping professions. No one would want a suicidal, bed-ridden, and biologically depressed relative treated by a psychiatrist who had never heard about Prozac, Zoloft, Paxil, or Effexor (see Table 6.1 Common Psychiatric and Psychotherapeutic Medications). Professional growth involves gaining the latest knowledge, strategies, and skills. It also means avoiding rote formulaic counseling, becoming stale, and burning out. There are myriad ways of broadening competency and upgrading knowledge and skills:

- Read addictions treatment journals in your specialty, which might include *Alcoholism Treatment Quarterly, Journal of Child and Adolescent Chemical Dependency, Employee Assistance Quarterly, Schizophrenia Bulletin,* and so on.
- Attend professional seminars. It is usually best to avoid the expensive lecture circuits and cruises for CEU credits that are advertised with glossy brochures and vague inspirational themes such as "Codependency and the Millenium."
- Attend agency networking events. Provider networks exist in many states or regions of states, but nonsupervisory staff are often unaware of their existence or are hesitant about asking to attend.
- Be active in the National Association of Drug and Alcohol Abuse Counselors (NAADAC), which has affiliate organizations in most states, and attend the regional and national conferences of NAADAC.
- Complete coursework in an addictions studies curriculum, or in criminal-justice or mental-health curricula as pertains to special populations such as addicted offenders and mentally ill chemical abusers.
- Judiciously peruse Internet resources, including those of the Center for Substance Abuse Treatment (SAMHSA), National Clearinghouse on Alcohol and Drug Information (NCADI), the Web of Addictions, and so on.

For professional growth, the areas of knowledge that counselors should pursue include

- biomedical knowledge and practice in regards to mentally ill chemical abusers.
- multicultural awareness and sensitivity. The *DSM-IV* addresses cultural sensitivity, both in diagnostic considerations for many long-recognized syndromes as well as in a special appendix of culture-bound syndromes. The American Psychological Association as well as the Addiction Counselor Competency document (CSAT 1997) consider cultural competency an ethical necessity.
- new medications such as antipsychotics, antidepressants, and drug antagonists, along with their therapeutic possibilities and side effects. Counselors also need to keep abreast of OTC medications that addicts and abusers use to supplement or substitute for street drugs, including legal stimulants contained in appetite suppressants and decongestants and "herbal" or "natural" energy boosters that contain ephedrine.
- new laws and regulations concerning confidentiality, liability, professional duties, insurance, and emergency treatment. Addictions staff can be effective advocates for constructive legislation that favors parity for substance-abuse and mental-health care. Counselors should be aware of their professional association's stance on and analysis of upcoming legislation so they can be resources for information on how to vote on these important issues.
- changes in the field such as the decline in inpatient rehabilitation in favor of intensive outpatient treatment, new screening and assessment tools such as the Addiction Severity Index, American Society of Addiction Medicine Patient Placement Criteria, and others.

Nondiscrimination

Service cannot be denied to eligible clients because of their gender, race, ethnicity, nationality, sexual orientation, age, or physical characteristics. Neither can the quantity or quality of services vary according to any of these client characteristics. Note the word *eligible*. It is not discriminatory for an agency specializing in the treatment of addicted, pregnant women to refuse to treat a male, nor is it discriminatory for an agency to refuse to treat a child, where such specialized care is not within the scope of services provided by the agency.

Taking this a step further, some ethics guidelines state that a tendency to decline cases based on counselor bias and aversion to or anxiety about certain client types constitutes discrimination. Certainly indigent, homeless, and mentally ill chemical abusers tend to suffer from discrimination, which creates an army of unwanted clients and people who are not getting the help they need. There is a lack of training for health professionals in addictions intervention and referral skills; and confrontation and intervention take more time and energy than may be available to the professional with a large caseload. An old expression among physicians and nurses concerned with alcoholism is the "ash can syndrome," an ironic reference to a derelict who was found out in back with the ash cans and who is treated for a host of ills directly or indirectly related to alcoholism, but never the alcoholism itself. Another expression for the undesirable or demented client is the "GOMER," or "Get Out of My Emergency Room."

The statutes of many states require agencies to accept and treat a number of indigent (nonpaying or charity care) clients. In such cases, it is discriminatory to set up a covert system whereby a referring agent must refer a certain number of paying clients for every nonpaying client.

Using the same logic, a caseload skewed toward types of clients from which the counselor derives the most personal satisfaction, or with whom he or she is most at ease, discriminates against others not in this category. This does not exclude an agency from assigning a counselor to work with a special population because he or she has the knowledge and skills required. For example, a Creole-speaking counselor may have a caseload of Haitians.

It has become accepted among most helping professions that discrimination and incompetence exist if a particular cultural or ethnic group is not being served because counselors lack cultural competency skills (see chapter 8).

Objectivity

There is an incredibly wide range of opinion, theory, and belief in the addictions field, perhaps greater than in the treatment of nonaddictive disorders. The definition of addictions, beliefs as to the origin and course of addiction, and opinions as to how recovery is to be achieved inevitably vary among counselors and between counselor and client. While counselors need not hide their views, the counseling role is not to preach, lecture, convince, argue a position, or disparage the position of clients or other staff. Any of these stances disrespects the rights of others and is certainly a sidetrack from the counseling process. This is another gray area because, as Rhodes (1992, 43) remarks, clients may want help and guidance in an ethical exploration of their issues. The undersocialized client needs habilitation, and the sociopath requires treatment that includes development of a value system. A skilled, objective counselor can facilitate values clarification and development of an ethical system with clients without imposing his or her belief system or disparaging that of others.

ACTIVITY 4.5   Can't Handle That God Stuff

Marcia, who comes from a Hasidic Jewish family and rebelled to marry a secular Jewish man, enters treatment under family pressure. She goes to a few AA meetings at the urging of her counselor, but feels she is being forced to go along with something she considers similar to her "repressive" family environment. "Another dogmatic in-group who only talk to themselves," is the way she puts it. She strongly declares her desire to recover from her alcoholism but does not want to be forced to go along with "the God thing."

Discuss

- How would you approach Marcia?
- Are these religious issues or family issues?
- Would you address her issues about religion in a treatment plan? If so, how?
- Would forcing Marcia to attend AA or denying her treatment be religious discrimination?
- Do you know anything about Hasidim?
- Would you need to know about Hasidim? Her family?
- Would it be ethical or appropriate to refer Marcia to another program or agency?

An Ethical Treatment System

It is important to identify systemic factors in ethical choices. The web of systemic influences (economic and regulatory systems, agency and societal cultures) reaches down to surround client and counselor, determining how policies and procedures are implemented in day-to-day counseling practice. An example (given above) is the screening function, that is supposedly an objective determination of appropriateness and eligibility for admission but, distorted by market competition and managed-care constraints, stretches or even invents a diagnosis for mercenary or altruistic reasons. A more complex example is the apparent fact that a client cannot make sufficient progress in a particular setting. It is the ethical responsibility of the counselor and agency to terminate and/or transfer the client, and to be knowledgeable about resources (NAADAC 1992, Principles 7c, 7d; ACA 1981,12). Or, within an agency, if a particular counselor is a bad match for the client, the client should be reassigned. All too often, however, clients are retained inappropriately. This situation may be caused by systemic factors such as the need to keep up client statistics, as well as countertransference issues such as anxiety about appearing a failure, overinvolvement, and the need to play a rescuer role. Obviously, a great deal of honest, critical thinking is required to tease out the strands of influence. A climate of secrecy and denial, antithetical to a therapeutic environment, makes it unlikely that accurate assessment of agency practice or personal and professional growth will take place.

References

AODACCBNJ (Alcohol and Other Drug Abuse Counselor Certification Board of New Jersey, Inc.) 1990. *AODACCBNJ Ethical Standards.* East Brunswich, NJ: Author.

ACA (American Counseling Association). 1981. *Ethical Standards.* Alexandria, VA: Author.

Anderson, B. S. 1996. *The Counselor and the Law*, 4th ed. Alexandria, VA: Author.

Bissell, L., and J. E. Royce. 1987. *Ethics for Addiction Professionals.* Center City, MN: Hazelden Foundation.

Brooks, M. K., et al. 1997. "Ethical and Legal Aspects of Confidentiality," in *Substance Abuse: A Comprehensive Textbook*, 3rd ed. J. H. Lowinson, P. Ruiz, R. B. Millman, and J. G. Langrod, ed. Baltimore: Williams & Wilkins.

Brown, S. D., and R. W. Lent. 1993. *Handbook of Counseling Psychology*, 2 ed. New York: Wiley-Interscience.

Code of Ethics for Professional Alcoholism Counselors: NIAAA Proposed Standards for Alcoholism Counselors by the Clinical Standards Commitee of the Regional Training Program for Alcoholism Counselors. 1974. Baltimore, MD: Johns Hopkins University Press.

"Confidentiality of Alcohol and Drug Abuse Patient Records." 1975. *Federal Register* 40, no. 127, Part 4 (1 July). Washington, DC: U. S. Government Printing Office.

Corey, G., and M. Schneider-Corey. 1993. *Issues and Ethics in the Helping Professions*, 4 ed. Pacific Grove, CA: Brooks/Cole.

CSAT (Center for Substance Abuse Treatment). 1994. *Confidentiality of Patient Records for Alcohol and Other Drug Treatment.* Technical Assistance Publication Series no. 13, by Felix Lopez. Rockville, MD: Substance Abuse and Mental Health Services Administration, U.S. Dept. of HHS.

———. 1996. Checklist for Monitoring Alcohol and Other Drug Confidentiality Compliance. Technical Assistance Publication 18, Rockville, MD: Center for Substance Abuse Treatment, Substance Abuse Mental Health Administration, U.S. Dept. of HHS.

———. 1998. *Addiction Counselor Competencies: The Knowledge, Skills and Attitudes of Professional Practice.* Technical Assistance Protocol Series 21. Rockville, MD: Substance Abuse and Mental Health Services Administration, U.S. Dept. of HHS.

Doyle, K. 1997. "Substance Abuse Counselors in Recovery: Implications for the Ethical Issues of Dual Relationships." *Journal of Counseling and Development* 75: 428-32.

Emerson, S., and P. A. Markos. 1996. "Signs and Symptoms of the Impaired Counselor." *Journal of Humanistic Education and Development* 34:108-17.

Hoffman, J. 1994. "Faith in Confidentiality of Therapy Is Shaken." *New York Times*, 15 June, p. 1.

Hogan, D. B. 1978. *The Regulation of Psychotherapists, 3: A Review of Malpractice Suits in the United States.* Cambridge, MA: Ballinger.

Hubert, M. 1996. "Guidelines for Avoiding Ethical Pitfalls." *Counseling Today* 10 (February): 14.

Hugman, R., and D. Smith. 1995. *Ethical Issues in Social Work.* London and New York: Routledge.

Krystal, H., and R. A. Moore. 1963. "Who Is Qualified to Treat the Alcoholic? A Discussion." *Quarterly Journal of Studies on Alcohol* 24: 705-20.

Lemere, F., et al. 1964. "Who Is Qualified to Treat the Alcoholic? Comment on the Krystal-Moore Discussion." *Quarterly Journal of Studies on Alcohol* 25: 558-60.

Lewin, T. 1996. "Issues of Privacy Roil Arena of Psychotherapy." *New York Times*, 22 May, p.1/D20.

Lowenberg, F., and R. Dolgoff. 1988. *Ethical Decisions for Social Work Practice*, 3rd ed. Itsaca, IL: Peacock.

Myers, P. 1990. "Sources and Configurations of Institutional Denial." *Employee Assistance Quarterly* 5, 3: 43-54.

————. 1991. "Cult and Cult-Like Pathways out of Adolescent Addiction," in *Special Problems in Adolescent Chemical Dependency.* E. E. Sweet, ed. New York: Haworth Press. (Orig. appeared in *Journal of Adolescent Chemical Dependency*, vol. 1 no. 4).

NAADAC (National Association of Alcoholism and Drug Abuse Counselors). 1992. *Ethical Standards of Alcoholism and Drug Abuse Counselors.* Arlington, VA: Author.

NIAAA (National Institute of Alcohol Abuse and Alcoholism). *Code of Ethics for Professional Alcoholism Counselors: NIAA Proposed Standards for Alcoholism Counselors by the Clinical Standards Committee of the Regional Training Program for Alcoholism Counselors.* 1974. Bethesda, MD: Author.

NASW (National Association of Social Workers). 1980. *Code of Ethics of the National Association of Social Workers.* Silver Spring, MD: Author.

NCRC/AODA (National Certification Reciprocity Consortium/ Alcohol and Other Drug Abuse, Inc.). 1991. *Role Delineation Study for Alcohol and Other Drug Abuse Counselors.* Raleigh, NC: Author.

Pope, K. S., and V. A. Vetter. 1992. "Ethical Dilemmas Encountered by Members of the American Psychological Association." *American Psychologist* 47, 3: 397-411.

Powell, D. 1980. *Clinical Supervision: Skills for Substance Abuse Counselors.* New York: Human Sciences Press.

Rhodes, M. L. 1992. "Social Work Challenges: The Boundaries of Ethics." *Families in Society,* (January): 40-7.

Scarf, M. 1996. "Keeping Secrets." *The New York Times Magazine,* 16 June.

Vermont Alcoholism Counselors Association, Inc. 1980. *Ethical Standards.* Reprinted in *Clinical Supervision: Skills for Substance Abuse Counselors.* D. J. Powell, ed. New York: Human Sciences Press.

White, W. L. 1993. *Critical Incidents.* Bloomington, IL: Light-house Training Institute.

5

Case Management — From Screening to Discharge

The term *case management* is used by helping professionals to denote activities that bring the client through a service-delivery system to a desired outcome. Beyond that very general definition, *case management* may refer to an aspect, task, or special emphasis in human and social services.

In many agencies case management is seen as an overarching model for the processing of addicted clients through the continuum of care from initial contact to closure, based on the specific treatment and recovery needs of each individual. Whatever the setting (inpatient, outpatient, halfway house, etc.) and whatever the intensity of services (40 hours per week, 10 hours per week, 1 hour per week, etc.), the counselor assists the client through a series of stages from initial contact to final discharge. According to Ballew and Mink (1986), the counselor helps the client navigate through a set of stages, which they identify as engaging, assessing, planning, accessing resources, coordinating (others would add monitoring), and disengaging. Individual, family, and group counseling processes and relationships are the motor that moves the client through these stages. (See Figure 5.1 for an illustration of case manangement.)

Figure 5.1 Case Management Framework

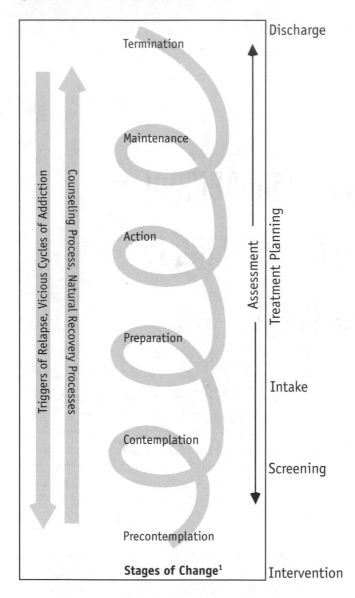

Discharge

Termination

Maintenance

Action

Preparation

Intake

Contemplation

Screening

Precontemplation

Stages of Change[1]

Intervention

Assessment

Treatment Planning

Triggers of Relapse, Vicious Cycles of Addiction

Counseling Process, Natural Recovery Processes

---

[1] As per Prichaska and DiClemente, discussed in Chapter 1.

In other agencies case management refers to a special emphasis on the coordinated and aggressive use of ancillary services to support all areas of individual life (housing, health care, mental-health services, financial services, etc.), in contrast to counseling or treatment of addiction alone. For example, Mejta and colleagues (1994) describe the Interventions Case Management Model. The underlying assumptions and philosophy of the model are that there are a "constellation of problems that encourage continued drug use and antisocial behavior" (303) and there is a limited period of time to initiate action before the motivation to change dissipates. These two variables necessitate a proactive, coordinated, and decisive system of client management. The expression "intensive case management services" (ICMS) is used throughout the social services, including welfare-to-work projects, workers' compensation, addiction treatment, and mental-health delivery systems. It refers to a consortium of programs working to provide comprehensive, integrated, or "wrap-around" services. ICMSs are seen as necessary to avoid fragmentation of care and to mobilize services for fragile and noncompliant populations such as chronic welfare recipients, the mentally ill, and the homeless. Consortia can range from small to large, regional systemwide efforts. In the addictions field, a prime example of the latter is the Target Cities Program, initiated by the federal Center for Substance Abuse Treatment in 1991 for several urban areas.[2] The funded cities use a Central Intake Unit to unify the various treatment providers of initial screening, assessment, and referral functions.

Addiction-counselor certification boards affiliated with the International Certification Reciprocity Consortium limit the definition of *case management* to coordination of service activities only, excluding such functions as screening, assessment, and treatment planning. According to this definition, case management responsibilities of addictions counselors include planning and coordinating with clients in recovery as they access, link with, and use supportive services; client advocacy to secure resources; and education of clients to increase their awareness of community services. This definition is also found in the addiction counselor competency consensus document (CSAT 1997).

The Marriage of Case Management and Counseling

Human services professions have often drawn a distinction between counseling, which focuses on process (client self-awareness, self-reflection, and decision making) and case management, which focuses on outcome (goals, objectives, action steps, plans, etc.). In social-welfare and offender services,

---

[2] The Center for Substance Abuse Treatment operates as part of the Substance Abuse and Mental Health Services Administration (SAMHSA) in the U.S. Department of Health and Human Services (HHS).

the titles Case Manager and Caseworker may, in fact, denote individuals who perform duties outside of or not primarily pertaining to the counseling or clinical realms. These two important aspects of treatment, however, depend on each other for successful treatment. Clients will not agree to a treatment contract, honestly follow a treatment plan, or use resources effectively if they do not see the need for them or are not working with the counselor. This commitment can develop only within an empathic, supportive counseling relationship. Active listening and communication skills such as reflection of content and feeling are also necessary to identify problems that need to be addressed in the treatment plan. It is a revolutionary experience for a client to work with someone who actually seems interested in hearing about his or her feelings, problems, and thoughts, rather than dealing with the formal and impersonal bureaucratic routines to which he or she may have been accustomed. In short, all of the counseling skills identified in chapters 2 and 3 come into play to carry out the various processing and management functions discussed in this chapter, and are crucial in their success.

Screening

All human services involve screening, which determines whether the client is eligible and appropriate for admission to an agency or needs referral to another agency to which he or she is eligible or appropriate for admission. Screening serves two major purposes:

1. attesting to the presence of a condition that may go unrecognized if not detected and
2. providing data to decide whether a client is appropriate for a specific treatment program or vice versa.

In the first purpose of *screening*, social, health, and criminal-justice workers determine if there is evidence for referral of a client to alcohol and/or drug treatment for further assessment. It is important that such screening take place because there is strong evidence that early intervention increases the success rate of treatment. Screening can have an active or passive connotation. That is, service-delivery systems can attempt to screen large segments of the population in order to identify individuals with a particular condition. In many health-care settings, this is known as "case finding." Addictions units at a medical center can work with emergency room or general medical staff to seek out addicted patients, just as all patients can be screened for tuberculosis.

The second purpose of *screening* relates to the initial process whereby it is determined that clients are appropriate for treatment or that they should be referred to other services. The counselor's recommendation depends on the client's clinical needs (such things as heath, living conditions, severity of symptoms, etc.) and the capacity of an agency to provide such treatment. In order to provide such screening and recommendations, a counselor not only needs to know the client's symptoms and social and health problems, but must clearly understand his or her agency's eligibility requirements and scope of services, as well as the eligibility requirements and capabilities of other treatment agencies in the region. It also means that the counselor has an ethical obligation to refer clients to the most appropriate treatment available (see chapter 4, which discusses ethics). Awareness of and a willingness to refer to a broad range of health and social-service agencies is necessary.

Engaging

In addition to gathering information and evaluating treatment options, the screening interview serves the following purposes:

- To establish as much rapport as possible during the first contact (see the discussion of these skills in chapter 2)
- To establish the boundaries of clients and counselors (see chapter 7)
- To explore the client's expectations and desired outcomes of treatment
- To describe the program

Remember that the screening or intake worker is usually the first person a client sees, and therefore the representative of the agency; indeed, of the entire concept and system of addictions treatment. The initial impression made on the highly ambivalent client may be crucial to accepting or delaying the first step on the road to recovery. When addictions screening of large populations in health or social-services settings is the method of clients' entry to treatment, attention must be paid to the attitudes, motivations, and active listening skills of screening personnel who are not primarily trained as addictions counselors.

Screening Tools

It is useful for addictions counselors to have a familiarity with some of the screening tools that general and social-service practitioners use. Although many clients abuse both alcohol and drugs, most screening tools are focused on either one or the other. Several instruments have been developed to detect alcohol problems such as the C.A.G.E., the Brief M.A.S.T., and the A.U.T.I.D. The C.A.G.E. is the shortest and has been demonstrated to be valid (Ewing, 1984). A physician, nurse, or social worker may integrate the C.A.G.E. questions into a medical interview. In a general interview, if clients indicate that they drink alcohol or have drunk in the past, the clinician can ask the following questions:

C = Have you ever thought you ought to **C**ut down on your drinking?

A = Have people **A**nnoyed you by criticizing your drinking?

G = Have you ever felt **G**uilty about your drinking?

E = Have you ever had an **E**ye-opener, a first drink, in the morning after a hangover?

Any positive response should be followed up with concerned interest. Two positive responses would indicate need for referral. Use of drugs and medications should also be investigated.

Kinney (1996) uses the mnemonics HALT and BUMP to list questions that can be helpful in gathering data to indicate alcohol or drug problems.

H = Do you usually use drugs and/or drinks to get **H**igh?

A = Do you sometimes drink or use drugs **A**lone?

L = Have you found yourself **L**ooking forward to drinking or using?

T = Have you noticed an increase in **T**olerance for alcohol or drugs?

B = Do you have memory lapses, **B**lackouts that occur during drinking?

U = Do you find yourself using drugs or drinking in **U**nplanned ways?

M = Do you drink or use when you feel anxious, stressed, or depressed, or for **M**edicinal reasons?

P = Do you work at **P**rotecting your supply, having drugs or alcohol available at all times?

A few positive responses to screening instruments are often taken as proof of addiction; however, they only indicate the need for further assessment. It is important that anyone who is doing screening realize that the results of screening are a preliminary indicator of a problem and not a diagnosis.

Figures 5.2 and 5.3 are examples of tools to screen for abuse of drugs and alcohol by adolescents and adults. (For more detail on specific screening tools, see CSAT, 1991 and 1997.)

Figure 5.2 Substance Abuse Screening Instrument

Please read carefully and circle the appropriate response.

Have you ever done something crazy while high and had to make excuses for your behavior later?	Yes No
Have you ever felt really burnt out for a day after using drugs?	Yes No
Have you ever gotten out of bed in the morning and really felt wasted?	Yes No
Did you ever get high in school?	Yes No
Have you gotten into a fight while your were high (including drinking)?	Yes No
Do you think about getting high a lot of the time?	Yes No
Have you ever thought about committing suicide when you were high?	Yes No
Have you run away from home, partly because of an argument over drug use?	Yes No
Did you ever try to stick to one drug after a bad experience mixing drugs?	Yes No
Have you gotten into a physical fight during a family argument over drugs?	Yes No
Have you ever been suspended because of something you did while high?	Yes No
Have you ever had a beer or some booze to get over a hangover?	Yes No
Do you usually keep a supply (of drugs) for emergencies, no matter how small?	Yes No
Have you ever smoked some pot to get over a hangover?	Yes No
Have you ever felt nervous or cranky after you stopped using for a while?	Yes No

Thank You for Your Cooperation.

ID#: _____ Age: _____ Gender _____ Race _____

Results: No. of yes answers: _____ No. of no answers: _____

Offense(s):_____

Comments:_____

_____

Referred for further assessment? Yes _____ No _____

Figure 5.3 Short Michigan Alcohol Screening Test

Screening Adults for Alcohol Abuse   **Answer Yes or No**

1. Do you feel that you are a normal drinker?
   (By "normal" we mean that you drink
   less than or as much as most other people.)   _____

2. Does your wife, husband, parent, or other near
   relative ever worry or complain about your drinking? _____

3. Do you ever feel guilty about your drinking?   _____

4. Do friends or relatives think you are a normal drinker? _____

5. Are you able to stop drinking when you want to?   _____

6. Have you ever attended a meeting
   of Alcoholics Anonymous?   _____

7. Has drinking ever created problems between you and
   your wife, husband, a parent, or other near relative? _____

8. Have you ever gotten into trouble at
   work because of your drinking?   _____

9. Have you ever neglected your obligations,
   your family, or your work for two or more
   days in a row because you were drinking?   _____

10. Have you ever gone to anyone for
    help about your drinking?   _____

11. Have you ever been in a hospital because of drinking? _____

12. Have you ever been arrested for driving
    under the influence of alcoholic beverages?   _____

13. Have you ever been arrested, even for a
    few hours, because of other drunken behavior?   _____

ACTIVITY (5.1) What do these people need?

Form groups of three. Assign each group a scenario and each person a role: client, counselor, or observer. Using the following scenarios, enact a screening interview to determine if the client needs a more in-depth assessment. As the counselor, you are working as an identification and referral counselor in a substance-abuse screening program. Using your listening and feedback skills, try to motivate the client to agree to further assessment. When playing the client, try to stay in character. Role-play each scenario for 10 minutes, allowing the observer 5 minutes to give observations. After all the role-plays are complete, process and discuss them in the large group for 15 to 30 minutes.

Scenario 1: The client is seeing this counselor as a result of a DWI arrest, the second. Following the first offense she attended DWI School. To be without her automobile would be a serious inconvenience, so she is anxious to do whatever it takes to get her license back. Therefore, she is determined to be cooperative, but she is not convinced she has a problem.

Scenario 2: The client has finally agreed to see a counselor, but only after an ultimatum from his wife that she would leave unless he seeks help. The precipitating problem is serious nightly quarrels that begin over dinner and end with the family in tears and his storming out of the house. He attributes the quarreling to the topic under discussion when the argument erupts (e.g., the children's grades, finances, the in-laws coming to visit) and his family's inability to listen to reason.

Scenario 3: A 65-year-old grandmother was referred by a visiting nurse. She was found in a stupor on her couch last week. Nearby were a bottle of pills (Darvon) and an empty bottle of sherry. She lives alone and sees her daughter about once a month. She has arthritis and is sometimes in pain. The nurse visits weekly and helps with some chores. The nurse insisted she come for help.

Assessment

Assessment is a broad term that encompasses a variety of critical knowledge and skills in addictions counseling. Assessment includes those activities, skills, and tools that facilitate the gathering of information throughout the case management and the treatment process.

- It is designed to bring out clients' concerns, desires, fears, beliefs, values, and life experiences.

- It is a means to determine clients' needs, strengths, and resources, and the impediments to successful treatment that might lay in misunderstanding, anxiety, perception, confusion, or denial.
- It uses tools and documents, each of which serve a specific purpose in the continuum of care, which may include a mental-health status exam, a suicidality assessment instrument, or a discharge summary. Client self-reporting is only one source of data. With the clients' informed consent the counselor will seek information from family, employers, referring agencies, and past treatment agencies.

Although assessment may appear to be a separate stage of case management, it is in fact an ongoing process that informs treatment planning and the clinical use of individual, group, and family treatment. Initial assumptions about clients may be supported or need to be revised as more data becomes available and the client evinces change and movement into recovery.

According to Hester and Miller (1995), there are six purposes for evaluation in addictions counseling (see Table 5.1).

Table 5.1 Purposes for Evaluation of Addicts

Type	Purpose
Screening	To determine whether the client needs further evaluation
Diagnosis	To determine if criteria are met to make a clear diagnosis
Ongoing evaluation	To determine the nature and extent of the client's problems
Motivation	To determine the ways in which the client is ready and able to change
Treatment Planning	To determine appropriate interventions and needs for services
Follow-up	To determine what has changed and which aftercare services the client needs

Source: Adapted from Miller, 1985.

Intake

The *intake* procedure is the point of formal admission to a treatment program. This assumes that initial assessment (e.g., through the screening process) has justified the step of admitting this client to this particular program. Also at this point, enough information should be available to prescribe the early critical components of treatment that are valuable and possible for this client. The intake procedures comprise a variety of documents and formalities, including those involving confidentiality that were described in chapter 4. Some minimal orientation to treatment usually takes place at this point. If screening has been done externally (e.g., at a referring social-service agency), the intake process becomes the client's first exposure to the treating agency and to treatment. Again, the intake person must pay attention to use of empathy, active listening skills, and other "human" aspects of this supposedly routine bureaucratic procedure.

Biopsychosocial Assessment

Biopsychosocial assessment provides a detailed overview of the social, biological, family, employment, and medical history of the client. It explores the critical issues in each major area of the client's life. It examines the client's functioning and negotiation of developmental problems that may have arisen in each of the areas. A thorough biopsychosocial assessment identifies the critical issues to be addressed in a treatment plan.

Components of Biopsychosocial Assessment

There is tremendous variation among the activities used to provide a comprehensive biopsychosocial assessment. The types of instrument employed vary in length, format, focus, detail, degree of specificity, and areas of knowledge to be elicited. Most biopsychosocial assessments address the following areas:

- *Childhood and adolescence*, including parental drug and alcohol use, loss of parent(s); relationships with parents, step-parents, or other caregivers, social and cultural beliefs, and messages given in the family.
- *History of substance use and abuse*, including first use of alcohol and drugs, the patterns and changes, and the experiences that occurred under the influence of drugs, up until the present. This should include use of tobacco and over-the-counter medications.
- *Health problems and medical treatments* past and present, including those related to drug use or abuse, withdrawal, hospitalizations and the reasons for them (physical or mental, alcohol- or drug- related, etc.), HIV status, other STDs and infections, and medications.
- *Mental-health history*, including previous evaluations and treatment summaries, as well as the client's evaluation of whether previous treatments were helpful, and why or why not.
- *Family and social functioning*, including marriage(s), divorces, relationships with children, friends, and the impact of alcohol and drug use on these relationships. There are two categories of family: present family (spouse, children, and significant others)

and family of origin (parent, other relatives, and significant others including peers or mentors that influenced life). Is there a family history of alcohol or drug abuse or mental problems? (See chapter 8 for methods of assessing the kin and social systems of clients.)

- *Employment, education, and recreation*, including past and present work and school problems and achievements, past and present ways client finds to relax and have fun, and the role of drugs and alcohol in these areas.
- *Sexual history*, including problems, sexual orientation, and the role of drugs and alcohol in this area.
- *Finances*, including income, sources of income, debts, changes in financial status, and the role of alcohol and drugs.
- *Legal issues*, including criminal history (probation, parole, having served time), incidence of DWIs, whether prior or present treatment is court stipulated, and the role of drugs and alcohol in a client's involvement in the criminal-justice system.

A C T I V I T Y (5.2) What's the best way to ask?

Break into groups of three to five. Choose one of the nine areas of biopsychosocial assessment outlined above. Develop assessment questions for that knowledge area. In doing so, consider the impact of each question on the client, the appropriate timing, and the effect on the development of empathy and a treatment alliance. For example, in the area of family and friends, you might ask, "Who was important to you as you grew up?" "Who could you turn to in your life?" "Who were you close to?" "Who did you have a problem or conflict with?" "Have you lost someone important to you?" "What are some good memories you have of your childhood/teen years?"

Diagnosis

Diagnosis is a medical term that means "1. a. the art of identifying a disease from its signs and symptoms b. the decision reached by diagnosis 2. a. concise description of a taxon" (Merriam-Webster 1993, 177). A diagnosis is also a categorization made after objective, standard diagnosing (diagnostic) activities. Diagnosis is done by matching clients' signs (observable objective data, such as are gathered in laboratory tests) and symptoms (information received from the patient) to established criteria that describe specific medical categories. A diagnosis of strep throat is made following a demonstration that streptococcus bacilli are found in a patient's throat, by obtaining a sample on a cotton swab and growing it in a culture.

Procedures to diagnose addictions, which are described variously as biological, psychological, and spiritual disorders, cannot be so simple and straightforward. Diagnosis should not be confused with a biopsychosocial assessment. It is only a part of such an assessment and does not give enough information to make important clinical decisions about clients. Diagnosis is performed usually by physicians or clinical psychologists. However, it is important that counselors be familiar with diagnostic criteria. The first reason is that physicians often rely on input from counselors and social workers to make diagnoses. Second, understanding signs and symptoms assists counselors in determining relevant data to explore in a clinical (biopsychosocial) assessment interview with clients. Third, and most important, being certain that a client has an addiction predicts reasonable therapeutic interventions that are necessary for counseling to be effective.

There are a number of diagnostic systems in behavioral health fields, but by far the most accepted and used system is the *Diagnostic and Statistical Manual, Fourth Edition (DSM-IV)* published by the American Psychiatric Association (APA, 1994). The *DSM-IV* does not use the terms *addiction* or *alcoholism* but rather refers to *substance dependence*. Inclusion of a condition or syndrome in the *DSM-IV* does not automatically imply mental illness. In fact, the *DSM-IV* is designed to accommodate any kind of adjustment, emotional, or learning problem conceivable. In the arena of chemicals, one can be diagnosed merely as drunk or high, known as "substance intoxication," for any of nine chemicals, or as following a pattern of substance "abuse," or as "dependent" on any of nine chemicals, the dependency category being equivalent to many concepts of addiction. A client can have a diagnosis of marijuana abuse and alcohol dependence, as well as any of a number of accompanying personality disorders, psychoses, and/or organic disorders that are related to chemical use, aging, and so on. The *DSM-IV* describes *substance dependence* as a "maladaptive pattern of substance use, leading to clinically significant impairment or distress, as manifested by three (or more) of the following, occurring at any time in the same 12-month period" (p.181):

1. Tolerance, either as an increased amount needed to achieve the desired state or diminished effect with continued use of the same substance
2. Withdrawal, characterized either by standard withdrawal symptoms specific to the substance used or by taking a similar drug to relieve or avoid withdrawal symptoms
3. Increased amount and time using substances than user had intended
4. Persistent desire and/or failure to cut down on use

5. Great deal of time spent in obtaining and using a substance or recovering from the effects of the substance
6. Substance use interfering with or disrupting important social, occupational, or recreational activities
7. Substance use continuing despite knowledge of having a persistent or recurrent physical or psychological problem that is likely to be caused by or exacerbated by the substance

These criteria can be clustered into three major areas: (1) loss of control, a progressive inability to predict the consequences of the use of a substance, (2) compulsive use, involving a strong craving or the need to drink or use drugs, and (3) problems in which alcohol or drug use is implicated as a cause. Often the client does not perceive that these symptoms mean he or she is addicted or dependent or has any problems whatsoever. This phenomenon is often referred to as denial, which is not a conscious effort to distort the truth. It is normal to expect that clients will minimize, rationalize, or in some other way deny they have a substance-abuse problem. (See chapter 7 for a discussion of denial.)

Although the *DSM-IV*, as well as any other diagnostic framework, establishes categories of severity, it is important to remember that addiction is a complex process that progresses from social or recreational use of substances to abuse to dependency. The amount of time that it takes an individual to progress through these stages depends on a number of variables:

- *Age of the user.* Adolescents who experiment with psychoactive substances tend to progress faster than adults into abuse and then into addiction.
- *The route of administration of the substance.* Individuals using drugs by snorting or injecting them tend to progress into abuse and addiction faster than those who use drugs that are drunk or eaten.
- *The purpose of use or expectation of the user.* The use of a substance to get high or "wasted" or to escape emotional pain lends itself to abuse and addiction more than when use of substance is shaped by social and cultural norms.

Treatment Plans

Like assessment, treatment planning is an ongoing process that begins with and builds on a core of information as treatment proceeds. On the basis of information gleaned from a sound assessment, a client and a counselor can collaborate to identify problems, goals, and objectives of treatment.

Once this is done, they can determine priorities, the methods of treatment, and a schedule, which are all part of the initial treatment plan. A treatment plan provides a framework for logical decision making by a joint effort of counselor and client, as well as reinforcement that clients are responsible for their recovery. In addition to input from the client and the counselor, the clinical supervisor and the agency's treatment philosophy influence treatment planning.

Some time and a considerable amount of paperwork are involved in writing and maintaining an effective treatment plan. Although counselors often avoid or resist doing paperwork, there are good reasons to document the treatment plan and treatment:

- To give direction and focus to the counseling process. Treatment plans provide the clients feedback on their progress and refocus them, if necessary. The documentation helps the counselor review the issues and progress with the client and supervisor.

- To give tangible evidence of progress toward recovery. Clients have an opportunity to see each step, no matter how small, of success and check it off the list. This increases the clients' sense of self-efficacy and reinforces commitment to treatment.

- To facilitate discussion of difficult issues that, if not addressed, would sabotage treatment. Often in writing out and implementing the plan, such issues are identified and clarified, and can be addressed effectively. Clients often leave treatment against professional advice because of failed expectations or concerns that were not identified or discussed.

- To give a clear picture of the client's issues, history, progress, and current situation to all in-house members (present and future) of a treatment team, such as a group leader, a family counselor, a supervisor, or anyone who needs to take over the case.

Treatment Planning Process

The treatment planning process can be seen as a series of ten steps:

1. *Identify issues.* The counselor uses the assessment results as a database. In addition, the counselor receives information from the client that helps to identify the primary concerns, problems, and issues.

2. *Identify needs.* After reviewing the client's case history, the counselor creates a list of the client's needs. Problems or obstacles identified by the client often can be reframed as needs.

3. *List strengths and resources.* From the history and from what the counselor knows of the agencies and community resources, he or she develops a list of the client's strengths and a list of

resources. It is important that the client review and internalize (own) these needs and resources. (See DeJong and Miller 1995)

4. *Set long-term goals.* Having an understanding of the client's problems and needs, the counselor and client set long-term goals. Goals are broad, general outcomes that, when achieved, indicate treatment is complete. These could include being free of drugs and alcohol, having stable family relationships, returning to employment, having solid support systems such as twelve-step groups, and so on. Goals provide beacons, purpose, and direction to the treatment process.

5. *Write objectives.* Each need of the client should translate into an outcome objective. Outcome objectives must be specific, concrete, measurable, and relevant to the goals. "Specific" means that it is clear what the client will do, say, or demonstrate in the treatment process. "Concrete" means there is no confusion about what constitutes the desired behavior of the client. "Relevant" means that it should lead toward attaining the identified goals.

6. *Prioritize.* Because there may be many, perhaps too many, objectives, it is important to prioritize them. Criteria can be weighted to establish priorities, for example: (a) How important is it to the client? The more valuable, the more likely the client will attempt to do what is necessary; (b) How realistic is it given the strengths and resources of the client?; (c) What must be accomplished before the next thing can be done? Is there a logical order to the objectives?; (d) How critical is it to the client's sobriety?

7. *List the steps.* The counselor develops with the client a set of steps that lead up to the objective. These are the activities that the client, the counselor, or significant others engage in to accomplish the objective. It is important to write concrete, specific, and do-able activities to accomplish the objective. For example, simply to state that Jim S., a chronically unemployed male, "will become employed during February" misses the point. An effective list of steps might include, but not be limited to, writing a résumé, having the résumé prepared attractively and duplicated, completing a course of vocational rehabilitation, identifying a number of possible employers, acquiring clothing appropriate for a job interview, and so forth.[3]

---

[3] For a long-time addict, such an organized series of relatively simple, concrete steps might be necessary to form "straight" relationships. Such a list might be to make two phone calls to (potential) friends you met at a meeting; write down how you felt before, during, and after each call; tell people in group meeting a feeling you have about them (like them, annoyed or hurt by something they said).

8. *Name the actors.* In each step toward the objective, it is critical to name the person who is responsible for carrying it out. It is important to give the client as much responsibility as possible. However, it is not always possible for the client to do everything. The counselor may have to make certain contacts or collect certain information. For example, if the client lost his driver's license, his wife may agree to take him to the clinic.

9. *Set deadlines.* It is not realistic to assume all deadlines will be met; but setting a deadline for each step and each objective allows an understanding between counselor and client of a reasonable timeline.

10. *Write a discharge summary.* When all objectives are met and they demonstrate that the client is ready for discharge, it is time to write a discharge plan. It summarizes what has been accomplished in treatment and, most important, provides a plan for the client to continue in recovery, and indicates the steps he or she must take if there is a need for more help.

This process requires refinement depending on the specific treatment setting (residential, outpatient, detox) and mission of the program or agency in which the counselor works. Realistic goals and objectives vary. It is important to remember that a treatment plan is not set in concrete. It is a guiding document that needs to be renegotiated with the client when unexpected problems arise or objectives prove too difficult to meet.

The formulation of treatment goals takes into consideration the stage of treatment and recovery. Addictions-counseling professionals are familiar with typical, common (almost invariable) issues of clients at each stage. For example, in very early treatment of a client who is barely post-detoxification, thought processes may still be confused, and motivation to stay sober and in treatment is threatened by uncomfortable and unfamiliar physical and psychological states. Overall treatment goals include the alleviation of anxiety and keeping the client focused on simple sobriety-maintenance steps and cognitions. Alcoholics Anonymous (not a treatment program) captures this in exhortations to novice members: "Don't drink, and go to meetings." "Stay away from people, places, and things connected to drinking/drugging." Objectives for the newly sober should be simple and concrete. Maintaining a drug-free state one day at a time is about all that one can reasonably put on the client's plate. When this treatment plan is successful, it reinforces the hopes for success in working with the counselor on future changes, personal growth, and challenges.

Because of the common pattern among clients in a given stage, some agencies follow a standard format for goals and objectives in early and middle treatment. Such a list can be helpful to prompt or remind counselors of items that may come into play, but treatment planning requires individualization of goals and objectives to correspond to the gender, culture, age, and characteristics of each client.

Relapse prevention continues to be a vital component of treatment planning throughout treatment, if not a life-long concern. Planning should take into account not only the learning of coping mechanisms for high-risk situations and self-efficacy for a sober lifestyle, but also planning what to do if a relapse has begun. (Chiazuzzi 1991; Gorski and Miller 1982; Marlatt and Gordon 1985).

ACTIVITY 5.3 What do we want to do here?

To practice writing treatment goals, write two treatment objectives you might have for a client. Then in groups of three or four members, pick three treatment objectives that best represent your ideas. Have each group report its objectives.

PROCESS

- Whose objective is it? Would the client take ownership of it?
- When in the treatment process would it be appropriate to address the goal?
- How would you or the client know when the objective is accomplished?
- What would the client need to do to accomplish the objective and what resources would he or she need?

ACTIVITY 5.4 Okay, how are we going to do this?

In small groups read the case of Lee C., then complete the following steps 1 through 8.

CASE: Lee C.

Lee C. is a 25-year-old, married, male, who is participating in an outpatient chemical dependency program. Lee is an electrician who had worked steadily until he was recently suspended from his job after a period of absenteeism and tardiness due to his drinking. Lee has been in treatment in the past and has maintained several periods of sobriety ranging from three to six months, with Alcoholics Anonymous participation. He often states that he drinks after arguments with his wife. They often fight about money and his running off to his mother's after they fight. He often drinks with his best friend and co-worker, Kim. Lee's wife does not permit him to live in the house when he is drinking, but his mother always allows him to stay with her. Lee recognizes he has "some kind of drinking problem" and wishes to stay sober because he is afraid of losing his wife and job. Following the steps, write a treatment plan for Lee C.

1. List Lee's strengths and resources.
2. List his needs.
3. Write a goal for Lee.
4. Write a problem statement for Lee.
5. Write an objective for him.
6. Write a set of steps to accomplish the objective.
7. Determine who will be responsible for each step.
8. Set a date for each step.

 ACTIVITY (5.5) **Are these good objectives?**

Review and evaluate the following treatment objectives. Which objectives do you feel are satisfactory and complete? Rewrite objectives that are unsatisfactory or incomplete.

1. Mr. A will improve his self-esteem.
2. Mrs. B will work on her sobriety.
3. Mr. C will attend five AA meetings per week for the next six weeks.
4. Ms. D will start attending community college.
5. Mr. E will improve his social skills by the end of group therapy.
6. Mrs. F will participate by the third week of group by describing how her dependence on pills affected her.
7. Mr. G will participate in treatment.
8. The H family will learn to communicate more effectively through therapy by the end of the next month.

Progress Notes

The frequency of meetings between client and counselor depends on the context and the level of care (inpatient rehabilitation, intensive outpatient treatment, outpatient treatment), the intensity of help the client needs, and of course the limitations imposed by third-party payers and managed-care organizations. There are important functions fulfilled by these meetings. First, the counselor checks with the client on the progress toward the objectives and goals of the plan. Second, regular individual, group, and family sessions are scheduled in order to work through problems and issues that the treatment plan has identified. And third, unforeseen crises that occur must be addressed in order for the plan to proceed. The plan must be renegotiated as circumstances and priorities change.

Each contact with a client requires documentation, whether it be a phone call, an individual meeting, or a group session. Continued accreditation of the agency, as well as a positive evaluation of the employee, often depends on careful documentation. Health-care and social services settings use the term *chart notes* or *progress* notes, which are kept in official files of the agency. Most addictions counselors do not keep private notes on clients, unless they are in private practice. Counselors record the particulars of a meeting, either immediately after it or on the same day, while it was fresh in the counselor's mind (so time and intervening circumstances don't warp memories). The counselor can use these notes to refresh his or her mind just prior to the next meeting—especially helpful if the counselor has a huge caseload or there is a long time between meetings.

One well-known way of organizing progress notes is through SOAP. This acronym stands for Subjective, Objective, Assessment, and Plan. It is in a sense a miniplan around each significant client contact. The Subjective (S) focuses on the client's perception of the problem. The Objective (O) is the factual data the counselor obtains about the situation, for instance, laboratory or other tests, counselors' observations, records and reports from reliable sources. Assessment (A) is an analysis of the factual data and the client's perceptions of the immediate issues. The Plan (P) is a description of steps to take to solve the problems or work through the issues. For more detail and material on case recording see Wilson (1976).

For example, using the case of Lee C., Lee agrees to avoid people who influence him to drink. Lee comes into a session to discuss this issue. The record of the meeting could look like this:

S—Lee is concerned that his friend Kim will stop by on Friday and ask him to go out drinking. He is concerned that he will have difficulty saying no because he has not been able to do this in the past.

O—According to the assessment and report from family members, Lee has demonstrated difficulty in asserting himself when pressured.

A—Clearly Lee's sobriety is at risk if he goes out with his friend Kim. Lee needs a strategy to assert himself and explain that he cannot go out with Kim.

P—In the counseling session, Lee practiced responses he could make to his friend Kim. In Thursday night group, Lee will discuss these issues and practice his responses with the group and ask for group support.[4]

An alternative and newer form of organizing progress notes is the SOAIGP format (Kagle 1991). In this format,

S = Supplemental (new or revised) information obtained from clients, kin, or peers.

O = the counselor's Observations and those of other staff.

A = the Activities or tasks of treatment.

I = Impressions, assessments, hypotheses, and so on.

G = current Goals.

P = the additional Plan or action steps to be taken.

Client information contained in agency documents such as treatment plans and progress notes are under the confidentiality guidelines described in chapter 4. The counseling field is beginning to grapple with the difficulties of ensuring confidentiality when information is filed and stored in a computerized management information system. Each agency should have guidelines for handling electronic files.

Resources and Services

Throughout the treatment process, the counselor must use his or her expertise to connect the client to the resources necessary to carry out the treatment plan. The counselor has this primary responsibility because he or she is the expert on the array of local health, educational, social, and economic resources that the client may use to address specific needs, in order to reach identified goals. This means that the counselor must have a thorough understanding of the social services in the communities served by the agency. It is useful for counselors to visit and get to know local programs and develop personal contacts within each program. This facilitates referrals and ensures that a client will not be sent to an agency that cannot or will not be helpful.

It is helpful for the counselor to develop a personal directory of social and health services. This directory should contain all agencies in the continuum of care for treatment of alcoholism and other addictions. Directories are available through the United Way, local counsils on alcoholism and addiction, and various state, county, and municipal agencies. They are good references to begin to develop a personal directory. The advantage of a personal

---

[4] Refusal skills that help Lee, which he can practice in a group setting, are "I statements," empathetic refusal, and limit setting ("I like you and I'd like to have some fun with you, but I really can't go out drinking"), which recognizes the feelings and needs of both parties.

directory is that it can be expanded with information the counselor learns about specific nuances of a program (e.g., which programs are most responsive to the cultural, ethnic, and personal needs of clients). Moreover, printed directories can become out of date in one year. To build a useful personal directory of resources, a counselor should include answers to the following questions:

- What are the eligibility requirements for the program?
- What services can a client expect from this agency? What is expected from the client?
- What is the cost of the service? Is it free? Is there a sliding fee scale? Does the program take insurance including Medicare and Medicaid?
- What is the protocol for referral?
- What is the culture, economic status, and ethnic makeup of the client population?
- Does the program provide services for needs such as disabilities (wheelchair access, deafness, blindness, etc.), foreign languages, babysitting, transportation, education, or job development skills?
- Who is the contact—name, telephone and fax numbers, e-mail and street addresses?
- What are the hours of operation? Does the agency provide services during business hours only, on weekends, on evenings, on holidays?
- How long has the agency been operating? What is its track record? Who funds it?

The case of Mrs. Harris is an example of case management from intake to discharge. It illustrates the need to know the offerings of other resources and their contact people in order to coordinate all aspects and stages of a client's care (this case was the basis for Figure 1.4).

Mrs. Harris was referred by the Human Resources (HR) Department of an urban college to the in-house Employee Assistance Program (EAP). The HR administrator had gathered information that documented decrements in Mrs. Harris's job performance, which warranted referral to the EAP. Mrs. Harris, a long-time, well-liked employee and a recent widow, was also approaching retirement. Screening by the EAP administrator indicated the strong possibility of a late-onset alcohol abuse or dependency syndrome. Mrs. Harris's depression and grief were obvious, but she clearly did not feel comfortable to divulge information about drinking to someone who represented her employer. The EAP administrator felt that it would be useless and possibly insulting or threatening to confront Mrs. Harris strongly. Therefore, he decided to refer her to an outpatient alcoholism program in the community. The initial EAP screening impressions were borne out when Mrs. Harris acknowledged to the agency's intake counselor the degree to which she had been drinking. That intake counselor recommended to the referring EAP administrator that Mrs. Harris undergo a medical detoxification prior to further treatment. Because she was consuming more than a pint of whiskey per day, and considering her age, outpatient detoxification was not indicated because of the possibility of medical complications. There being no local detoxification facility, the EAP administrator contacted a medical center in a neighboring city and arranged Mrs. Harris's admission. At the same time, because of the waiting period for admission to inpatient rehabilitation, the EAP staff contacted the admissions department of an inpatient alcoholism rehabilitation program specializing in EAP referrals so that upon completion of a five-day detox stay, Mrs. Harris could be transported without a hiatus to the rehabilitation setting. The EAP also notified the HR department. that Mrs. Harris would require a five-week medical leave.

After determining that Mrs. Harris's sister was a relative whom he trusted with information about her planned treatment, the EAP administrator worked with her to ensure a bag of clothes would be packed and that Mrs. Harris would be present the next day, at the time scheduled for the medical center van to pick her up from her sister's home and transport her to the detoxification unit. She detoxified from alcohol in four days, and was transported to the inpatient rehab setting. Following discharge, Mrs. Harris was cleared to return to work, and she had to attend the outpatient program for continuing care (aftercare). The EAP administrator monitored her aftercare via telephone and sent a monthly report to the HR department that Mrs. Harris was meeting the requirements of the EAP. None of the details of diagnosis and treatment went into Mrs. Harris's HR file, nor were they communicated to her supervisors. Mrs. Harris had become isolated from her church, an affiliation which she greatly valued. She was ashamed of her drinking and sought to avoid humiliation by a self-imposed ostracism. In discussions with the EAP staff and in treatment, her desire to find a way out of this situation emerged as a motivation for recovery, in addition to the formal requirements of the HR department for continued employment. Following treatment, she felt encouraged to forge anew her contacts with church and community. In this way, she also renewed a social support she needed to negotiate the stages of grief and loss of her husband. These steps successfully cemented her sobriety, which she maintained until retirement two years later, at which time contact with the EAP staff ended.

Impediments to Treatment

Some impediments to entering treatment are posed by caretaker roles, such as parent, breadwinner, household manager, and caretaker of ill or elderly parents. It is difficult to find time to attend an outpatient program, and seemingly impossible to find a way to enter intensive outpatient or inpatient rehabilitation. There are specialized programs for women and their children and for pregnant women. Components of such programs often include child care, compensatory special-education programs for children, screening for fetal alcohol syndrome, neonatal withdrawal units, parenting skills, vocational-educational rehabilitation, personal and social skills development, nutritional counseling and augmentation, and transportation. Some of these services are provided by social-services agencies working with the addictions agency to provide integrated case management. Staff should be aware of them to make appropriate referrals.

Physical and Mental Abuse

Especially with women, it is necessary to assess whether the client has been or is being battered or sexually abused, usually by a relative or mate. Unfortunately, it is unlikely for women who are being abused to enter treatment.[5] While rates vary by population and among studies, many agency directors state that at least half of the females in treatment with their agencies have histories of physical, sexual, or emotional abuse. At the least, a battered client brings associated guilt, anger, or shame. Worse, a battered client may qualify for a diagnosis of post traumatic stress disorder (PTSD). In one study of addicted women at Amity House, a long-term theraputic community in Tucson, Arizona, 35 of 55 residents had been raped or molested before the age of 21, and an additional 15 after the age of 21

---

[5] One of the elements of battered woman syndrome is that the dominating abusers isolate the woman from family and social relationships that might propel them in the direction of help. Moreover, the woman's sense of self is so low that she seldom thinks of getting help without outside encouragement. The tendency is to drink and drug more to numb out, escape, and get through the day. Of course, the abuser is highly threatened by the prospect of the woman entering treatment, and usually forbids such thoughts. Often, an abused woman seeks or accepts help only when her children's lives and safety are at risk, and when children's protective services enter the picture.

(Stevens and Gilder 1994). A valuable manual for screening, assessment, and case management of battered and abused women is available from the Center for Substance Abuse Treatment (1997).

Ethnicity and Social Class

The ethnic background and social class of clients also affects use and abuse of substances. Middle-class Caucasian women fit a bell curve of normal distribution in which moderate drinking is the modal or most typical pattern. In lower income African American females, the distribution is flatter, with more nondrinkers and more heavy drinkers than moderate drinkers. Nondrinking is associated with women in middle age, and has a high correlation to church affiliation (Cahalan, Cisin, and Crossley 1969). Chapter 8 discusses considerations of ethnicity in treatment.

Self-Assessment

Counselors usually make assessments of self-image, self-esteem, and self-efficacy from their general observations of a client's presentation, affect, body language, and oral reports. Psychosocial assessment of female addicts should rate self-efficacy and self-esteem because powerlessness, shame, and stigma are more often a major concern for female than for male substance abusers. Personal history many reveal depression, common in female alcoholics, as antecedent to alcoholism, secondary to it, or antecedent to but worsened by it.

Treatment planning for female addicts needs to address trauma, abuse, shame, and self-efficacy as issues in their own right and in relapse prevention. Many women recovering from alcoholism and other addictions report women's groups as a setting where such issues can be addressed and links shown, and where they can build a positive image and identity of recovering womanhood. In later stages of treatment, they need to construct models of a positive occupational and social role, interacting with recovering and nonrecovering individuals.

Criminal Offenses

As is well documented, the vast proportion of crime is alcohol- and drug-related, and treatment reduces recidivism (Lipton 1995). Treatment of criminal offenders must not be cursory and must include a meaningful, long-term relapse-prevention component. Even where treatment has occurred in prison, continuing care upon release is a priority. Offenders are especially at risk for relapse. They are the archetypal "hot-house" plant, coming from a "total institution" setting and flung into a chaotic, overstimulating environment with multiple requirements, stressors, decisions, and lack of support, as well as the task of being responsible for themselves (CSAT 1993, vii). They must look for jobs with little but jail time on their résumés, and the stigma of "felon." They may have been involved in criminal activity and the criminal-justice system since adolescence, and never learned appropriate adult financial, occupational, and interpersonal skills. They need not so much a rehabilitation as a habilitation. Contrary to the common image of the offender as a hulking, snarling brute, the average offender who receives help from organizations such as The Fortune Society or Offender Aid and Restoration has a defeated, lost, and fragile quality. Such organizations generally provide or give a referral to vocational training, achievement of high school equivalency diplomas, addictions counseling, job-seeking skills, parenting skills, and child care for those attending program services. Many employ ex-offenders, which provides positive role-models for those who may feel destined to stay in the role of chronic recidivist.

Treatment and case management of an addicted offender require an integrated system. This involves the court, prison officials, probation and parole authorities, and the treatment network. Collaborative planning between criminal-justice and treatment systems can make an effective joint effort to treat addicted offenders (CSAT 1995). Drug courts, which are often the link between the systems, have been spreading from Florida, to Texas, and north.

There are many points of contact between the criminal-justice and addictions-treatment systems. Offenders who are addicts are processed in a variety of ways, at the judge's discretion. Factors in disposal of a criminal case by the judge include the offense and its severity; criminal history of the offender; evaluation and the recommendations made by prosecutors, special court staff, or external social-services agency; plea-bargaining efforts by attorneys for the defendant; and the options available in the area, such as the following:

1. Pretrial hearing, with charges dropped or delayed contingent on entry into treatment for substance abuse
2. Presentencing plea bargaining, with placement in a diversion or treatment program
3. Probation to a treatment program
4. Treatment in prison
5. Serving of sentence in a halfway house, day-reporting center, or therapeutic community
6. Parole contingent on entry into treatment

Although a large proportion of clients has always entered treatment through mandated referrals from the criminal justice system, the proportion grew much larger in the United States during the late 1990s because state and federal funding for addictions treatment has declined, as has the ability to seek reimbursement from managed-care entities and third-party payers. At the same time, criminal-justice funds have increased. Agencies began to scramble for government contracts to process offenders, and many either started new components for that purpose or shifted the overall focus of the agency. These system changes have implications for the development of addictions counselors. Many counselors who entered the profession as an extension of their own recovery have been dismayed that the offender population is less motivated to enter recovery than they had expected, and that their role in offender treatment amounts to noncharismatic case management or "babysitting" of clients. Although there are many excellent programs for addicted offenders, often adaptations of the therapeutic-community model, some privatized correctional behavioral health services have not met clinical standards to which addictions professionals are accustomed.

There are a very wide variety of subpopulations of addicts, beyond the scope of this text to cover. These include the homeless, veterans, clergy, prostitutes, celebrities, and the terminally ill. Treatment planning for most of these individuals calls for concurrent services such as financial and living skills training, child-welfare services and parenting skills, nutritional and medical attention, vocational and educational rehabilitation. Treatment planning can attempt to incorporate attention to the special needs of each of the subpopulations to which a client belongs, but all information about the client will not come at the onset. The treatment plan is a "living document" open to modification as more knowledge is available and as treatment progresses.[6]

---

[6] A large variety of free publications on treatment of addicted offenders are published by the Center for Substance Abuse Treatment, and are available from the National Clearinghouse for Alcohol and Drug Information (NCADI) in Rockville, MD.

References

APA (American Psychiatric Association). 1994. *Diagnostic and Statistical Manual*, 4th ed. (DSM-IV). Washington, DC: Author.

Allen, J.P., Eckardt, M. J., and Wallen, J. 1988. "Screening for Alcoholism: Techniques and Issues," *Public Health Reports* 103: 586-592.

Cahalan, D., I. H. Cisin, and H. M. Crossley. 1969. *American Drinking Practices*, Monograph no. 6. New Brunswick, NJ: Rutgers Center of Alcohol Studies.

Chiazuzzi, E. 1991. *Preventing Relapse in the Addictions: A Biopsychosocial Approach*. New York, Pergamon Press.

Cohen, J., and S. J. Levy. 1992. *The Mentally Ill Chemical Abuser: Whose Client?* New York: Lexington Books.

CSAT (Center for Substance Abuse Treatment). 1991. *Screening and Assessment for Alcohol and Other Drug Abuse in the Criminal Justice System*. Treatment Improvement Protocol, no. 7. Rockville, MD: Center for Substance Abuse Treatment, Substance Abuse and Mental Health Services Administration, U.S. Dept. of HHS.

CSAT (Center for Substance Abuse Treatment). 1993. *Screening and Assessment of Alcohol- and Other Drug-Abusing Adolescents*. Treatment Improvement Protocol, no. 3. Rockville, MD: Center for Substance Abuse Treatment, Substance Abuse and Mental Health Services Administration, U.S. Dept. of HHS.

CSAT (Center for Substance Abuse Treatment). 1993. *Relapse Prevention and the Substance-Abusing Criminal Offender*, Technical Assistance Publication no. 8. T. A. Gorski et al. Rockville, MD: Center for Substance Abuse Treatment, Substance Abuse and Mental Health Services Administration, U.S. Dept. of HHS.

CSAT (Center for Substance Abuse Treatment). 1994. *Assessment and Treatment of Patients with Coexisting Mental Illness and Alcohol and Drug Abuse*. Treatment Improvement Protocol, no. 9. Rockville, MD: Center for Substance Abuse Treatment, Substance Abuse and Mental Health Services Administration, U.S. Dept. of HHS.

CSAT (Center for Substance Abuse Treatment). 1994. *Combining Substance Abuse Treatment with Intermediate Sanctions in the Criminal Justice System.* Treatment Improvement Protocol, no. 12. Rockville, MD: Center for Substance Abuse Treatment, Substance Abuse and Mental Health Services Administration, U.S. Dept. of HHS.

CSAT (Center for Substance Abuse Treatment). 1995. *The Role and Status of Patient Placement Criteria in the Treatment of Substance Abuse.* Treatment Improvement Protocol, no. 13. Rockville, MD: Center for Substance Abuse Treatment, Substance Abuse and Mental Health Services Administration, U.S. Dept. of HHS.

CSAT (Center for Substance Abuse Treatment). 1995. *Planning for Alcohol and Other Drug Abuse Treatment for Adults in the Criminal Justice System.* G. Vigdal, ed. Technical Improvement Protocol, no. 17. Rockville, MD: Center for Substance Abuse Treatment, Substance Abuse and Mental Health Services Administration, U.S. Dept. of HHS.

CSAT (Center for Substance Abuse Treatment). 1996. *Counselor's Manual for Relapse Prevention with Chemically Addicted Offenders.* Technical Assistance Publication, no. 19. Rockville, MD: Center for Substance Abuse Treatment, Substance Abuse and Mental Health Services Administration, U.S. Dept. of HHS.

CSAT (Center for Substance Abuse Treatment). 1998. *Addiction Counselor Competencies: The Knowledge, Skills and Attitudes of Professional Practice.* Technical Assistance Publication, no. 21. Rockville, MD: Center for Substance Abuse Treatment, Substance Abuse and Mental Health Services Administration, U.S. Dept. of HHS.

CSAT (Center for Substance Abuse Treatment). 1997. *Substance Abuse Treatment and Domestic Violence.* Treatment Improvement Protocol Series no. 25. Rockville, MD: Center for Substance Abuse Treatment, Substance Abuse and Mental Health Services Administration, U.S. Dept. of HHS.

De Jong, P., and Miller, S. D. 1995. "How to Interview for Client Strengths." *Social Work*, 40, 6 (November): 729-736.

Doweiko, H. E. 1997. *Concepts of Chemical Dependency*, 3rd ed. Pacific Grove, CA: Brooks Cole.

Evans, K., and M. Sullivan. 1990. *Dual Diagnosis: Counseling the Mentally Ill Substance Abuser.* New York: Guilford Press.

Ewing, J. A. 1984. "Detecting Alcoholism: The CAGE Questionaire." *Journal of the American Medial Association* 252: 1905-1907.

Gorski, T., and Miller, M. 1982. *Counseling for Relapse Prevention.* Independence, MO: Herald House/Independence Press.

Hester, R. K., and Miller, R. M. ed. 1995. *Handbook of Alcoholism Treatment Approaches: Effective Alternatives,* 2nd ed. New York: Simon and Schuster.

Johnson, V. 1998. *I'll Quit Tomorrow.* New York: Harper and Row.

Kagle, J. D. 1991 *Social Work Records,* 2nd ed. Belmont, CA: Wadsworth.

Kinney, J. 1996. *Clinical Manual of Substance Abuse,* 2nd ed. St. Louis, MO: Mosby.

Kivlahan, D. R., et al. 1991. "Treatment Cost and Rehospitalization Rate in Schizophrenic Outpatients with a History of Substance Abuse." *Hospital and Community Psychiatry* 42, 609-614.

Krupnick, L. 1983. *Rx Intervention: Something That Works.* Palm Springs, CA: Plaintalking Press.

Lehman, A., C. P. Myers, and E. Corty. 1989. "Assessment and Classification of Patients with Psychiatric and Substance Abuse Syndromes." *Hospital and Community Psychiatry* 40: 1019-1025.

Lipton, D. S. 1995. "The Effectiveness of Treatment for Drug Abusers under Criminal Justice Supervision." *NIJ Research Report.* Washington, DC: U.S. Department of Justice, Office of Justice Programs, November.

Marlatt, G. A. and Gordon, J. R. 1985. *Relapse Prevention.* New York: Guilford Press.

Mejta, C. L., et al. (1994). "Approaches to Case Management with Substance-Abusing Populations," chap. 21 in *Addictions: Concepts and Strategies for Treatment.* J. A. Lewis, ed. Gaithersburg ed., MD: Aspen.

Miller, R. M. 1991. *Motivational Interviewing: Preparing People to Change Addictive Behavior.* New York: Guilford Press.

Merriam-Webster's Medical Desk Dictionary 1993. Springfield, MA: Merriam-Webster, Inc.

Myers, P. L. 1991. "Cult and Cult-Like Pathways out of Adolescent Chemical Dependency," in *Special Problems in Counseling the Chemically Dependent Adolescent*. E. E. Sweet, ed. New York: Haworth Press (originally appeared in *Journal of Adolescent Chemical Dependency* 1, no.4, 1991).

NIDA (National Institute on Drug Abuse). 1993a. *Diagnostic Sourcebook on Drug Abuse Research and Treatment*. NIH Pub. 93-3508. Rockville, MD: U. S. Dept of HHS.

NIDA (National Institute on Drug Abuse). 1993b. *Assessing Clients Needs Using the ASI: Resource Manual*. Pub. 93-3620. Rockville, MD: HHS NIH

Schuckit, M. A. 1973. "Alcohol and Sociopathy: Diagnostic Confusion" *Journal of Studies on Alcohol* 34, 157-164.

Stevens, S. J., and P. J. Gilder. 1994. "Therapeutic Communities: Substance Abuse Treatment of Women," in *Therapeutic Community: Advances in Research and Application*, F. M. Tims, G. DeLeon, and N. Jainchill, eds. NIDA Research Monograph series, no. 144, Rockville, MD: National Institute of Public Health, NIH, Public Health Service, US HHS.

Wilson, S. J. 1976. *Recording: Guidelines for Social Workers*. New York: Free Press.

6

Considering Client Populations

Introduction

Age, gender, sexual orientation, ethnicity, and mental illness can be associated with characteristic patterns of alcohol and drug use and misuse. Various combinations of an encyclopedic array of neurobiological, genetic, developmental, and environmental factors can predispose a person to substance abuse (Hanson and Venturelli 1998). This chapter provides a brief sketch of items to consider while assessing a client and before establishing the treatment plan. It does not substitute for a comprehensive description of drug use in all diverse groups, which is usually covered in one or more chapters of a text that addresses addictions (Hanson and Venturelli 1998). Counselors must be aware of risk factors and patterns of use, abuse, and abuse progression that are typical of demographic and cultural subgroups. In addition, these items *cannot* be used to create a grid of stereotypical expectations to which the clients will be fitted, or encouraged to conform. Rather, open-ended questions about these issues in the context of a supportive and empathic relationship should elicit information for psychosocial, addictive, and interpersonal assessment.

Age

Childhood

Addiction is culturally defined as an adult enterprise. The vast majority of addictions agencies do not admit individuals aged twelve or younger. Nevertheless, children do smoke cigarettes and marijuana, drink, and engage in inhalant abuse. Statistical patterns of substance abuse have inched downward into childhood and preadolescence in the 1980s and 1990s. Experimentation or casual use progresses and solidifies into a pattern of abuse especially among neglected, abused, or isolated children, and children suffering from undiagnosed and untreated learning or behavioral disabilities. The abuse of inhalants, vapors emitted by volatile substances such as solvents, glues, and correction fluids is a special issue among counselors working with the child and preadolescent population. Inhalant abuse is common among hungry and homeless children in a variety of nations from Central America to southern Asia as well as among children in inner-city districts of North America. Inhalant abuse among children is often associated with a total lack of nurturing family structure. The use of many other substances, such as tobacco and alcohol, are also motivated by a desire to augment status by appearing sophisticated and adult. Thus, their use can serve as a rite of passage. Admission to and participation in gangs are also often linked to drinking and drugging. When gang membership is seen as a logical self-protective strategy as well as a normative peer activity, prevention messages alone do not have much influence.

A general awareness of the typical developmental issues, conflicts, and stressors found in various age groups can facilitate assessment of critical issues facing clients.

Adolescence

Individuals from ages 13 to 20 are in a special risk period for use of alcohol and other drugs. Individual risk factors are compounded by the confluence of developmental conflicts and stressors that occur during adolescence, and the desire to try out symbols of adult freedom. It is imperative that developmental issues be assessed, especially conflicts in maturational tasks, independence, sex, romance, and intimacy (Filstead and Anderson 1983).

The clinical observations of Levine (1984) found adolescent substance abuse to be associated with a "developmental logjam" of unfaced dilemmas, which result in some combination of boredom, drift, malaise, inability to conceive of a future for themselves, social isolation, separation problems, meaninglessness, difficulty in achieving intimacy, and dissatisfaction with their own impulsive behaviors (28-38, 41). Attention-deficit hyperactivity disorder (ADHD) or other learning disabilities, depression, and family problems can aggravate this logjam (see the section "Attention-Deficit Hyperactivity Disorder" later in this chapter). Taking risks, rebelling, and abusing substances are often linked to adolescents' attempts to resolve these conflicts. Initial assessment of these issues is difficult when clients find these topics painful and threatening, cannot articulate them, and are slow to trust a counselor who is associated with disliked authority structures.

In addition, addictions counselors need to learn the skill of diagnostically differentiating the youth who is experimenting or using as a rite of passage, and the youth who is seriously abusing substances. On college campuses, the situation is complicated by an entrenched and ancient tradition of binge drinking. This practice remains fairly constant even as prevention programs make gains against use of cocaine and marijuana in college populations. Among high school and college-aged youth, heavy drinking is associated with a majority of driving fatalities, sexually transmitted diseases, academic failure, accidents, unwanted sexual encounters, violence, property damage, and insurance claims. Case-finding and appropriate referrals are difficult due to institutional denial, participation of adult role models in heavy drinking, campus tradition, and encapsulated subcultures of abuse in fraternity settings. Counselors must consider an appropriate level of care in referring an adolescent: Experimentation or casual use does not warrant referral into an intensive rehabilitation program. It is understandably difficult to convince students or their parents to accept an inpatient referral during the academic year. There is no shortage of role models of recovery for adults in addictions treatment, nor of subcultures of recovery (e.g., AA, NA, therapeutic communities, Smart Recovery). In the treatment of adolescents, however, one dilemma is the dearth of a recovery subculture. Even individual role models are relatively scarce, because adolescent substance abusers either mature out of addiction or, following treatment, tend to get on with their lives rather than remain in a self-help milieu. Substance-abusing adolescents are often in environments in which users set the tone and in which successful clean-and-sober adult role models are lacking. It is especially difficult for these young people to think through the consequences for their entire life, leave the "using society" (which may be the majority of their family and friends), and stay clean and sober. Some treatment programs have a group of graduates who have "made it," whom clients can trust and identify with, and who can give them hope and pointers on how to get there.

Experimentation with or abuse of substances is seldom the only problematic areas for adolescents. It is often part of a constellation of so-called acting-out behaviors. Other parts of the picture include depression, learning disabilities, suicidal ideation or gestures, truancy, DWI charges or convictions, history of family addictions, child abuse or molestation, vandalism, and petty (or not-so-petty) crimes. Counselors must beware of assumptions underlying assessment that lead to imagining a greater role for substance abuse in adolescents' problems than is actually the case. For example, the depressed, learning-disabled adolescent will not magically prosper when she stops using marijuana. Although depression and learning disabilities are worsened significantly and masked by chronic use of marijuana, eliminating the marijuana will not eliminate them as well. Failure to address such other issues jeopardizes recovery.

Adolescent treatment walks a fine line between treatment per se and prevention. It needs to capture their imaginations, excite them, and offer alternatives to using drugs. Programs that treat adolescents as a major component of their services need activities that

- are age-appropriate
- are attractive
- offer the opportunity to attain developmental milestones
- help them identify and reach some maturational goals such as obtaining a high school equivalency degree and acquiring occupational skills
- build a positive self-image.

These activities may be recreational, educational, vocational, artistic, journalistic, or athletic, depending on the needs of the client.

Some troubled and substance-abusing adolescents find an Outward Bound-type program helpful. Such programs are physically, socially, mentally, and emotionally challenging outdoor group adventures in a remote area (Gillis and Simpson 1994). However, because of costs, space availability, and the status of the client, Outward Bound is not appropriate to all adolescent addicts. Project Adventure incorporates many of the same features, but with minimal travel requirement. Local variations came into existence in many states during the 1990s, but their growth has been stymied by limited funding. Special sports programs that incorporate therapeutic elements and antidrug messages have also been successful in creating an alternative to subcultures of abuse. These programs are sponsored by local government, social-service agencies, the Police Athletic League, and community coalitions. An example is the Midnight Basketball Coalition programs, which originated in 1986 in Atlanta, Georgia, and now exist in a dozen cities.

The Middle-Aged and Elderly

Middle-aged and elderly are categories that cannot be delineated precisely. However, late middle age is often defined as age 55+, and senior citizens, or the elderly, often defined as 65+. Another pothole in the highway of life is late middle age and retirement, not so much a logjam as too few logs to stand on. The empty nest and the losses of body image, friends and family, and occupational role bring grief, regret, disappointment, loneliness, and isolation. Counselors must teach and facilitate processing of losses and encourage new involvements and initiatives. The EAP client in chapter 5, Mrs. Harris, was a widow approaching retirement, whose drinking went from social to abusive after her husband's death. Her Pentecostal church peers were by-and-large teetotalers who disapproved of her drinking alcohol; her shame isolated her from the church, which she longed to rejoin. In assessment, it is important to differentiate between a late-onset alcoholic as in the case of Mrs. Harris and an addict who has simply aged along with his or her long-time addiction. The late-onset addict is less deteriorated and less antisocial and has fewer coexisting problems than the long-term addict.

Assessment of an elderly client must be informed by diagnostic issues typical of this age group. These issues include the differentiation among symptoms of alcohol or illicit drug use, use of prescription and over-the-counter drugs, and any combination thereof (Figure 6.1). This is compounded by the fact that the elderly frequently are overmedicated and often self-medicate. The bodies of the elderly do not detoxify substances quickly, which results in high levels of psychoactive substances lingering in the blood and brain. Medical care for the elderly is often compartmentalized. More than one physician may be involved in prescribing medications and some seniors have difficulty keeping track of them. Possible overmedication or medication interactions are not always monitored adequately. Depression in the elderly can be generated or compounded by prescribed depressants and by alcohol use. Especially in this age group it is important to determine whether problems with memory and cognition are results of alcohol and illegal drugs, incorrect use of prescriptions, or senile dementia.

Figure 6.1 Screening Senior Citizens for Substance Abuse

What are the risk factors for seniors?

Problems, pain, and anxieties

Retirees sometimes feel the loss of a meaningful part to play in society, feelings of worthlessness and obsolescence, loss of an occupational identity, the loss of friends on the job, loss of earned income, stress of living on a fixed income, and boredom.

Children "leave the nest," parents have passed away, and people may feel lonely. The illness and deaths of family and friends create loss and grief, which may be difficult to bear.

People may feel disappointed when life expectations don't pan out.

Physical pain and fatigue often accompany the aging process, as well as stress and loss of body functions and skills.

Chronic illnesses are accompanied by restricted activity, pain, stress, and fear.

Possible reactions

Depression

Denial

Repression or restriction of feelings

Withdrawal from others

Use of alcohol or other drugs to "numb" or deny feelings

Medication problems

Losing track of prescriptions

Forgetting how much was taken

Seeing several physicians who prescribe

Overprescription of sedatives.

Other aspects of alcohol and other drug use

It is often hidden and private, not often in a bar or at a party.

It is often rapid in onset.

The effects are often worsened by use of prescribed medications and over-the-counter medications, which may contain sedating substances.

The effects of substance abuse may be hard to differentiate from memory and thinking problems of some elderly.

The effects are often compounded by decrease in liver function so that it becomes harder to eliminate substances from the body.

Older drinkers tend to attribute negative physical symptoms of drinking to aging.

Source: Courtesy of Essex County College Senior Alcohol and Drug Abuse Prevention Project, with support from the Newark Municipal Alliance.

Sexuality

Gender

Women are underrepresented in treatment in proportion to their numbers in the addict population, and programs addressing their special needs are also relatively few. A national survey by Johnston, Bachman, and O'Malley (Johnston et al.1996. 64-5) indicates that 22 percent of females report binge drinking (five drinks in a row in the last two weeks), compared to 43 percent of males; 23 percent of females report any illicit drug use during the past year, compared to 31 percent of males. When assessing a female client, it is important to explore relationships with significant others, support systems, impediments to treatment, and issues of abuse, shame, and stigma.

The degree to which an addicted woman associates with a chemically abusing spouse or boyfriend is an important factor in her patterns of use. Hser and colleagues (1987 a, b) found that women tend to stay with addicted males, perhaps participating in the drug use, whereas nonusing mates are more likely to abandoned addicted females. In addition, they found that the most important reason for first use and increase in use by women is an intimate relationship with a chemical abuser.

The degree of social support for entering treatment is significant. Females have much less support to enter treatment than do males. The variety of reasons include social stigma, the history of alcoholism as a men's disease, and denial of women's addictions (Beckman and Amaro 1986). Counselors must remember the distinction between social support and support to enter treatment. All kinds of helping, sympathizing, and supporting of an addict can amount to enabling or buffering the addict against the consequences of addiction, and keeping her or him away from treatment when that is an option. Alcoholism among women tends to be kept hidden in the house by both the drinker and her family. When questions are asked about a woman's functioning, answers are given in terms of fatigue, minor illness, or even depression. Men are more likely when drunk to get into public displays that eventually become noted in a police or hospital report. Statistics, therefore, tend to hide the proportion of female drinkers.

Homosexuals

Chemical abuse among homosexuals can be linked to their social status as outcast, stigmatized, and deviant, which contributes to pain and isolation and can lead to substance abuse. For many decades, the "gay bar" was a secret gathering place, the only setting where homosexuals could interact, be open about their sexuality, safely explore possible relationships, and be themselves. Gay Pride marches in the 1970s and 1980s in New York City featured many contingents that marched behind the banners of their bars. Although the bar scene continues to be important in the lives of many gays and lesbians, its continued importance as the critical locus of interaction is controversial (McNeese and DiNitto 1994, 195-7).

While the old stigmatized, outcast status has changed a great deal in recent decades, it is still true that a majority of homosexuals have suffered some form of ostracism, discrimination, or family rejection. Clinicians with competency in the area of gay and lesbian alcohol and drug use agree that treatment must provide a framework for the client not only to acknowledge sexual orientation, but also to explore unresolved sexual issues.

The Counselor, the journal of the National Association of Alcohol and Drug Counselors, published a special issue to focus on gay, bisexual, lesbian, and transgender (GBLT) issues. In it, Amico and Neisen (1997) stress that shame interferes with sobriety, and that counselors should create an environment that provides an opportunity to release shame and reclaim pride. It is not surprising that recovery and "coming out" often go hand in hand; a counselor's assessment should recognize that this wrenching period can be a time of increased risk of alcohol and other drug abuse. Addicted gays are an underserved population, according to Amico and Neisen, because of a spectrum of antigay attitudes in treatment agencies, ignorance of gay issues, or anxiety about gay issues.

Clients in the treatment facility are a microcosm of their culture, which, unfortunately, includes homophobia. One can imagine the stress and conflict of either concealing or acknowledging a homosexual orientation in group treatment. Yet it is far too glib simply to recommend referral to a facility that specializes in treating gays and lesbians. Given the fact that facilities specializing in treating homosexuals are few and far between, and reimbursement may be difficult, counselors would generally limit such special referrals to those whose recovery seriously requires it. Gay and lesbian AA, NA, and Al-Anon groups are more accessible, especially in medium-sized and large cities. Kus and Latkovich (1995) point out that some individuals prefer to start out in gay groups and then "come out" in regular groups, and others take the reverse route.[1]

Mentally Ill Chemical Abusers

One of the curiosities in the history of science is the separation of addiction and psychiatric disorders as fields of study and treatment. Contributing to this dilemma is that medicine has found alcoholics and other addicts difficult to treat, uncooperative, and unremunerative, and that addictions

---

[1] A valuable resource is the National Association of Lesbian and Gay Alcoholism Professionals (NALGAP), located in New York City (see Finnegan and McNally 1995).

treatment began as an outgrowth of self-help ideologies. Those who qualify for diagnoses in both areas (the "dual-diagnosis" clients) suffer from the division of thought and labor. Training and education of mental-health and addictions personnel often gives short shrift to the other wing of the behavioral universe. Problems of the mentally ill chemical abuser are interpreted too often according to a single, limited perspective. Many individuals in substance-abuse treatment have an undiagnosed, overlooked, or untreated psychiatric problem. The opposite is also true: "Mental patients" are often abusers of psychoactive substances, seven to ten times more often than those not suffering from mental disorders (Kivlahan et al. 1991)

Mentally ill chemical abusers are commonly referred to by the acronym MICA, the convention we follow in this text. Other acronyms include CAMI (chemically abusing mentally ill) and MISA (mentally ill substance abuser).

Among MICAs with severe psychiatric disorders, there are high rates of suicide and suicidality, homelessness, legal and medical problems, and longer and more frequent hospitalizations (Baker 1991). Because it is uncommon for simultaneous and effective attention to be paid to all of their many, varied, and complex needs (Cohen and Levy 1992), MICAs receive fewer services than other client populations in proportion to their needs. MICAs belong to two stigmatized social categories. They are underdiagnosed, undertreated, and often dumped from one system to another, or discharged early from treatment as soon as they have been stabilized for the moment. Their experience of treatment is less successful than that of single-diagnosis clients. Where they do receive treatment for both psychiatric and addictive disorders, it is often sequential (first for one disorder, then the other) or parallel treatment (ping-pong style between units and services), rather than in a single integrated model or facility. The chronic, cyclic nature of symptoms, poor prognoses, noncompliance, behavioral disorganization of clients, and the limited nature of goals in treatment are frustrating to helping professionals.

In the 1990s the behavioral health field increasingly recognized and began to plan for integrated case management and treatment of MICA clients (Baker 1991; Mueser et al. 1998). The degree to which treatment models are integrated, however, still varies greatly among states, counties, and municipalities. On the down side, cost-containment and managed-care trends tend to cause MICAs to be released from the treatment system before sufficient time has elapsed to address or even properly assess their problems. Funding for inpatient treatment has been cut continuously since the 1960s without the provision of adequate community support systems.

The mentally ill in the criminal-justice system outnumber those in state hospitals by three to one. In the private sector, although employer funding for employees' general health services dropped 7.4% from 1988 to 1997, funding for mental-health and substance-abuse benefits was 54.1% (Kennedy 1999; Winerip 1999).

Myriads of Dual Diagnoses

Given the range and severity both of addictive and psychiatric phenomena, there are a near-infinite variety of combined syndromes. In terms of the primacy of addiction or psychiatric illness, they range from those who suffer primarily from psychiatric disorders and who "self-medicate" with alcohol or illegal drugs, through complex cases in which psychiatric and addictive symptoms are hard to tease apart, to addicts whose chemical use causes organic brain syndromes such as stimulant psychoses, alcoholic hallucinosis, or psychotic conditions associated with the use of hallucinogens.

It is almost always the case that unless the chemical-dependency counselor is also credentialed in psychiatric social work, psychiatric nursing, or medicine, he or she is expressly denied the role of diagnosing a client. Nevertheless, because the counselor must treat the chemical abuse and dependency of persons suffering from other psychiatric conditions, he or she must be aware of behavior that suggests serious psychiatric disorder in order to alert the agency to the necessity of psychiatric consultation.

Issues of Medication

Because the counselor may be counseling clients who are taking medications prescribed for psychiatric conditions, he or she must be familiar with the categories and names of commonly prescribed medications (see table 6.1). It is important to distinguish antipsychotic, antimanic, or antidepressant medications from drugs of abuse. Although some "garbage head" abusers or experimenting teenagers might take a Prozac or a Haldol, drugs in these categories are rarely abused. Some recovering persons distrust psychiatric medications for a variety of reasons: they have been misdiagnosed as psychotic and misprescribed these medications; they have been given major tranquilizers as a behavioral control strategy (e.g., in prison); they have a drug-free philosophy; or the medications have undesirable side effects. Yet these drugs are frequently lifesavers, and permit the social integration of the severely disabled.

Table 6.1 Common Psychiatric and Psychotheraputic Medications

Category	Brand Name	Generic Name
ANTIDEPRESSANTS		
Monoamine oxidase inhibitors (MAOI)	Parnate	Tranylcypromine sulfate
Tricyclics	Norpramin	Desipramine
	Tofranil	Imipramine
Selective serotonin reuptake inhibitors (SSRI)[1]	Effexor	Venalfaxine
	Paxil	Paroxetine
	Prozac	Fluoxetine
	Zoloft	Sertraline
Miscellaneous	Desyrel	Trazodone
	Wellbutrin	Buproprion
ANTIMANICS[2]	Depakene, Depakote	Valproic acid
	Eskalith, Lithobid, Lithonate, Lithotab	Lithium carbonate
	Tegretol	Carbamazepine
ANTIPSYCHOTICS[2]		
Phenothiazines	Stelazine	Trifluoperazine
	Thorazine	Chlorpromazine
Other	Haldol	Halperidol
	Navane	Thiothixene
	Prolixin	Fluphenazine
Newest (atypical)[4]	Clozaril	Clozepine
	Loxitane	Loxepine
	Risperdal	Risperidone
	Zyprexa	Olanzapine
SEDATIVE-HYPNOTICS		
Benzodiazepines[5]	Ativan	Lorazepam
	Dalmane	Flurazepam
	Halcion	Triazolam
	Librium	Clordiazcpoxide
	Rohypnol	Flunitrazepam
	Tranxene	Clorazepate
	Valium	Diazepam
	Xanax	Alprazolam
Barbiturates[6]	Butisol	Butabarbital
	Nebutal	Pentobarbital
	Seconal	Secobarbital

Table 6.1 cont.

Category	Brand Name	Generic Name
Barbiturate-like	Doriden	Glutethimide[7]
		Chloral hydrate
	Placidyl	Ethchorvynol
	Quaalude	Methaqalone
Antianxiety[8]	Ambien	Zolpidem tartarate
	BuSpar	Buspirone
OPIOIDS[9]	Demerol	Meperidine
	Dilaudid	Hydromorphone
	Percocet, Percodan	Oxycodone
	Roxanol	Morphine
Fentanyl, fentanyl-like	Alfenta	Alfentanyl
	Darvocet, Darvon	Propoxephone
	Sublimaze Duragesic	Fentanyl
	Sufenta	Sufentanil
	In various compounds	Codeine
STIMULANTS[10]		
Amphetamines	Cylert	Pemolin
	Dexedrine	Dextroamphetamine
	Desoxyn	Methamphetamine
	Ritalin	Methylphenidate
Amphetamine-like	In appetite suppressants	Phenmetrazine
		Phendimetrazine
Sympathomimetics[11]	In OTCs for cold, flu, allergy	Pseudoephedrine
		Phyloproponalomine
		Aminophylline
		Theophylline

1. SSRI antidepressants have fewer side effects and take effect more quickly than MAOIs.
2. For treatment of bipolar disorder
3. For treatment of schizophrenia
4. Have fewer side effects and help with apathy and avolition
5. Commonly prescribed for insomnia and anxiety; high potential for abuse
6. Narrow window between effective and lethal doses
7. Commonly combined with codeine as a substitute for heroin, and known as "C&C," "hits," or "loads"
8. A relatively low potential for abuse
9. Legitimate for control of pain, but potential for abuse and addiction; frequently sought as substitutes for heroin
10. Prescribed for ADHD and weight loss, and as decongestants and bronchodilators
11. Found often in combination with antihistamines and non-narcotic pain relievers (ibuprofen, aspirin, acetaminophen)

Diagnostic Issues

Clients arrive for treatment with any of a number of prior diagnoses, usually according to the categorization system in the *Diagnostic and Statistical Manual of Mental Disorders*, fourth edition, or *DSM-IV* (APA, 1994). The DSM is a human, multicommittee attempt at comprehensive categorization or taxonomy of mental disorders. It is a guide to systematic diagnosis and classification of clients. It does not pretend to substitute for, nor does it espouse a theory of mental disorders. It does not explain why someone is schizophrenic, or kleptomaniac, or attention-deficited. The categories are not "basic" underlying conditions, but terms found useful over the years that have some discrete validity about them in that they describe recurring clusters of symptoms. Some diagnoses may be symptoms of others, or they may be ideal types rarely found in nature. Some are more discrete than others: The disorganized schizophrenic or the bipolar mood disorder are fairly clear biologically based brain disorders, almost as clear as "strep" throat or a broken leg. Why someone is a "pathological gambler" or an "avoidant personality" is less clear and perhaps reflective of some deeper, as yet unfathomed syndrome or imbalance.

Misdiagnosis can occur in psychiatry even without the complicating factors of addiction. In a survey of bipolar members of a national support organization for depressive and manic-depressive patients (Lish et al. 1994), three-quarters of respondents stated it had taken an average of eight years to get a correct diagnosis. The similarities of psychiatric and addictive phenomena outlined in table 6.2, the fragmentation of the behavioral health fields, and the spotty interaction of MICA clients with the heathcare system make it all but inevitable that MICA clients will be underdiagnosed and misdiagnosed. To establish a valid psychiatric diagnosis, the symptoms must manifest long after intoxication has abated.

Table 6.2 Similarities of Addictive and Psychiatric Phenomena

Drug Syndromes	can be confused with	Psychiatric Syndromes
High dosage amphetamines		Paranoid schizophrenia
Chronic cocaine use		Paranoid schizophrenia
Cocaine withdrawal		Major depression
PCP overdose		Schizophrenia
Cocaine intoxication		Mania

Alcohol and other drug abuse (AODA) and psychiatric symptoms (PS) can interact in the following ways:

1. AODA may prompt the emergence or re-emergence of PS.
2. AODA may worsen pre-existing PS.
3. AODA may ameliorate, dampen, hide, mask, or disguise PS
4. AODA may mimic PS.
5. Cessation of AODA following development of tolerance or dependence results in a withdrawal syndrome that may mimic psychiatric symptoms.
6. PS must be distinguished from denial, resistance, and lack of motivation associated with AODA.
7. PS increases the risk of AODA.
8. Side effects of antipsychotic medications (i.e., sedation, involuntary physical movements) may be mistaken for symptoms of either PS or AODA.
9. Relative primacy and severity of PS and AODA symptoms may wax and wane, diminish, or re-emerge. Case management functions such as screening, assessment, and treatment planning are ongoing with MICA clients.

For example, one cannot take as evidence of psychosis the paranoia of an active crack addict, the hallucinations of an active LSD or PCP user, or the fevered imaginings of a client in the throes of delirium tremens. In 1987 such misdiagnoses resulted in an inpatient psychiatric unit in Brooklyn, New York, being filled with more "paranoid schizophrenics" than might be found in the state of Texas. This was due to the newness of crack cocaine, which was epidemic at the time, and the unfamiliarity with the symptoms of acute cocaine intoxication and abuse by psychiatric staff who had been trained abroad.

A factor that confounds assessment is that in MICAs substance use may mask pathology, numb its sharpest points, exacerbate it, or simultaneously improve and worsen different symptoms. Depressants blunt the mania of the bipolar client but drive the depressed deeper down. Alcohol or marijuana is the drug of choice of some schizophrenics. Marijuana soothes anxieties and holds demons at bay, without the agitation of alcoholic hangovers and withdrawal; yet alcohol and marijuana make cognition and memory all the more fuzzy. Crack and "angel dust" (PCP) are the absolutely worst things for schizophrenic, paranoid, and violence-prone people. Within the MICA treatment community, there is considerable controversy about how long to wait with a clean-and-sober client in order to determine whether his or her symptoms constitute a "real" psychiatric problem (Evans and Sullivan 1990, 58-9). With today's short-term treatment limits, it may be next to impossible to make such a determination.

The MICA client population presents several specific treatment problems:

- Instead of feeling better after detoxification, as the nonpsychiatric alcoholic does, the self-medicating MICA client may feel the full force of his or her schizophrenic, PTSD, or other symptoms.

- A MICA client may focus on psychiatric problems while in addictions treatment, but explain his or her problems in terms of drugs while with the mental-health professional. With such interchangeable or free-floating denial, both conditions may be denied (Doweiko 1997, 275).

- To the MICA client, chemical use is the means of coping with a devastating mental affliction. Chemicals seem to provide some sense of control, even though the underlying syndrome is not addressed, or is worsened. Counselors must recognize and empathetically reflect these motives if a treatment alliance is to be made.

- Most categories of MICA are quite fragile; traditional confrontational methods would not be appropriate (Evans and Sullivan 1990, 30).

Schizophrenia

Schizophrenia is a biologically based brain disorder. Like cancer, it is not just one well-defined disease. Schizophrenia results from some combination of inherited neurological vulnerability, and any of a number of external risk factors, including some in utero (usually second-trimester) environmental stressors (Andreasen 1999).

Identical (monozygotic) twins have a concordance rate of 30 percent to 50 percent for schizophrenia. This shows that schizophrenia is in part based on an inherited predisposition or vulnerability. Starting in the late 1980s, structural differences in the brains of schizophrenics were demonstrated. These observations also applied to twin studies. That is, where one identical twin is schizophrenic, there are significant differences in the brain structures of the two (Andreasen et al. 1990; Barta et al. 1990; Shenton et al. 1992; Suddath et al. 1990), and even subtle differences in fingerprints (Mellor 1992). However, if schizophrenia were based totally on genetics, identical twins would always be both schizophrenic, or not. Family history is probably a necessary factor in a majority of cases, but not a sufficient explanation. A variety of pregnancy, delivery, and perinatal problems have also been implicated, which may include nutritional problems and viruses. A greater incidence of schizophrenia has been found in influenza epidemics, even among those without a family history of schizophrenia (O'Callaghan,

Gibson, et al. 1991; O'Callaghan, Sham, et al. 1991). Schizophrenia, then, is a neurodevelopmental disorder with variations in etiology to the extent that genetics or environmental insults are involved.

Schizophrenia has an age of onset usually between 16 and 23 years. The major symptoms of schizophrenia include

- delusions (distortions of inferential thinking). One common set of delusions is those in which unrealistic associations are made between events in the world and the client. An example might be that a person seen on television is perceived to be talking to or about the schizophrenic client. Such delusions are called "ideas of reference." They include but are not limited to paranoid persecutorial delusions.
- major perceptual distortions (hallucinations), which are more likely to be auditory than visual in schizophrenic patients.
- disorganized speech, thought, and behavior.
- flat affect (restricted range and intensity of emotional expression), affect that is incongruous to the situation, and apathy or avolition.
- other neurocognitive deficits such as difficulty in concentrating, sensory overload, and difficulty in sorting, integrating, organizing, and responding to sensations and information.

Schizophrenia is *not* caused by bad parenting, disordered family communication, or mothers who send double messages. Family members of schizophrenics have no more role in creating this disease than they do in cases of multiple sclerosis or Alzheimer's disease among their relatives. Neither is it caused by the surfacing of unconscious and unbearable thoughts or feelings, the alienation of modern society, or traumatic losses. Finally, abuse of alcohol or other drugs can cause any number of emotional or mental problems, but not schizophrenia proper.

The treatment of schizophrenia involves antipsychotic medications (also known as neuroleptics or major tranquilizers), which can reduce greatly the severity of psychotic symptoms such as hallucinations and bizarre behavior. Medications do not cure this brain disease, and some have side effects such as tremors, twitching, and tics. Psychiatrists call such behaviors extrapyramidal symptoms.

In addition to medication, schizophrenic MICA clients and their families require education on the nature of their conditions, as well as supportive case management, which may include monitoring medications, supportive group apartment programs, day treatment programs, occupational training, and programs to train clients in activities of daily living. Formulating or carrying out a treatment plan with a disorganized addicted schizophrenic is obviously more difficult than with ordinary addicts.

Confrontive treatment and "tough-love" forms of intervention are not recommended for this population (Loneck and Way 1997). The simple and concrete nature of twelve-step slogans and suggestions, and the non-confrontive and nonjudgmental quality of Alcoholics Anonymous and Narcotics Anonymous make these groups a congenial environment for many MICA clients. Supportive group therapy and topical groups that focus on medication or daily living skills are also useful components of a MICA program. However, not all AA/NA members and groups are sophisticated as to the necessity for antipsychotic medications. In some areas, specialized "double-trouble" groups, such as Dual Diagnosis Anonymous groups, exist.

Mood Disorders

The two overall categories of mood disorders are depression and bipolar disorder (manic-depression), which manifests in unusual swings or fluctuations between extremes of mood. Depression must be differentiated from simple exhaustion, normal grief, thyroid disease, dementias, and the "crash" at the end of a stimulant "binge." Although depression itself is broken down into dysthymia (formerly neurotic depression), which is the relatively mild variety, and major depression, there is a continuum of pathology, the true nature of which may be masked or exaggerated when presented to a counseling professional. Depression is a complex phenomenon, and each depressed client probably suffers from a unique mix of etiological variables, which may include

- biochemical predisposition, which often has a genetic basis
- biological stressors such as fatigue and pain
- cognitive and behavioral factors such as lack of self-efficacy, learned helplessness, and problematic thinking patterns and beliefs (see table 6.3)
- unresolved, impacted grief and anger
- interpersonal factors such as lack of support systems and poor interpersonal skills, which lead to isolation
- depressants such as alcohol, barbiturates, or benzodiazepines

Antidepressant medications are often successful in the alleviation of severe depression. These medications are not stimulants, and may require several weeks to take effect. The client may also require trials of various antidepressants before the most efficacious drug is identified. The vast majority of individuals treated for severe depression are now prescribed medications belonging to the SSRI category (see table 6.1). Varieties of talk therapy are also helpful in the resolution of emotional, cognitive, and behavioral aspects of depression.

Table 6.3 Depressive Thinking Patterns

Dichotomous thinking such as "all-or-none" self-statements
Awfulizing or catastrophizing
Jumping to conclusions, especially negative extrapolations and expectations
"Should" or "must" statements, demandingness
Self-referential guilty, codependent thinking
Feeling helpless, powerless
Believing that one cannot tolerate frustrations, anxieties, or pain
Overgeneralizing about failures

Source: Summarized from the work of Aaron Beck, Albert Ellis, and others.

Bipolar (manic-depressive) affective disorder is based on one or more biochemical vulnerabilities and can be triggered by trauma, substance abuse, fatigue, or stress. In the manic phase of the disorder, thoughts race and tend toward grandiosity, behavior is reckless, and energy is boundless. Sooner or later the patient "crashes" into a phase of depression. There are several subtypes of bipolar disorder with which the counselor should become acquainted. At least one-half of people with this disorder go on to substance-abuse syndromes, and are at great risk for suicidal attempts. The simple chemical lithium carbonate enables many to stabilize their mood swings, as do a number of medications first used as anticonvulsants.

Case in Point

Ups and Downs

Mr. K., a middle manager at an accounting firm, burst into an office, perched on a desk, and began to demonstrate his karate techniques. He described his plans to enroll in medical as well as law school, and his activities as a director of motion pictures. Two weeks later, his demeanor was totally different: His speech was slowed, his affect dejected, and his gaze averted. Mr. K. was put on medical leave and successfully referred into psychiatric treatment. He was correctly diagnosed as having bipolar mood disorder. His mood was stabilized through a course of lithium carbonate, and he returned to work in three months. His medication (lithium carbonate) is monitored carefully because it has a very narrow therapeutic index, that is, a small window between ineffective and toxic. He also attends a support for people who have bipolar disorder.

Personality Disorders

Chemical abusers often have diagnoses that fit the category of personality disorders (formerly called character disorders). In the listing of diagnoses in the *DSM-IV*, personality disorders are coded separately as Axis II, as if they are on a separate dimension. In view of spatial limitations, this discussion addresses only the most common personality disorders diagnosed among chemical abusers—antisocial personality disorder (ASPD) and borderline personality disorder (BPD).

Antisocial Personality Disorder

Antisocial personality disorder (*DSM-IV* 301.7), also referred to as sociopathy, may be diagnosed only in individuals who are at least 18 years old, who manifest a "pervasive pattern of disregard for and violations of the rights of others, as indicated by three or more of the following: unlawful behaviors, deceitfulness, impulsivity, irritability and aggressiveness, reckless disregard for safety, consistent irresponsibility, lack of remorse" (APA 1994, 645-50). Addict sociopathy is a complex phenomenon, and the diagnosis of addicts as sociopaths raises more issues than it settles (Gerstley et al. 1990). It is important to avoid describing social problems in psychiatric terms. Clients who grew up in addictive family environments probably lacked proper role models and had inadequate or abusive parenting, and thus are insufficiently socialized or habilitated. Others turn to crime for lack of job skills or economic opportunity. Addicts especially may be incapable of sustaining regular employment, and turn to criminal behavior to raise funds for survival needs and drugs. Other addicts participate in fighting, vandalism, stealing, and unwanted sexual behavior while intoxicated, which can also appear as antisocial behavior.

A quarter century ago, addictions researcher Marc Schuckit differentiated sociopathy proper, which precedes alcoholism, from "secondary sociopathy" of the alcoholic (Schuckit 1973). The *DSM-IV* offers guidelines on this issue of differential diagnosis, stating that the diagnosis of ASPD is not made unless signs were also present in childhood. It also states that the diagnosis may be misapplied to urban settings where "seemingly antisocial behavior may be part of a protective survival strategy" (647). However, if both substance abuse and antisocial behavior began in childhood, the client may be diagnosed as suffering from both a substance-related disorder and antisocial personality disorder, "even though some antisocial acts may be a consequence of the substance-related disorder" (648-9). To complicate the picture, both sociopathy and substance abuse are linked to other disorders. It is mentioned, almost as an aside, that the likelihood of developing ASPD is increased when there is early onset of attention-deficit hyperactivity disorder, or ADHD (647). Many individuals who have ADHD and/or periodic depression find it difficult to attain or sustain employment and drift into extralegal or manipulative means of survival. Such individuals are also at risk for substance-abuse disorders.

Counselors should pay attention to one of the trademark features of the true, early onset sociopath: "lack of remorse, as indicated by being indifferent to or rationalizing having hurt, mistreated, or stolen from another" (APA 1994, 645-50). People who have ADHD and/or are substance abusers who act in ways verging on the sociopathic are less likely than a true sociopath to be conscienceless about predation against members of their families. Crack addicts are portrayed in the media as engaging in horrific abuse and neglect of their own families, yet numerous recovering crack cocaine addicts are truly remorseful about the effects of their addictions on their families. Also, some professionals falsely assume that a client who has multiple convictions or who has been incarcerated for long periods of time is a hardened sociopath not amenable to treatment for personality disorder. Yet many clients, once freed from the matrix of extralegal economic systems, subcultures of drug abuse, and the prison environment, are rehabilitated in offender programs within a frame of time that suggests that their core personality traits are not those of a basic sociopath.

The true antisocial personality is difficult to engage in chemical-dependency treatment. He or she is likely to feign insight and personal change to escape sanctions and mandates of the criminal-justice system. Group treatment and therapeutic milieux (e.g., application of the therapeutic-community model to addicted offenders) are more likely to address underlying sociopathy than is individual counseling.

Borderline Personality Disorder

In popular parlance, a "borderline" often refers to someone on the edge of insanity. But the borderline personality disorder (BPD) is not a point on a continuum from normality to insanity or from neurosis to psychosis, but a separate entity entirely. Most borderlines represent a "stable instability," a severe disturbance in personality development and integration with a distinct cluster of symptoms. Many authors and schools of thought have contended with the borderline personality; in the universe of possibilities, each major author has delimited a slightly, or more than slightly, different subset of the psychiatrically disordered (Stone 1986, 492).

According to the *DSM-IV*, borderline personality disorder (301.83) is marked by a "pervasive pattern of interpersonal relationships, self-image, and affects, and marked impulsivity" (APA 650). Clients with borderline personality disorders are intense and unstable. They also have sudden, dramatic, or impulsive shifts in occupational or educational goals.

Clients with BPD often engage in impulsive, dangerous behaviors in the areas of sexuality, substance abuse, and suicidality. Borderline chemical abusers vary tremendously along the Global Assessment of Functioning, or GAF, scale (O'Connell 1988), ranging from those with stable jobs and relationships to those who are severely self-destructive and who have psychotic episodes, often triggered by substance abuse, that require hospitalizations.

According to the neopsychoanalytic object-relations theorist Otto Kernberg (1975), the client with BPD "splits" contradictory ego states: He or she may seem to like and idealize someone one day, but hate and devalue the same person the next day. To make this work, the client also uses the mechanism of denial, manifesting an "emotional amnesia" about the preceding attitude or feeling. The client may switch from the "all-good" evaluation to the "all-bad" one when an individual cannot meet all of his or her considerable needs.

Many modern psychiatric authorities agree that BPD has no single origin (Gabbard 1995). Some researchers (Akiskal et al. 1985) have concluded that the preponderance of biologically based problems among borderline diagnoses (affective disorders, attention deficit, substance abuse) warrant removing it from the realm of "personality" problems and the *DSM-IV* Axis II. Still, despite its origins, it describes a type or level of personality functioning familiar to many clinicians.

There are a variety of possibilities to consider when confronted with a diagnosis of borderline personality disorder. The borderline personality can be an adaptation to any combination of mood disorder, ADHD, or chemical dependency.

Chemical dependency (CD) can appear as a borderline personality disorder. Alcoholic mood swings, alcoholic amnesia, "blackouts," impulsive behavior while intoxicated, and massive use of denial and confabulation to construct an account of this chaotic, out-of-control situation can present a clinical picture not unlike that described as BPD. At the very least, BPD can contribute to chemical abuse and dependency as a result of the need to self-medicate, relax, and numb pain.

Many problems of clients with BPD may be symptoms of mood disorders. People who are depressed may manifest extreme irritability and flashes of hostility, coloring of thought, rationalizing, or confabulating. Clients may also receive a diagnosis of major depression or dysthymia on Axis I and a diagnosis of BPD on Axis II, and be intricately bound up with chemical use and abuse as well.

The experiences of the mentally ill addict contribute to a difficult relationship with counselors. There may be a long and conflicted relationship with authority figures in the criminal- justice or social-services systems.

The counseling experience in early recovery may release a flood of unmet or untapped emotional needs, which creates a feeling of vulnerability and helplessness. It is natural to defend against this by denying the feelings and by devaluing or attacking the counselor

Chemical abuse can be a "keystone" in the archway of borderline personality. Sobriety can afford the opportunity to grow and heal. Indeed, to avoid relapse, clients and counselors must address previously masked, powerful emotions, painful anxieties and conflicts.

Post-Traumatic Stress Disorder

For more than a century, it has been observed that severe trauma (e.g., a train wreck, a wartime massacre, rape, child neglect, and spousal abuse) can take its toll in ways that persist long after the event (Young 1995). The combined result has been named post-traumatic stress disorder (PTSD). The major symptom clusters of PTSD involve re-experiencing the trauma (sometimes called having flashbacks), persistent arousal (insomnia, rage, hypervigilance, startle response), and numbing, avoidance, and detachment (APA 1994: 424-9). In addition to experiential causes, a neurobiological basis for PTSD has been described (Krystal et al. 1991; van der Kolk 1991).

Many major theoretical writings on PTSD do not delve into its connections with abuse of alcohol or other drugs. Nevertheless, the two conditions often coexist; sufferers of both have the need to calm or numb themselves (Bremner et al. 1996). Some treatment programs that do deal with both conditions switch addicted PTSD clients from their drugs of choice to legal, prescribed medications such as the benzodiazepines (if these are not already their drug of choice), then wean them off medications as anxiety abates in treatment. Although the classic PTSD client is a veteran, many other populations suffer. For example, a large proportion of addicted prostitutes suffer from PTSD, being victims of rape and violence perpetrated by clients as well as pimps. Herman (1992) feels that PTSD underlies many other conditions, such as the borderline personality. Others (Young 1995) caution against overdiagnosing the disorder.

Attention-Deficit Hyperactivity Disorder

Attention-deficit hyperactivity disorder is a genetically based neurological disability. Although it is thought of as a childhood learning disability, it affects many aspects of functioning and often persists in some form into adulthood. ADHD is marked by inattention, disorganization, distractibility, impulsivity, and inability to concentrate, sustain, and follow through on efforts. There may also be motor hyperactivity and "fidgetiness" (APA 1994 78-85), which are really less of a disability than the other features. Although ADHD varies in its severity, it often results in impaired educational and career efforts (Kelly and Raimundo 1995; Wender 1986). This, together with the relationship problems and social rejection experienced by many ADHD sufferers, may result in depression, self-esteem and self-efficacy problems—typical risk factors for chemical abuse (Biederman et al. 1995; Horner and Scheibe 1997). Added to this is the need to damp down (i.e., self-medicate) "high-strung," frustration-intolerant, hot-tempered, anxious, and sometimes insomniac temperamental qualities.

A majority of clients with ADHD report some, even significant, help from medications, including (paradoxically) stimulants such as Ritalin (methylphenidate) and antidepressants such as Nopramin (desipramine). Support groups are often beneficial. Clients with ADHD badly need to learn about their condition, to reduce guilt and shame, to learn drug-free coping strategies, and to educate their families, teachers, and peers.

The client with ADHD often has a history of chaotic and unstable relationships, which were based in impulsivity and mood swings. In addition, having experienced pervasive relationship failures, even including childhood scapegoating, rejection, and abuse, the ADHD client may be tremendously ambivalent about relationships. This is reminiscent of the borderline personality discussed above, which makes diagnosis challenging. When the individual is also a chemical abuser, it may be difficult indeed to untangle the skein of behaviors.

There is tremendous variation in approaches to diagnosis of ADHD. In some areas it appears that ADHD is underdiagnosed, yet parent groups in some parts of the United States claim that ADHD is overdiagnosed and stimulant medications are overprescribed. Addictions educators occasionally encounter bright, recovering students with undiagnosed ADHD or other learning disabilities.

References

Akiskal, H. S., et al. 1986. "Borderline: An Adjective in Search of a Noun," in *Essential Papers on Borderline Disorders*, M. H. Stone, ed. New York: New York University Press.

Amico, J., and J. Neisen. 1997. "Sharing the Secret: The Need for Gay-Specific Treatment." *The Counselor* 5, 3:12-5.

Andreasen, N. C. 1999. "Understanding the Causes of Schizophrenia." *New England Journal of Medicine* 340, 8 (25 February): 645-7.

Andreasen, N. C., et al. 1990. "Ventricular Enlargement in Schizophrenia Evaluated with Computer Tomographic Scanning: Effects of Gender, Age, and Stage of Illness." *Archives of General Psychiatry*, 47, 11 (November): 1008-15.

APA (American Psychiatric Association). 1994. *Diagnostic and Statistical Manual of Mental Disorders*, 4th ed. (DSM-IV). Washington, DC: Author.

Baker, F. 1991. *Coordination of Alcohol, Drug Abuse, and Mental Health Services*. Center for Substance Abuse Treatment Technical Assistance Pub. 4, Rockville, MD: U.S. DHHS, Substance Abuse and Mental Health Services Administration.

Barta, P. E., et al. 1990. "Auditory Hallucinations and Smaller Superior Temporal Gyral Volume in Schizophrenia." *American Journal of Psychiatry* 147: 1457-62.

Beckman, L.J., and H. Amaro. 1986. "Personal and Social Difficulties Faced by Women and Men Entering Alcoholism Treatment." *Journal of Studies on Alcohol* 47:135-45.

Biederman, J., et al. 1995. "The Psychoactive Substance Use Disorder in Adults with Attention Deficit Hyperactivity Disorder: Effect of ADD and Comorbidity." *American Journal of Psychiatry* 152: 1652-58.

Bremner, J. D., et al. 1996. "Chronic PTSD in Vietnam Combat Veterans: Course of Illness and Substance Abuse." *American Journal of Psychiatry* 153, 3: 369-75.

Cohen, J., and S. J. Levy. 1992. *The Mentally Ill Chemical Abuser*. New York: Lexington Books.

Doweiko, H. E. 1997. *Concepts of Chemical Dependency*, 3rd ed. Pacific Grove, CA: Brooks/Cole.

Evans, K., and M. Sullivan. 1990. *Dual Diagnosis: Counseling the Mentally Ill Substance Abuser*. New York: Guilford Press.

Filstead, W. J., C. L. Anderson. 1983. "Conceptual and Clinical Issues in the Treatment of Adolescent Alcohol and Substance Misusers," in *Adolescent Substance Abuse*. R. Isralowitz and M. Singer, ed. New York: Haworth Press.

Finnegan, D., and E. McNally. 1995. "The National Association of Lesbian and Gay Alcoholism Professionals: A Retrospective," in *Addiction and Recovery in Gay and Lesbian Persons*. R.J. Kus, ed. New York: Harrington Park Press (Haworth Press). (originally vol. 2, no. 1 of the *Journal of Gay and Lesbian Social Services*).

Gabbard, G. 1995. "Researchers Study Causes and Treatment of Borderline Personality Disorder." *The Menninger Letter* 3, 5 (May): 1-2.

Gerstley, L. J., et al. 1990. "Antisocial Personality in Patients with Substance Abuse Disorders: A Problematic Diagnosis?" *American Journal of Psychiatry* 147, 2: 173-8.

Gillis, H.L., and C.A. Simpson. 1994. "Working with Substance-Abusing Adolescents through Project Adventure," in *Addictions: Concepts and Strategies for Treatment*. J. E. Lewis, ed. Gaithersburg, MD: Aspen.

Hanson, G., and P. Venturelli. 1998. *Drugs and Society*, 5th ed. Sudbury, MA: Jones and Bartlett.

Herman, J. 1992. *Trauma and Recovery*. New York: Basic Books.

Horner, B. R., and K. E. Scheibe. 1997. "Prevalence and Implications of Attention Deficit Hyperactivity Disorder among Adolescents in Treatment for Substance Abuse." *Journal of the American Academy of Child and Adolescent Psychiatry* 36, 1: 30-6.

Hser, Y., M.D. Anglin, and M.W. Booth. 1987a. "Sex Differences in Addict Careers 3: Addiction," *American Journal of Drug and Alcohol Abuse* 13, 3: 231-51.

———. 1987b. "Sex Differences in Addict Careers 4: Treatment," *American Journal of Drug and Alcohol Abuse*, 13, 3: 254-80.

Johnston, L.D., P.O. O'Malley, and J.G. Bachman. 1996. "National Survey Results from the Monitoring the Future Study." Rockville, MD: National Institute on Drug Abuse.

Jonas, J. M., and H. G. Pope. 1992. "Axis 1 Co-Morbidity of Borderline Personality Disorder: Clinical Implications," chap. 7 in *Borderline Personality Disorder: Clinical and Empirical Perspectives*. J. F. Clarkin, E. Marziali, and H. Munroe-Blum, ed. New York: Guilford Press.

Jones, P. B., et al. 1998. "Schizophrenia as a Long-Term Outcome of Pregnancy, Delivery, and Perinatal Complications: A 28-Year Follow Up of the 1966 North Finland General Population Birth Cohort. *American Journal of Psychiatry* 155 (3 March): 355-64.

Kelly, K., and P. Raimundo. 1995. *You Mean I'm Not Lazy, Stupid or Crazy? A Self-Help Book for Adults with Attention Deficit Disorder.* New York: Scribner.

Kennedy, R. 1999. "Desperate for Treatment, and Battled Every Step: Addicts and Mentally Ill Seen as Vulnerable to H.M.O's." *New York Times* (26 May): B1, 5.

Kernberg, O. 1975. *Borderline Conditions and Pathological Narcissism.* New York: Jason Aronson.

Kivlahan, D. R., et al. 1991. "Treatment Cost and Rehospitalization Rate in Schizophrenic Outpatients with a History of Substance Abuse." *Hospital and Community Psychiatry* 42: 609-14.

Kreisman, J. J., and H. Straus. 1989. *I Hate You, Don't Leave Me: Understanding the Borderline Personality.* Los Angeles: Body Press.

Krystal, J. H., et al. 1991. "Neurobiological Aspects of PTSD: Review of Clinical and Preclinical Studies," in *Essential Papers on Posttraumatic Stress Disorder.* M. J. Horowitz, ed. New York: New York University Press.

Kus, R.J., and M.A. Latkovich. 1995. "Special Interest Groups in Alcoholics Anonymous: A Focus on Gay Men's Groups," in *Addiction and Recovery of Gay and Lesbian Persons.* R.J. Kus, ed. New York: Harrington Park Press (Haworth Press). (originally vol. 2 no. 1 of the *Journal of Gay and Lesbian Social Services*).

Levine, S. 1984. *Radical Departures: Desperate Detours to Growing Up.* New York: Harcourt, Brace Jovanovich.

Lish, J. D., S. Dime-Meenan, P. C. Whybrow. 1994. "The National Depressive and Manic-Depressive Association Survey of Bipolar Members." *Journal of Affective Disorders* 31, 4: 281-94.

Loneck. B., and B. Way. 1997. "A Conceptual Model of a Therapeutic Process for Clients with a Dual Diagnosis." *Alcoholism Treatment Quarterly* 15: 33-46.

McNeese, C. A., and D. M. DiNitto. 1994. *Chemical Dependency: A Systems Approach.* Englewood Cliffs, NJ: Prentice-Hall.

Mellor, C. S. 1992. "Dermatoglyphic Evidence of Fluctuating Asymmetry in Schizophrenia." *British Journal of Psychiatry* 60: 467-72.

Mueser, K., R. E. Drake, and D. Noordsy. 1998. "Integrated Mental Health and Substance Abuse Treatment for Severe Psychiatric Disorders." *Journal of Practical Psychiatry and Behavioral Health* 4: 129-39.

Murray, R. M., P. Jones, E. O'Callaghan. 1991. "Fetal Brain Development and Later Schizophrenia (Review)." *Ciba Foundation Symposium* 156, 155-63.

O'Callaghan, E., T. Gibson, et al. 1991. "Season of Birth in Schizophrenia: Evidence for Confinement of an Excess of Winter Births to Patients without a Family History of Mental Disorder." *British Journal of Psychiatry* 158: 764-9.

O'Callaghan, E., P. Sham, et al. 1991. "Schizophrenia after Prenatal Exposure to 1957 A2 Influenza Epidemic." *Lancet* 337 (8752): 1248-50.

O'Connell, D. F. 1988. "Managing the Borderline Patient in Addiction Treatment Settings." *Alcoholism Treatment Quarterly* 5, no. 1/2: 61-71.

Pakkenberg, B. 1990. "Pronounced Reduction in Total Neuron Number in Mediodorsal Thalamic Nucleus and Nucleus Accumbens in Schizophrenics." *Archives of General Psychiatry* 47, 11 (November): 1023-28.

Paris, J. 1994. *Borderline Personality Disorder: A Multidimensional Approach.* Washington, DC: American Psychiatric Press.

Schuckit, M. A. 1973. "Alcohol and Sociopathy: Diagnostic Confusion." *Journal of Studies on Alcohol* 34: 157-64.

Shenton, M. E., et al. 1992. "Abnormalities of the Left Temporal Lobe and Thought Disorder in Schizophrenia: A Quantitative Magnetic Resonance Imagining Study." *New England Journal of Medicine* 327, 9 (27 August): 604-12.

Stone, M. H. 1986. "The Borderline Syndrome: Evolution of the Term, Genetic Aspects, and Prognosis." in *Essential Papers on Borderline Disorders.* M. H. Stone, ed. New York: New York University Press.

Suddath, R. L., et al. 1990. "Anatomical Abnormalities in the Brains of Monozygotic Twins Discordant for Schizophrenia." *New England Journal of Medicine* 322: 789-94.

van der Kolk, B. A. 1991. "The Body Keeps the Score: Memory and the Evolving Psychobiology of Posttraumatic Stress," in *Essential Papers on Posttraumatic Stress Disorder.* J. M. Horowitz, ed. New York: New York University Press.

Wender, P. H. 1986. *The Hyperactive Child, Adolescent, and Adult: Attention Deficit Disorder through the Lifespan.* New York: Oxford University Press.

Winerip, M. 1999. "Bedlam on the Streets." *New York Times Magazine* (23 May): 42-9.

Young, A. 1995. *The Harmony of Illusions.* Princeton, NJ: Princeton University Press.

7

Clinical Treatment Issues

Introduction

Treatment issues are framed by the dynamic encounter of the counseling process. Interpersonal context shapes intrapersonal responses: clients construct and communicate accounts of their situations (oversimplified as "denial"); strong emotional responses occur; and intimacy and professionalism are juxtaposed (boundary issues). Competent addiction counseling requires familiarity with these treatment issues, self-awareness, and a willingness to think openly and critically. [1]

---

[1] Powell (1993) recalls that clinical supervision concerning these treatment issues was rooted originally in psychoanalytic training, and aimed to develop "sensitivity to transference, countertransference, drives, and defense mechanisms" (85).

Denial: A Multifaceted Phenomenon

A central principle of the addictions field is that denial is intrinsic to addiction—that addicts refuse to acknowledge reality, or that they deny the magnitude and severity of the problem (minimization) and/or their responsibility (rationalization). Counselors certainly do report that chemical abusers and their associates often attempt to refute or neutralize many self-evident aspects of their situations (see Table 7.1).

TABLE 7.1 Facts Addicts May Deny

Use or abuse of mind- or mood-altering substances
Consumption of large and ever larger amounts of mind-altering substances
Inability to abstain from using substances for any meaningful length of time
Having little control over how much they use, once they start
Sneaking or hiding drinks or drugs
Feeling anxious, depressed, or angry just before they use
Feeling anxious, depressed, or angry during the counseling session
Being under the influence of a substance during the counseling session
Harming, upsetting, or annoying others
Missing work or school as a result of substance use
Experiencing impaired performance of their duties
Belief that their problems (those that they acknowledge) are due to abuse or addiction
Facing an impending crisis
Impaired health
Social withdrawal or a switch to a peer group of users
Rejection by family or friends
Loss of ambition and motivation
Spending a large portion of their funds on alcohol and/or other drugs
They have been helped by treatment
Emotional needs for the counselor (may act out with a show of independence or devaluation of the counselor)
Guilt about their abuse or addiction

There have been many accounts of denial in the history of psychiatry and psychoanalytic thought and in contemporary writings on trauma, recovery, and self-help designed for general audiences. In early psychoanalytic theory, *denial* referred to a primitive means of negating external reality, normal in infants, but seldom found in adults except those suffering from psychosis (Fenichel 1972, 144-46). To block out reality, in fact, is a desperate adaptation characteristic of dissociative disorders. On the other end of the spectrum, some consider denial a normal aspect of coping with an otherwise immobilizing, crushing horror (Kübler-Ross 1997). Most writers do not attempt a sharp, technical delineation of terms, but use the expression as a variant on concepts of repression, self-deception, avoidance, and dishonesty. Denial has had a special place in traditional addictions treatment and self-help programs, where it was a cornerstone throughout the 1960s and 1970s. Overcoming denial was considered an obstacle or a fortress that required demolition through confrontation, "hitting bottom," or both. Though that view is not so dominant in the addictions field as it once was, it is still encountered often.

The traditional view of denial began to be questioned in the 1980s. The work of John Wallace (1985 a, b) influenced counselors to consider working with the defense structure of the alcoholic or addict rather than engaging in a wholesale assault on it, especially early in treatment. Behavioral, motivational, and solutions-oriented clinicians advanced the opinion that it was counterproductive to engage clients in arguments on the label of "addict" as a part of conquering denial. Many addicts are willing to try counseling because of work, health, relationship, or financial problems, but they do not appreciate the labeling or stigma of addiction (Morgan 1996, 222). Chapter 1 mentions Miller and Rollnick's identification (1991, 64-71) of the confrontation–denial trap. They hold that the counselor's assumption of the client's denial creates a combative or antagonistic attitude on the part of the counselor. This attitude imparted in the counseling setting is in conflict with the goal of establishing a therapeutic *alliance* with the client. The more a confrontational counselor insists a client admit to being an addict, the more a denying client resists anything the counselor says. Some professionals who train addictions counselors go so far as to declare, "Let's deny that denial is so basic to addiction theory. Let's let it die" (Taleff 1994, 52).

It is undoubtedly true that some clients' behavior which counselors call denial are artifacts of (produced by) counseling dogma and expectations. It is also true that a one-size-fits-all approach to denial misses the subtleties in the mix of reasons presented for the denials, and in the changing day-to-day thinking of clients. Few go so far as to jettison the entire concept of denial.

Counselors must recognize that denial is a common expression of a wide variety of physiological, cognitive, and cultural phenomena. To attempt to "treat" denial and ignore its source (e.g., psychological, cognitive, cultural phenomena) would be like trying to stop hallucinations without determining their cause (e.g., fever, syphilis, dementia, ingestion of LSD or PCP). Although it is no easy task, counselors need to deconstruct, dissect, and get to the roots of denial. Counselors strive to elicit which of a multiplicity of phenomena is taking place, what the client is denying to the counselor, what the client denies to himself or herself, and the etiology of each area of denial. Counselors should also consider the degree to which each is defended, linked to other areas of pain, or easily given up. To construct a strategy to address this treatment issue, a counselor should consider doing a thorough "denial assessment." This, of course, requires a little time and some well-honed skills.

Denial by Chemically Dependent Individuals

Many explanations of denial delve into unbearable inconsistencies between reality and ideals—what should be and what is, advantages and disadvantages, pleasures (or pain abated) and the pain of addiction. Cognitive and motivational conflicts cannot be tolerated in the same conscious mind without unbearable dissonance. Many researchers and therapists believe that these conflicts engender the need for people to engage in denial (Orford 1985; Saunders et al. 1996). Addictions counselors can help clients deal with denial by exploring its manifestations and employing some effective strategies.

Motives for Treatment

Many clients suffer from a "double approach-avoidance conflict," (as shown in Figure 1.2) which manifests itself in a client's momentary insights, advances, and retreats. Contradictory motives for entering treatment and for using toxic substances are confusing, dissonant, and anxiety-producing. The account the client attempts to construct while confused and anxious will predictably be one that attempts to skirt the core issues and makes use of some denial.

A related phenomenon is simply the reaction against involuntary attendance to treatment, especially when the client is in the precontemplative stage. This is a normal reaction to the loss of freedoms, whatever the ultimate benefits to the client. In the era when so many clients are drafted into treatment from the criminal-justice system, this simple explanation should not be overlooked (Taleff 1997: 40-1).

Many addictions professionals feel that their clients are "incompetent" to assess their situations, and should be hauled into a drug-free situation using whatever leverage is available. Many recovering addicts, in fact,

who fought tooth and nail against entering treatment now express grati-
tude that someone had the concern and the tenacity to initiate this
process. (Thus the slogan "Bring the body and the mind will follow.")

Some individuals who deny their addictions appear to concur with a
diagnosis of addict as a means of getting through some sanctioning process.
For example, an employee referred by an EAP administrator may cleverly
"admit" to a problem to escape demerits, demotion, or dismissal; a person
referred by the criminal-justice system may be anxious to avoid "hard time"
and thus cooperate in counseling (in jailhouse argot, "talk and walk").
Another type of client who only seems to agree with the diagnosis is the homeless person who is seeking shelter in cold weather; he or she "admits" alcoholism but loses this insight when warmer weather ensues. Nevertheless, some
of these winter admissions seeking "two hots and a flop" discover after a week
that they do want to avail themselves of the recovery program.

Counselors who attack the denial symptoms only elicit more fervent
denial by the client. Counselors can help clients explore motives for substance abuse or abstinence by working with clients to create motivational
or decisional balance sheets. As suggested by MET and cognitive therapies,
balance sheets list the positives and negatives associated with the use of alcohol
and drugs. These can be modified or expanded as the client gains more insight
(Miller and Rollnick 1991, 23-4, 78-80, 95; Beck et al. 1993, 137-9).

Active addicts are motivationally and cognitively conflicted, confused,
and often filled with anxiety and pain. Their cognitive functions are compromised, and they fear treatment, change, and institutions more than the
"devil they know." A quarter of a century ago, Paredes (1974) used sociological constructs to explain how addicts are simply trying to construct an
account of themselves to present to themselves and the world, which is
designed to get them through the day. The account is unlikely to be consistent, or to agree with a clinical assessment. Addictions counselors should
not waste energy struggling with that account. It is not necessary to convince addicts of a diagnosis as an initiation into treatment. The priority is
to assess the underlying causes and construct a creative treatment plan to
change a situation that needs illusions and self-deceptions. Eventually,
with an unclouded opportunity to sort out cognitions, motives, and feelings, addicts can arrive at an intellectual understanding of the disease.

Just as addictions treatment now recognizes a multiplicity of factors
that predispose or enable addiction (and each individual possesses a
unique mix of factors), it seems that a similar "paradigm shift" is long
overdue in the analysis of and approach to the complex phenomenon
formerly known simply as denial. Taleff (1997) comprehensively reviews
the varieties of resistance and denial phenomena, and the ideological and
dogmatic impediments to addressing them adequately.

Labels and Stereotypes

Many individuals hold false stereotypes as to what constitutes an addict, such as that an alcoholic is a "bum" or not a functional individual, that an addict is someone who takes illegal or "hard" drugs, or that binge users aren't really addicts. (The binge drinker is a major subtype of alcoholic.)

The terms *addict* and *alcoholic* are associated with shame and stigma. Although there is better understanding of addictions among professionals and the public, many still associate addiction with immorality, weakness, or laziness. People understandably resist suggestions that they belong in such a category. Clients who are not ready to be identified as addicts are affronted by labels and require extra time to establish a working relationship with a counselor.

One effective strategy for dealing with stereotypes of addicts is to offer information; for example, only 5 percent of alcoholics are homeless or unemployed. Attendance at AA, NA, or other support groups will introduce clients to persons of similar level or type of addiction who self-identify as addicted, but who do not fit the stereotype.

Some counselors have a hard time bypassing the label because their own recovery depends on acceptance of themselves as addicts or alcoholics (see AA's Step 1 in appendix B). To omit this self-identification seems to some to cut out the heart and soul of recovery. In reality, it is not crucial to accept the label addict; it is crucial to separate oneself from the world of active addicts, associate with a healthier peer group, and adopt a healthier, drug-free perspective.

Counselors should not insist that the client accept the label. Through active listening skills (see chapter 2), a counselor helps the client become aware of and accept his or her conflicted motives and goals. The very acceptance of ambivalence helps the client move into the contemplative stage.

A client engaged in a recovery process who starts to change addictive behavior patterns will gain insight into the nature of his or her disorder through exposure to recovering role models and nonthreatening education on the disease concept of addictions.

Social Standing

Addiction can conflict with a socially defined self-concept associated with an occupation or gender. Examples include a male alcoholic personnel director who had no concern about the obvious intoxication he exhibited to colleagues; a female high school teacher who carefully concealed her secret drinking; and a male lawyer who was humiliated when a cab driver remarked that he was drunk, which prompted him to seek counseling.

Lederer (1994, 264-66) has examined gender roles in denial from a feminist perspective. These issues may be summed up as follows:

- Women's thoughts and feelings are discounted by their spouses and others, which lowers women's self-esteem and leads to denial of their perceptions of the family situation.
- Women are held responsible for the emotional well-being of the family, which leads women into self-blaming, enabling roles, and to denying situations that "must be," ipso facto, their fault.
- Women go along with their husbands' denial due to the secondary gains of power in the addictive family (executive authority), but, paradoxically, a power they cannot acknowledge because it relies on their husbands' underfunctioning!

Such addictive family roles are discussed frequently in alcoholism recovery, children of alcoholics movements, and Al-Anon, but not always tied directly to the problems of the client in denial.

The loss of physical, psychological, and social control in addiction is an extremely traumatic experience. It has been compared to post-traumatic stress disorder. Even when losses are extensive, denial can remain strong, Paradoxically, a substance abuser may resist help because he or she has "a right to control my own life," when the sad reality is that the substance is increasingly controlling and determining the abuser's life. As Bean describes:

> What generates the psychological position which the drinker takes? The person who develops an addiction is faced with a strange subjective experience. Addiction is an organic assault on the physical and psychological integrity of the person.
>
> He has had repeated experiences of painful consequences of drinking. He ought to make the terrifying discovery that he cannot control his drinking, but he resists and denies it. He realizes that a catastrophe is afoot, and is bewildered and afraid. But he does not know what has happened to him. He does not say, "I drink because I have no control over alcohol use, withdrawal makes me sick, and drinking has been repetitively reinforced." . . . His usual intellect and judgment are not available to help him understand what has happened to him because alcohol has so often impaired them. . . . Because of the experience of loss of control, the despair that he cannot stop, the lack of understanding how to stop, and the terror of the consequences of stopping, the alcoholic sets up an elaborate psychological protective structure to preserve his drinking, a system of denial. (Bean 1978, 74-75)

A counselor must judge the proper timing to determine whether to simply reflect the feelings sensed by the counselor (an active listening skill) or to lead the client into grieving his or her losses. The counselor must sense whether the greater risk to growth and sobriety lies in failure to air painful losses or in being overwhelmed by too much pain at one time. Agencies sometimes ritualize "saying goodbye" to the bottle in a group setting, the equivalent of a funeral for alcohol, with an actual bottle present.

Fear

Fear of Exposure

Many addicts are afraid of exposure and humiliation, and the consequences (e.g., losses of job, status in community, custody of children). This can lead to reluctance to discuss the behaviors that need to be addressed. In organizational settings, fear of exposure and ridicule may be a predominant factor in refusal to acknowledge addiction. An EAP client seen by one of the authors was terrified of disclosure within the gossip-ridden institution where he worked. He resisted the idea that his drinking was a problem, but immediately responded when referred to an outside agency, where he was referred to other services. He was placed in a detoxification unit, completed a stay in inpatient rehabilitation, and returned to work. He remained sober until retirement.

To allay clients' fear of exposure, an agency can prominently display the federal regulations that address confidentiality and provide printed confidentiality forms and disclosure forms. When a client signs forms, a member of the agency (usually the counselor) should sign them, too, then provide a copy to the client. It is very important to educate clients about the privileged nature of the counseling relationship.

Fear of Rejection

Even when fears about confidentiality are not a problem, the client may expect rejection or humiliation after self-disclosure to family, peers, or a therapy group. The shame of behavior, such as unwanted or inappropriate sexual encounters, that took place while the client was intoxicated contributes to the fear of being judged negatively.

Counselors can encourage clients to observe others who engage in self-disclosure in group settings. This often brings great relief to anxious clients. They see that rejection is not forthcoming, and that the disclosure makes the speaker feel better. Finally, the fearful observer identifies with what is said, and feels, "I'm not alone and many people have the same problems that I do."

Fear of Change

Some clients are operating according to an unrecognized logic that "if I give up my denial, then I'll have to look at what I've become, and face the prospect or demand to change. Since I don't think I can change, and I'd just have to live forever with the horrible knowledge of what I am, I'd better keep the lid on everything, avoid the issue, and even avoid people who might suggest looking at the problem." Or, as Karl Marx put it, "The demand to give up illusions about one's condition is the demand to give up a condition that needs illusions" (1988). This paradox is particularly hard to unravel in later stages of addiction, when negative self-perceptions and firmly held ideas of hopelessness have developed after repeated failed attempts to stop using (Kovacs and Beck 1978).

To ease the fear of change, counselors recommend participation in recovery programs. These groups involve considerable exposure to role models who were at least as badly off as any fearful clients who are clinging to denial. Talking with and listening to other addicts—both their failures and successes—offers hope, at least for the possibility of change. Letting go of denial is only possible with hope. In addition, collaborative treatment planning translates the fearful demands of recovery into a list of manageable "bits," showing a way out of a helpless, hopeless situation.

Impaired Memory

Chemical impairment of memory, judgment, and perception operate as anesthetics that allow the improbable hypotheses or denial systems to seem reasonable. Some alcoholics have blackouts, periods of time for which they cannot recall what happened or what they did. The medical term for this is alcohol amnestic disorder. It reflects a "pickling" of the brain's ability to encode long-term memories, a result of high blood alcohol levels. Chemical impairment of memory and perception is a mental environment that allows improbable hypotheses and denial systems to appear reasonable.

In advanced stages of addiction, denial is tied to impacted painful and threatening feelings (Johnson 1980). Removing such an addict's denial opens these wounds, and keeping the denial avoids the pain. Some addicts have partially or totally repressed memories of sexual abuse, or of damaging behavior they committed while intoxicated. Introspection or open discussion may threaten to bring this material dangerously close to awareness. While counselors do not force clients to delve into painful, threatening material while they are just getting a toe-hold on sobriety, there comes a time when such issues have to be aired. Repressed memories may surface in group treatment while listening to an account of abuse related by another client. The group facilitator should anticipate the reactions of other clients, allow time for them to share them, and follow up in individual sessions.

It is good to remember that addictions treatment is just that; designed to help clients get and stay clean and sober, and avoid triggers of relapse. Deeply rooted areas of pain are best relegated to later stages of treatment. In the twelve-step programs of AA and NA, clients learn to concentrate on simple and concrete tasks for the sake of sobriety, remembering to put first things first, take it easy, and to turn problems over to a higher power. Barging into painful areas of denial in early recovery can precipitate a relapse. Wallace (1985a) recognizes the importance of working with denial rather than demolishing it, acknowledging that the counselor treads a fine line between allowing dangerous denial to continue and precipitating premature self-disclosure (1985b).

Underdeveloped Social and Emotional Skills

Some individuals are unused to and unskilled at the business of dealing with emotions, which is not the same thing as denying or repressing them. Such persons need help in identifying, acknowledging, managing, interpreting, and accepting their emotions, and finding the words to communicate them appropriately to others. These skills are called "emotional intelligence" by Goleman (1995) and "emotional literacy" by Steiner (1997); their absence is a sort of "psychological naïveté" (Taleff 1997, 39). This naïveté can reflect growing up in an emotionally isolated setting or in a family with addiction problems, and can be compounded by the chronic, numbing use of depressants.

Interactive group treatment usually results in progress in acquiring emotional skills, as does the practice of the active listening described in chapter 2. If a client persists in evincing a "flat" affect (no flickers of emotion seen) after weeks of treatment, a psychiatric consult is indicated to screen for disorders such as schizoid personality.

Neurological Impairment

The existence of severe psychiatric disorders that are not secondary to intoxication, abuse, addiction, or withdrawal indicate status and needs that differ from those of other addicts (see "mentally ill chemical abuser" section in chapter 6). Delusions and other cognitive distortions, dissociative states, and sociopathy are severe disorders, not denial as therapists have come to understand it.

Advanced alcoholics may have some permanent neurological impairment that compromises cerebral functions. It is important to assess brain damage with information provided by both medical history and an up-to-date medical assessment. Even elementary knowledge of medical syndromes such as Wernicke-Korsakoff syndrome, alcoholic cerebral atrophy, and the effects on the brain secondary to cirrhosis of the liver help counselors interpret information from medical workups. Continuing education can enable the counselor to stay up to date on brain research. Even so, specialized medical assessment of long-term, advanced alcoholics is necessary to determine their neurological status.

Case in Point

Do I know you?

The family of a severe alcoholic called upon an addictions counselor to help them get him into treatment. As the alcoholic's drinking worsened, so did the unpredictability of his behavior. His employer, although an old friend, had about "had it" with him as well. When the counselor arrived at the home, the alcoholic greeted him and offered him a drink. The counselor refused the drink and spent several hours discussing the need for treatment and its salutary effects, and reassuring the alcoholic that treatment did not involve forced consumption of noxious substances, and so forth. The alcoholic finally consented to treatment. Because of the amount of alcohol he had consumed, it was deemed appropriate to initiate treatment with inpatient detoxification. The counselor accompanied the alcoholic to the detox, which was a forty-five minute drive; they waited in the reception area for quite a while; and the counselor was present during the intake procedure. One week later, the detoxification phase being completed, the client was referred to the rehabilitation unit where the counselor was employed. The counselor greeted his client effusively, but to his consternation, the client had absolutely no memory of him and all the time they had spent together getting him into treatment!

Denial by Members of Addicts' Social Networks

Family members and peers of addicts often deny, minimize, or rationalize the addictive syndrome, and/or rescue the addicts from the consequences of their behavior. Such denial and rescuing enables an addict to avoid facing reality and to continue the destructive behavior. At best, this buffer facilitates denial, and at worst, it is a symbiosis of irrational, even delusional thinking. (This is discussed in greater detail in chapter 8.) A peer or relative may participate in denial for direct, indirect, or perceived benefits garnered from the relationship with the addict. Perceived benefits include augmentation of self-esteem from playing the role of rescuer, power and control as a manager, or even attention and pity as a martyr. Such an individual might even sabotage recovery efforts for fear of losing the addict and upsetting the applecart. Finally, the family itself is suffering from a form of post-traumatic stress disorder; the family can be so traumatized by the experience of living with an active addict that it needs to dissociate from or block out the knowledge, memory, and experience, much as those who survive other types of catastrophe.

Organizational or institutional denial is often overlooked as an impediment to recovery. At the workplace, in school, or in other organizational contexts, a variety of motives serve to deny, minimize, or explain away an alcohol or drug problem, as well as the responsibility to act (Myers 1990).

Table 7.2 Motives for Institutional Denial

The need to maintain appearances.
The need to protect funding or accreditation.
An unspoken agreement not to "step on toes."
"Protected classes" of individuals. When some are immune, then the entire problem must be swept under the carpet to avoid inconsistency.
The desire to avoid the extra work of prevention or intervention programs.
Embarrassment and anxiety about confronting someone.
The corporate culture that defines heavy drinking as normal, "time out" behavior.
Social traditions that do not view heavy chemical use in terms of a disorder, disease, or deviant act.
Unwillingness or inability to fund a prevention or intervention program.
Peer or codependent relationships that prohibit disloyalty or "ratting."

In seeking or managing referrals from other organizations, it is important to analyze the roots of institutional denial, as well as its intensity among members of the organization. Often, denial is especially strong in "encapsulated subcultures" such as the insufficiently regulated fraternity house. Chancellor Edward Bloustein of Rutgers University remarked in anger following a death due to alcohol poisoning that fraternities were "an organized conspiracy dedicated to the consumption of alcohol."

When individual, group, and institutional denial come together in an interlocking triad, then the treatment professional has a complex impediment to treatment of addictions.

Recurring Denial

Not only is addiction a relapsing syndrome, but so are the cognitive processes associated with it. Any long-term, powerful, and stable coping mechanism can return given the right set of variables.

Denial may diminish as the motivational scale tips toward acceptance of treatment, yet it can revive when things are not quite so bad or the pressure is off. Almost immediately after contact with some type of treatment, a client will "bounce off the bottom" he or she had reached before getting help. A client who was ready to enter treatment may decide suddenly to "do it on my own." He or she might express honest, yet dubious, hopes like "I can control it now." A helping setting that provokes anxiety (e.g., a medical detox) can tip the scale back so that a client wants to steer clear of formal treatment. Clients may ride up and down on this scale for quite a while.

People who appear to be in stable recovery may resurrect old patterns of thinking, minimizing the severity of their former use, rejecting the need to stay sober, resisting the need to stay active in self-help, and so on. Signs of these old patterns are the first stages of impending relapse. Alcoholics Anonymous succinctly describes the phenomenon as "stinking thinking" and "BUDing" (building up to drink).

Case in Point

It wasn't me!

Sergio was an addictions counselor and a recovering addict, the kind of person who interpreted the tenets of his recovery program very rigidly and literally. He never admitted to angry feelings, and always said he "turned it over." He so believed that his Higher Power intervened in everyday affairs at his behest that another counselor kidded Sergio that he probably thought his Higher Power would levitate an ashtray over to him if he prayed. Sergio was also noted for his impeccable honesty and sincerity. However, when he was assigned to work in an offender program that required routine background checks, Sergio declared, against all reality, that he had no criminal-justice record. When the facts of his record turned up, he explained the discrepancy by declaring, "That was another person."

There is often a sense of well-being and euphoria in early recovery when the newly clean-and-sober addict seems to be walking on a pink cloud. This euphoria may create a "flight into health." An attitude that "I'm all better now" may diminish vigilance, and the remaining range of problems, not yet touched, is avoided and even denied.

A desire to move beyond the identity of "recovering addict" may be a natural progression for some; new career and personal involvements may take precedence over avid self-help attendance. However, it is important to "keep the memory green" to prevent relapse and its denial.

A step beyond the pink cloud is a dissociation of the new recovering addict from the old active addict, a refusal to consider the past (Wallace 1985b) that comes closer to the primitive denial of neurotics described by Fenichel (1972) or that of borderline personalities described by Kernberg (1975).

Emotional Issues of the Counseling Relationship

Both clients and counselors carry emotional baggage into the counseling relationship. The imprint of experiences affects perceptions, attitudes, feelings, and expectations in treatment. A useful metaphor is that early experiences are elements of a lens through which people view each other in distorted images. Another metaphor is that the clients *project* their expectations onto the counselor so that what the client sees is his or her own production. Psychotherapy uses the term *transference* for the effects of emotional baggage brought by the client into the counseling relationship. *Countertransference* reflects the counselor's reactions to the client, through his or her own transference.

Transference and countertransference derive from traditional psychoanalysis—the theory and practice of psychotherapy founded by Sigmund Freud. The phenomenon of transference was considered outside of the awareness or conscious mind of the client, in an "unconscious" domain. Psychoanalytic writings dwell in great detail on transference; resolution of the transference neurosis, as it was once called, was in fact considered a prime mechanism of psychoanalysis in aiding personal growth. Today most schools of counseling and psychotherapy do not think of these phenomena as operating in some mysterious unconscious limbo, but use the terms to refer to a broad range of prior issues that color the counseling relationship (Brockett and Gleckman 1991; Kernberg 1975). Although some feelings and thoughts truly are repressed, most psychotherapists do not find it helpful to relegate psychological phenomena that are outside of people's awareness to a separate subconscious realm of the mind. For example, in Freud's Vienna of a century ago, hostility toward parents was much harder to illuminate than today.

Clinical concern with transference phenomena is found in therapeutic approaches that have some connection, however indirect, to a psychoanalytic perspective. Addictions treatment has emerged primarily from a different historical legacy. Therefore, transference has not been a major focus of addictions treatment. In addition, the association of transference with psychoanalysis raises the fear that it is the kind of drawn-out, "talky" concern that might take the focus off the immediate, life-and-death issues of addiction and recovery. Transference is actually a powerful presence in addictions treatment and it is also very useful as a clinical tool in illuminating patterns of thinking and relating.

Recognizing transference in addictions treatment does not mean that treatment time is spent analyzing the phenomenon; the term may never be used in treatment. Nevertheless, addictions counselors must be aware of it and become skilled in processing and coping with the advantages or impediments of transference in the helping process.

Regardless of theoretical preferences, counselors can all agree that clients import issues into the counseling process, whether it is
- a learned response such as defensiveness
- cognitions such as the expectation of rejection or criticism
- emotional needs and responses from prior relationships
- the propensity to play an accustomed part in a group, such as the super-responsible one or the scapegoat

The understanding of transference is a searchlight into the psyche and a means of identifying impediments to the facilitation of growth through the counseling process.

Transference

Positive Transference

Positive transference refers to positive feelings and emotional needs being transferred from another person or relationship to the counselor. Transference of positive feelings has the advantage of keeping the client in treatment, even when the counselor is confronting, challenging, or pressuring the client to an uncomfortable extent.

Positive transference can be intense in early recovery. With release from anesthesia comes awareness of formerly muted emotions and needs. The "emotional rebound" includes affiliative, intimacy, and affectional needs. Recovery offers relief from a lonely, often stigmatized existence. Many addicts who are new to treatment have been estranged from family, friends, and community. The new counseling relationship in individual and those in group treatment also contribute to reawakening feelings and needs, both positive and negative. A chronically, chemically encapsulated client may not have resolved some dependency conflicts at an age typical for this society. The client may naturally "imprint" on the counselor. Therefore, positive transference may involve unrealistic expectations of help, love, or protection, at times involving a fantasized relationship (of which the client is not altogether aware). When taken to the extreme the counselor is idealized and invested with the powers and qualities of some sort of omnipotent, omniscient superparent.

For the counselor, there are interrelated traps in runaway positive transference: It is flattering and ego enhancing to be a rescuer. This meets a counselor's emotional needs for validation and importance. Thus, the counselor may unwittingly "leak" cues that subtly reinforce this message (see the section "Countertransference" later in this chapter). Unfortunately, in doing so, the counselor is encouraging the client's unrealistic expectations and fantasies, which are bound to be dashed at some point. This often results in extreme disappointment and devaluation of the counselor, and in some cases of the entire counseling experience.

At the same time, the client may feel shame, guilt, anxiety, panic, or loss of control at having strong positive feelings and intense needs (a colleague calls this an "intimacy freak-out"). Therefore, the client may develop denial and resistance strategies (so-called counterdependent behavior), flee treatment entirely, or even relapse.

A skilled counselor recognizes when clients are resisting their own emotional needs, and handles intense emotional needs by setting limits without appearing rejecting or wreaking emotional devastation. One counselor asked, "How do you chill them out without sending them out?" Judicious self-disclosure that humanizes the counselor can avert deification. Assertive refusal skills that recognize the needs of the client while stating the limits within which they must operate can mitigate impossible expectations. Finally, transference to a variety of individuals, a group, and to the entire program should always be encouraged.

A special situation is one in which the client is flirtatious or sexual. A rereading of the psychosocial assessment, preferably in a supervisory setting, can help the counselor understand the meaning of this behavior. Flirtatious behavior may be the result of transferring onto a counselor the relationship with a seductive parent or a parent who demanded appeasement. Such behavior may be the only method the client knows to achieve intimacy, to manipulate people into meeting his or her needs, or a combination. It may also indicate the client's inability to distinguish between a sexual relationship and other types of close relationships.

A crucial phase in which transference occurs is termination of treatment. As termination approaches, clients may become anxious and begin anticipatory grieving for the loss they are about to experience. Some try to avoid or negate this unbearable loss by being hostile, denigrating the formerly idealized counselor, or leaving treatment and possibly relapsing. Treatment planning should attempt to anticipate and plan for a healthy means of separating and moving on. Counselors should lead clients into an exploration of how they will feel when time in the program is up, and help them weave a new emotional safety net.

Negative Transference

Clients get angry, hostile, resentful, and jealous. It is wonderful in fact if clients feel free and safe enough to show these feelings. Counselors must respect the clients' rights to have any feelings without risk of repercussion. Clients must learn to communicate feelings appropriately in order to maintain sobriety and prevent relapse. One of the next tasks in treatment and recovery is to sort out, as much as possible, the factors contributing to this anger or hostility.

In the emotional rebound of early sobriety, the rejections, resentments, abuse, and disappointments of a lifetime may be piled onto the counselor. Many clients have a history of conflicts with authority, of misdiagnosis, or of punishments by the agents of authority, whom a counselor may represent. In addition, many have experienced trauma, loss, pain, and abandonment as children of addicts. Again, the counselor can become the target.

Of course, it is no fun to be the scapegoat. While it may be an uncomfortable situation for the counselor, it may be the first time that the client has felt safe in feeling and expressing anger or rage. In allowing this to happen, counselors provide a substitute for "drinking about it," and an opportunity to practice coping with negative feelings in a healthy way, without chemicals. Despite the discouragement, the counselor must maintain his or her professional role, remain emotionally detached, and not personalize the client's behavior. It is dangerous to take this anger personally and react defensively to it. It is also dangerous to jump too quickly to explore, interpret, and explain the negative transference, which short-circuits the counseling process. The first task is to verify that the counselor is not the cause of such anger. It is appropriate for a client to be angry with a counselor who is always late, hostile when the counselor allows other clients to cut in on his or her meeting time, or resentful of a counselor who regularly answers phone calls during sessions. Having eliminated elements in the counselor–client relationship as causes, it is necessary to explore other causes of these emotions. For example, is the client's irritability a result of withdrawal syndrome, an imbalance of medications, or transference? Is a client's anger a mask for the fear that he or she cannot be helped by this human agency? This fear may convert into rage at the counselor, even if the client has fantasized an omnipotent counselor.

There are indeed powerful sources of both positive and negative transference among addicted clients, both sets of feelings being threatening to the client. The transference is not only strong but also marked by ambivalence, conflicts, and shifts (Wallace 1985a, 16).

Countertransference

This somewhat cumbersome term is variously used to refer to all reactions to clients. More restrictively and more accurately, *countertransference* describes those reactions to clients that stem from the counselor's own needs, relationships, or recovery issues. Counselors' skills in identifying personal reactions are imperative in ethical treatment. Counselors must keep clients' needs and welfare as the primary concern and avoid acting upon emotional reactions to clients in ways that are not helpful to the client or the counseling process. Examining countertransference can also reveal important information as to what messages the client is sending: A counselor may be resonating to a client's powerful feelings not yet out in the open.

One of the toughest tasks facing the counselor is staying in touch with his or her feelings, especially when dealing with challenging and difficult clients. Being aware that a client is causing emotional reactions may make a counselor feel out of control, or at least a loss of self-control. However, that awareness is critical. When a counselor is not fully aware of these reactions, or how they influence his or her behavior, that counselor truly is not in control.

Positive Countertransference

Positive countertransference may arise from the counselor's experience as a codependent, or as a way of making amends for abuse or neglect suffered when he or she was actively addicted. A need to be worshipped and loved by a client (narcissism) masks low self-esteem, terror of abandonment, dependency needs, and a lack of gratifying relationships in the counselor's life.

Sorting through countertransference is often difficult. For example, if a counselor finds the client romantically interesting, is this
- a normal reaction to an attractive client?
- an indication of the counselor's need for intimacy or love?
- a response to the client's idealization of, or love for, the counselor, which feeds a need for praise, validation, and flattery?
- a response to a client's need for affection and intimacy being communicated via nonverbal cues, subtle flattery, or seduction?
- a romantic rescue fantasy arising from the counselor's codependency?
- a reaction to a client's skillful manipulation?
- a combination or intermediate form of two or more of the above?

Counselors must, with the aid of individual or group supervision, sort through their own feelings and needs. Exploration and evaluation of the role in the counselor–client relationship contribute to the client's progress in treatment, and can help avoid the following pitfalls:

- encouraging inappropriate levels of transference, which result in disappointment, rage, or relapse
- failing to maintain appropriate boundaries
- falling into an enabling or infantalizing role
- holding on to clients when it is time for them to move on
- establishing a "pet" client to the disadvantage of all.

Negative Countertransference

Being human, counselors can have angry or hostile feelings toward clients. Having negative emotions about clients is normal. Being vigilant and rigorously honest about these reactions is an ethical imperative, so as to ensure that counselors do not unwittingly act on them or send double messages to the client. Where possible, counselors should strive to understand the basis of client feelings. Aside from simple reactions to provocation, attack, or unpleasant characteristics of a client, a wide variety of personal issues and experiences of counselors can result in negative perceptions and emotional reactions. Signals that clients maybe be communicating through voice qualities or body language can also cause discomfort. These reactions are called negative countertransference. *Negative countertransference* reactions occur when a counselor's reactions to a client are rooted in the counselor's own issues. A counselor may have a need to control or may expect a client to meet needs for validation, love, and so on. Unrealistic expectations may echo a counselor's negative experiences and prompt negative feelings toward a client who rejects help, or who is resistant, critical, or provocative.

Counselors may become angry and disappointed when clients have setbacks or relapse, since these seem to signal their own inadequacy. Relatively new, recovering counselors may overidentify with a client, and feel anxious and out of control when things do not go as planned. If a counselor identifies with a client's undesired character trait, he or she might, as the addiction aphorism goes, "attack in others what we faintly perceive in ourselves."

A counselor might associate the client with a negative experience or relationship in the counselor's past. What if the client is a rapist or child abuser, and the counselor has suffered from such individuals? What if the counselor is parenting or has parented a problem child, like the client? Negative countertransference can be caused by reactions to body language or voice qualities. Facial expressions, gestures, postures, and voice qualities can be inconsistent with what a person is saying, which creates tension and discomfort. Counselors may also react negatively to clients' rigid or overcontrolled body language or speech qualities, talking in a monotone, lack of affect (which suggest hidden content or difficulties), and rejection of attempts at engagement. Unexpressed strong feelings in a client who is making a valiant attempt to present a cheerful or stoic face, but whose tension and strain "leaks through" in contradictory signals can also make the counselor tense.

Case in Point

Everything's fine.

Marge, the wife of a severe alcoholic, was enrolled in an addiction counseling training program. She maintained a controlled, cheerful, "chatterbox" persona behind which lay great tension, and probably great pain. The internship/practicum course included a weekly seminar class in which the trainees aired their concerns, feelings, and problems in reference to their fieldwork placements, and discussed clinical issues as well. The cheerfulness manifested by Marge was clearly forced. This "got on the nerves" of the other students, who found it difficult to deal with the facade. As often happens in a group learning to be counselors, the interactions among the group members became material to the process. The students gently and respectfully confronted Marge and encouraged her to talk about her life and problems. Through honest expression and exploration of feelings (positive and negative), the group resolved the situation—an excellent learning experience.

Unexplored negative countertransference is dangerous. Counselors always run the risk of acting out their countertransference without realizing it. Especially a newly recovering counselor, prematurely thrust into a counseling role, may have intense reactions that could cause burnout and be harmful to the client by disrupting the treatment process. If the agency atmosphere does not encourage ventilation, insight, or mutual support, such a counselor may defend, deny, or guard against countertransference. A counselor in recovery may make the recovery of each client his or her personal mission and responsibility. Personal emotional investment in a client ruins the counselor's perspective and his or her ability to behave in a professional way. For example, such a counselor may be too easy on a client, or push too hard! (Those who have "worked" the twelve steps of

AA/NA have gone through a process of purging themselves of this pain by accepting that they were powerless over their disease, and "making amends." They have also learned that they can support and aid another person's recovery, but they cannot control it.)

Unrecognized and unexplored negative countertransference reactions may lead a counselor to

- subtly push away a client
- withhold support
- make incorrect negative interpretations
- participate in scapegoating
- feel guilty about hostile or negative feelings and act "nice"
- be anxious when negative feelings threaten to surface

Some of these reactions may lead a counselor to reject or avoid the patient, or quickly take away strong feelings by staying in a nonfeeling realm ("numbing out"), or move too quickly to explain a problem or "resolve" an issue. Or a counselor might spend a great deal of energy avoiding his or her feelings, which leads to burnout and depression.

Before resorting to obscure or exotic interpretations of their feelings, counselors should always look at concrete things that are going on to which they may be responding. The excerpt from a student's process recording (Figure 7.1) provides a simple example of anxiety provoked by a client.

Figure 7.1 Process Recording: Anxiety

During the course of the session, the client talked loudly and was very animated. He maintained eye contact to a point that I thought he was trying to stare me down. We were seated in a closed-door, narrow, and rectangular conference room and sat across from each other. However, even though we were seated some distance apart, the client's demeanor and behavior was so overwhelming that his presence seemed to fill the entire room. Since both doors to the conference room were closed and locked from the outside, I began to experience some feelings of claustrophobia to the point that I wanted to run out of the conference room.

In the real world of counseling, emotional reactions are not sorted neatly into positive and negative transference and countertransference. The client's reactions to the counselor are a mixture of positive and negative feelings, sometimes ambiguous and shifting. So are the counselor's reactions to the client. Ambiguity, in self and others, is difficult to process and often provokes anxiety. Learning to work with and tolerate ambiguity is a necessary skill in the world of relationships—a counselor is his or her own most difficult client (Ellis 1985).

Loss, Grief, and Regrets

Loss and grief are issues throughout the addiction and in the recovery process. Drinking can be initiated or drastically increased following a loss. This reaction is often linked to an inability to accept and integrate the experience because of an inability to go through the grieving process. Addiction itself brings many losses—of relationships, self-esteem, physical health, employment, and so forth. The coming of sobriety and healing paradoxically brings one face-to-face with these losses. Grieving losses of the pre-addictive and addictive periods is part of the work of recovery. Finally, giving up alcohol itself is a significant loss (Goldberg 1985).

Feelings of loss and grief can be generated when a client leaves treatment prematurely. For example, at a general meeting at an adolescent intensive outpatient facility, which was part of the therapeutic-community movement, the counselors and senior clients gave a client the option of making a difficult change or leaving the program. The client picked up her sweater and left. As one of the clients later described it, "There was not a dry eye in the house."

The spread of HIV/AIDS has resulted in thousands of deaths among recovering IV drug users, including more than a few working as addiction counselors. The pain to colleagues and friends can be compounded when AIDS dementia occurs in late stages of the infection. Working with HIV-infected clients means re-experiencing those losses, which might generate any number of countertransferential reactions, such as withdrawal, anger, and tenderness.

Many jobs now involve alternatives to sentencing in which the agency contracts to be an extension of the criminal-justice system. This can cause tremendous role conflicts and painful decisions when a client violates rules, as the Case in Point "Sam's Story" illustrates.

....

Case in Point

Sam's Story

When I was a counselor at the halfway house (for addicted offenders), one of the clients, Charles, went out on a job interview and returned acting out of character. Usually quiet and soft-spoken, Charles was singing, dancing, and talking loudly. Suspecting he had gotten high, my supervisor assigned me to administer a urine test. Charles stalled around until I told him that he had thirty minutes to comply (Noncompliance with urine tests result in getting sent back to prison). I cut him some slack since I felt, well, he's never given me a problem before. Finally Charles showed up, chatted about getting his GED and job training. I handed him the urine sample test cup, he entered the bathroom and turned on the tap, saying it helped him urinate. At that moment I heard anxiety in his voice, and began to watch him closer. With his back towards me it looked like he was pulling something out of his sweat pants. When Charles handed me the sample, I felt it was cold through my rubber gloves. I told him that unless he was dead, this did not just come out of his body. I then noticed a black string hanging from his sweat pants, and asked him what it was for. He replied that he needed it to keep his pants up. I ordered him to give it to me. It came out with a test tube attached. Charles fell to his knees and began to pray and cry. He said, "I'd rather escape then go back to prison." I told him to get up, stop crying, and go to his room, and everything would be all right.

I asked myself, Could I turn him in? I liked Charles and couldn't stand to send him back. I couldn't separate my feelings from the job. Finally I told myself this wouldn't help him in the long run, and I called my supervisor. The dirty urine and the escape threat were too much, and Charles was called down to the office. Charles told me he'd let his family and friends down. I was instructed to empty out his pockets, change him out of his street clothes into the regulation orange prison jumper, and wait with him in the conference room until someone from the Department of Corrections came to pick him up. Also, I had to put the chains and cuffs on him. This was the hardest thing I have ever done. Charles told me that he understood and had no anger towards me. This didn't make it any easier for me because I don't like putting chains on any man. I believe he said this to help me ease the pressure of feeling like crying myself.

Source: courtesy of Samuel Nelms

🄰🄲🅃🄸🅅🄸🅃🅈 **7.1 Is it OK if I feel this way?**

Break into groups of six. Designate a person as recorder and reporter for each group. Consider the process recording in Figure 7.1. Discuss the student's reaction to the client. Consider the following questions:

- What, if anything, could the student do about these feelings? Discuss them with a supervisor? Confront the client?
- Have you had similar feelings during or after a discussion with someone?

- Are there some feelings that a person should not have? That a counselor should not have? If so, what are they?
- Do some of your feelings make you anxious or ashamed?

After brief (about 15 minutes) discussions, the recorder from each group can report to the class on the results of the discussions.

Setting Limits and Boundaries

Boundary rules provide a framework for relationships, the parts that people play in groups, and the positions that they occupy. Setting limits and establishing boundaries are important issues in counseling, in helping the client to learn appropriate, mature, sober, and successful behaviors and in establishing the appropriate relationships between counselors and clients.

These issues frequently generate problems for counselors and clients at addictions agencies. Some clients are emerging from such personal disintegration that they seem to have a "bottomless pit" of need; others are habituated only to manipulative relationships. Counselors, especially those whose experience has been limited to participation in self-help fellowships, are not always prepared to set definite boundaries and abide by them.

Counselors must think through and establish limits, expectations, guidelines, and frameworks in advance. It is important to anticipate that clients may push beyond what is possible, realistic, ethical, or appropriate for them or their counselors. Without clearly stated boundaries, counselors also can, without realizing it, go beyond acceptable limits.

If counselors are not aware of these issues and not aware of their own motives or attitudes that may contribute to inappropriate limit-setting, a wide range of consequences might occur for the client, the counselor, and the counseling process. Demands might be made or expectations created that are unrealistic, excessive, or inappropriate. This is a no-win situation. The counselor has the choice of allowing excessive demands or intimacy, or going along for a time and then shifting position to reject such demands. This turns out to be a somewhat of a Hobson's choice. Going along with a client's inappropriate or unrealistic expectations can lead to resentment or burnout for the counselor, failure to help the client learn to manage his or her needs appropriately within society, and blurred roles of counselor and client. Failure to establish and respect boundaries can also lead to the counselor's being drawn into manipulation, which may include finances, sexuality, housing, and other favors. Such actions, regardless of good intentions, are dangerous, and violate professional ethics. A counselor who lets a client stay at his or her house, for example, might face any number of disastrous consequences. A counselor who ignores or disregards a client's behavior that pushes or exceeds limits will eventually feel stressed or resentful. The resentment may begin to show, and the double message will confuse and disturb the client. In such situations, either alone or as a result of clinical supervision, the counselor must set new limits and boundaries, which changes the nature of the counselor–client relationship. Although this is necessary, it often leaves the client feeling disappointed, rejected, or even infuriated. Honest exploration of the client–counselor relationship must lead to renegotiation of the boundaries and rebuilding of the working alliance.

Personal Space

People have powerful attitudes and feelings concerning their "turf" or "personal space." This is the area immediately around their bodies as well as extensions of them such as belongings and spaces they occupy (e.g., supermarket carts, beach blankets, and telephone booths). When people, especially strangers, enter someone's personal space, that person feels intruded upon, even if there is no physical contact. An individual may define the intrusion as bad manners, unacceptable, wrong, or even mentally unstable or criminal behavior.

Case in Point

What is that supposed to mean?

Crosscultural training for doing business abroad attempts to preclude such problems as North American businesspeople being defined as unfriendly and withdrawn by their Latin American counterparts. Such seminars were not provided to small businessmen in New York City during the early 1990s. Then, there was tension between Korean greengrocers and members of low-income communities in which the Koreans had recently set up shop. These tensions were exacerbated by the fact that the Koreans consider it impolite to smile at strangers, which made them seem standoffish and unfriendly to their Hispanic and African American customers.

Definitions of personal space, rules about emotional expression, and acceptable ways to display information are contained in cultural customs. People send information to one another about boundaries by the way they say things (voice qualities, choice of words), and through gestures, postures, and facial expressions. These vary among societies and among groups, or subcultures, in large societies. Edward Hall, one of the first to study personal space, reported that Northern Europeans and North Americans required greater personal space than Southern Europeans, Latin Americans, and Arabs. He pointed out that behavior that is understood as friendly and polite in Culture A can be perceived as flirtation in Culture B (Hall 1959, 1966, 1974).

In large societies, all kinds of groups have their own codes and customs. There are real differences that counselors should not ignore; for example, Hispanic members of NA in Brooklyn, New York, hug more after meetings than middle-class, Caucasian, Protestant AA members in Akron, Ohio. While recognizing the subcultural traits, counselors must not assume all members of a group conform to a certain code.

ACTIVITY 7.2   How would you feel?

Visualize the following situations:

- You're in a large hotel lobby at midnight. The only other person in the lobby, a stranger, comes up and stands right next to you.
- At a movie, you went to the restroom and someone threw your coat on the floor and took your seat.
- A casual acquaintance saw your wallet or purse laying on a table in the library and went through it, looking for a pen.
- A colleague is annoyed about a memo you wrote. While talking to you, he taps you on the shoulder repeatedly for emphasis.
- You are having a tense discussion on the phone with a loved one. A client walks into your office without knocking, and starts to ask a question.
- You are under the gun to finish neglected paperwork. Several clients on your caseload need to be seen in the next two hours, and notes entered in their charts. As you walk down the hall toward your office, Oliver, a resident of the facility, announces that he is in another emotional crisis and needs to talk with you immediately.

Discuss: How do you think you would feel? What do you think your reaction would be? Do you have any responsibility to the other person in the situation? If so, how could you respond to meet the other's persons need and your own?

Physical Contact

In the addictions recovery setting, hugging especially brings up the question of physical boundaries. Hugging provides support, reduces isolation, has a healing quality, and can help someone learn to trust and build toward emotional intimacy. Between counselor and client, however, and even among clients at an agency, hugs can be hidden traps. They can

- be used as a "quick fix" that avoids looking at some painful truths or the need to make some difficult changes in entrenched behavior patterns.
- encourage clients to look within the treatment system to have essential needs met. Then termination can be very painful and might have to be postponed.
- prematurely open up a long-repressed "Pandora's box" of emotional needs early in sobriety, which can be threatening and result in departure or even relapse. Or the client can develop a "crush" on a counselor.
- result in sexual arousal, then guilt, and possible departure.
- cause jealousy in clients who receive fewer hugs.

The type of program that to one extent or another has a "hugging" culture that emphasizes love and acceptance may seem like heaven on earth to many. But some individuals abuse this and become intrusive or smothering. In such a setting, people who prefer not to hug are defined as withdrawn, unfriendly, or deviant. Also the "lovey-dovey" technique can cover resentments or make it difficult, if not impossible, for individuals to explore anger and other uncomfortable or "negative" emotions within the group or program. In fact, it will cause them to feel conflicted or guilty when these feelings crop up. Finally, the real world is not always a loving environment. A counselor who fosters a client to be ill-equipped to cope with *negative* emotions and reactions sets him or her up for relapse.

Intangible Boundaries

In addition to personal space and physical boundaries, people establish intangible boundaries around their private selves. People set limits beyond which others should not intrude (Goffman 1971). For example, people limit

- the amount or type of information other people can have
- the amount of time they are willing or able to devote to one person
- the amount of work they put into one task or project
- the degree of intimacy with each person

People do "step over the line" and go beyond the limits or boundaries of others, which creates discomfort. It is not always easy to tell whether they do this out of poor judgment, insensitivity, arrogance, cultural differences, neediness, or unfamiliarity with a normal or nonaddicted lifestyle, or if the limits were not communicated clearly. Counselors should have the ability to identify what they are feeling about a client, and how this may relate to an issue about limits and boundaries. Figure 7.2 is an excerpt from a process recording that describes a "pal-sy" relationship between a client and a counselor.

Figure 7.2 Process Recording: Questionable Boundaries

The student records her observations and her reactions, and her possible countertransference.

R. A. is entering detox for the fourth time. For the intake, the male staff counselor and I went to meet him and take the information prior to admitting him to the floor. The counselor did mention casually that he knew R. A. When we approached, and the two saw each other, it was "old home week." "Hey man, what's happening! What you been up to?" said the counselor . . . and he and the client continued with the patter.

ME: What's going on? This display is a typical male bonding ritual. I immediately felt on the edge of the circle. I felt left out and slightly resentful. This does not seem to be the way an intake is supposed to go.

After we're all seated, I introduced myself to R. A. as a counselor-in-training, and asked if he minded that I would be doing the intake. Counselor and R. A. both said "Naah, no problem. He knows the routine." They started back on their reunion, "Man it's good to see you, you're looking good." R. A. was talking a mile a minute about his various businesses. "I'm still producing."

ME: If he knows the routine, if he's so smart, why is he here? This guy and the counselor act as if he has just checked into the Hilton for a vacation. What a crock! He thinks he's so *smooth and yet he comes back again and again. I feel that obviously giving him treatment as a favorite son is not the key. I hope that my expression and my demeanor did not betray the negative feelings I was having toward this patient. I wonder why he turned me off. He is clean, courteous, and articulate. Was it his swagger? Was it fathering eight children with three mothers?*

Skills in Setting Limits

In reality, counselors all learn through error. They sometimes miss signals or clues that a client is developing expectations that cannot or should not be met; then the counselor must "back off" gracefully. There are all kinds of hidden traps that counselors cannot always anticipate. When boundaries are crossed, their renegotiation need not be a total disaster. The situation can be discussed honestly with the client, and the counselor's taking responsibility for the situation humanizes and explores the nature of this collaborative relationship. It can be reframed as an opportunity for growth in the area of relationship skills.

Although every scenario cannot be anticipated, counselors should keep a number of guidelines in mind in order to negotiate the reefs and shoals of the counseling relationship as it pertains to boundaries and limits:

- Identify the appropriate and realistic boundaries that are consistent with legal and ethical guidelines. Know your employer's standards and guidelines. Consult your supervisor about all unclear areas.
- Identify your attitudes and motives for not setting limits assertively. (Do you feel guilty or anxious? Are you confused about the role of fellowship member and the role of professional counselor? Do you need to protect or rescue clients?)
- Set limits in a manner that is assertive, direct, honest, and open as well as empathetic. Keep it simple and friendly, pertaining to a single, specific behavioral area rather than a comprehensive denunciation.

Examples of assertive statements to set limits are

"I have ten minutes for you today."

"I know you need more time with me today, and I wish I had it, but I have other clients who also must see me. One is waiting for me now."

"It makes me uncomfortable when you leave your coat in my office. I'd appreciate it if you could arrange for another place to put it."

🅐🅒🅣🅘🅥🅘🅣🅨 (7.3)   **Should I or shouldn't I?**

Is it ever advisable to do any of the following? If yes, under what circumstances? If no, why not?

- Lend money to or borrow money from a client
- Give your home phone number to clients
- Send a client on a personal errand for you
- Let clients have their packages left with you for them
- Let clients leave their coats or hats or purses in your office while at the agency but not in session with you
- Develop a pet client
- Spend a lot of time helping a client in an area outside of your job function, when there are others at the agency who do this (e.g., get food stamps, arrange transportation, pick up medications)

References

Bean, M. 1978. "Denial and the Psychological Complications of Alcoholism," in *Dynamic Approaches to the Understanding and Treatment of Alcoholism*. M. H. Bean et al., ed. New York: Free Press.

Beck, A. T., et al. 1993. *Cognitive Therapy of Substance Abuse*. New York: Guilford Press.

Berg, I. K., and S. D. Miller. 1992. *Working with the Problem Drinker: A Solution-Focused Approach*. New York: Norton.

Brockett, D. R., and A. D. Gleckman. 1991. "Countertransference with the Older Adult." *Journal of Mental Health Counseling* 13(3): 343-355.

Ellis, A. 1985. *Overcoming Resistance: Rational-Emotive Therapy with Difficult Clients*. New York: Springer-Verlag.

Fenichel, O. 1972. *The Psychoanalytic Theory of Neurosis* (1945). New York: Norton.

Goffman, E. 1971. *Relations in Public*. New York: Harper Colophon.

Goldberg, M. 1985. "Loss and Grief: Major Dynamics in the Treatment of Alcoholism," in *Psychological Issues in the Treatment of Alcoholism*. D. Cook, ed. New York: Haworth Press.

Goleman, D. 1995. *Emotional Intelligence*. New York: Bantam Books.

Hall, E. T. 1959. *The Silent Language*. Garden City, NY: Doubleday.

———. 1966. *The Hidden Dimension*. Garden City, NY: Doubleday.

———. 1974. *Handbook for Proxemic Research*. Washington, DC: Society for the Anthropology of Visual Communication.

Johnson, V. 1990. *I'll Quit Tomorrow*. New York: Harper and Row.

Kernberg, O. 1975. *Borderline Conditions and Pathological Narcissism*. New York: Jason Aronson.

Kovacs, M., and A. Beck. 1978. "Maladaptive Cognitive Structures in Repression." *American Journal of Psychiatry* 135: 525-33.

Kübler-Ross, E. 1997. *On Death and Dying*. New York: Simon and Schuster.

Lederer, G. S. 1994. "The Use of Denial and Its Gender Implications in Alcoholic Marriages," in *Addictions: Concepts and Strategies for Treatment*. J. A Lewis, ed. Gaithersburg, MD: Aspen.

Marx, K. 1988. *Economic and Philosophical Manuscripts of 1884.* M. Mulligan, trans. New York: Prometheus Books.

Miller, W. R., and S. Rollnick. 1991. *Motivational Interviewing.* New York: Guilford Press.

Morgan, T. J. 1996. "Behavioral Treatment Techniques for Psychoactive Substance Use Disorders," in *Treating Substance Abuse: Theory and Technique.* F. Rotgers, D. S. Keller, and J. Morgenstern, ed. New York: Guilford Press.

Myers, P. L. 1990. "Sources and Configurations of Institutional Denial." *Employee Assistance Quarterly* 5(3): 43-54.

Orford, J. 1985. *Excessive Appetites: A Psychological View of Addiction.* Chichester, England: Wiley.

Paredes, A. 1974. "Denial, Deceptive Maneuvers, and Consistency in the Behavior of Alcoholics," in *The Person with Alcoholism,. Annals of the New York Academy of Sciences,* vol. 33. F. A. Seixas, R. Cadoret, and S. Eggleston, ed.

Powell, D. J. 1993. *Clinical Supervision in Alcohol and Drug Abuse Counseling: Principles, Models, Methods.* San Francisco, CA: Jossey-Bass.

Saunders, B., C. Wilkinson, and T. Towers. 1996. "Motivation and Addictive Behaviors: Theoretical Perspectives," in *Treating Substance Abuse: Theory and Technique.* F. Rotgers, D. S. Keller, and J. Morgenstern, ed. New York: Guilford Press.

Steiner, C. 1997. *Achieving Emotional Literacy.* New York: Avon.

Taleff, M. 1994. "The Well-Deserved Death of Denial." *Behavioral Health Management* 14, 3 (May/June): 51-2.

———. 1997. *A Handbook to Assess and Treat Resistance in Chemical Dependency.* Dubuque, IA: Kendall-Hunt.

Wallace, J. 1985a. "Working with the Preferred Defense Structure of the Recovering Alcoholic," in *Practical Approaches to Alcoholism Psychotherapy,* 2nd ed. S. Zimberg, J. Wallace, and S. B. Blume, ed. New York: Plenum.

———. 1985b. "Critical Issues in Alcoholism Therapy," in *Practical Approaches to Alcoholism Psychotherapy,* 2nd ed, S. Zimberg, J. Wallace, and S. B. Blume, ed. New York: Plenum.

Family, Community, and Cultural Systems

Social Systems

We are elements of social systems that shape and mold our behavior, and we in turn influence them. The systems aspect of addictive behavior is crucial, yet it is often overlooked, over-simplified, or fragmented. The topics of family, community, and culture have been the property of separate disciplines, which gives the impression that they are distinct phenomena. Yet these levels of social organization cannot, in reality, be disentangled.

Family therapists, trained to focus on the impact of systems on individuals, who became pioneers in cultural competency skills for counselors. The introduction to the landmark work Ethnicity and Family Therapy (McGoldrick et al. 1982, 4) states that "just as family therapy . . . concluded that human behavior could not be understood in isolation from its family context, family behavior also makes sense only in the larger cultural context in which it is embedded." In other words, although there are general principles of family systems organization, actual family systems vary culturally, just like language, music, and cuisine vary among cultures.

In 1973 the American Psychological Association declared "that the provision of professional services to persons of culturally diverse backgrounds by counselors not competent in understanding and providing professional services to such groups shall be considered unethical. It shall be equally unethical to deny such persons professional services because the present staff is inadequately prepared. It shall therefore be the obligation of all service agencies to employ competent persons or to provide continuing education for the present staff to meet the service needs of the culturally diverse population it serves" (Korman 1973, 105).

The 1998 addictions competencies consensus document recognizes that one of the transdisciplinary foundations of competency in the professional treatment of substance abuse is knowledge and appreciation of "the role of family, social networks, and community systems as assets or obstacles in the treatment and recovery process" (CSAP1998, 18).

The Family as a System

Families are social systems. Three general principles of systems are that
- each element (in this case, person) plays a part or role in the system,
- the elements of systems (here, persons) influence each other, and
- systems tend to strive for balance and to maintain the status quo.

Like group counseling, family counseling focuses on process. Unlike a group of strangers together in a room, however, a family has a long-established system of rules, traditions, rituals, and modes of communication. Every family member knows the rules and plays his or her role. A good metaphor for the difference between individual and family counseling is the choice of seat at a football game. You can sit up close and see individual plays or sit farther back in the bleachers and see the entire team play as a unit. In family counseling, the counselor focuses on the way the "team" plays as a unit rather than on each individual's actions.

ACTIVITY (8.1) **In my family . . .**

Form groups that correspond to your family's size (only child, two children, three to five, etc.). Discuss the rules, taboos, and family rituals of your childhoods. Consider issues of drinking, sex, and secrets. Discuss who had power in the family, who drank or took drugs, who supported whom,

> how you were disciplined and by whom, who came into conflict with
> whom and how conflict was handled. Were there family secrets, things
> kept within the family? What happened on special occasions like birth-
> days, holidays, and anniversaries? Share only what you wish to share!

To help a family with an addicted member, counselors need skills in
assessing, understanding, and facilitating change in a number of areas (see
Table 8.1).

Table 8.1 Topics of Concern for Addictive Families

Status, power, and authority
Elements of the system
Definitions of relationships
Conflict—hidden and open
Styles of communication
Family belief systems
Harm to nonaddicted family members
Expectations of treatment
Concepts of privacy and boundaries

Status, Power, and Authority

It is important to determine who has power and authority in the family.
Observations of who makes decisions are necessary, but not always sufficient. Who determines if a referral will be implemented, or aftercare recommendations followed? It may be the oldest child, an uncle, a
grandparent, a grandaunt, or even someone not living in the continental
United States. In some urban communities, teenagers involved in dealing
drugs acquire unusual power in the family. If there are two languages or
cultures involved, the use of a child to translate for parents may transform
the child into a "family hero" or "cultural broker," on whom the family
depends for information and representation. Even a counselor's intervention
can play a role in the family power system. The counselor can play a part
in reinforcing the status and power of individuals who are neglected or
suppressed within the family constellation by looking to them for responses
and comments, and by encouraging and rewarding their participation.

Elements of the System

Referring to the roles played by and the interdependency of family members, Minuchin and Fishman (1981) use special terms to characterize family
relationships. Enmeshment describes excessive or intrusive involvement

where there is no personal space, autonomy, or sense of personal competence. The term fused is almost synonymous. Enmeshment may be a reaction to trauma or loss, a "circling of the wagons," or a coalescing against a perceived threat. Quite typical in the family with an addicted parent is a pattern of enmeshment between the non-using spouse and the children (Edwards 1990, 17). Enmeshed and fused relationships go beyond mere coalitions or alliances; people inter-twine to the point of losing their autonomy, a condition that is necessary for personal growth. Keeping up appearances in the family with an active addict or other disabled person can involve an adaptation where everything revolves around the addiction of another person. To be enmeshed is also to be *dependent*. Enmeshment, then, comes close to the popular if overused concept of 'codependency.'

The opposite of enmeshment is *disengagement*, an abnormal lack of involvement, communication, loyalty, and sense of belonging (Minuchin 1974). Many family members disengage from a problematic, untrustworthy, or troublesome member (living at home or not). An addict may drift away into an addictive netherworld and become disengaged, or may pop in and out of a family or other social system when he or she needs help or wants to resume a normal role. Al-Anon teaches that to avoid codependency and maintain some autonomy and individual identity, a nonaddicted family member must learn to "lovingly detach" from the addict. When individuals or systems are destructive or prevent someone's personal growth, disengagement is a healthy response. This may range from someone refusing to let the other person's addiction be the center of his or her life (for example, refusing to lie for him, clean up her mess, or bail him out) to making it clear that a relationship is not possible as long as the addict is not making an investment in recovery.

The degree of disengagement from addiction varies considerably by ethnicity. Fitzpatrick's study of Puerto Rican addicts (1990) found that their families did not reject addicted members, or, if the addict *was* isolated from the family and later went into recovery, he or she could re-enter with relative ease (119). However, the addict's family may have to put up with a great deal of exploitation (120). This acceptance may not extend to the disgraced or degraded female crack cocaine addict, particularly the crackhouse habitué who exchanges sex for crack (Williams 1989).

Definitions of Relationships

An addictive family system often has its own definitions of the way families are supposed to be, such as what constitutes a "good child" or a "normal marriage." Families may hold sharply contrasting views of what constitutes "good" and "normal." A "good" child may be a passive or quiet child, or one who waits hand and foot on the parents, or one who excels in sports or academics. For some families, "talking back" to parents is a sign of spunk, spirit, and intelligence; for others, it is a sign of disrespect. Cultural norms shape many of these definitions. For example, in the film *Lovers and Other Strangers* a young man complains that he and his wife do not love each other anymore and are planning a divorce. In response, his father explains that romantic love is not necessary in a marriage, that he and the mother were "content" with each other. Not only do family patterns vary among ethnic groups, but also historical changes in all societies affect concepts of love and the family.

Conflict

There are innumerable sources of conflict, hidden or open, in a family, as well as various methods of resolution. Reactions to conflict are based both on norms of appropriate emotional expression and on the propriety of conflict. There may be interminable "cranky" verbal recrimination and accusations, "cut offs" of family members (McGoldrick 1982), or a fused and enmeshed but conflicted relationship. Conflict may take the form of verbal violence, physical violence, indirect sarcasm, nonverbal signals, or attempts to manipulate (by guilt, loyalty, or fear). Conflict may be expressed in the form of verbal battering by a man who resents his wife for earning more money than he does. Disowning a grown sister may be the result of a conflict arising from her upsetting the family system by seeking help and talking about family issues in therapy. If a teen is the focus of conflict, he or she might be "sent back" to his or her country of origin if it is feasible. This might be a combination of a "geographic cure" and a way to minimize conflict. It also functions to remove the "problem teen" from the family and from peer groups that may be perceived as negatively influencing him, and perhaps to transport him to a stricter environment to "straighten him out." A family that has migrated may experience "transgenerational stress," when members of the family do not adhere to traditional norms of deference and respect.

Styles of Communication

Families have many methods and styles of communication, which vary on many axes and dimensions: the degree to which communication is direct or indirect; the attitude such as assertive, playful, passive, hostile, or passive-aggressive; the "channels" employed (words, voice qualities, gesture, posture, and facial expression); and the degree to which emotion is displayed or shared. Some families air important issues at the dinner table; some post notes on the refrigerator; others ignore issues until a crisis erupts. Certain family members may have "permission" to communicate emotion (e.g., only Dad can get angry). An example of cultural differences in family interactions is a scene in the film *Hannah and Her Sisters*, which presents an exaggerated, stereotypical portrayal of ethnic differences for the sake of humor. A split screen contrasts arguments and discussion of medical problems at the main character's urban Jewish family dinner and the reticent and "proper" behavior at dinner with his fiancée's family, who is of old mainline American stock.

Addiction superimposes dysfunctional patterns onto an existing cultural pattern. To cope with pain and anxiety, denial among family members is practiced, resulting in an emotional climate where, as described in detail by Claudia Black (1981, 24–48), the unspoken rules are "Don't talk. Don't trust. Don't feel." Thus, there is noncommunication, incongruent communication (double messages), or destructive communication, and family secrets.

It is important to distinguish between cultural patterns and addictive patterns, or their interaction. One common clinical situation is that a wife demurs from confronting a husband or refuses to confirm what is evident to the counselor about the family's sorry state of affairs. This might be a manifestation of required family loyalty/secrecy found in their culture, the exaggeration of a tendency toward that behavior, or an addictive adaptation.

Family Belief System

The addictive family constructs an *account* of its functioning that family members believe and present to others. The addiction and codependency in the family are often denied, rationalized, excused, or blamed on others. Families in general think of their own behavioral patterns as the norm, a kind of micro-ethnocentrism. This is also true of the dysfunctional family: The abnormal is perceived as normal. Its thinking patterns are also typically helpless and hopeless. Table 8.2 shows some irrational statements or internal dialogues, which may not be consciously realized. Some of the items are adapted from the "alcoholic family rules" summarized by Wegscheider (1989, 80-4).

Table 8.2 Irrational Thoughts of Addictive Families

use as overhead?

The alcoholic's drinking or the drug abuser's using is the most important thing in family life.
Use of alcohol or drugs is not the cause of our family's problems.
Someone or something else caused the problems; the addict is not responsible.
Keep the status quo at all costs.
Everyone pitch in and enable the addict.

Table 8.2 cont.

Don't discuss what's going on with one another or with outsiders.

Don't say what you feel.

If we stop enabling, something terrible will happen.

Things will get better when . . .

Harm to Nonaddicted Family Members

The addicted family is a host to all sorts of problems growing out of addiction and codependency. These problems affect all members of the family including the nonaddicted and extended family members. The harm, which may be short-term, long-term, or both, includes sexual dysfunction, marital paranoia, emotional and physical neglect, and nutritional problems. Family life is traumatic and inconsistent: After an outbreak of violence to which the children and other family members bear witness, there may be a brief honeymoon period where the perpetrator feels remorse, then the nightmare resumes. Chaotic functioning and not knowing what trauma is about to occur generate a great deal of anxiety. Family alliances shift as the system frantically attempts to cope with addictive loss of control. Other aspects of trauma to children include witnessing sex, being molested themselves, and being witness to police intervention in the home. Another harmful effect on families is that out of isolation or preoccupation the family itself, or a subsystem within it, an individual member often gets "stuck" in the normal process of development (Edwards 1990, 59; Sweet 1990).

Expectations of Treatment

Family members coming into recovery hold many myths and unrealistic expectations. Among many working-class and poor populations, for example, the concept of family therapy is alien. They expect individual addictions treatment to be short-term, as in a detox unit. Family counseling, to the extent that this concept is accepted, is also expected to be very short-term. The family may expect primarily concrete instructions and advice. They may believe that "Everything will be OK now that he or she has stopped." They need orientation about the process of family therapy. They need to know that all of the family members will have to work hard to avoid enabling and to communicate honestly and directly, both in treatment and at home. (See the section "Sober Family Living Skills" later in this chapter.)

Privacy and Boundaries

Concepts of boundaries around the family vary greatly. Discussion of intimate relationships with people outside of the family and public expressions of anger or discord may not be permissible. Families act as units, putting up boundaries around themselves. (Chapter 7 discusses boundaries and preserves of the individual.) Concepts of privacy vary among families, as well as among groups in society to which families belong. Topics that are considered privileged information include annual income, sexual orientation of members, psychiatric or legal status, adoptions, even ethnicity. The degree to which privacy about a topic is an issue varies, and is expressed by reactions ranging from discomfort to absolute secrecy. Further, information may not be shared even with individuals in the family, such as children and adolescents. Again, addictive dysfunction is superimposed on regular cultural norms: In the addictive family, there is a great discrepancy between what goes on "backstage" and what is presented "frontstage" in order to "keep up appearances." The family tends to encapsulate, putting up thick boundaries.

Orientation to the concept of family therapy can precede the attempt to elicit such self-disclosure. The need to use a child to translate, mentioned earlier, can make certain topics even *more* taboo, and in general seem disrespectful. Counselors must find out about these customs and attitudes before treading into unknown territory.

Counselors need to gather information in the above areas in order to help family members develop self-understanding of their work together as a system, and to help facilitate a healthier, recovery-oriented system. There is a wide variety of "normal" families, and the counselor may find that he or she must tread a line between respecting the cultural norms of families (and not alienating the clients) and encouraging changes out of the need to facilitate honest communication, individual autonomy, and growth. For example, a counselor may want to bring children into an intervention to confront destructive or enabling behavior on the part of adult family members, but that may conflict with norms of respect for elders.

Enabling, Codependency, and Roles in Families

Family systems tend to adjust themselves around a member's dysfunction. If this happens during caretaking for a cancer victim, at least it is beneficial for the sufferer. In the case of chemical abuse, however, it makes it easier to progress onward in addiction. In treatment of families with addicts, behavior that contributes to continuance and progression of chemical abuse is called enabling. It may include cleaning up the mess made by a drunk, or cleaning up the drunk, bailing an addict out of jail, paying his or her debts, getting out of dinner invitations, calling in sick to the addict's boss, and so on. In its more subtle manifestations, it may be playing peacemaker when conflicts erupt as a result of the addict's behavior. The family often does not see how its "helping" is injurious. A closely related term in the addictions self-help vocabulary is *codependency*. Codependency refers not only to the enabling role played by a significant other or family member of an active addict, but also to the overinvolved investment in playing that role and in making the addict and/or addiction the center of his or her life, like a small satellite circling a planet. Prominent examples of such codependent roles are the rescuer, the martyred caretaker, and the eldest child who takes on parental functions.

The term *codependency* has struck a chord with those who came to believe that their lives were overly circumscribed and defined by the needs of others, and the concept has spread to encompass or explain a multitude of phenomena in society, although rarely grounded in clinical observation or research. In this text, we limit the use of *codependency* to those who adjust their lives around addiction, and who receive gain or benefit to themselves or to the system as a whole, although this gain may seem very indirect and, in fact, be injurious in the long run.

Edwards (1990, 196-7) remarks that he never ceases to be amazed at the "sincere and abysmal ignorance" he encounters in family members who, for example, greet the returning, newly dried-out member with a drink. Moreover, telling family members *not* to allow the drunk back into the house or scrape him or her up off the front lawn and clean him or her up, may run smack dab up against family norms of loyalty and protectiveness that are almost sacred in its culture.

Stress and Trauma

Counselors must take care not to ascribe all enabling to a pathological codependency. Stress, trauma, conflict, and disabilities can lead to adaptations, which are imposed onto existing patterns of behavior.

Pain, difficulty, and special needs are posed by a variety of familial situations:

- death
- physical or mental disability or illness
- absence of a parent
- an addicted family member
- major life events such as migration, job change, and unemployment
- addition of a family member such as a new baby, a sick grandparent, a newly migrated aunt

All of these situations can contribute to some extent to the development of abuse or addiction, which augments the existing dysfunction.

Family Roles

It is normal for families to assign all kinds of roles, often predicated on birth order. The birth-order effect was discussed in detail as early as 1931 by Alfred Adler. Often an eldest child, particularly in a family where there do not seem to be many achievements, goes on to relative success and is pointed to as a family hero. Often a youngest child is the beloved baby or mascot. The middle child may have no special part to play, being neither the first born nor the baby, and may become invisible and/or depressed, misbehave to get attention, and become the identified patient or the scapegoat (Adler 1988).

Whatever the combination of factors, trauma or increased stress may cause even more need for a hero, a mascot, or one less person to bother about. In addition, the family frequently needs someone to "take up the slack"; one person must then do more than necessary and usually take on more decision-making authority, often at the expense of his or her own needs. Salvador Minuchin (1974) describes a "parental child" who carries decision-making authority in a family whose parent is unavailable (absent or unable to function). Virginia Satir (1964) describes a similar concept, the "super-responsible one." All of these adaptations need to be seen against the backdrop of family relationships typical of the culture of which this family is a part.

Scapegoating

Families, like other groups, may actually *need* someone to draw fire, to be a tension-reducer, to take the blame. (The phenomenon of group scapegoating is discussed in chapter 3.) The "Palo Alto group" of family therapy systems researchers (Don Jackson, Jay Haley, Virginia Satir, and Gregory Bateson) as early as 1959 described the way the family often acts as a unit, the communication disturbances, and the process by which the family creates a scapegoat, often a child who is identified as the patient (Kolevzon and Green 1985; Satir 1964; Vogel and Bell 1960). In one respect, however, the Palo Alto group came to a conclusion that was not borne out by later medical research. They reasoned that scapegoating caused childhood psychiatric illness, which does not apply, for example, to childhood autism or schizophrenia, although such an ill individual may indeed be scapegoated for other problems. We know now, however, that schizophrenia and other brain diseases are not caused by poor parenting. A family with an addicted member often directs its anger and frustration at the weakest, most deviant, or problematic member. The hyperactive child may be scapegoated, even abused. The chemically dependent member of a family may become the scapegoat for problems not of his or her creation. By scapegoating, the family is telling itself (Edwards 1990, 31), "If he didn't use, we'd be fine."

Parental children, scapegoats, and other such roles are especially typical of enmeshed families, whose members are overinvolved with each other and underinvolved with their own identities and outside relationships. However, many inner-city family systems beset by addictions do not fit any sort of enmeshed pattern; at the extreme the caregiver is a burnt-out grandparent or there is a no-parent family, which some inner-city schools estimate to be the plight of one-half of their students.

Popular Views

In modern, popular writing on addiction in the family and on codependent roles of children that are carried into adulthood, all of these roles are depicted as especially characteristic of *addicted* families (Wegscheider 1989). There is usually no citation of the earlier researchers and clinicians who observed these roles in *non-addicted* families. (For example, the Palo Alto group's research was not focused on addicts and addictive families.) Moreover, the cultural context that determines family roles is also overlooked, as if there were one type of addicted family that transcended culture. These popular writings are the basis of what might be called a folk model of addicted family roles, subscribed to by many within the adult children of alcoholics movement. Since such roles are so common, many individuals identify with them and ascribe a variety of ills to their being the offspring of a particular variety of addict. To be sure, many individuals suffer tremendously from the legacy of family addiction, and some have indeed been cast in one of these roles as a by-product of addiction in the family. The testimony of such stars as Suzanne Somers has been helpful to those who had not recognized their pain, compulsive behaviors, and the origin of their emotional baggage. Still, there is the real danger that a counselor may identify behavior as that of an adult child of an alcoholic or a codependent when the behavior is actually grounded in other disorders, birth order, cultural patterns, or acculturative stress.

Case in Point

Codependent or Mentally Ill?

A 32-year-old recovering addict who had an alcoholic parent enrolled at a community college. He functioned quite erratically, became a student activist, drifted into irritability, then dropped out for the semester. He entered an expensive rehabilitation clinic for treatment of mood swings caused by "codependency issues." He was later diagnosed as suffering from bipolar disorder; the original interpretation was unhelpful and even dangerous.

Other Disorders

Merlene Miller (personal communication) commented to an addictions-studies newsgroup in 1998 that the chaos in addicted families is sometimes the result of family members who have attention-deficit hyperactivity disorder (ADHD), some of whom self-medicate. Since ADHD has a genetic component, there may be a parent and a child who suffer from problems of hyperactivity, organization, staying on task, and losing and forgetting things, and who also may serve as role models for other children. Yet addiction specialists tend to look only at the substance abuse as culprit for the chaos.

Cultural Patterns

A counselor who is familiar with a client's regular cultural patterns might be guilty of ethnocentrism, that is, looking through cultural blinders and evaluating another culture by the standards of one's cultural rules. For example, McGoldrick's description of the Irish family roles also sounds like the roles that have been described as typical of addicted families. She says that the typical Irish family (not necessarily alcoholic) as described by the mother, contains "My Denny, Poor Mary, and That Kathleen"— a family hero, lost child, and scapegoat (McGoldrick 1982). Scheper-Hughes (1979) provides many examples of the Irish family's "pattern of mythmaking whereby each family in the village seemed to have its successful, high-achieving (usually first-born) 'pet son,' as well as its black-sheep alcoholic, or its shy, incompetent (often last-born) bachelor son" (Scheper-Hughes 1982, 179). These patterns are rooted in both birth order and economics; they are not results of addictive family systems.

As another example, the partially assimilated Mexican American family "retains" and infantalizes the youngest child as a defense against assimilation that has claimed other children. This role is similar to the mascot described by Wegscheider and colleagues (Falicov and Karrer, 1980).

Assessment of Addictive Family Roles

Actress Suzanne Somers describes her father's vacillation between the drunken, violent monster one night and a benign parent the following day. Living with such a wild inconsistency generates tremendous cognitive dissonance and anxiety, which necessitates the need for considerable denial to self and others. On a less catastrophic (nonetheless disruptive) level, the addicted member may simply drift in and out of people's lives. The binge-drinking or chronically relapsing addicted single parent may vacillate between a "normal" parental role and an infantalized childlike role (Edwards 1990, 76-8).

When assessing a family's roles, counselors must take into consideration its community and culture. If counselors are not familiar with them, they should consult someone who is. It is wrong to assume that a role derives from an addictive or dysfunctional adaptation. In trying to locate and identify the roles of the family members of addicts, counselors have found the checklists in figures 8.1, 8.2, and 8.3 helpful.

Figure 8.1 Role of the Spouse or Significant Other

Check one or more of the following if they apply to the spouse or partner of the identified addict. It may be useful to draw an arrow indicating current transition from one role to another or, if the role vacillates, as may be the case when the addict's behavior vacillates, draw a two-headed arrow between the two roles. Indicate whether this role deviates from the typical role of the spouse or significant other in nonaddicted families of this ethnic group.

____ *rescuer: "Love conquers all."*

____ *caretaker: "The poor man, he needs my help."*

____ *long-suffering martyr and saint: "Poor me, I do it all myself for their sake."*

____ *overextended super-responsible one: "I'll take care of it."*

____ *chief enabler: "I'm just trying to help."*

____ *scapegoat: "We'd all be better off if she'd just give up the booze."*

____ *hypochondriac, somaticizing: "I just don't feel well at all."*

____ *joiner in addiction: "Let's get high and stay together."*

____ *placater or peacemaker: "It wasn't that bad. He didn't really mean it."*

____ *blamer, conscience: "You're ruining our lives!"*

____ *battler, limiter: "Don't drink more than one drink tonight."*

____ *disengaged and hostile: "I don't care. After that last fiasco, I'm not having any more to do with my family."*

____ *recovering from codependency, lovingly disengaged from addiction, and/or attempting to achieve referral into treatment: "I love you but I can't be with you until you start getting better."*

____ *other _____*

Figure 8.2 Role of the Active Addict

Check one or more of the following descriptions if they apply to the addict. If the addict, as is often the case, cycles between two behavior patterns depending on his or her state of intoxication, it is important to indicate this. This can be done by drawing a two-headed arrow between the two roles.

___ *absent, disengaged*

___ *baby and/or sick one*

___ *kept out of sight, encapsulated in family*

___ *not encapsulated*

___ *scapegoat*

___ *good, depressed caretaker*

___ *good, depressed dependent*

___ *out of control, but not particularly threatening*

___ *out of control and threatening or abusive*

___ *attempting relapse*

___ *other* _____

Figure 8.3 Roles of the Children of Addicts

Indicate which children play which role, by birth order and gender. A simpler technique is to enter the children's names and ages next to their roles. You can also draw an arrow to indicate transition or growth from one role to another, or a double-headed arrow to indicate vacillation. The binging or relapsing parent, for example, may propel a child repeatedly into "pseudoparent to parent" status and back out again. An individual can play one or more of the following roles:

___ *pseudoparent to other children*

___ *pseudoparent to parent*

___ *pseudospouse to nonaddicted parent*

___ *family hero*

___ *scapegoat, rebel who acts out*

___ *scapegoated child (some are colicky, hyperactive, or have fetal alcohol syndrome)*

___ *invisible one*

___ *placater*

___ *co-abuser who joins the parent in abuse*

___ *battler with addiction who attempts to limit someone's use*

___ *codependent in recovery, lovingly detached*

___ *other* _____

A C T I V I T Y (8.2) **How do I describe this family?**

Solicit volunteers to play family members in a mini-drama, taking roles from the assessment schedules. Identify a situation or a theme for enactment. Other class members then guess which roles are being played.

Addiction or Cultural Norm?

Counselors must take care not to confuse codependency with normal cultural roles, ADHD, bipolar disorder, or birth-order roles. For example, in many African American families, the so-called executive authority over younger children can be the normal role of an eldest daughter as part of a broader pattern of role flexibility (Brisbane 1985a; Brisbane and Womble 1985). Family addiction and codependency literature has patented this role, the family hero, as typical of the addictive family. Such a role may not flow from an addictive framework. When a counselor sees an older child playing a parental part in the family, he or she must be careful to determine, as much as possible, whether this is culturally routine behavior or indicative of a response to addiction in the family.

According to Brisbane (1985), the African American female family hero elaborates upon a normal second-mother role, one who is in charge, and is preparing for her (assumed) adult role. Unfortunately, in the addicted family, the executive/parental child has no adequately functioning mother figure to emulate. The addicted or codependent mother can, perhaps, provide concrete needs, but is less likely to be capable of fulfilling psychological needs. The African American female family hero may not complain about her plight. She is proud of her tenacity and ability; alcoholism is but one more problem to cope with, not to correct (Brisbane and Womble 1985). She is likely to leave home early, via a job or marriage, although she continues to be a source of emotional support for younger siblings and may provide a refuge or safe place for them. These pseudoparents are themselves victimized by not having the opportunity for nurturance, play, and age-appropriate dependence.

The questionnaire in figure 8.4 attempts to gauge whether the child who appears to have parental authority is playing a normal, culturally assigned role, or whether it is forced upon him or her by the circumstances of having an addicted parent. In the instrument, this role is abbreviated as PC for "parental child," using Minuchin's term.

Figure 8.4 Assessment of Parental Child Role

1. *Is the parenting done by the parental child (PC) adequate?*
   A. *good to fair* ___ **B.** *not sure* ___ **C.** *clearly inadequate* ___

2. *Does the PC receive any nurturing or support? If so, is it an*
   A. *adequate amount?* ___ **B.** *minimal?* ___
   C. *clearly inadequate?* ___

3. When authority is delegated to the PC, is it systematic and explicit or does the child pick up tasks by default or via vague instructions?
A. Detailed and explicit ___ B. minimal ___ C. unsupervised ___

4. Does the PC have time to spend with peers?
A. typical amount of time as other peers ___
B. fair to minimal amount of time ___ C. little or no time ___

5. In separate interviews of members of the family, do they have similar and consistent responses (e.g., as to who is in charge of various functions and tasks, who gives orders, etc.)?
A. consistent ___ B. a bit inconsistent ___
C. highly inconsistent ___

6. Do the younger children dress and act in ways that are consistent with other children in their community? For example, an infantalized six-year-old who drinks from a baby bottle would not be consistent with behavior of others in the community.
A. consistent ___ B. a bit inconsistent ___
C. not culturally appropriate ___

7. Does punishment follow some set of clear rules or is it capricious and unpredictable?
A. consistent ___ B. a bit inconsistent ___
C. capricious and unpredictable ___

Scoring: As a crude rule of thumb, three or more checks of option C suggest a poor authority-assignment system. This case is likely to be found in families whose parental figures are not in a condition to conceptualize or assign a system of tasks appropriate to the ages and needs of their children.

Charting the Family

Discussions about the family often focus on examples from movies rather than the participants' own families. Part of this is due to the fact that film exaggerates stereotypes for the purposes of entertainment, which makes it easy to separate personalities and dynamics. But it is also true that it is hard to reflect on one's own patterns of relationships. Sometimes people need help conceptualizing patterns and structures, especially their own, yet it is important. Genograms and family maps help counselors and clients see the patterns in their behavior. Figure 8.5 shows the symbols used in family charts to indicate relationships.

Edwards points out that family charts (genograms and maps) are no more than working hypotheses, one that may need correction or amplification, or that may change. He warns that counselors "must guard against elevating it to the status of a fact" (1990, 50). It is a model of the

Figure 8.5 Symbols for Family Systems Charts

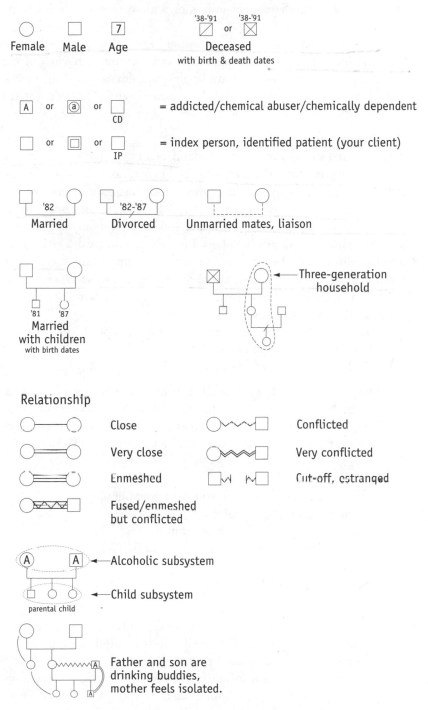

Note: The size of a symbol indicates a person's level of power and authority.

family, which counselors may embellish with meanings that are not there, based on countertransferential identification with some role or ethnocentric assumption.

Culturally competent family assessment must also identify the generations since immigration, if appropriate: bicultural behaviors of the family as manifested in their identity, language, health care, and other areas; transgenerational gaps, if any; and the economic and educational status of family members.

The Genogram

A genogram is a family tree that includes data on the relationships among family members across the span of several generations. It is an efficient way to assess a family by recording information and gaining an overview and summary of relationships that reveal patterns of functioning. Genograms also generate new questions. It is useful not only to the counselor, but also to the family members themselves, who are drawn into fascinating glimpses of their past and present. Very important, a genogram illustrates and underscores the nature of the family as a social system.

Many agencies use preprinted genogram charts with the nuclear family as the baseline. This has two drawbacks:

1. The traditional nuclear family is not the typical structure in many client populations.
2. It unduly focuses attention on the nuclear family.

The geogram should include all significant kin, informally adopted kin, stepkin, and persons referred to or treated as kin who are not legally or biologically related. To elicit information, counselors ask these kinds of questions (Garrison and Podell 1981; McGoldrick and Gerson 1985, 3, 33):

- Who raised you?
- Whom did you have when you were growing up?
- Who is important to you?
- Have you gotten help from the community?
- Has anyone else ever lived with your family? Where are they now?
- On whom do you rely?
- To whom can you go for help?
- Who listens to you?

The nuclear family, defined as the normal family in the dominant culture of the United States, is out of the ordinary as families go, if one surveys cultures around the world. In more societies than not, the unit of family organization is some form of extended family; that is, it contains more than two generations, or other relatives such as nieces, nephews, unmarried or widowed uncles or aunts, and so on. In fact, an extensive web of kinship alliances is found in a large proportion of societies. In the United States it is difficult to maintain common residence for all of these individuals, because of the vicissitudes of employment as well the size of apartments in cities.

While assessing the family, the counselor must take care to identify significant relatives who are not in the immediate household, or in the vicinity, or in the same country. Absent relatives might play a large part in making decisions for the family, which may include encouragement of a referral into treatment or to an alternative, folk healing system.

....

Case in Point
Extended Families

One of the authors (PM) grew up in a largely Irish and Italian neighborhood where extended families continued to exist, but were spread out over several blocks. Many adult men worked on the nearby waterfront, and congregated in the neighborhood bars after work. Their wives, wives' unmarried sisters, and mothers spent many daytime hours working together and visiting without having to walk more than a block or two. Later, while working in a tenant organizing program in the 1960s on the Lower East Side of New York City, PM found members of extended Puerto Rican families occupying two or more apartments in the same or adjacent buildings. Members of the extended family walked in and out of any of the apartments as if they were contiguous. Babies and young children were watched by mothers, aunts, or grandmothers, so that their mothers could work or complete high school.

The genogram can bring out powerful repetitive patterns within family lineages. One student, reporting on the book *Genograms and Family Assessment* (McGoldrick and Carter 1985), read a genogram and accompanying text stating that the Kennedy family males had a pattern of taking risks, violent accidents, sexual impulsivity, and substance abuse. Students raised four more such incidents that had occurred in the Kennedy "clan" since the book was published.

The Family Map

Mapping a family is simpler than constructing its genogram. It takes a few key family members and indicates their relationships. It may be an alternative or ancillary tool to the genogram of a large family system for which the number of lines necessary to indicate biological relations and the quality of relationships grows out of control. A family map is certainly

quicker and easier to draw than a genogram. To create a family map, simply
put down male and female symbols separated by a line to show who are
the parents and who are the children, and do all of the relationship chart
symbols between them. A square or circle can be bigger or smaller to show
power and influence. Figures 8.6 and 8.7 are charts of Hanna's family that
illustrate the case study.

Figure 8.6 Hanna's Genogram

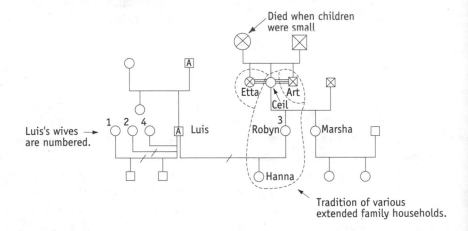

Figure 8.7 Hanna's Family Map

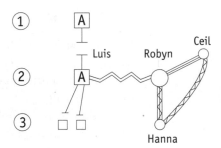

Clinical Case: Hanna and Her Family

The patient is Hanna, a fifteen-year-old female referred to the clinic
by the Student Assistance Program at her high school because of her truancy and alcohol abuse. Her parents, Robyn and Luis, were divorced in
1992. Robyn returned to live with her widowed mother, Hanna's grandmother, and Luis remarried a few years later. Hanna's genogram (Figure

8.6) and family map (Figure 8.7) identify two "strains" of problems in Hanna's heritage, depression and enmeshment on Robyn's side and disengaged and substance-abusing fathers on Luis's side.

Depression and Enmeshment. Hanna's grandmother and Robyn's mother was Ceil, whose father worked in another city while she grew up, leaving three teenaged daughters and three teenaged sons to fend for themselves. Ceil's mother, the functioning parent, died in 1929 at the start of the Great Depression when Ceil was 15. Many of the siblings continued to live together as young adults throughout the 1930s. Ceil married in 1940 and Art, an unmarried uncle, lived with the couple and their children until his death in 1968. Two other uncles (Ceil's brothers) were compulsive gamblers. When Ceil's husband died the following year, a widowed sister, Etta, moved in. The extended family household tradition encouraged enmeshment. Robyn recalled an incident involving her sister Marsha who had moved out and married at 19. Marsha and her husband planned to go to a New Year's Eve party with friends and Ceil, enraged at being denied their company, screamed at her, "Who are they to you, anyway?"

Ceil was described by her daughter Robyn as intelligent, but cynical, gloomy, and morose. She did Robyn's homework for her. When Robyn moved out, it was to an apartment above her mother's store, and her mother set up her utility accounts. Both Robyn and Marsha were diagnosed with dysthymic disorder, but in Robyn's case it was compounded with passivity and indecisiveness. She worked for many years at a clerical job that she despised.

Disengaged, Substance-Abusing Father. Hanna's father Luis, a Hispanic, had an alcoholic father who drifted in but mostly out of the family's lives. Luis's father did not attend his son's wedding, although he was living in the same city at the time and saw Luis shortly before, as well as after the wedding. Luis, an intelligent man proficient in film technology, was a heroin addict for many years, including during his marriage to Robyn. He has two estranged adult sons from a previous marriage. Luis had financed his habit with the rent money and sale of Robyn's jewelry while she was pregnant. She also endured occasional violent outbursts and bailed him out of jail when he was arrested for possession of drugs. Luis entered a methadone-maintenance program after the divorce from Robyn, but augmented the synthetic narcotic with liberal amounts of beer. He married for a third time and, although technically skilled and stabilized on methadone, he did not seek employment but depended on his new wife's income.

The series of events that led to the referral of Hanna include conflict with her grandmother, Ceil, who developed Alzheimer's disease and pestered Hanna. Hanna appeared devoted to Ceil, but reacted with rage at her forgetfulness and pestering and seemed on the verge of violence.

Robyn also was irritable and shouted at Ceil. Some of Hanna's anger seemed based on the neglect by Luis, her newly married father, who often failed to see her even on holidays. When Ceil died after years of decline, Robyn was devastated. Hanna found a bottle of vodka and got drunk at the funeral. In the following year, Hanna frequently exploded with rage at her mother and stayed out all night with her friends. She developed problems with lateness, truancy, and academics. Eventually, she started to "crash" at Luis's house, despite his neglect, which allowed her to escape from her conflicted, fused yet combative relationship with her mother. Robyn resented Hanna's new bond with her father, and complained that she was left alone in the house. Hanna was referred by the student assistance counselor in her high school, after she had appeared in class twice with alcohol on her breath, and had shown signs of marijuana intoxication after lunch period.

𝔸ℂ𝕋𝕀𝕍𝕀𝕋𝕐 ⟨8.3⟩ How do you relate?

Form pairs to serve as interviewer and interviewee, for the purposes of constructing a genogram. Make sure that each pair contains an individual who feels comfortable being the subject of a genogram. As a class, discuss such questions as, What patterns of relationship were uncovered as a result of the genogram? What questions were helpful in eliciting information for the genogram? Were there times that the interviewee was uncomfortable, and if so, why?

Treatment. Family sessions with Hanna and Robyn, using genogram and mapping techniques, followed by individual sessions with Hanna, helped her to identify the conflicted feelings she had about each parent. The genogram and map also helped her understand the guilt she had about their divorce and her relationship with her grandmother. All of this was a very confusing, painful, and emotional situation for a young person who had a familial predisposition to depression. The genogram showed her the pattern of relationships in the family, and how people had a hard time building their autonomous identities. The charting gave a name and an identifiable design to nameless pain and confusion, and enabled Hanna to talk about it rather than drink about it. Robyn was encouraged to go past the delayed developmental milestone of individuation, and develop extrafamilial relationships and activities.

Family Intervention Skills   Sonya include here p.216 of S&S

Vernon Johnson is the name most closely associated with the formal intervention. The term _intervention_ is used in two ways in the human services field: (1) as a general term to refer to any remark, technique, confrontation, or helping effort and (2) to refer to a specialized technique of group confrontation by friends or loved ones to convince an addict to go into treatment. A group intervention can break through denial, at least for the time necessary to get the client into a chemical-free setting.

All addictions counselors have the opportunity to interact with their clients one on one and in group. Unfortunately, family counseling is not always on the agenda, due to agency priorities, lack of reimbursability for family sessions, or the short amount of time during which the agency treats the client. Moreover, the family may be dispersed, or members may be deceased, abroad, or alienated from the client to an extent that cannot be remedied during his or her association with the agency. All members of the family could benefit from even a brief exposure to the possibility of doing things differently. At the very least, counselors should be able to plant some seeds that will germinate when the family is able to listen. A treatment plan should include some family goals and objectives, but it has to be realistic in view of the limited time available for treatment. Lifelong patterns will not be reversed so easily, and counselors should not encourage clients to expect this to happen.

Family treatment has three governing principles:
1. Be aware of process rather than focus on the topic or content under discussion or argument. What is going on between and among people? What is happening in the here and now?
2. Help the clients become aware of these processes and learn to recognize the roles and patterns in their family system.
3. Empower clients to change. In an addictive family, members must learn to disengage from codependent roles, build autonomy, and help get the addicted member into treatment.

The counselor facilitates awareness of the parts that each member plays in the family system, what everyone gets out of it, and if and how members communicate. The counseling skills are the same as some of those for individual and group counseling: listening, reflection, restatement, gentle probing, disputation, establishing a rapport, creating a safe place, and so on. The counselor attempts to facilitate change in the features of the system that thwart growth, individual autonomy, and recovery from addiction. Counselors should not simply give lectures and advice, but encourage members to talk with each other and tell each other their feelings, bring silent members into the conversation, and eventually empower family members to take charge of this process themselves. The counselor needs to be aware of his or her feelings about different family members (possible countertransference) and how they affect the family. For example, counselors should be aware of a tendency to play favorites.

Earlier chapters contain discussions of counseling traps. One of the easiest traps to fall into is accepting the roles that the family communicates. Some examples are letting the invisible "lost child" hide out and be left out, going along with the notion that only the "identified patient" needs help, and letting the helpful, overextended, protective member avoid the necessity for change (e.g., avoid letting go of some of his or her tasks). One trap is arguing about labels early in treatment. It is a poor strategy to try to convert the family to a set of labels, such as "enabling" and "codependency." If counselors provide educational materials about addiction as a family disease, and counselors facilitate honest self-reflection, the family's awareness will grow. Certainly counselors may have to probe or challenge family members by asking questions such as, "Do you think it helps Don face the consequences of his behavior when you bail him out of jail every time he is arrested for public intoxication?" Such a focused or specific question is different from "Do you see how you are an enabler?" The latter can be perceived as name-calling and damning by a person who has shown up to help the addict. The latter question is likely to elicit defensiveness and resistance rather than self-reflection and self-awareness.

The ways in which counselors help families can be broken down into five subprograms: family education, family self-understanding, personal growth, intervention skills, and sober family living skills.

Family Education

Families of addicts may know they are in pain, but they may not know "the nature of the beast" they are facing. Family education is actually the beginning of enlisting kin in the recovery process. Some of the basic elements of such a program include

- basic knowledge of addictions, very basic psychopharmacology, addictive behaviors, and behavior patterns of addicts and their families and friends.
- the nature of enabling and codependency: Letting an addict face the consequences of his or her behavior—which might include embarrassment, loss of income, employment, or jail time—may actually save the addict's life. Keeping addicts from pain by bathing drunks and putting them to bed, mopping up a mess, making excuses, doing their jobs, or bailing them out enables them to continue and progress in addiction.

- the nature of family systems; the "family mobile," a moving sculpture of interdependent parts, is a concrete tool for showing a system and demonstrating that changing one part changes the system, which strives for balance.
- the importance of direct, assertive, honest communication of needs and feelings; "I" statements.
- the role of Al-Anon, Nar-Anon, and other supportive groups that provide hope, identification, positive role models, and a surrogate family and support system to buffer stress and give strength.

see handout

Family Self-Understanding

Awareness is a critical first step to changing. Counselors need to help families come to self-awareness. For example, reasons for enabling that they need to identify may include guilt, shame, fear of hurting the addict, fear of losing the addict's love, misguided sense of loyalty, fear of humiliation, need to feel important or have a meaningful role as protector, fear of change. This situation is delicate because it is a lot to ask people to "confess" motives they are not so proud of in front of their entire family. Some things are best discussed initially in individual sessions or in support groups without other family members present. The counselor must be sensitive to each person's status; some will be ready for self-divulgence before others. Counselors also have to help the family visualize other options and possibilities. What would actually happen if you didn't cover for her with her boss? If you revealed the situation to your child's guidance counselor?

To help families of addicts gain self-understanding, counselors facilitate
- understanding of enabling and codependent behaviors and other adaptations of the family to addiction; how "helping" hurts
- identification of roles played in the family
- understanding of the investment that each person has in his or her role
- understanding of the investment others have in one member's staying in his or her role
- understanding of alliances and subsystems
- understanding of communication patterns in the family, or the lack of communication
- understanding of how the family resists change
- identification of self-statements, internal dialogue, and hidden assumptions

Individuation and Personal Growth

Nonaddicted family members contribute enormously to the family's recovery by focusing on their own individual growth into a healthier person. Counselors facilitate and encourage this by supporting the nonaddicted individuals in learning the following skills:

- *Communicate using "I" statements.* When one person has something to say, he or she can learn to "say it straight." That means speaking for oneself without waffling or talking all around what he or she really wants to say. It also means keeping statements simple and concrete. While this kind of communication does depend on having a clear sense of self, it is also true that repeated practice of assertive "I" statements can contribute to self-empowerment and taking responsibility for self. Practice beginning statements with "I want" or "I feel" or "I need," or "I don't like" or "I won't accept," rather than with "you," "they," or "we."
- *Acknowledge* feelings and needs—emotional, physical, mental, and spiritual. Acknowledge each person's right to have his or her own feelings and needs.
- *Set limits.* Don't let one member's addiction be the center of your life. Examples of setting limits are refusing to fight, refusing to cook at 11 p.m., and refusing to clean up spills caused by a drunken family member.
- *Practice doing things for yourself.* Examples include building relationships and support for yourself, joining a group, and taking a class.
- *Detach lovingly from the active addict.* People who find it impossible to stay in an ongoing relationshiop with an active addict while maintaining reasonable limits may have to go a step farther and detach from the addict. They should make it clear that they are still concerned with the addict, but need to distance themselves for the time being.
- *Dispute negative self-statements* underpinning guilt when detaching from enmeshment, codependency, and enabling. "I got myself into this, so I'm stuck with it" can be countered with "I can't change the addict, but I can change myself and build a better life." Another example is, "He needs my help and protection or he'll die" can be countered with "My help is hurting him by keeping him from the consequences and reality of addiction; he'll die if I continue it."

- *Recognize abuse and losses* that may not be apparent (past and present), grieve them, and move forward. For example, taking care of a drunken mother and four younger children denied one woman a childhood.
- *Build personal responsibility.* Build self-awareness and learn to take care of yourself. Admit mistakes and make amends if possible.

Intervention Skills and Techniques

Johnson (1989) describes the steps in preparing a formal intervention:

1. *Gather the intervention team,* which consists of meaningful people who surround the chemically dependent person. They can be family, friends, or colleagues.

2. *Form and inform the intervention team.* Each person must be willing to risk his or her relationship with the addict, be knowledgeable about the nature of addiction, and be emotionally strong enough to perform as interveners. Part of this step may be addictions education for team members.

3. *Gather the data.* Each person writes a list of incidents or conditions related to the victim's drinking that illustrate his or her concerns. The counselor may need to guide the team to write concrete, first-hand incidents, not general gripes or statements. Johnson suggests using a video of the client while intoxicated (1989, 73). At this time, local treatment options must be explored. The intervention cannot proceed without this information because there will be a short window of opportunity to refer the addict to appropriate treatment.

4. *Rehearse the intervention.* Prepare an agenda and practice the scenario over and over, with someone designated as the client, and plan how to deal with the addict's likely or probable reactions during the intervention. Also think of realistic, yet firm statements of future non-enabling stands by associates of the addict.

The tone of the intervention must be objective, unequivocal, non-judgmental, and caring (61). It is *not* a therapeutic-community confrontation or "haircut." Significant others who cannot control their anger should be excluded and the reasons explained to them in an empathic, non-blaming manner.

Sober Family Living Skills

The rules of engagement change as the family moves from "wet" to "dry"; there is a different set of tasks and dilemmas. Presumably, the addict has been through treatment. Roles and rules are changing. Some of the areas that need to be addressed include the following.

Build healthy communication. Re-establish channels of communication and teach healthy communications skills that are assertive rather than passive, hostile, or aggressive. Assertiveness skills (sometimes know as say-it-straight skills) are important in all types of families. In the "wet" family they help people survive as individuals, set limits, and undermine the conspiracy of silence. In the "dry" family, they further and strengthen the recovery process and help to explore options for a new "family mobile."

Develop sober relationships. If a member of a couple was actively addicted when the two became involved and is now sober, it is almost as if they never were introduced. If one of them has been addicted for a long time and gets clean and sober, it is like starting over. In couples therapy, one technique is to assign a "date" as homework. This provides the opportunity to fashion a relationship, to process the changes they're going through, and, if there are children, to allow some space and intimacy for themselves as a couple outside of the larger family system.

Stay in the here and now. Concentrate on family processes and feelings in the here and now, not content or details of arguments. Chapter 3 discusses skills in distinguishing process from content. Group therapy skills of staying in the here and now can be generalized successfully into work with the family systems. If a member can reflect on what he or she is feeling, and to what underlying issues these feelings pertain, he or she is less likely to pour it all into an argument over who was responsible for letting the toast burn.

Learn appropriate parenting skills. Parents need to take back the responsibility and authority from whomever they gave it to, whoever took it from them, or whoever took over for them—parental child, grandparents, aunts, neighbors, teachers, and so on. They need to set boundaries, get help, distinguish themselves from their children, and distinguish their children from friends or other adults. Parents must support their children's growth through their understandable resistance, anger, built-up hostility, and fears. They must be patient as children develop trust of a parent who betrayed and abandoned them by not being a parent and being unavailable. Parents must also learn that children will test to see whether it is really safe to express their feelings. Parents should not respond to their children's challenges the same way they would to being challenged by another adult.

Children learn or relearn to be children. They must relinquish pseudo-parental or pseudospousal roles and acknowledge how that feels. They may have to grieve the loss of the old role with which they felt comfortable. They may also have to redefine relationships with siblings, and learn to make friends with peers.

Adapt to the new personality of a recovering member. Relating to the new personality of a recovering member is often very difficult for his or her family. Out from under a chemical haze, the sober member may be unexpectedly assertive, argumentative, irritable, demanding, or needy. People in recovery have to try out new ways of being and dealing with all of the other family members. Often, when the family resents the changes and wants to return to its old ways, someone will say "We like you better drunk!" They may sabotage or undermine the real changes that go with recovery, or even go from blaming all problems on the addict for being an addict to blaming all problems on the addict for his new qualities in sobriety and recovery!

Adapt to the new personality of the recovering codependents. The addict's codependents are developing a more assertive style, less controlled. Recovering codependents or enablers are discovering that they have feelings, opinions, and the right to express them. They may have a great deal of difficulty in doing so, and feel guilty the first few times. Another possibility is that their feelings, having been held in or repressed for a long time, are likely to be extreme and not expresssed well when they are trying new methods of communication.

Adapt to a new family structure. Derail arguments about child rearing and finances: "I was used to doing the checkbook alone." "I can't believe you let him watch so much TV." The counselor can help clients turn arguments into discussions about the possibilities of handling these things, helping them brainstorm new and different strategies, and saying, "Why not at least try it? The old ways were not working in healthy or satisfactory ways, were they?"

Adapt to new activities and relationships of family members. "All those damn meetings." "Some of your new friends sure look seedy." Loved ones of people in recovery have to deal with feelings about twelve step or other support groups, fears of infidelity, unfamiliar beliefs and rituals, unavailability of the recovering member of AA/NA who is attending the recommended 90 meetings in 90 days, and resentment of the counselor. "Now that you have your new friends, I suppose you don't need us anymore" or "I guess we're not good enough anymore" or "So now you just do everything she says?" Friends or extended relatives often interpret recovery-milieu involvements as dangerous or strange: "If she keeps going to those meetings, you're gonna lose her for sure. All those feminists giving her ideas. She'll leave you and take you for all you're worth—and you'll never see those kids again," or "She'll take off and leave you with the kids." More astute family members can be enlisted to educate the rest on the importance of growth, autonomy, and outside involvements of the recovering codependent.

Learn to express anger and sexuality in healthy ways. Some clients have difficulties expressing anger or sexuality because in the past these were associated with alcohol, drugs, or violence. Some fear that the loss of control over feelings will precipitate a relapse. In fact, trying to control all of your feelings all of the time, or any form of obsessive perfectionism, is so exhausting and anxiety-producing that a relapse could threaten.

Let go. Once resentments, anger, and pain about the past have been acknowledged and ventilated, all family members (each in his or her own time) must let go of grudges and make direct amends to people they've hurt or offended. Even if drink or drugs were dominating when offenses were committed, an addict's acknowledging the hurt he or she has done clears the air, and, even if it doesn't, helps relieve the offender of guilt.

Deal with the emergence of masked problems. For example, some addicts never had sober sex. Others didn't think much about sex when they were using. Learning to come to terms with this as an adult can be terrifying. Therefore, although some experience sexual dysfunction while addicted, others experience it when clean and sober!

paraphrase

Continue involvement in new support systems. Ongoing participation in fellowships (e.g., AA, Al-Anon, Nar-Anon, Gam-Anon, parenting classes, Al-A-Teen, and Smart Recovery) offer a great deal of support as the family goes through the changes that come with sobriety.

Describe handout →

Stop "walking on eggs" with the recovering member. Addicts who were very out of control during their addiction, or who've had several relapses, may have relatives who are afraid of antagonizing or upsetting them.

Build trust. Having had good reasons to mistrust the recovering addict, the family finds it hard to shed the stigma and fear associated with addiction. On some level, kin may be saying to themselves, "We can never trust him or her again." The recovering addict may sense this mistrust, and think, "They should recognize my recovery and treat me differently."

Abandon unrealistic expectations. Addicts and their families may think that the end of drinking/drugging means the end of problems when actually the journey has just begun. There are still problems with children, layoffs and downsizing, health problems, crime, pollution, and all of the emotional problems that people have who never had a drink or put a needle into their arms.

Counselors must be very patient while addictive family systems are changing. In working with couples especially, counselors have to stay in touch with their own countertransference, and take care not to have an unstated, hidden agenda such as "saving the marriage" as a primary goal.

Some counselors on some level may fear that if a couple separated, this would be a counseling failure; others have experienced their own or their parents' divorce and those feelings come up in treating couples who have children.

Community Systems   *Laura*

Communities are intermediate between individuals and their families and the larger society. They come into being wherever people gather regularly, regardless of the reason. Characteristics and elements shared by communities may not involve society-at-large, or may be a concrete expression of society and culture on a local level. For treatment purposes, it is important to locate social networks and subgroups of addicts and chemical abusers. Major examples of communities include the following:

- *Family and social networks.* The peers of family members are an interface with the community at large. The social networks within the community are often organized according to social class, ethnicity, age, and subcultural differentiation according to style, sexual preference, or other involvement such as "bikers," "street gangs, homosexual teenagers, and devotees of "goth" or "hip-hop" styles.
- *Places where people congregate to interact informally.* Such places include stoops, corners, playgrounds, and stores such as barbershops and grocery stores, which may serve the purpose of community "mini-institutions." Another crucial community institution is, of course, the bar or saloon.
- *Local institutions.* More formal interactions occur in sub-communities such as places of worship, block associations, tenant councils, community precinct groups, trade associations, sports and social clubs, schools, businesses, professional organizations, and police departments.

Öetting and colleagues (Öetting 1982; Öetting and Beauvais 1987) describe how small, close-knit peer clusters influence drug use. Other research has shown how students exaggerate the extent of chemical use among their peers. Imitating these "imaginary peers" contributes to drug use, and many prevention programs now attempt to correct these misperceptions (Perkins and Berkowitz 1986; Perkins Wechsler 1996).

Outreach Work

To be effective, counselors must learn about the local culture(s) of their clients and achieve cultural competence and gain familiarity with norms of family systems, drinking and drugging, and concepts of deviance. They must also learn the best ways to achieve rapport and establish collaborative helping relationships with clients and their families. Contacts with community systems are crucial for a variety of reasons:

- For the counselors to learn about local cultures
- To identify the community's strengths and weaknesses
- To build a referral network
- To house meetings of AA, NA, Al-Anon, Smart Recovery, Nar-Anon, and other recovery fellowships
- To enlist other community institutions to send prevention and intervention messages
- To support applications to government and other institutions for funding

Treatment and prevention programs may espouse values, definitions, and norms concerning alcohol and other drugs that are not congruent with those of the occupational or residential community. It is difficult to intervene in "cultures of drinking" in which the environment defines heavy use as normal and even expected. This is true not only of skid-row or economically marginal communities. California's 1997 ban on smoking in bars ran afoul of long-entrenched norms in which smoking is almost as intrinsic to the bar scene as alcoholic beverages.

The philosophy, mission, and method of addictions treatment agencies is unfamiliar, strange, and even threatening to many newly arrived immigrants. Their resistance to seeking or accepting addictions services is compounded by the fact that large numbers of immigrants are undocumented and illegal. They are understandably fearful of governmental or quasi-governmental agencies who might disclose their status to the immigration authorities.

Case in Point

A Different Culture

This is but one simple example of the barriers between some immigrant subcultures and the majority culture. A block association in Brooklyn, New York, included African Americans, Puerto Ricans, and Caucasians. A large tenement building on the corner housed a large number of newly arrived Mexican and Guatemalan immigrants. Despite posting signs in Spanish up and down the block, the association failed to attract them to block events because the immigrants perceived that they were not wanted, they could not speak English, and they had no personal ties to block association members.

Strengths and Weaknesses

Identification of a community's strengths and weaknesses regarding addiction is critical. A community system is not always a "community support system." In fact, the peer network may be a major enabler of addictive progression or relapse. For example, the support systems of Hispanics may reduce or elevate the possibility of alcoholism (Barrera and Reese 1993). The erosion of social support removes a buffer to acculturative stress, which, as is well documented, leads to chemical abuse. However, social networks and communities that define heavy drinking as normal may induce, encourage, and camouflage patterns of heavy use (Cosper 1979; Fine et al. 1982). Joan Moore (1990) describes a drug-using population in the Chicano "cholo" underclass gang subculture in East Los Angeles, in which several generations of family members featured gang involvement, illegal income, and incarcerations. This subculture is entrenched because it provides the equivalent of an extended family and many easy, immediate rewards. Alternatives to this lifestyle seem relatively remote and unattainable.

A Professional Network

A referral network among community institutions is invaluable. Because many individuals turn to clergy in crises, informed clergy can recognize early addiction in individuals and signs of addiction in families even if it is not the addict who comes for help. Treatment can complement reintegration into the community via religious affiliation (Mariz 1991). Clergy can be an important bridge to treatment not only by referral, but also by preliminary pastoral counseling and education and by supporting formal intervention by family members. As trusted and respected authorities in a community, clergy can also be very influential in an ongoing system that supports recovery. Although *clergy* may be defined habitually to include only mainstream denominations, it should include alternative religions and healers such as the *espiritistas, santeros,* and *curanderos* among the Latino community. Addictions agencies can conduct training and educational efforts among clergy, or they can import trainers from their local councils on alcoholism and addiction, to enable clergy and other influential community figures to acquire skills in identifying and referring problem users.

An elementary task of any treatment agency is to establish a formal, ongoing, collaborative relationship with school administrators and counseling staff for timely intervention and referral of students. If the school has no drug counselor (Student Assistance Counselor or Coordinator), the agency could help the school establish this office, bring in other resources, or establish a satellite office at the school, depending on the needs and desires of the school.

It is critical to enlist the aid of community institutions in sending prevention and intervention messages. At the very least, agency literature can be made available on site. Again, a formal relationship with the school system is a must for treatment agencies. Regardless of how hard the addict and/or the addict's family have worked, maintaining sobriety is an uphill battle in a community that has no supporting role. Established institutions should conciously and actively give out messages that support, admire, and perhaps reward prevention and that encourage appropriate intervention and treatment. Counselors and agencies can, at the very least, provide literature to churches, stores, movie theaters, libraries, grocery stores, and other places where the public gathers. The literature, such as pamphlets or posters, will succinctly inform readers about signs of addiction and give a telephone number to call for further information.

Community Profiles

It is important to create a profile of the community to identify clusters of addicts and their support systems. The prototype community of substance abusers and addicts that flourished until the middle of this century was the traditional "skid row" such as existed on New York City's Bowery, and mini skid-row groupings and "bottle gangs" around railroad stations, in railroad tunnels, and in similar locations. Today's equivalent is the "crackhouse." Starting in the second half of the 1980s, groups of crack cocaine users "squatted" in abandoned buildings, or occupied apartments by either paying off or intimidating landlords or tenants of record. They were environments where crack could be obtained, and where one could stay for days on a crack-using binge or "run." A system of roles developed around the crackhouse, including an individual who went out on "missions" to obtain the drug, a lookout, a proprietor, and addicted women who exchanged sexual favors for drugs. The number of crackhouses declined in the mid 1990s along with the popularity of crack cocaine.

Case in Point

A Drinking Community

One of the authors (PM) interviewed Inuit males from Nain in subarctic coastal Labrador. These men had been incarcerated in the provincial capital of St. Johns, Newfoundland, following stabbings and fights that had resulted in serious injuries. As a result of alcoholic amnestic disorder, the men could not remember the fights. Immediately upon discharge they headed home by coastal steamer, obtained alcohol en route, and became so intoxicated that they walked down the gangplank (lashed to the ship) after the ship had set sail, and had to be rescued from the ocean.

The following are three examples of marginal underclass communities in which drinking and drunkenness are central in social life and communal identification:

1. Some shantytowns in the vast Mexico City urban region, as described by Lomnitz (1977), in which close friendship, or *cuatismo*, is inseparable from drinking. A loner reported, "I do not drink so I don't have any friends" (177).

2. Migrant agricultural worker camps in the Northeastern United States (Friedland and Nelkin 1973, 140-8, 167-72) that feature weekend binging and interpersonal violence.

3. Some Native American and Inuit communities with high levels of addiction.

In some poverty-stricken communities many people are driven into a drug economy, which in turn influences and/or devastates the social fabric (Bourgeois 1995; Ratner 1992; Williams 1989). Many women in urban centers are forced to raise their grandchildren when their children become addicted. The parents abandon their parental responsibilities, have their offspring removed by the child-welfare authorities, or contract HIV through intravenous drug use or sexual relationships with intravenous drug users.

Substance-abusing groups and networks are not always so visible. For example, one urban community of mixed subcultures includes

- newly arrived Central Americans and Mexicans
- lower middle-class African Americans and Hispanics
- young ethnically mixed gay and lesbian couples
- liberal middle-class professionals upgrading the decrepit housing stock
- Euro-American gay men who are underemployed, middle-aged, and typically homeowners who support themselves with rental income and minor investments
- adult alcoholic Euro-Americans who are tenants or subtenants of the professional homesteaders or Euro-American gay men.

A neighborhood tavern in this community is a gathering place for many, but especially for alcoholics. It works as an informal referral system for jobs, not only among themselves, but for homeowners who seek cheap plumbing and contracting workers. This economic support system is of very limited utility, because the plumber, carpenter, or construction worker often fails to appear, disappears with a deposit, or provides incomplete services.

Cultural Systems *Laura*

In 1973 the American Psychological Association declared it unethical for clinical services to overlook the cultural backgrounds of their clients, and for services to be denied or unavailable because staff lack "cultural competency."

In setting standards for professional training in clinical psychology, the American Psychological Association declared

> the provision of professional services to persons of culturally diverse backgrounds not competent in understanding and providing professional services to such groups shall be considered unethical. It shall be equally unethical to deny such persons professional services because the present staff is inadequately prepared. It shall therefore be the obligation of all service agencies to employ competent persons or to provide continuing education for the present staff to meet the service needs of the culturally diverse population it serves. (Korman 1973, 105)

To engage clients in treatment and understand their thoughts about drug use and expectations of treatment, counselors need information about the lifestyles of the groups to which clients belong. Culture is a learned, shared, changing map of reality and system of rules concerning behavior, ideas, communication, and values. Lifestyles of segments of society such as ethnic groups, age groups, social classes, and regions form subcultures. Culture shapes beliefs and behavior regarding chemical use, abuse, intoxication, problems, user roles, and curing. Being familiar with cultural patterns helps a counselor get to know clients. To this end, in 1999 several new treatment programs for new immigrants in New York City were designed to dovetail with gender and family patterns of the ethnic populations served. Korean clients, for example, were reported to be open to female counselors. Treatment for Russian teenagers was aided by involving grandparents, to whom the youth are more likely to listen than their parents (Sachs 1999).

Unfortunately, cultural competency skills have had trouble becoming part of standard practice in the human services; culture tends to remain a peripheral or exotic concern. Until the last decade or so, multicultural awareness, or rather cultural competency, has not been a major concern of the addictions field, where it is often felt that "a drug is a drug," and an "addict is an addict." This can result in overlooking key variables in engaging and treating addicts. To build multicultural awareness the Center for Substance Abuse Prevention (CSAP) has published a cultural competency series for drug-prevention workers, volunteers, and program-evaluation specialists. Professionals in higher education now recognize that binge drinking is deeply rooted in the organizational culture of college, and federally sponsored programs that teach prevention practices emphasize changing the campus culture.

Research

Many studies of the cultural contexts of chemical abuse have investigated how and why beliefs and behaviors vary, and how they shape addicts. However, due to the wide variety of subgroups and the constant cultural change that occurs, a comprehensive, clear map of chemical use among United States subgroups does not exist. Another problem is that ethnographers tend to study the most "pure" cultures in order to obtain neat, clear descriptions of rules and customs, while addictions counselors work among the *least* pure cultures—those that are constantly changing and are blended, disorganized, and often alienated from cultural roots. The client population varies from those who, for example, drink heavily within their standard cultural context to crack users whose ethnic affiliations are on the back burner. As a result of this lack of research, some assumptions about ethnic behaviors are based on observations made decades earlier. Rather than rely on old assumptions or informal observations of others, counselors must develop their own cultural competency.

Cultural Competence

Counselors are ethically mandated to build their awareness and knowledge of their clients' cultures. A counseling skill that must be developed is the ability to elicit information regarding mental maps and categories; value systems regarding alcohol and other drugs; concepts of normality and deviance; models of addiction, abuse, and curing in the client culture or subculture; and other symbolic and ceremonial importance of drug use.

Culture defines drug use. Cultural and subcultural baggage includes mental maps, charts, and categorizations of reality-of colors, kinship categories, roles, and even of chemicals. Consider the following actual interviews:

COUNSELOR: Do you consider yourself a heavy drinker?
CLIENT: No, I only drink beer.
COUNSELOR: You were drunk when you came in here last week.
CLIENT: No, we only had a few beers.

This interview illustrates a mental map shared by many Americans, one that places beer almost outside the domain of alcoholic beverages, a step above soda. A prevention message aimed at modification of that mental map is, "When you drink a lot of beer, you drink a lot!" A beer has same amount of alcohol as a shot of bourbon.

"I would never use drugs. I only drink." is the kind of statement made by a large proportion of Americans who put alcohol and drugs in different categories. Alcohol and other drug-abuse education counters this mapping by pointing out that alcohol is a drug. Similar to the way people do not consider beer alcohol, many people do not consider marijuana a drug. For example, Rita, a 22-year-old crack addict and prostitute, said while discussing her first "date" as a prostitute:

INTERVIEWER: Did you buy drugs with the money?

RITA: No, I wasn't using drugs yet—I bought reefer (Ratner 1992).

While placing a drug "off the map" may be simply naive, it contributes to denying or defining away abuse and addiction. Treatment personnel need to be alert to the words clients use. Just as *drug* meant anything stronger than marijuana to Rita, the word *alcoholic* is sometimes used by alcoholics in reference to more severe alcoholics. Their definition agrees with an aphorism, "An alcoholic is anyone who drinks more than I do."

Culture includes evaluations of and values associated with drugs. People put drugs into "good" and "bad" categories. Cultures weave myths, which are sometimes totally fallacious, or merely exaggerate or misinterpret some real effect. In the 1930s American college students acquired a "reverence for strong drink" (Room 1984) and considered heavy use romantic and adult. American culture in general evaluates beverages containing ethanol as sexy, mature, sophisticated, facilitating of socializing, and enhancing of status if a prestigious brand. In the 1930s and 1940s many people thought that marijuana was literally a "killer weed." In the rather exaggerated portrayal in the film *Reefer Madness*, marijuana resulted in homicidal psychoses and suicides, as if it were a large, combined dose of crack and angel dust.

In the 1960s and 1970s many young members of the "counterculture" called the information-distorting effects of hallucinogenic drugs "mind-expanding," "psychedelic," and "fun." Barbiturates have been considered "thrill pills," "gangster pills," or "sleeping pills," depending on the set, setting, and expectation. Marijuana was thought "sexy" in the 1960s, as the sedative methaquaalone (Quaalude) was in the 1970s. In 1978 five billion minor tranquilizers ("good" drugs) were prescribed, and many people became addicted to them. Cocaine is thought to have special euphoriant qualities, yet in the laboratory cannot be differentiated from other stimulants. Methadone, a highly addictive synthetic opiate, is now accorded the status of a medication, although its street analogues are still the purview of "dope fiends."

Another example of cultural evaluations of drugs appears in Gilbert's (1993) review of literature on Mexican-American drinking patterns, which reveals consistent findings that men conceive of alcohol as having many positive effects. Men have more positive expectations and fewer restrictions of use than women do. This gender gap closes significantly in studies of Mexican-Americans born in the United States.

Cultural rules tell us when, where, and how much drugs can be taken. Many cultures, such as the traditional Italian, French, and Jewish cultures, permit moderate drinking within the family, especially at meals, but disapprove of "drunken" behaviors. Along with such commonalities, there are many differences among groups. Italians consider wine a food, while Orthodox Jews use wine for ritual. In one study of Scandinavian nations, drinking was considered absolutely separated from work. Where drinking was permitted, however, it was allowed to go on to the point of intoxication (Mäkelä 1986). In the United States there are a vast variety of subgroups: some heavy-drinking clients may live in a community where it is not considered excessive to drink with their friends, out of paper bags, or on the street in the morning. Other clients may belong to a "workplace culture of drinking," at a post office or construction site, for example. If a client's drinking is not much greater than that of his or her peers, to be "treated" for this behavior might seem as strange as going into rehab for eating birthday cake!

Culture often gives ceremonial meaning to use of alcohol. In a variety of cultures, rituals involve the use of alcohol, hallucinogens, or stimulants to alter states of consciousness for healing or spiritual purposes, or during a "time out" when normal rules are suspended. It is important to note that this behavior involves no social disruption and is culturally sanctioned. Hallucinogen use by practitioners of Native American religions and cannabis use by Rastafarians have met with legal sanctions. The first notable work on ceremonial use and ethnicity among Americans was by Robert Bales (1946) who attempted to explain the different rates of drinking among an earlier generation of Jews (low) and Irish (high) in the United States in terms of symbolic and ceremonial meanings. For Jews, drinking had familial and sacramental significance, whereas for the Irish it represented male convivial bonding. There was a high rate of heavy drinking among Irish in the 1800s. It was said that they drank because they were Irish. Now, for those who live up to the stereotype, drinking represents Irishness; they are Irish because they drink. Many Jews, on the other hand, think that Jews can't be alcoholic. By that logic, if they are Jewish, even though they drink a lot, they are not really alcoholics. If they give up denial, however, and admit alcoholism, then they can't be Jewish (Blume, Dropkin, Sokolow 1980). Cultural definitions of "not drunks" can contribute to denial (Haberman 1970), especially if alcohol is part of a culture's rituals.

Culture defines "problem behavior" associated with chemical use. A person's use of drugs is identified as a problem when it has negative effects on a cultural group or subgroup. Californians in one study emphasize drunken driving as a major problem, whereas Poles in Poland and Mexicans in Mexico focus on family disturbances and productivity (Österberg 1986, 13). Some U.S. campus cultural maps do not define drunken brawling on Spring Break as "problematical."

Culture defines the origin of drug-related problems. When it is generally recognized that some problems are drug related, a cultural group looks for the cause. United States citizens define alcoholism as a disease far more than the French Canadians or French (Babor et al. 1986). Some South Bronx Hispanics ascribe alcoholism to "spells," spirits, *mal ojo* (the evil eye), and *brujeria* (witchcraft) (Myers 1983). On the other hand, a group may ignore or bypass the entire addiction and attribute it directly to supernatural influence, ulcers, divorce, and car accidents that the counselor recognizes as alcoholism-based. If a problem is traced back to a supernatural cause, a supernatural solution can be called upon. Thus, many seek the help of a folk healer (*espiritista, santero,* etc.).

Highly religious individuals and groups believe that God will solve their problems or they interpret their problems as a punishment from God (Knox 1985). A religious or moral model of addiction may make it difficult to accept a diagnosis founded on medical or psychological concepts. Many health and human-services professionals declare, "I've never had a client with these beliefs." However, a client with such beliefs is unlikely to share them with the helping professional. Also, the client may be influenced by older members in the extended family who interpret the symptoms, make folk diagnoses, and suggest or plan action. These significant others are frequently less acculturated than the client, and adhere to traditional belief systems.

Cultures have elements that can be used to encourage healthier choices. For example, although it is commonplace to cite Latino *machismo* as an incentive to drink, it is also *macho* to take care of your family. Many religious bodies that a client may wish to join or rejoin support healthy behaviors in individuals and families.

Culture shapes addictive careers. For example, African Americans are diagnosed as alcoholic at an earlier mean age than Caucasians (James and Johnson 1996) and may progress into extremely heavy "gamma" alcoholism at an earlier age. Based on a Caucasian model, it would be unlikely to see a 35-year-old with alcoholic organic brain syndrome (AOBS). Clinicians working with such expectations could misdiagnose clients with AOBS as suffering from, say, schizophrenia.

Cultural variations in the "gateway drug" effect have also been reported. That is, the first drug, which becomes the gateway to other drugs, can differ by culture. In the 1970s various researchers found African Americans more likely to progress from marijuana to heroin, while Caucasians moved from marijuana to hallucinogens, barbiturates, and amphetamines (Kleinman and Lukoff 1978). Trends in drug use among various subgroups change continually, and addictions counselors should participate in in-service or other training to ensure that their knowledge of such patterns is not out of date.

Culture shapes personality and psychiatric symptoms, responses of the kin network, and diagnostic decisions based on those symptoms. There is a universal structure and chemistry in the human nervous system that is vulnerable to characteristic disorders. Major mood disorders (clinical or major depression and bipolar, or manic-depressive, illnesses) are related to abnormal neurotransmitter functioning at the synapse. Conversion reactions, dissociative and trancelike states, and sociopathy are also found in many cultures. Although schizophrenia, depression, and manic-depression, and perhaps conversion hysteria are universals, culture shapes the symptoms and manifestations of these diseases through the basic personality structure (modal personality) of each society and its behavior and belief patterns. For example, suspicious personalities will manifest more paranoid ideation, those who have learned helplessness will suffer from more depression. Schizophrenics in tribal societies will not have delusions about flying saucers or the CIA (Torrey 1989). Characteristic clustering or skewing of psychiatric symptoms that are fairly unique to a particular culture are known as culture-bound disorders. The *DSM-IV* lists some of these for the first time in a special appendix, although it does not link them to the taxonomy of disorders in the main body of the text. (See the section "Mentally Ill Chemical Abusers" in chapter 6.)

The psychiatric labeling of a client begins with the ways deviance is assessed by his or her family and peers. In one study, significantly more Irish families than Jewish families tolerated deviant thinking in a psychotic relative, while significantly more Jewish families than Irish families tolerated out-of-line verbal emotionality (Wylan and Mintz 1976). *The psychiatric mislabeling of a client can continue with mental health professionals and medical institutions.* Blacks with AOBS are misdiagnosed as schizophrenic (Bell et al. 1985). Minorities with bipolar disorder are misdiagnosed as schizophrenic (Mukherjee et al. 1983). Hispanic females with dramatic emotional expression are commonly misdiagnosed as suffering from psychiatric or neurological syndromes (Myers 1983). In the 1980s New York City psychiatric wards were filled with what should have struck clinical administrators as a disproportionate number of "paranoid schizophrenics"; those patients were, in fact, suffering from crack paranoia.

Ethnic Subgroups and Acculturation

Counselors must watch for statements that claim to describe the behavior of a cultural group as a whole. Any description of typical cultural behavior is only a description of the most common or most frequent behavior, the mode or center of the bell curve. For example, many Norwegians cry less than Italians do, but there are still some Italians who cry less than some Norwegians! With groups in the process of changing, there is an even greater range of variation. Counselors must take into account subgroups: rich and poor, urban and rural, male and female, and the degree to which groups have been absorbed. It would be a tremendous disservice, for example, to make statements about "Black" drinking patterns, which runs the gamut from middle-class cocktail lounges, to blue-collar wakes, to birthday parties, to the "bottle-gang" of homeless and poor. African American female middle-class drinkers are not so different from the Caucasian middle-class female drinkers, who are typically "moderate," with few nondrinkers and few heavy drinkers. Poorer African American female groups have a larger proportion of nondrinkers; but among those who do drink, there are more heavy than moderate drinkers. African American men are more tolerant than women of heavy drinking. Breaking it down further, being married, older, and church affiliated also were associated with nonacceptance of heavy drinking (Gary and Gary 1985).

Gordon (1981) studied three Hispanic groups, all new to the United States and all blue-collar workers. Dominicans drank less after migration than before migration. They emphasized suave or sophisticated drinking and saw drunkenness as *indecente* (not respectable). Alcoholics were believed to be sick, perhaps from some tragic experience. Guatemalans drank more after migration than before migration; one third of the males were often drunk and binged most weekends. Being drunk was glamorous, sentimentalized. They boasted of hangovers, even when they didn't have one. The Puerto Ricans broke down into middle-class American-style moderate drinkers; depressed, wife-abusing, alcoholic welfare recipients; and various sorts of polydrug abusers, including diffusion from mainland "druggie" youth culture (Gordon 1981). This represents only a fragment of the subcultural and acculturative spectrum.

Blane (1977) surveyed Italian-American drinking patterns. He compared four subcultural groups; recent arrivals in the United States, those born abroad but were living in the United States longer than ten years, children of immigrants, and grandchildren of immigrants. Among males, the percentage of daily drinkers declined from 92 percent among recent immigrants to 15 percent among the grandchildren of immigrants, as did wine and cordial consumption. Any heavy use (5 drinks at one sitting) rose from 1 out of 5 to 3 out of 5 and once-a-week heavy use went from 1 out of 8 to 1 out of 3, moving from generations. Daily drinking by women declined from 73 percent to 9 percent, and wine and cordial use was decreased by more than half. Occasional heavy use by women went from 6 percent to 32 percent, and weekly heavy use from 3 percent to 10 percent.

Biculturalism and Code-Switching

Many individuals live a bicultural existence because they live in two cultural worlds. This may be because their work or school is in a different cultural context from their home (family and peers), or because each generation in their families lies at a different spot on an acculturative continuum. Biculturalism may be a combination of both of these factors. In some areas, biculturalism is not a case of one person living in two cultures but of the two cultures having blended. Many urban, mainland Puerto Ricans in New York live in a blended culture which has developed its own dialect, known as "Newyorkian" or "Spanglish." For example, one counselor active in a tenant organizing program among Hispanic urbanites found that his high school Spanish did not help him to understand the complaints of tenants relative to the *rufo* and the *elevador*, translations of *roof* and *elevator* that contrasted with the standard Spanish *techo* and *ascensor*. They worried that their children were going to *flunkear* (flunk) and that they had no place to *parquear* (park).

Another familiar phenomenon in urban areas with large numbers of new arrivals who do not speak English is code-switching. The term *code-switching* usually applies to communicative behaviors such as speech or body language. For example, people change from English to their native language and back again during a conversation, a paragraph, even a sentence. One of the authors (PM) observed Italian physical plant personnel using typical Italian gestures in a small group discussion, but their arms dropped to their sides like puppets with strings suddenly cut when their Irish supervisor joined the group.

The concept of code-switching deserves applicability beyond communication, and can shed light on help-seeking and help-rejecting behaviors of clients in mental-health and addictions treatment settings. This can be a function of an individual fluctuating between health resources of folk and "official" medical culture. In one study, Chinese patients alternated between the hospital emergency room and the herbalist, depending on the perceived success of the treatments or by disease entity (Myers 1983). Code-switching can also reflect the participation of several "cooks" in preparing the treatment "meal." For example, a well-known addictions administrator recounted how he was brought to an *espiritista* for both his heroin addiction and a bone infection that gave him a permanent limp, before he was recruited to a therapeutic community (personal communication to Peter Myers, 1980).

Bell and Evans (1981, 20-2) point out that the addictions counselor, like the teacher or any other staff member in a helping or human-services system, may not be aware of a bicultural identity, since they only see one "face" of the client. The seemingly successfully bicultural individual may, in fact, be adrift between the two cultures and flee from one to another when uncomfortable. In addition, if the "home" culture is the substance-abusing milieu and the counselor and/or treatment system is predominantly identified with the majority culture, this adds a motivational or cognitive disadvantage to the clean-and-sober road. Bell and Evans further note (28-9) that cultural identity has different "faces": how individuals see them-selves, how they think others see them, and how they see themselves in relation to others.

Acculturative Stress

Families undergoing "acculturative stress" are at risk for development of chemical abuse and dependency. It is stressful and frustrating when indi-viduals and families are no longer in their traditional culture, but cannot successfully assimilate into the new culture. Some stress-inducing factors are denial of meaningful participation in the social structure, especially in a way that communicates a "loss of face"; reversal of power roles; lack of deference to elders; denial of culturally important roles such as bread-winner; isolation; lack of support systems; and communication or role pat-terns that result in not using support systems. Acculturation is uneven within the ethnic subculture: the poor, women, older persons, and city-dwelling families may be more immersed in traditional behavior patterns than economically stable men, youth, and rural families. This can lead to strain within the peer or family network (Avanzo, Frye, and Froman 1994).

Although acculturative stress is often associated with poverty, among some relatively affluent Miami Cubans, use of drugs was associated with upward mobility and overwork, which led to parental neglect (Page 1990, 172), weakening of parental influence, and the actual breakup of many nuclear families.

Behavioral problems, including drug use, are linked in many studies not only to intergenerational differences due to different stages of accul-turation, which accentuates family conflict, distance, and alienation, but also to inflexibility of parents to the traits of the new culture (Adrados 1993; Page 1990, 176; Rio et al. 1990, 211-2; Szapocznik and Kurtines 1989).

Suspended Ethnicity

Many addicts seem to lose their affiliation to any ethnic group, reli-gion, and community of origin while they are actively addicted; they regain their roots, or grow new roots, during recovery. Westermeyer (1981) gives us the term *suspended ethnicity*. The lifestyle devoted to obtaining and using alcohol and/or other drugs supersedes ethnic values and affiliations, and may lead to exploiting the group, and to acquiring like-minded peers (46). With disease progression, progressively less time and fewer resources are devoted to ethnic-pertinent relations and institutions. Westermeyer cites Chippewa, Irish-American, and African American examples (47). User sub-cultures, which are fragile, exploitive of members, and relatively interethnic, are alternatives into which one is initiated (48). During suspended ethnicity, though, norms, mores, and values may be kept on as ideals or symbols (e.g., Navaho jewelry, Catholic religious medal) (48-9).

A C T I V I T Y (8.4) What's the neighborhood like?

1. Identify the sociocultural groups in the catchment area served by your agency or an agency in your neighborhood.
2. What are the beliefs (expectations of use, definitions/explanation/degree of acceptable or of problem use) and behavior patterns regarding alcohol and other drugs among each sociocultural group served by the agency? Consider heavy drinking for release on weekends, after-hours social drinking, stigmatization of heavy users, and so on.
3. Identify community institutions and subgroups.
4. Identify social networks of substance abusers and their interface with the community.
5. Who are the potential allies in the community who are or could be part of a support system?

References

Ablon, J., and W. Cunningham. 1981. "Implications of Cultural Patterning for the Delivery of Alcoholism Services." *Journal of Studies on Alcohol,* suppl. 9, part 3, Special Populations, 5.

Adler, A. 1998. *What Life Could Mean to You.* Center City, MN: Hazelden Educational Materials.

Adrados, J-L. 1993. "Acculturation: The Broader View," in *Drug Abuse among Minority Youth: Advances in Research and Methodology.* M. R. De La Rosa and J-L. Adrados, ed. NIDA Research Monograph 130. Rockville, MD: U.S. Dept. of HHS, Public Health Services.

Avanzo, C. E., V. Frye, and R. Froman. 1994. "Culture, Stress, and Substance Use in Cambodian Refugee Women." *Journal of Studies on Alcohol* 55: 420-26.

Babor, T. F., et al. 1986. "Concepts of Alcoholism among American, French-Canadian, and French Alcoholics," in *Alcohol and Culture: Comparative Perspectives from Europe and America. Annals of the New York Academy of Sciences* 472, T. F. Babor, ed.

Bacon, M. K., H. Barry, III, and I. L. Child. 1965a "A Cross-Cultural Study of Drinking 2: Relations to Other Features of Culture." *Quarterly Journal of Studies on Alcohol,* suppl. 3: 29-48.

———. 1965b. "A Cross-Cultural Study of Drinking 5: Detailed Definitions and Data." *Quarterly Journal of Studies on Alcohol,* suppl. 3: 78-111.

Bales, R. F. 1946. "Cultural Differences in Rates of Alcoholism." *Quarterly Journal of Studies on Alcohol* 6: 489-99.

Barrera, M., and F. Reese. 1993. "Natural Support Systems and Hispanic Substance Abuse," in *Hispanic Substance Abuse.* R. S. Mayers, B. L. Kain, and T. D. Watts, ed. Springfield, IL: Charles C. Thomas.

Bell, C. C., et al. 1985. "Misdiagnosis of Alcohol-Related Organic Brain Syndromes: Implications for Treatment." *Alcohol Treatment Quarterly* 2, (fall/winter): 45-65.

Bell, P., and J. Evans. 1981. *Counseling the Black Client.* Center City, MN: Hazelden.

Black, C. 1981. *It Will Never Happen to Me.* New York: Ballantine Books.

Blane, H. 1977. "Acculturation and Drinking in an Italian American Community." *Journal of Studies on Alcohol* 38, 7:1324-44.

Blume, S., D. Dropkin, and L. Sokolow. 1980. "The Jewish Alcoholic: A Descriptive Study." *Alcohol Health and Research World* 4, 4:21-6.

Bourgeois, P. 1995. "Workaday World: Crack Economy." *The Nation* (4 December): 706-11.

Boyd-Franklin, N. 1989. *Black Families in Therapy: A Multisystems Approach.* New York: Guilford Press.

Brisbane, F. L. 1985a. "Understanding the Female Child Role of Family Hero in Black Alcoholic Families," *Bulletin of the New York State Chapter of the National Black Alcoholism Council, Inc.* 4, 1 (April): 47-53.

———. 1985b. "A Self-Help Model for Working with Black Women of Alcoholic Parents," *Alcoholism Treatment Quarterly* 2, (fall/winter): 47–53.

Brisbane, F. L., and M. Womble. 1985. "Afterthought and Recommendations." *Alcoholism Treatment Quarterly* 2, (fall/winter): 54-8.

Chavez, E. L., and R. C. Swaim. 1992. "Hispanic Substance Use: Problems in Epidemiology," in *Ethnic and Multicultural Drug Abuse.* J. E. Trimble, C. S. Bolek, and S. J. Niemcryk, ed. New York: Harrington Park Press.

Colon, F. 1980. "The Family Life Cycle of the Multiproblem Poor Family," in *The Family Life Cycle, A Framework for Family Therapy.* E. A. McGoldrick and M. McGoldrick, ed. New York: Gardner Press.

Cosper, R. 1979. "Drinking as Conformity," *Journal of Studies on Alcohol* 40 (September): 868-91.

CSAP (Center for Substance Abuse Prevention). 1998. "Addiction Counselor Competencies: The Knowledge, Skills, and Attitudes of Professional Practice," *Technical Assistance Publication Series* 21. Rockville, MD: U.S. Dept. of HHS, Substance Abuse and Mental Health Administration.

Dennis, P. A. 1975. "The Role of the Drunk in an Oaxacan Village," *American Anthropologist* 77: 856-63.

Edwards, J. T. 1990. *Treating Chemically Dependent Families.* Minneapolis, MN: The Johnson Institute.

Falicov, C. J., and B. M. Karrer. 1980. "Cultural Variations in the Family Life Cycle: The Mexican American Family," in *The Family Life Cycle: A Framework for Family Therapy.* E. A. McGoldrick and M. McGoldrick, ed. New York: Gardner Press.

Field, P. B. 1962. "A New Cross-Cultural Study of Drunkenness," in *Society, Culture, and Drinking Patterns*. D. Pittman and H. White, ed. New York: Wiley.

Fine, M., S. H. Akabas, and S. Bellinger. 1982. "Cultures of Drinking: A Workplace Perspective." *Social Work* 26, (September): 436-42.

Fitzpatrick, J. P. 1990. "Drugs and Puerto Ricans in New York City," in *Drugs in Hispanic Communities*. R. Glick, and J. Moore, ed. New Brunswick: Rutgers University Press.

Friedland, W. H., and D. Nelkin. 1973. *Migrant Agricultural Workers in America's Northeast. Case* Studies in Cultural Anthropology. New York: Holt, Rinehart, and Winston.

Garbarino, M. S. 1981. "Life in the City: Chicago," in *The American Indian in Urban Society*. J. O. Waddell and O. M. Watson, ed. Boston: Little Brown.

Garrison, V., and J. Podell. 1981. "Community Support Systems Assessment for Use in Clinical Interviews." *Schizophrenia Bulletin* 7:1.

Gary, L. E., and R. B. Gary. 1985. "Treatment Needs of Black Alcoholic Women." *Alcohol Treatment Quarterly* 2, (fall/winter): 97-113.

Gilbert, M. J. 1993. "Intracultural Variation in Alcohol-Related Cognitions among Mexican-Americans," in *Hispanic Substance Abuse*. R. S. Mayers, B. L. Kain, and T. D. Watts, ed. Springfield, IL: Charles C. Thomas.

Gonzalez, D. H., and J. B. Page. 1981. "Cuban Women, Sex Role Conflicts, and the Use of Prescription Drugs." *Journal of Psychoactive Drugs* 13: 47-51.

Gordon, A. J. 1981. "The Cultural Context of Drinking and Indigenous Therapy for Alcohol Problems in Three Migrant Hispanic Cultures." *Journal of Studies on Alcohol* suppl. 9: 217-40.

Graves, T. D. 1967. "Acculturation, Access, and Alcohol in a Tri-Ethnic Community." *American Anthropologist* 69: 309-21.

Greeley, A. W., W. C. McCreadym, and G. Theisen. 1980. *Ethnic Drinking Subcultures*. New York: Praeger/J. F. Bergin.

Haberman, P. W. 1970. "Denial of Drinking." *Quarterly Journal Studies of Alcoholism* 31, 3: 711-20.

Horton, D. 1943. "The Functions of Alcohol in Primitive Societies: A Cross-cultural Study." *Quarterly Journal of Studies on Alcohol* 4: 199-320.

James, W. H., and S. N. Johnson, ed. 1996. *Doin' Drugs: Patterns of African American Addiction.* Austin: University of Texas Press.

Jilek, W. G. 1981. "Anomic Depression, Alcoholism, and a Culture-Congenial Indian Response." *Journal of Studies on Alcohol,* suppl. 9, part 3, Special Populations, 149-58.

Jilek-Aall, L. 1981. "Acculturation, Alcoholism, and Indian-Style Alcoholics Anonymous." *Journal of Studies on Alcohol,* suppl. 9, part 3, Special Populations, 143-48.

Johnson, V. 1989. "Intervention: How to Help Someone Who Doesn't Want Help." Minneapolis, MN: The Johnson Institute.

Kleinman, A., and B. Goode. 1985. *Culture and Depression.* Berkeley: University of California Press.

Kleinman, A., and T-Y. Lin, ed. 1981. *Normal and Abnormal in Chinese Culture.* Higham, MA: Reidel (Kluwer).

Kleinman, P. H., and I. F. Lukoff. 1978. "Ethnic Differences in Factors Related to Drug Use." *Journal of Health and Social Behavior* 19 (June): 190-99.

Knox, D. H. 1985. "Spirituality: A Tool in the Assessment and Treatment of Black Alcoholics and Their Families." *Alcohol Treatment Quarterly* 2, (fall/winter): 31-44.

Kolevzon, M. S., and R. G. Green. 1985. *Family Therapy Models.* New York: Springer.

Korman, M. 1973. *Levels and Patterns of Professional Training in Psychology* (Recommendations of APA Vail Conference). Washington, DC: American Psychological Association.

Leighton, A. 1959. *My Name Is Legion.* New York: Basic Books.

Leighton D. 1971. *The Empirical Status of the Integration–Disintegration Hypothesis in Psychiatric Disorder and the Urban Environment.* New York: Behavioral Publications.

Leighton D. et al. 1963. *The Character of Danger.* New York: Basic Books.

Lomnitz, L. A. 1977. *Networks and Marginality: Life in a Mexican Shantytown.* New York: Academic Press.

Madsen, W. 1967. "The Alcoholic Agringado." *American Anthropologist* 66: 355-61.

Mäkelä, K. 1986. "Attitudes Towards Drinking and Drunkenness in Four Scandinavian Countries," in *Alcohol and Culture: Comparative Perspectives from Europe and America,* Annals of the New York Academy of Sciences, vol. 472, T. F. Babor, ed.

Mariz, C. L. 1991. "Pentacostalism and Alcoholism among the Brazilian Poor." *Alcoholism Treatment Quarterly* 8, 2: 75-82.

Marshall, M. 1979. *Weekend Warriors: Alcohol in a Micronesian Culture*. Mountain View, CA: Mayfield.

Mayers, R. C., B. L. Kail, and T. D. Watts. ed. 1993. *Hispanic Substance Abuse*. Springfield, IL: Charles C. Thomas.

McGoldrick, M. 1982. "Ethnicity and Family Therapy: An Overview," in *Ethnicity and Family Therapy*. M. McGoldrick, J. K. Pearce, and J. Giordano, ed. New York: Guilford Press.

Minuchin, S. 1974. *Families and Family Therapy*. Cambridge, MA: Harvard University Press.

Minuchin, S., and N. D. Fishman. 1981. *Family Therapy Techniques*. Cambridge, MA: Harvard University Press.

Moore, J. 1990. "Mexican-American Women Addicts: The Influence of Family Background," in *Drugs in Hispanic Communities*. R. Glick, and J. Moore, ed. New Brunswick: Rutgers University Press.

Mukherjee, S. M., et al. 1983. "Misdiagnosis of Schizophrenia in Bipolar Patients: A Multiethnic Comparison." *American Journal of Psychiatry*, 140: 1571-74.

Myers, P. L. 1983. "Cautionary Notes on Ethnic/Psychiatric Stereotypes." *Medical Tribune*, September 28.

Öetting, E. R. 1992. "Planning Programs for Prevention of Deviant Behavior: A Psychosocial Model" in *Ethnic and Multicultural Drug Abuse*, J. E. Trimble, C. S. Bolek, and S. J. Niemcryk, ed. New York: Harrington Park Press.

Öetting, E. R., and F. Beauvais. 1987. "Peer Cluster Theory, Socialization Characteristcs, and Adolescent Drug Use: A Path Analysis." *Journal of Counseling Psychology* 34: 205-13.

Österberg, E. 1986. "Alcohol-Related Problems in Cross-National Perspective: Results of the ISACE Study." *Alcohol and Culture: Comparative Perspectives from Europe and America*, Annals of the New York Academy of Sciences, vol. 472, T. F. Babor, ed.

Page, J. B. 1990. "Streetside Drug Use among Cuban Drug Users in Miami," in *Drugs in Hispanic Communities*. R. Glick and J. Moore, ed. New Brunswick: Rutgers University Press.

Panitz, D. R. 1983. "The Role of Machismo and the Hispanic Family in the Etiology and Treatment of Alcoholism in Hispanic American Males," in *American Journal of Family Therapy* 11, 1: 31-44.

Perkins, H. W., and A. D. Berkowitz. 1986 "Perceiving the Community Norms of Alcohol Use among Students: Some Research Implications for Campus Alcohol Education Programming." *International Journal of the Addictions* 21, 9-10: 961-76.

Perkins, H. W., and H. Wechsler. 1996. "Variation in Perceived Drinking Norms: Its Impact on Alcohol Abuse: A Nationwide Study." *Journal of Drug Issues* 26: 961-74.

Ratner, M. 1992. *Crack Pipe as Pimp.* Lexington, MA: Lexington Books.

Rio, A., D. A. Santisteban, and J. Szapocznik. 1990. "Treatment Approaches for Hispanic Drug-Abusing Adolescents," in *Drugs in Hispanic Communities*, R. Glick and J. Moore, ed. New Brunswick: Rutgers University Press.

Room, R. 1984. " 'A Reverence for Strong Drink': The Lost Generation and the Elevation of Alcohol in American Culture." *Journal of Studies on Alcohol* 45, 6: 540-5.

Rubington, E. 1990. "Drinking in the Dorms." *Journal of Drug Issues,* 20, 3: 451-61.

Sachs, S. 1999. "Treatment Rooted in Culture: Typing Drug and Alcohol Programs to Immigrants' Backgrounds." *The New York Times* (16 June): B1, B10.

Satir, V. 1964. *Conjoint Family Therapy.* Palo Alto: Science and Behavior Books.

Scheper-Hughes, N. 1979. *Saints, Scholars, and Schizophrenics.* Berkeley: University of California Press.

Simons, R. C., and C. Hughes, ed. 1985. Culture-Bound Syndromes. Dordrecht: Reidel (Kluwer).

Spindler, G., and L. Spindler. 1971. *Dreamers without Power: The Menomini Indians.* New York: Holt, Rinehart, and Winston.

Sweet, E. E. 1990. "Unattained Milestones in Chemically Dependent Adolescents from Dysfunctional Families." *Journal of Adolescent Chemical Dependency* 1, 2: 139-47.

Szapocznik, J., and W. Kurtines. 1989. *Breakthrough in the Family Therapy of Drug Abusing and Behavior Problem Youth.* New York: Springer.

Szapocznik, J., Rio, A., et al. 1986. "Bicultural Effectiveness Training (BET): An Experimental Test of an Intervention Modality for Families Experiencing Intergenerational/Intercultural Conflict." *Hispanic Journal of Behavioral Sciences* 8: 303-30.

Szapocnik, J., Santisteban, D., et al. 1984. "Bicultural Effectiveness Training: A Treatment Intervention for Enchanting Intercultural Adjustment." *Hispanic Journal of Behavioral Sciences* 6: 317-44.

Torrey, R. F. 1989. *Schizophrenia and Civilization.* New York: Jason Aronson.

Vogel, E. F., and N. B. Bell. 1960. "The Emotionally Disturbed Child as the Family Scapegoat," in *The Family.* N. W. Bell and E. F. Vogel, ed. New York: The Free Press.

Wegscheider, S. 1989. *Another Chance.* Palo Alto: Science and Behavior Books.

Westermeyer, J. 1981. "Research on Treatment of Drinking Problems: Importance of Cultural Factors." *Journal of Studies Alcohol,* suppl. 9, part 2, issue 1, pages 40-53.

———. 1989. *Mental Health for Refugees and Other Migrants.* Springfield, IL: Charles C. Thomas.

Westermeyer, J., and J. Neider. 1986. "Cultural Affiliation among American Indian Alcoholics: Correlations and Change over a Ten-Year Period," *Alcohol and Culture: Comparative Perspectives from Europe and America.* Annals of the New York Academy of Sciences, vol. 472, T. F. Babor, ed.

Williams, T. 1989. *The Cocaine Kids.* Reading, MA: Addison-Wesley.

Wylan, L., and N. Mintz. 1976. "Ethnic Differences in Family Attitudes Towards Psychotic Manifestations with Implications for Treatment Programs." *International Journal of Social Psychiatry* 22, 2 (summer): 86-95.

Suggested Reading on Multicultural Counseling

Atkinson, D. R., G. Moren, and D. W. Sue, ed. 1989. *Counseling American Minorities: A Cross Cultural Perspective*, 3rd ed. Dubuque, IA: William C. Brown.

Axelson, J. A. 1985. *Counseling and Development in a Multicultural Society*. Pacific Grove, CA: Brooks/Cole.

Baruth, L. G., and M. L. Manning. 1991. *Multicultural Counseling and Psychotherapy: A Lifespan Perspective*. New York: MacMillan.

Lee, C. C., and B. L. Richardson, ed. 1991. *Multicultural Issues in Counseling: New Approaches to Diversity*. Alexandria, VA: American Association for Counseling and Development.

Lum, D. 1992. *Social Work Practice and People of Color: A Process-Stage Approach*. Pacific Grove, CA: Brooks/Cole.

Pedersen, P., ed. 1985. *Handbook of Cross-Cultural Counseling and Therapy*. Westport, CT: Greenwood Press.

Pedersen, P., et al., ed. *Counseling Across Cultures*, 3rd ed. Honolulu: University of Hawaii Press.

Ponterotto, J. G. 1991. *Handbook of Racial/Ethnic Minority Counseling Research*. Springfield, IL: Charles C. Thomas.

Rebach, R. 1992. "Alcohol and Drug Use Among American Minorities," in *Ethnic and Multicultural Drug Abuse*. J. E. Trimble, C. S. Bolek, and S. J. Niemcryk, ed. New York: Harrington Park Press.

Sue, D. W., and D. Sue. 1985. *Counseling the Culturally Different: Theory and Practice*, 2nd ed. New York: Wiley.

Vacc, N. A., J. Wittmer, and S. B. DeVaney, ed. *Experiencing and Counseling Multicultural and Diverse Populations*, 2nd ed. Muncie, IN: Accelerated Development.

Resources

Selected Journals

Addiction
Carfax Publishing Co.
PO Box 25
Abingdon, Oxfordshire, OX143UE
England

Addiction Research
Harwood Academic Publishers
c/o STBS Order Dept.
P. O. Box 786
Cooper Station, NY 10276

Alcohol and Alcoholism Journal
  Oxford University Press,
  2001 Evans Road
  Cary, NC 27513
  www.oup-usa.org/journals

Alcoholism Treatment Quarterly
  Haworth Press, Inc.
  10 Alice Street
  Binghampton, NY 13904
  www.haworthpressinc.com

American Journal of Drug and Alcohol Abuse
  Marcel Dekker, Inc.
  270 Madison Avenue
  New York, NY 10016

Contemporary Drug Problems
  Federal Legal Publications, Inc.
  157 Chambers Street
  New York, NY 10016

The Counselor
  National Association of Alcoholism and Drug Abuse Counselors
  3717 Columbia Pike, Suite 300
  Arlington, VA 22204-4254

Drugs and Society
  (new title in 2000: *Journal of Ethnicity in Substance Abuse*)
  Haworth Press, Inc.
  10 Alice Street
  Binghampton, NY 13904
  www.haworthpressinc.com

Employee Assistance Quarterly
  Haworth Press, Inc.
  10 Alice Street
  Binghampton, NY 13904
  www.haworthpressinc.com

International Journal of the Addictions
(new title: *Substance Use and Misuse*)
Marcel Dekker, Inc.
170 Madison Avenue
New York, NY 10016

Journal of Alcohol and Drug Education
Alcohol and Drug Prevention Association (ADPA)
1555 Wilson Blvd., Suite 300
Arlington, VA 22209

Journal of Chemical Dependency Treatment
Haworth Press, Inc.
10 Alice Street
Binghampton, NY 13904
www.haworthpressinc.com

Journal of Child and Adolescent Substance Abuse
Haworth Press, Inc.
10 Alice Street
Binghampton, NY 13904
www.haworthpressinc.com

Journal of Drug Issues
P. O. Box 4021
Tallahassee, FL 32315-4021

Journal of Maintenance in the Addictions
Haworth Press, Inc.
10 Alice Street
Binghampton, NY 13904
www.haworthpressinc.com

Journal of Studies on Alcohol
Rutgers University
P. O. Box 969
Piscataway, NJ 08850

Journal of Substance Abuse Treatment
    Pergamon Journals, Ltd.
    Headington Hill Hall
    Oxfordshire, OX3 OBW
    England

NIDA Notes
    National Institute for Drug Abuse
    U.S. Department of Health and Human Services (DHHS)
    Parklawn Bldg, Room 10-39
    5600 Fishers Lane
    Rockville, MD 20857
    www.nida.nih.gov/NIDA_Notes/NNIndex.html

Substance Abuse
    Association for Medical Education and
        Research in Substance Abuse
    Manisses Communication Group, Inc.
    P.O. Box 3357
    Providence, RI 02906-0757

Web Resources

GOVERNMENTAL SITES

Addiction Technology Transfer Centers
www.views.vcu.edu/vattc/Atcs.html

Center for Substance Abuse Treatment (CSAT, SAMHSA)
www.samhsa.gov/csat/csat.htm

Indian Health Service
www.tucson.his.gov

National Clearinghouse on Alcohol and Drug Information
www.health.org/aboutn.htm

National Institute on Alcohol Abuse and Alcoholism
www.silk.nih.gov/silks/niaaa1

National Institute for Drug Abuse
www.nida.nih.gov/NIDAHome.html

NIDA Notes
www.nida.nih.gov/NIDA_Notes/NNIndex.html

Treatment Improvement Exchange
www.treatment.org/

INFORMATION AND REFERRAL

Center on Addictions and Substance Abuse (CASA)
www.casa.columbia.org/home.htm

Center for Substance Abuse Research (CESAR)
www.bsos.umd.edu/cesar.html

Hazelden Publishing Company publishes a wide
   variety of publications on addictions
www.hazelden.org

National Council on Alcoholism and Drug Dependency
(affiliate councils on alcoholism and drug dependency exist in
   every state)
www.ncadd.org/index.html

Partnership for a Drug-Free America
www.drugfreeamerica.org

"Treatment Works" fact sheets from CSAT; very helpful in
   advocacy efforts
www.health.org/csat/tx_final/fact_sheets/fact1_7.htm

COUNSELOR AND COUNSELOR CERTIFYING BODIES

ICRC/AODA (International Consortium and Reciprocity
   Commission on Alcohol and Other Drug Abuse)
www.icrcaoda.org/
www.icrcaoda.org/icrclist.htm

National Association of Alcohol and Drug Abuse Counselors (affiliates in most states)
www.naadac.org

LINKS TO ADDICTION SITES

Addiction Treatment.com
www.addiction-treatment.com/site_menu.htm

Substance Abuse Links
www.smu.edu/~alc_edu/links.html

Web of Addictions
www.well.com/user/woa/index.html#return_point

SELF-HELP GROUPS

Al-Anon and Alateen
www.Al-Anon-Alateen.org/

Alcoholics Anonymous
www.aa.org/

Gamblers Anonymous
www.gamblersanonymous.org/index.html

Narcotics Anonymous
www.wsoinc.com/

Smart Recovery
www.smartrecovery.org/

Women for Sobriety
www.womenforsobriety.org/body.html

OTHER SITES OF INTEREST

Addiction Counselor Competencies Consensus Document (TAP 21)
www.views.vcu.edu/nattc/tap21.html

American Society of Addiction Medicine
www.asam.org/

Dual Diagnosis Website
www.erols.com/ksciacca/

Harm Reduction
www.cts.com/crash/habtsmrt/hrmtitle.html
www.ex.ac.uk/~dregis/hitlist1.html

Higher Education Center on Alcohol and other Drug Abuse
www.edc.org/hec/

International Coalition for Addiction Studies Education
www.homestead.com/INCASE/

National Addiction Centre (GB)
www.iop.bpmf.ac.uk/home/depts/psychiat/nac/nac.htm

Project CORK (major reference and bibliographic site)
www.dartmouth.edu/dms/cork/

Therapeutic Communities of America
www.tcanet.org/

Instructors may request a copy of this resource list with embedded hypertext links by e-mailing Peter Myers at myers@essex.edu. Inquiries about networking with addiction studies educators will be forwarded to the appropriate regional or task force coordinator of the International Coalition for Addiction Studies Education.

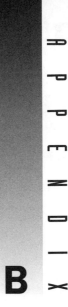

Self-Help Groups

Alcoholics Anonymous

Preamble

Alcoholics Anonymous is a fellowship of men and women who share their experience, strength, and hope with each other that they may solve their common problem and help others to recover from alcoholism.

The only requirement for membership is a desire to stop drinking. There are no dues or fees for A.A. membership; we are self-supporting through our own contributions.

A.A. is not allied with any sect, denomination, politics, organization, or institution; does not wish to engage in any controversy; neither endorses nor opposes any causes. Our primary purpose is to stay sober and help other alcoholics to achieve sobriety.

Source: Reprinted with permission of the A.A. Grapevine, Inc.

The Twelve Steps

1. We admitted we were powerless over alcohol—that our lives had become unmanageable.
2. Came to believe that a Power greater than ourselves could restore us to sanity.
3. Made a decision to turn our will and our lives over to the care of God *as we understood Him.*
4. Made a searching and fearless moral inventory of ourselves.
5. Admitted to God, to ourselves and to another human being the exact nature of our wrongs.
6. Were entirely ready to have God remove all these defects of character.
7. Humbly asked Him to remove our shortcomings.
8. Made a list of all persons we had harmed, and became willing to make amends to them all.
9. Made direct amends to such people wherever possible, except when to do so would injure them or others.
10. Continued to take personal inventory and when we were wrong promptly admitted it.
11. Sought through prayer and meditation to improve our conscious contact with God *as we understand Him,* praying only for knowledge of His will for us and the power to carry that out.
12. Having had a spiritual awakening as the result of these Steps, we tried to carry this message to others, and to practice these principles in all our affairs.

The Twelve Traditions

1. Our common welfare should come first; personal recovery depends upon A.A. unity.
2. For our group purpose there is but one ultimate authority—a loving God as He may express Himself in our group conscience. Our leaders are but trusted servants; they do not govern.
3. The only requirement for A.A. membership is a desire to stop drinking.
4. Each group should be autonomous except in matters affecting other groups or A.A. as a whole.
5. Each group has but one primary purpose—to carry its message to the alcoholic who still suffers.

6. An A.A. group ought never endorse, finance or lend the A.A. name to any related facility or outside enterprise, lest problems of money, property and prestige divert us from our primary purpose.

7. Every A.A. group ought to be fully self-supporting, declining outside contributions.

8. Alcoholics Anonymous should remain forever nonprofessional, but our service centers may employ special workers.

9. A.A., as such, ought never be organized, but we may create service boards or committees directly responsible to those they serve.

10. Alcoholics Anonymous has no opinion on outside issues; hence the A.A. name ought never be drawn into public controversy.

11. Our public relations policy is based on attraction rather than promotion; we need always maintain personal anonymity at the level of press, radio and films.

12. Anonymity is the spiritual foundation of all our Traditions, ever reminding us to place principles before personalities.

Source: The Twelve Steps and Twelve Traditions are reprinted with permission of Alcoholics Anonymous World Services, Inc. (A.A.W.S.) Permission to reprint the Twelve Steps and Twelve Traditions does not mean that A.A.W.S has reviewed or approved the contents of this publication, or that A.A.W.S. necessarily agrees with the views expressed herein. A.A. is a program of recovery from alcoholism *only*—use of the Twelve Steps and Twelve Traditions in connection with programs and activities which are patterned after A.A., but which address other problems, or in any other non–A.A. context, does not imply otherwise.

Smart Recovery: Self-Management and Recovery Training

Purposes and Methods

1. We help individuals gain independence from addictive behavior.

2. We teach how to
   A: enhance and maintain motivation to abstain
   B: cope with urges
   C: manage thoughts, feelings, and behavior
   D: balance momentary and enduring satisfactions

3. Our efforts are based on scientific knowledge, and evolve as scientific knowledge evolves.

4. Individuals who have gained independence from addictive behavior are invited to stay involved with us, to enhance their gains and help others.

Commentary

1. We assume that addictive behavior can arise from both substance use (e.g., psychoactive substances of all kinds, including alcohol, nicotine, caffeine, food, illicit drugs, and prescribed medications), and involvement in activities (e.g., gambling, sexual behavior, eating, spending, relationships, exercise, etc.). We assume that there are degrees of addictive behavior, and that all individuals to some degree experience it.

For some individuals the negative consequences of addictive behavior (which can involve several substances or activities) become so great that change becomes highly desirable. To individuals who are, or think they may be, at this point, we offer our services. Our groups are free of charge (although a donation is requested). Our Internet listserve discussion group is free to those who can access it. There is a nominal charge for our publications.

2. Gaining independence from addictive behavior can involve changes that affect an individual's entire life, not just changes directly related to the addictive behavior itself. Consequently there appear to be as many roads to gaining independence from addictive behavior as there are individuals. For many the road will lead somewhere other than using our services. We recommend they follow the direction they have chosen, and we wish them well. They are always welcome to return.

Individuals who have been successful in gaining independence from addictive behavior appear to have made changes in all four areas we teach about. These four areas could also be described as maintaining motivation, coping with craving, thinking rationally, and leading a balanced lifestyle. Although we teach important information in each of these areas, ultimately it is the individual's determination and persistence to keep moving forward that will determine how much success is achieved.

Our services are provided for those who desire, or think they may desire, to achieve abstinence. Individuals unsure about whether to pursue abstinence may observe in our group discussions how abstinence can be achieved, and how it can help. Even those whose ultimate goal is moderated involvement with their substances or activities may benefit from participation in abstinence-oriented discussions. Benefit could occur if the individual aims to engage in selected periods of abstinence, or frames the goal as abstaining from overinvolvement (as opposed to all-involvement).

Much of the information imparted by us is drawn from the field of cognitive-behavioral therapy (CBT), and particularly from Rational Emotive Behavior Therapy, as developed by Albert Ellis, Ph.D. In general, CBT views addictive behavior more as a complex maladaptive behavior than as a disease. Use of the CBT perspective allows us to use a rich and easily accessible body of ideas, techniques, and publications. Some of these publications we are able to make available directly to our participants, and others are available through bookstores and other sources.

3. What we offer is consistent with the most effective methods yet discovered for resolving emotional and behavioral problems. As scientific knowledge advances, our teachings will be modified accordingly. Individuals with religious beliefs are likely to find our program as compatible with their beliefs as other scientifically derived knowledge and applications.

4. The length of time an individual will derive help from our services is variable. For many sincere participants there will come a time when attending our groups, or participating in our other services, is more in conflict with the pursuit of their life goals than enhancing them. Although these participants will always be welcomed back if they want to come, this conflict signals that the time for graduation has arrived.

One of the most enduring satisfactions in life is helping others. The individuals who have nurtured SMART Recovery® thus far have reported intense satisfaction at witnessing the positive changes our participants have experienced, and at witnessing the influence we are having on professional addictive behavior treatment. We offer to others, whether graduates of our efforts or not, the opportunity to join us in experiencing that satisfaction.

SMART Recovery® Self-Help Network
24000 Mercantile Road, Suite 11
Beachwood, OH 44122
Phone: 216/292-0220
Fax: 216/831-3776
E-mail: SRMAIL1@aol.com

Source. Reprinted with permission from the Web site of SMART Recovery® Self-Help Network.

A

Abstinence Violation Effect, 32
Abuse. *See also* Alcohol and other
drug abuse
of children, 117–118
physical and mental, 164–165
polyabuse, 2, 20–21
recognizing, 259
sexual, 209
stages of, 154
Accreditation, 11–12
Acculturation
in ethnic subgroups, 274–275
stress of, 276
Action stage, 39
Active listening skills, 63–66
*Addiction Counseling Competencies:
The Knowledge, Skills, and Attitudes of
Professional Practice*, 2–3, 57
Addictions. *See also* Treatment
diagnosis of, 152–154
dual diagnoses of, 182
misdiagnosis in, 185–187
in peer groups, 7
religious model of, 272
similarities to psychiatric
symptoms, 185–187
Addictive voice concept, 27
Addicts. *See also* Clients
attitudes about, 54–56
detachment from, 258
roles of, 245–246

shame and stigma of, 206
Addict sociopathy, 191–192
ADHD. *See* Attention-deficit
hyperactivity disorder
Adler, Alfred, 242
Adolescents
as clients, 174–177
treatment placement criteria for, 14
Advertising, ethics of, 128
Affect, behavior and cognition, 36–38
Affect management, 34
African Americans
alcohol use in, 274
roles in families, 247
Age of clients
adolescents, 174–177
children, 174
middle–aged and elderly, 177–178
Agreements, covert, 85
AIDS
losses from, 222
prevention of, 19, 21
Al-Anon, 26, 236
Alcohol amnestic disorder, 209
Alcohol and other drug abuse (AODA)
in adolescents, 174–176
binge drinking, 175, 269
in children, 174
cultural variations in, 269–272,
274–275
detoxification from, 17
as a disease, 32, 272
in homosexuals, 179–180

Alcohol and other drug abuse (AODA)
(*continued*)
   in mentally ill, 180–195
   methadone and, 20–21
   in middle aged and elderly, 177–178
   natural recovery from, 6–8
   polyabuse, 2, 20–21
   psychiatric symptoms and, 186
   in women, 179
Alcohol-efficacy expectation, 36
Alcoholic organic brain syndrome
(AOBS), 272, 273
Alcoholics
   cultural definitions of, 269–270
   neurological impairment in, 210–211
   shame and stigma of, 206
Alcoholics Anonymous (ΛΛ)
   desperation in members, 5
   as a disease model, 31–33
   inpatient rehabilitation and, 27
   start of, 25, 58
   therapeutic communities and, 28
   twelve-steps and traditions, 25–26,
   295–297
American Psychological Association,
234, 268
American Society of Addiction Medicine
(ASAM), 12–13, 14
Anger, expressing, 29–31, 217, 219, 262
Antisocial personality disorder (ASPD),
191–192
AODA. *See* Alcohol and other
  drug abuse
Approach–avoidance conflicts, 8–9, 204
ASPD. *See* Antisocial personality disorder
Assertiveness skills, 260
Assessments
   biopsychosocial, 151–152
   described, 149–150
   diagnosis in, 152–154
   of families, 244–246, 250–251
   intake procedure in, 150–151
   purposes of, 150
   of self, 165
Attending skills, 62, 63
Attention-deficit hyperactivity disorder
(ADHD)
   in addicted families, 244

antisocial personality disorder
   and, 191–192
   clients with, 194–195
Attitudes, 53–59
   about addicts, 54–56
   categories of, 56–59
   defined, 53
Authority in families, 235
Avoidance behavior, 8–10
Awareness
   of feelings, 31
   of group process, 84–86
   multicultural, 268
   self-awareness, 257
Awfulizing, 35, 73

B

BEAST concept, 27
Behavior
   affect, cognition and, 36–38
   avoidance, 8–10
   defensive, 98–102
   flirtatious or sexual, 216
   in group process, 84
   polyabuse, 2, 20–21
   relapse, 10–11
Behavioral change, 35
Belief systems of families, 238–239
Biculturalism, 275–276
Binge drinking, 175, 269
Biopsychosocial assessment, 151–152
Bipolar disorder, 189–190
Birth-order effect, 242
Blackouts, 209
Borderline personality disorder (BPD),
   192–194
Boundaries
   of counseling relationships, 115–116,
   224–229
   of families, 240
   guidelines on, 229
   intangible, 227–229
   personal space and, 225–226
   physical contact and, 227
   skills in, 229–230
BPD. *See* Borderline personality disorder
Brain damage, 210–211, 272, 273
BUMP questions, 146

C

C.A.G.E. questions, 145–146
CAMI (chemically abusing mentally ill).
  See Mentally ill chemical abusers
Case management
  assessment in, 149–154
  counseling and, 143–144
  described, 141–143
  impediments to treatment in,
    164–167
  progress notes in, 159–161
  resources and services in, 161–164
  screening in, 144–148
  treatment plans in, 154–158
Case presentations, 76
Casriel, Daniel, 28
CBT. *See* Cognitive–behavioral therapy
Certification of counselors, 11
Change
  adapting to, 261–262
  behavioral, 35
  cognitive, 35–36
  fear of, 209
  impediments to, 105–107
  motives for, 8–11
  stages of, 38–39, 41, 62
Charting families, 248–254
  case study of, 252–254
  family maps, 251–252
  genograms, 250–251
  symbols in, 249
Chart notes, 76, 159–161
Checkbook diagnosis, 127
Chemical dependency (CD). *See
  also* Alcohol and other drug abuse
  borderline personality disorder
    and, 193
Children. *See also* Families
  abuse of, 117–118
  adolescents, 14, 174–177
  birth-order in, 242
  as clients, 174
  in family roles, 242–243, 246
  harm to, 239
  informed consent for, 120–121
  in parental roles, 247–248, 260–261
  parenting skills and, 260
Class clown role, 95

Clergy, 265
Client-centered counseling, 60
Clients
  age of, 174–178
  "career" of, 76
  ethnicity and social class of, 165,
    274–275
  flirtatious or sexual, 216
  gender of, 164–165, 179, 206–207
  as impediment to change, 106
  legally incompetent, 120–121
  mentally ill chemical abusers,
    180–195
  relationship with counselor, 3–4
  romantically interesting, 218
  sexuality of, 179–180
  variations in, 2, 173–174
Clinical discussions, 121
Codependency
  adjusting to new personalities in, 261
  enabling and, 240–241
  enmeshment and, 236
  family roles and, 242–247
  stress, trauma and, 239, 241
Code-switching, 275–276
Cognition, affect and behavior, 36–38
Cognitive-behavioral therapy (CBT)
  for alcoholism, 32
  described, 33
  session formats, 60–61
Cognitive change, 35–36
Cognitive therapy
  approach to counseling, 36
  downward arrow technique of, 67–68
  in listening skills, 65
  session structure for, 61
Communication
  building skills, 260
  code-switching, 275–276
  of feelings, 30–31
  styles of, 237–238
  using "I" statements, 258
Community systems
  examples of, 263
  outreach work in, 263–264
  profiles of, 266–267
  referral networks in, 265–266
  strengths and weaknesses of, 265

Competence of counselors
    impairment of, 129
    lack of preparedness of, 129–131
    lack of responsibility of, 131–132
Compulsory treatments, 6
Confidentiality, 116–126. *See also* Ethics
    of clinical discussions, 121
    of disclosure and redisclosure,
        119–120
    Duty to Report and, 117–118
    Duty to Warn and, 117
    Informed Consent and, 118–119
    of legally incompetent clients,
        120–121
    medical emergencies and, 122–123
    pending legislation and, 125
    qualified service organizations
        and, 124
    of records, 118, 121, 161
    regulations for, 116–117
    statistical aggregates and, 124
    of subpoenaed information, 122
    training and, 124
Conflicts
    approach-avoidance, 8–9, 204
    in families, 237
Confrontation-denial trap, 41, 203
Confrontations
    elements of, 71–74
    in group treatment, 29
    in Synanon, 28
Consent for Release of Information, 113,
    118–119
Consultations, 114–115
Contemplation stage, 38
Content of group process, 84
Continuing education, 132–133
Continuum of care, 13, 18, 19
Cooling-down phase, 93
Cooperative living arrangements, 18
Cost-containment, 13, 15, 16, 166–167
Counseling. *See also* Families
    boundaries in relationships, 115–116
    case management and, 143–144
    countertransference in, 218–222
    dealing with loss, grief and regrets,
        222–224
    defined, 2
    directive, 3–4, 62

limited perspectives of, 59
    in methadone programs, 21
    mystique of, 58–59
    pitfalls of, 219
    practice dimensions of, 2–3
    relationship with client, 3–4
    setting limits and boundaries in,
        224–229
    transference in, 214–217
Counseling approaches, 33–41
    affect management, 34
    behavioral change, 35
    cognitive change, 35–36
    integration of affect, behavior and
        cognition, 36–38
    motivational interviewing, 40–41
    stages of change in, 38–39, 41, 62
Counseling psychology, 60
Counseling skills
    attitudes in, 53–59
    engagement, 62
    formats for, 60–61
    for individual addictions, 59–60,
        61–62
    influencing, 71–74
    leading, 66–71
    listening, 63–66
    process recording, 75–77
    timing, 74
Counselors
    attracted to clients, 218
    credentials of, 128
    job titles of, 128
    nondegreed, 11, 12
    preparation of, 11–12
    self-disclosure of, 69–71
Countertransference, 218–222. *See
    also* Transference
    negative, 219–222
    positive, 218–219
Crackhouses, 266
Credentials of counselors, 128
Criminal justice system
    emotional conflicts and, 222–223
    offenses and treatments, 165–167
    trends in treatment of offenders, 15
CSAT document, 2–3, 57
Cultural competence, 269–273

Cultural customs
    of drinking, 264, 266–267
    of family relationships, 237–238
    family roles and, 244, 247
    of groups, 82–83
    personal space and, 225–226
Cultural systems, 268–277
    acculturative stress, 276
    biculturalism and code-switching,
        275–276
    competency skills in, 269–273
    ethnic subgroups and acculturation,
        274–275
    multicultural awareness in, 268
    research of, 269
    suspended ethnicity, 276–277

D

Daytop Village, 28–29
Day treatments, 16
Decisional balance sheets, 205
Dederich, Charles, 28
Defensive behavior
    against emotion, 100–102
    in groups, 98–100
    as impediment to change, 106–107
Deitch, David, 28
Demandingness, 35
Denial
    by addicts' social networks, 211–212
    confrontation–denial trap, 41, 203
    in family, 238
    fear and, 208–209
    impaired memory and, 209–210
    labels and stereotypes and, 206
    neurologic impairment and, 210–211
    as a part of addictions, 202–204
    in psychiatric history, 203
    recurring, 213–214
    social and emotional skills in, 210
    social standing and, 206–208
    in treatment motives, 204–205
Depression
    in families, 253
    learned helplessness model of, 37
    in mood disorders, 189–190
Desperation, 5–6
Detachment from addicts, 258

Detoxification units, 17
Diagnosis of addictions, 152–154
    dual diagnoses, 182
    misdiagnosis in, 185–187
*Diagnostic and Statistical Manual, Fourth
    Edition (DSM–IV)*, 153–154, 185
Diagnostic creep, 127
DiClimente, Carlo, 38–39
Directive counseling, 4, 62
Disclosure and rediscfosure, 119–120
Disease models, 31–33
Disengagement, 236, 253–254
Disputing technique, 73
Documentation
    Consent for Release of Information,
        113, 118–119
    process recording, 75–77, 107
    progress notes, 76, 159–161
    record confidentiality, 118, 121
    of treatment plans, 154–158
Dominator role, 96–97
Double approach-avoidance conflict, 204
Drinking. *See also* Alcohol and other
    drug abuse
    binge, 175
    cultures of, 264, 266–267
Drug Abuse Survey Project, 28–29
Drug use. *See also* Alcohol and other
    drug abuse
    cultural variations in, 269–273,
        274–275
    values associated with, 270–271
Dry drunk, 35
*DSM–IV. See Diagnostic and Statistical
    Manual, Fourth Edition*
Duty to Report, 117–118
Duty to Warn, 117

E

EAP. *See* Employee Assistance Programs
Eclectic counseling approach, 33, 39
Education of family, 256–257
Elderly clients, 177–178
Ellis, Albert, 37
Emotional illiteracy/literacy, 34, 101, 210
Emotional intelligence, 210
Emotions
    affect management and, 34

Emotions (*continued*)
   countertransference, 218–222
   defense against, 100–102
   loss, grief, regrets, 222–224
   models of, 29–31
   transference, 214–217
   underdeveloped skills, 210
Empathy
   in client-centered counseling, 60
   in cognitive-behavioral therapy, 37, 40
   in listening skills, 63
Employee Assistance Programs (EAP),
   6, 13
Enabling
   codependency and, 240–241
   denial and, 211–212
   examples of, 6
   family roles and, 242–247
   stress, trauma and, 241
Engagement skills, 62, 145
Enmeshment, 235–236, 243, 253
Ethics
   boundaries in, 115–116
   competence in, 129–132
   of family therapy, 234
   financial, 126–127
   legal issues in, 116–126
   moral dilemmas in, 113–114
   nondiscrimination in, 133–134
   objectivity in, 134–135
   principles and standards of, 111–113,
     114
   professional growth in, 132–133
   of representation of services, 127–129
   of supervision and consultation,
     114–115
   of treatment system, 135–136
Ethnicity
   of clients, 165
   disengagement and, 236
   of subgroups, 274–275
   suspended, 276–277
Ethnocentrism, 244
Evaluations. *See* Assessments
Evidentiary privilege, 122
Expectations
   alcohol-efficacy, 36
   of treatment, 239
   unrealistic, 262

Experimentation in adolescents, 175–176
Expert trap, 41
Exposure, fear of, 208

F

Facilitators, group, 86 , 96
Facilities, treatment
   continuum of care in, 13
   levels of care in, 12–13, 14
   methadone-maintenance, 19–23
   models of treatment in, 12
   recent changes in, 13, 15
   types of, 15–19
Families
   adapting to changes in, 261–262
   assessment of, 250–251
   attention-deficit hyperactivity
     disorder in, 244
   belief systems of, 238–239
   charting, 248–255
   communication in, 237–238
   conflict in, 237
   cultural patterns of, 237–238, 244
   denial by, 207, 211–212
   education of, 256–257
   enabling and codependency in,
     240–241
   harm to non-addicted members, 239
   individuation and personal growth in,
     258–259
   intervention skills for, 255–263
   privacy and boundaries of, 240
   relationships in, 235–237
   roles in, 207, 235–236, 242–248
   scapegoating in, 242–243
   self-understanding of, 257
   sober living skills, 260–263
   as a social system, 234–235
   status, power, and authority in, 235
   stress and trauma in, 241
   treatment expectations of, 239, 262
   treatment principles, 255
Family maps, 251–252
Fear
   of change, 209
   of exposure, 208
   of rejection, 208
Feedback, 92

Feelings. *See also* Emotions
　　acknowledging, 258
　　awareness of, 31
　　blunting or negating, 101
　　communication and awareness of,
　　　30–31
　　painful and threatening, 209–210
　　reflection of, 63–64
Fellowships. *See* Self-help groups
Financial ethics, 126–127
Flirtatious behavior, 216
Focusing
　　in confrontations, 72
　　in listening skills, 68
Formats
　　counseling, 60–61
　　of groups, 91–93
　　for group treatment plans, 103–105
FRAMES acronym, 41
Frustration tolerance, low, 36
Funding for treatment, 13, 15, 166–167
Fused relationships, 236

 G

Gateway drug effect, 272–273
Gender of clients, 179, 206–207
Generalizing, 36
Genograms, 248, 250–251, 252
Goals
　　for group treatments, 103–104
　　of treatment plans, 157–158
Grief, 34, 222
Group culture, 82–83
Group leaders, 86–88
Group process
　　awareness of, 84–86
　　as impediment to change, 105–106
　　intervening in, 86–88
　　involving marginal members, 86–87
　　peer leadership in, 87–88
　　understanding process, 88
Group treatment
　　confrontations in, 29
　　defensive behavior in, 98–102
　　defined, 81–82
　　formats of, 91–93
　　group culture in, 82–83
　　group process in, 84–86

intervening in, 86–88
intimacy in, 89–91
keeping on task, 91–93
process recording in, 107
roles in, 93–98
treatment plans in, 102–107

H

Halfway houses, 18
Hall, Edward, 225–226
HALT questions, 146
Hero, family, 235, 247
Hispanics, alcohol use in, 274
HIV/AIDS
　　losses from, 222
　　prevention of, 19, 21
Holistic counseling approach, 33
Homosexuality, 179–180
Hospitalization, partial, 16
Hostile role, 95
Hugging, 227
Hydraulic model of emotion, 30

I

ICMS. See Intensive case management
　　services
Identification with others, 92
Ideologies, 24
Immigrants
　　alcohol use in, 274–275
　　cultural patterns of, 268
　　resistance to treatment in, 264
Impairment of counselors, 129
Incompetent clients, legally, 120–121
Individuation of family members,
　　258–259
Influencing skills, 71–74
Informed Consent, 113, 118–119
Inpatient rehabilitation, 16–17, 27–28
Institutions
　　in community systems, 263
　　denial by, 212
Intake procedure, 150–151
Integrative counseling approach, 33
Intensive case management services
　　(ICMS), 143
Intensive inpatient rehabilitation, 16–17

Intensive outpatient programs (IOPs or IOTPs), 16
International Certification Reciprocity Consortium (ICRC), 11, 62
International Coalition for Addiction Studies Education, 12
Internet resources, 132, 290–293
Interpretation, 71
Interventions Case Management Model, 143
Intervention skills
    family education, 256–257
    family self-understanding, 257
    in group process, 86–88
    individualization and personal growth, 258–259
    principles of, 255
    sober family living, 260–263
    steps and techniques of, 259
Intimacy, group, 89–91
IOP. *See* Intensive outpatient programs
IOTP. *See* Intensive outpatient programs
Irish
    family roles of, 244
    use of alcohol by, 271, 273
Isolation of group members, 86–87
Italian-Americans, alcohol use in, 274

 J

Jews, use of alcohol by, 271, 273
Job titles, 128
Johnson, Vernon, 255
Joker role, 95
Journals, 287–290

 K

Kennedy family, 251

 L

Labeling trap, 41
Labels
    denial and, 206
    of family roles, 256
Leader role, 94–95
Leading skills, 66–71
Legal issues
    clinical discussions, 121
    confidentiality, 116–126
    disclosure and redisclosure, 119–120
    Duty to Report, 117–118
    Duty to Warn, 117
    Informed Consent, 118–119
    legally incompetent clients, 120–121
    medical emergencies, 122–123
    pending legislation, 125
    qualified service organizations, 124
    statistical aggregates, 124
    subpoenaed information, 122
    training, 124
Legislation, pending, 125
Levels of care, 12–13, 14
Limits
    in families, 258
    intangible boundaries and, 227–229
    personal space and, 225–226
    physical contact and, 227
    setting, 224–229
Listening skills, 63–66
Literature, prevention, 266
Long-term residential care, 18
Losses
    issues in recovery, 34, 222
    recognizing, 259

 M

Maintenance stage, 39
Manic-depression, 189–190
Maps
    family, 251–252
    mental, 269–270
Marlatt, Alan, 37
Medical emergencies, 122–123
Medications
    antidepressants, 189
    in elderly, 177
    for psychiatric conditions, 182–184
Member Assistance Programs, 13
Memories, repressed, 209
Memory, impaired, 209–210
Mental abuse, 164–165
Mentally ill chemical abusers (MICA)
    as clients, 180–182
    attention-deficit hyperactivity disorder in, 194–195
    diagnostic issues with, 185–187

Mentally ill chemical abusers (MICA) (*continued*)
   dual diagnoses in, 182
   mood disorders in, 189–191
   personality disorders in, 191–194
   post-traumatic stress disorder in, 194
   schizophrenia in, 187–189
   treatment facilities for, 18
   treatment problems with, 187
Mental maps, 269–270
MET. *See* Motivational enhancement therapy
Methadone-maintenance treatment (MM), 19–22
Mexican-American families, 244
MI. *See* Motivational interviewing
MICA. *See* Mentally ill chemical abusers
Middle-aged clients, 177–178
Miller, William, 40
Minnesota Model, 27
Minors. *See* children
MISA (mentally ill substance abuser). *See* Mentally ill chemical abusers
MM. *See* Methadone-maintenance treatment
Models
   of change, 38–39, 41, 62
   of counseling, 33–41
   defined, 23
   disadvantages of, 23–24
   disease, 31–33
   of emotion, 29–31
   Interventions Case Management Model, 143
   limits and evolution of, 42
   Minnesota, 27
   of treatment, 12, 23–29
Monopolist role, 96–97
Monti, Peter, 37
Mood disorders, 189–190
   borderline personality disorder and, 193
   cultural variations in, 273
Motivational balance sheets, 205
Motivational enhancement therapy (MET)
   general principles of, 40–41
   in listening skills, 65
   motives for change and, 10

Motivational interviewing (MI), 40–41
Motives
   for change, 8–11
   for confrontation, 72
   for treatment, 204–205
Multicultural awareness, 268

N

Narcotics Anonymous (NA), 26
National Association of Alcohol and Drug Abuse Counselors (NAADAC), 11
National Steering Committee on Addiction Counseling Standards, 2
Natural recovery, 6–8
Negative countertransference, 219–222
Negative self-statements, 258
Negative transference, 217
Neurologic impairment, 210–211
Nondiscrimination, 133–134

O

Objectivity, 134–135
Organizational denial, 212
Orientation
   of clients, 62
   confidentiality guidelines in, 113
   to group treatment, 83
Outpatient treatment programs, 15–16
Outreach work, 263–264
Outward Bound program, 176
Overgeneralizing, 36
Oxford Houses, 18

P

Pacing the client, 64
Palo Alto group, 94, 242
Paradigm, defined, 24
Paraphrasing, 63
Parental children, 242, 243, 247–248
Parenting skills, 260
Partial hospitalization, 16
Passages program, 21
Peer groups
   addiction as part of, 7
   denial by, 211–212

Peer groups (*continued*)
  as enablers, 265
  leadership in, 87–88
  in social network, 263
Personalities
  adapting to new, 261
  dynamics in groups, 82–83
Personality disorders
  antisocial, 191–192
  borderline, 192–194
Personal space, 225–226
The Philosophy, 90
Physical abuse, 164–165
Physical contact, 227
Polyabuse behavior, 2, 20–21
Positive countertransference, 218–219
Positive transference, 215–217
Post-traumatic stress disorder (PTSD),
  194
    denial and, 207
    in families, 211–212
    treatment by therapeutic communities,
    28
  Power in families, 235
  Practice dimensions, 2–3
  Preadolescent clients, 174
  Precontemplation stage, 38
  Preparation stage, 38–39
  Preparedness, lack of, 129–131
  Privacy of families, 240
  Privileged information, 122
  Probing, 68–69
  Process recording
    of groups, 107
    of individual clients, 75–77
  Process skills. *See* Counseling skills
  Prochaska, James, 38–39, 62
  Professional growth, 132–133
  Profiles, community, 266–267
  Progress notes, 76, 159–161
  Prohibition, 25
  Project Adventure, 176
  Protector role, 94–95
  Provocative role, 95
  Pseudoparental/pseudospousal role. *See*
    Parental children
  Pseudotherapist role, 94–95
  Psychiatric disorders
    attention-deficit hyperactivity
      disorder, 194–195

cultural variations in, 273
dual diagnoses in, 182
medications for, 182–184
mood disorders, 189–190
neurological impairment, 210–211
personality disorders, 191–194
post-traumatic stress disorder, 194
schizophrenia, 187–189
similarities to addictions, 185
symptoms and AODA, 186
Psychoanalysis, 2, 4, 203, 214–215
Psychology
  cognitive, 36
  counseling, 60
PTSD. *See* Post-traumatic stress disorder

Q

Qualified service organizations, 124

R

Rational-emotive–behavioral therapy
  (REBTor RET), 26, 35, 37
Rational Recovery (RR), 26, 27, 37
REBT. *See* Rational-emotive-behavioral
  therapy
Records, confidentiality of, 118, 121, 161
Recovery
  fellowships for, 25–26
  models of, 23–29
  natural, 6–8
  second year of, 102–103
Rediclosure, 119–120
Re-entry residences, 17–18
Referrals, 6, 13, 265–266
Reflection of feelings, 63–64
Reframing, 66
Regrets, 222
Regulations
  on child abuse, 117–118
  for confidentiality, 116–117
  managed-care, 11
  pending legislation, 125
Reimbursement, third-party
  in cost-containment, 13, 15, 16,
    166–167
  financial ethics and, 127
Reinforcing, 65–66
Rejection, fear of, 208

Relapses, 10–11, 32–33
Relationships
    counseling, 3–4, 115–116, 224–229
    enmeshed/fused, 235–236, 243, 253
    in families, 235–237, 236–237
    sober, 260
Religion
    model of addiction in, 272
    as support in recovery, 7, 265
Representation of services, 127–129
Repressed memories, 209
Research of cultures, 269
Resentful role, 95
Resources
    developing personal directory of,
        161–164
    journals, 287–290
    web sites, 290–293
Responsibility, lack of, 131–132
Restating, 63
RET. See Rational-emotive-behavioral
    therapy
Roles
    class clown, joker, 95
    in defense of emotions, 101
    defined, 93
    in families, 235–236, 240–247
    group facilitators, 86, 96
    in group process, 85
    as impediment to change, 105
    leader, protector, pseudotherapist,
        94–95
    provocative, hostile, resentful, 95
    scapegoat, 94, 98–99, 242–243
    self-oriented, 96–97
    weakest, sickest member, 96
Rules, group, 83

S

Salvation Army residences, 18
Scapegoats
    counselor as, 217
    in families, 242–243
    in groups, 94, 98–99
Schizophrenia, 187–189
Schools, support from, 265–266
Screening
    engaging in, 145

purposes of, 144–145
tools for, 145–148
Self-assessments, 165
Self-awareness of families, 257
Self-disclosure, 69–71
Self-efficacy, 35, 68, 165
Self-help groups. See also Alcoholics
    Anonymous
    Al-Anon, 26
    models of, 25–27
    Narcotics Anonymous, 26
    Smart Recovery, 297–299
    in support of family, 262
Self-understanding of families, 257
Seniors. See Elderly
Service coordination, 2. See also Case
    management
Services, representation of, 127–129
Sexual abuse, 209
Sexual behavior, 216
Sexuality
    of clients, 179–180
    expressing in healthy ways, 262
Shame, 206
Sickest member role, 96
Simplifying, 64
Skills. See also Counseling skills
    active listening, 63–66
    assertiveness, 260
    attending, 62, 63
    competency, 269–273
    engagement, 62, 145
    in group process, 86–88
    influencing, 71–74
    intervention for families, 255–263
    leading, 66–71
    parenting, 260
    in setting boundaries, 229–230
    sober living, 260–263
    underdeveloped social and emotional,
        210
Smart Recovery, 26, 27, 37, 297–299
Smith, Robert, 25, 58
SOAIGP format, 161
SOAP plan, 160–161
Sober family living skills, 260
Social class of clients, 165
Social interactions, 84–85
Social services, 161–164

Social Services Law, 118
Social skills, 210
Social standing, 206–208
Social systems, 233–234. *See also*
  Community systems; Cultural
  systems; Families
Sociopathy, 191–192
Sponsoring, 57–58
Spouse, role of, 245
Stages
  of abuse, 154
  of change, 38–39, 41, 62
  of treatment, 4
Statistical aggregates, 124
Status in families, 235
Stereotypes, 206
Strategies for group treatments, 103–105
Stress, 241
Student Assistance Programs, 6, 13
Subcultures
  addiction as part of, 7
  in cultural systems, 268, 269–275
  personal space and, 225–226
Subpoenaed information, 122
Substance dependence, 153–154. *See also*
  Alcohol and other drug abuse
Summarizing, 64–65
Supervision, ethics in, 114–115
Support systems
  clergy as, 265
  community as, 263–267
  family as, 240–248, 255–263
  peers as, 263, 265
  in recovery, 7
  schools as, 265–266
  for women, 179
Suspended ethnicity, 276–277
Symbols for charting, 249
Synanon, 28

T

TC programs. *See* Therapeutic
  community model
Temperance movements, 25
Termination stage
  anxiety about, 103, 216–217
  in stages of change, 39

Therapeutic community (TC) model,
  21, 28–29
Therapeutic leverage, 6
Throwing a bone, 106, 107
Timing
  of confrontations, 72
  in counseling skills, 74
  denial and, 208
Training, 124
Transdisciplinary foundations, 3
Transference, 214–217. *See also*
  Countertransference
  negative, 217
  positive, 215–217
Transtheoretical model of change, 38–39
Traps, therapeutic, 41, 256
Trauma, 239, 241
Treatment. *See also* Group treatment;
  Treatment plans
  for adolescents, 14, 176–177
  for children, 174
  client in, 2
  compulsory, 6
  counseling approaches in, 33–41
  counseling relationship in, 3–4
  disease models in, 31–33
  diversity of, 11–12
  effectiveness of, 5
  emotional models in, 29–31
  ethics of, 135–136
  evolution of, 42
  expectations of, 239, 262
  for families, 254, 255–256
  focus of, 1–2
  funding and, 13, 15, 166–167
  for homosexuals, 179–180
  immigrants' resistance to, 264
  impediments to, 164–167
  initiation of, 5–8
  leaving prematurely, 222
  for mentally ill chemical abusers,
    180–195
  methadone-maintenance, 19–22
  for middle-aged and elderly, 177–178
  models of, 12, 23–29
  motives for, 204–205
  motives for change in, 8–11
  practice dimensions of, 2–3

Treatment (*continued*)
  settings of, 12–23
  stages of, 4
  termination of, 216–217
  for women, 179
Treatment plans
  described, 154–155
  documentation of, 155
  goals of, 157–158
  for group members, 102–107
  planning process of, 155–158
Trouble-shooting group treatments,
  103–105
Trust, building, 262
Twelve-step programs, 25–26. *See also*
  Alcoholics Anonymous; Self–help
  groups
    counselor attitudes and, 58
    as a disease model, 31–33
    expressing emotions in, 30
    relapses and, 36

 V

Values associated with drugs, 270–271

 W

Weakest member role, 96
Web sites, 132, 290–293
Wilson, William Griffith, 25, 58
Women
  as clients, 179
  denial and, 207
  physical and mental abuse in, 164–165
  role in families, 247
  self-assessment of, 165
  in Temperance movement, 25